Technological Innovation in Global Cultural Tourism

Ahmad Albattat
Asia Pacific University of Technology and Innovation, Malaysia

Vice President of Editorial	Melissa Wagner
Director of Acquisitions	Mikaela Felty
Director of Book Development	Jocelynn Hessler
Production Manager	Mike Brehm
Cover Design	Jose Rosado

Published in the United States of America by
IGI Global Scientific Publishing
701 East Chocolate Avenue
Hershey, PA, 17033, USA
Tel: 717-533-8845
Fax: 717-533-7115
Website: https://www.igi-global.com E-mail: cust@igi-global.com

Copyright © 2025 by IGI Global Scientific Publishing. All rights reserved. No part of this publication may be reproduced, stored or distributed in any form or by any means, electronic or mechanical, including photocopying, without written permission from the publisher.

Product or company names used in this set are for identification purposes only. Inclusion of the names of the products or companies does not indicate a claim of ownership by IGI Global Scientific Publishing of the trademark or registered trademark.

Library of Congress Cataloging-in-Publication Data

Names: Ismail, Fathilah, 1969- editor. | Zulkiffli, Siti Nur 'Atikah, 1983- editor.
Title: Technological innovation in global cultural tourism / edited by Fathilah Ismail, Siti Nur 'Atikah Zulkiffli, Nur Amalina Mohamad Zaki, Jumadil Saputra, Noor Hussin.
Description: Hershey, PA : Business Science Reference, [2025] | Includes bibliographical references and index. | Summary: "In an era where connectivity and digital advancements are at the forefront, technology serves as a catalyst, transforming traditional tourism into an immersive, interactive, and deeply enriching venture"-- Provided by publisher.
Identifiers: LCCN 2024007186 (print) | LCCN 2024007187 (ebook) | ISBN 9798369331965 (hardcover) | ISBN 9798369331972 (ebook)
Subjects: LCSH: Heritage tourism. | Globalization and tourism. | Tourism--Technological innovations.
Classification: LCC G156.5.H47 T427 2024 (print) | LCC G156.5.H47 (ebook) | DDC 338.4/791--dc23/eng/20240424
LC record available at https://lccn.loc.gov/2024007186
LC ebook record available at https://lccn.loc.gov/2024007187

British Cataloguing in Publication Data
A Cataloguing in Publication record for this book is available from the British Library.

All work contributed to this book is new, previously-unpublished material.
The views expressed in this book are those of the authors, but not necessarily of the publisher.
This book contains information sourced from authentic and highly regarded references, with reasonable efforts made to ensure the reliability of the data and information presented. The authors, editors, and publisher believe the information in this book to be accurate and true as of the date of publication. Every effort has been made to trace and credit the copyright holders of all materials included. However, the authors, editors, and publisher cannot assume responsibility for the validity of all materials or the consequences of their use. Should any copyright material be found unacknowledged, please inform the publisher so that corrections may be made in future reprints.

Editorial Advisory Board

Adnan ul Haque, *Yorkville University, Canada*
Azizan Marzuki, *Universiti Sains Malaysia, Malaysia*
Sebastian Kot, *Czestochowa University of Technology, Poland*
Kamariah Ismail, *Universiti Teknologi Brunei, Brunei Darussalam*
Isfenti Sadalia, *Universitas Sumatera Utara, Indonesia*
Mohd Hafiz Mohd Hanafiah, *Universiti Teknologi MARA, Malaysia*
Sr. Mastura Jaafar, *Universiti Sains Malaysia, Malaysia*
Prof. Beata Ślusarczyk, *Czestochowa University of Technology, Poland*
Ir. Bob Foster, M.M, *Universitas Informatika dan Bisnis Indonesia, Bandung, Indonesia*
Katarzyna Szczepańska-Woszczyna, *WSB University, Dabrowa Gornicza, Poland*
tefan Cristian Gherghina, *Bucharest University of Economic Studies, Romania*
Yunieta Anny Nainggolan, *School of Business and Management, Institut Teknologi Bandung, Indonesia*
Raad Mahmoud Al-Tal, *The University of Jordan, Amman-Jordan*
Awangku Hasanal Bahar Pg Bagul, *Universiti Malaysia Sabah, Malaysia*
Jassim Ahmad Al-Gasawneh, *Applied Science Private University, Amman, Jordan*
Marina Hassan, *Universiti Malaysia Terengganu, Malaysia*
Mazni Saad, *International Islamic University Malaysia, Malaysia*
Namhyun Kim, *Dongguk University, South Korea*
Noor Azimin Zainol, *Universiti Utara Malaysia, Malaysia*
Siti Falindah Padlee, *Universiti Malaysia Terengganu, Malaysia*
Arifiani Widjayanti, *Politeknik STIA LAN Jakarta, Indonesia*
Jookyung Kwon, *Dongguk University, South Korea*
Ranjith Ihalanayake, *Victoria University, Melbourne, Australia*
Sergio Ibez-Snchez, *Universidad de Zaragoza, Spain*

Table of Contents

Preface xvi

Acknowledgment xxi

Introduction xxiii

Chapter 1
Navigating the Dark Side of Tourism: Ethical Dilemmas, Impacts, and Cultural Reflections - A Narrative Review 1
    Priyanka Kanjilal, Asansol Engineering College, India
    Nilanjan Ray, JIS University, India
    Soumya Mukherjee, Swami Vivekananda University, India
    Nirmal Chandra Roy, The University of Burdwan, India

Chapter 2
Integrating Artificial Intelligence in Enhancing Cultural Tourism Experiences 23
    Amrik Singh, Lovely Professional University, India

Chapter 3
Ability of Virtual Tourism to Enhance Tourists' Engagement and Satisfaction in the Middle East: Moderating Role of Virtual Influencers 41
    Tareq Nael Hashem, Applied Science Private University, Jordan
    Ahmad Albattat, Asia Pacific University of Technology and Innovation, Malaysia
    Firas Alotoum, Applied Science Private University, Jordan
    Hanan Suleiman, Talal Abu Ghazaleh University Collage for Innovations, Jordan

Chapter 4
Purchase Intention and Tourism Strategy in the Post-COVID-19 Era: Lessons and Perspectives From the Moroccan Experience 65
    Badr Bentalha, National School of Business and Management, Sidi Mohammed Ben Abdellah University, Morocco
    Ahmed Benjelloun, National School of Business and Management, Sidi Mohammed Ben Abdellah University, Morocco
    Hajar Slimani, National School of Business and Management, Moulay Ismail University, Morocco
    Bouteïna El Gharbaoui, National School of Business and Management, Moulay Ismail University, Morocco

Chapter 5
Exploring the Socio-Economic Effects of Rural Cultural Tourism: A Case Study of Shantiniketan, West Bengal.. 87
    Nilanjan Ray, JIS University, India
    Tapas Kumar Chatterjee, IMT Nagpur, India
    Indranil Bose, MIT University, Shillong, India

Chapter 6
Investigating Sustainable Tourism in Indonesia: A Way Forward for the Tourism Industry.. 107
    Augustin Rina Herawati, Universitas Diponegoro, Indonesia
    Nina Widowati Widowati, Universitas Diponegoro, Indonesia
    Teuku Afrizal, Universitas Diponegoro, Indonesia

Chapter 7
Tech Tales of Travel: The Confluence of Technology and Tourism Decision Making 143
    Shubhra Mishra, Babu Banarasi Das University, India
    Rinki Verma, Babu Banarasi Das University, India

Chapter 8
Cultural Tourism in Digitalization Era: The Case of AR Glasses 183
    Mario Ossorio, University of Campania "Luigi Vanvitelli", Italy

Chapter 9
The Use of Technology in Enhancing Pilgrimage Tourism Experiences and Hospitality Services 199
    Md Shamim Hossain, Hajee Mohammad Danesh Science and Technology University, Bangladesh

Chapter 10
Positive and Negative Aspects of Cultural Heritage Tourism: An Insight Story 219
> Rohit Thakur, Central University of Himachal Pradesh, India
> Suman Sharma, Central University of Himachal Pradesh, India
> Sahil Gautam, Central University of Himachal Pradesh, India

Chapter 11
Investigating the Effect Dynamic Interplay of Social Media Promotion on Tourist Revisiting Intention Through Tourist Satisfaction at Sepilok Orangutan 251
> Noor Fazliza Rasim, Universiti Malaysia Terengganu, Malaysia
> Zaliha Zainuddin, Universiti Malaysia Terengganu, Malaysia
> Sofea Cheah Azlan, Universiti Malaysia Terengganu, Malaysia
> Nurul Najwa Napatah, Universiti Malaysia Terengganu, Malaysia

Chapter 12
Impact of Customers' Interpersonal Interactions in Social Commerce on Purchase Intention of Tourism Products and Services 277
> Md Shamim Hossain, Hajee Mohammad Danesh Science and Technology University, Bangladesh
> Rafi Ahmed Reza, Hajee Mohammad Danesh Science and Technology University, Bangladesh
> Md. Abdullah Al Noman, Hajee Mohammad Danesh Science and Technology University, Bangladesh

Chapter 13
Decision to Visit Ecotourism Among Generation Z: The Role of Environment Sustainability and Social Sustainability 311
> Genoveva Genoveva, President University, Indonesia
> Tandi Gunadi, President University, Indonesia

Chapter 14
Emerging Technologies in Metaverse Tourism: Opportunities and Challenges 333
    Nilanjan Ray, JIS University, India
    Tanmoy Majumder, JIS University, India
    Moumita Roy, JIS University, India

Compilation of References 349

About the Contributors 411

Index 421

Detailed Table of Contents

Preface xvi

Acknowledgment xxi

Introduction xxiii

Chapter 1
Navigating the Dark Side of Tourism: Ethical Dilemmas, Impacts, and
Cultural Reflections - A Narrative Review 1
    Priyanka Kanjilal, Asansol Engineering College, India
    Nilanjan Ray, JIS University, India
    Soumya Mukherjee, Swami Vivekananda University, India
    Nirmal Chandra Roy, The University of Burdwan, India

This systematic literature review explores the shadows of tourism by examining its impact, ethical considerations, and cultural narratives through a critical lens. Tourism, while economically beneficial, often masks negative consequences, including environmental degradation, cultural commodification, and socio-economic inequalities. The review synthesizes research from various disciplines, focusing on how tourism can exploit local communities, exacerbate inequality, and contribute to the erosion of cultural identity. It highlights ethical concerns surrounding issues like overtourism, sustainability, and the responsibilities of both tourists and industry stakeholders. The review also investigates the narratives constructed around tourism, where cultural traditions are often commercialized to cater to visitors, leading to questions about authenticity and appropriation. The review advocates for a paradigm shift in how tourism is approached, calling for policies that prioritize the well-being of host communities and respect for their cultural heritage, rather than purely economic gain.

Chapter 2
Integrating Artificial Intelligence in Enhancing Cultural Tourism Experiences 23
    Amrik Singh, Lovely Professional University, India

The rapid advancement of Artificial Intelligence (AI) is reshaping the cultural tourism sector, offering unprecedented opportunities to enhance visitor experiences and promote heritage preservation. This chapter explores the transformative role of AI in cultural tourism, focusing on its applications, benefits, and challenges. AI-powered tools such as virtual assistants, chatbots, and recommendation systems are revolutionizing how tourists interact with cultural sites by providing personalized and immersive experiences. The integration of machine learning and natural language processing allows for dynamic translation, real-time navigation, and context-aware storytelling, ensuring accessibility and engagement for diverse audiences. This chapter aims to conclude integrating AI into cultural tourism to create inclusive, sustainable, and enriched visitor experience.

Chapter 3
Ability of Virtual Tourism to Enhance Tourists' Engagement and Satisfaction in the Middle East: Moderating Role of Virtual Influencers 41
Tareq Nael Hashem, Applied Science Private University, Jordan
Ahmad Albattat, Asia Pacific University of Technology and Innovation, Malaysia
Firas Alotoum, Applied Science Private University, Jordan
Hanan Suleiman, Talal Abu Ghazaleh University Collage for Innovations, Jordan

We aimed in current study to realize the hypothesis that virtual influencers moderate the relationship between virtual tourism (Interactivity, Realism, Multimedia Content, Social Interaction, Personalization, User-Friendly Interface) and tourists' engagement and satisfaction. For that reason, we have depended on quantitative methodology through uploading a self-administered questionnaire online through Google Forms. Total of (968) customers from EMNA region, Gulf countries and Egypt responded to the questionnaire which enabled us to screen and analyze collected primary data through SPSS. Results indicated that acceptance of the main hypothesis as there appeared a moderating influence of virtual influencers on the relationship between virtual tourism and tourists' engagement and satisfaction as the incorporation of Virtual Influencers and Virtual Tourism variables led to a significant increase of 1.4% in the overall interpretation variable, as evidenced by the $R2$ value.

Chapter 4
Purchase Intention and Tourism Strategy in the Post-COVID-19 Era: Lessons and Perspectives From the Moroccan Experience 65
 Badr Bentalha, National School of Business and Management, Sidi
  Mohammed Ben Abdellah University, Morocco
 Ahmed Benjelloun, National School of Business and Management, Sidi
  Mohammed Ben Abdellah University, Morocco
 Hajar Slimani, National School of Business and Management, Moulay
  Ismail University, Morocco
 Bouteïna El Gharbaoui, National School of Business and Management,
  Moulay Ismail University, Morocco

The COVID-19 pandemic has had an unprecedented impact on the global tourism industry, including Morocco. This article examines purchase intentions and tourism strategies in the post-COVID-19 era, drawing lessons from the Moroccan tourism experience. The empirical study shows that tourists' intention to buy has changed considerably as a result of the COVID-19 pandemic. Whereas price and destination used to be the decisive criteria, health concerns, social distancing, booking flexibility and safety now take priority. The research shows that tourists' purchasing intentions have changed considerably as a result of health concerns. he article concludes that post-COVID success will depend on agile, innovative strategies and strong public-private partnerships, as exemplified by Morocco. Tourist confidence will be crucial and will rely on transparent management of health risks. An analysis of decision-making criteria will enable us to identify the levers on which to act to win back the confidence of tourists in an uncertain health context.

Chapter 5
Exploring the Socio-Economic Effects of Rural Cultural Tourism: A Case Study of Shantiniketan, West Bengal 87
 Nilanjan Ray, JIS University, India
 Tapas Kumar Chatterjee, IMT Nagpur, India
 Indranil Bose, MIT University, Shillong, India

This study explores the diverse effects of rural cultural tourism on the socio-economic circumstances of local communities within the region. The objective of this research is to investigate the effects of tourism on the local economy, lifestyle, and socio-cultural dynamics within the host community in and around the tourist location. The results suggest that rural cultural tourism has propelled the advancement of infrastructure, bolstered local entrepreneurship, and attracted investment, consequently augmenting household incomes and alleviating poverty. Nevertheless, the research also emphasizes challenges, such as the imperative for sustainable tourism practices, equitable distribution of benefits, and the preservation of cultural integrity. The study underscores the significance of community engagement, governmental support, and the establishment of effective policy frameworks in optimizing the beneficial impacts of rural cultural tourism while mitigating potential adverse effects.

Chapter 6
Investigating Sustainable Tourism in Indonesia: A Way Forward for the
Tourism Industry 107
    Augustin Rina Herawati, Universitas Diponegoro, Indonesia
    Nina Widowati Widowati, Universitas Diponegoro, Indonesia
    Teuku Afrizal, Universitas Diponegoro, Indonesia

Sustainable tourism is a type of tourism that comprehensively considers its present and future economic, social, and environmental impacts while addressing the needs of visitors, industry, environment, and communities. Tourism plays a significant role in achieving three Sustainable Development Goals (SDGs). SDGs-8 focuses on creating conditions for quality jobs and promoting local culture and products, with sustainable tourism serving as a driver for these objectives. Goal 12 emphasizes the need for clean and environmentally friendly products, particularly in the context of tourism, to enhance the health of forests and oceans. Goal 14, addressing life below water, calls for careful management of global resources, with a specific focus on monitoring sustainable development impacts in tourism. The Sustainable Tourism Development (STDev) program in Indonesia prioritizes the implementation of Sustainable Tourism Observatories (STO) as a fundamental approach.

Chapter 7
Tech Tales of Travel: The Confluence of Technology and Tourism Decision
Making 143
    Shubhra Mishra, Babu Banarasi Das University, India
    Rinki Verma, Babu Banarasi Das University, India

The travel industry is going through an incredible era of innovation and change due to confluence of technology and tourism decision-making. This research explores the field of TechTales of Travel, with a particular emphasis on how tourism decision-making processes use Artificial Intelligence (AI), Big Data Analytics, Social Media/User-Generated Content, and Information and Communication Technology (ICT) infrastructure. Through surveys and multiple regression analysis conducted on a sample of 212 respondents involved in travel, the study explores how these technologies influence consumer perceptions and behaviours in trip planning. Findings reveal a significant positive relationship between technology integration and consumer decision-making, underscoring the importance of strategic technology utilization for enhancing travel experiences and meeting evolving customer expectations. The study emphasizes the need for continuous innovation, data-driven strategies, and ethical considerations to navigate the digital landscape effectively and ensure sustainable growth in the travel sector.

Chapter 8
Cultural Tourism in Digitalization Era: The Case of AR Glasses 183
   Mario Ossorio, University of Campania "Luigi Vanvitelli", Italy

The chapter illustrates the main charachteristics of cultural tourism, categories and preferences of cultural tourists and how digital technologies have improved internal processes of cultural tourism industry. The chapter also highlights the increasing role of the experience and the growing function of technologies as support for firms and travellers. Lastly, the chapter describes an immersive experience that tourists can live in Pompeii sites by using Augmented Reality glasses by AR Tour, through which they can walki through twenty must-see sites in the ancient Roman city.

Chapter 9
The Use of Technology in Enhancing Pilgrimage Tourism Experiences and Hospitality Services 199
   Md Shamim Hossain, Hajee Mohammad Danesh Science and Technology University, Bangladesh

This paper investigates how technology can be utilized to enhance pilgrimage tourism and hospitality services. The article gives an overview of technology use in the pilgrimage tourism business, with a focus on technology's role in improving pilgrim experiences and the quality of hospitality services provided by hotels, restaurants, and other service providers. The report underlines the benefits of integrating technology in pilgrimage tourism, such as greater efficiency, convenience, and service personalization. Overall, the assessment shows how technology has the potential to dramatically improve the experiences and services supplied in the pilgrimage tourism business, as well as the need for future research to fully fulfill that potential. There hasn't been a lot of research done on pilgrimage tourism, and the current study focused on the potential use of technology to improve pilgrimage tourism experiences and hospitality services.

Chapter 10
Positive and Negative Aspects of Cultural Heritage Tourism: An Insight Story 219
   Rohit Thakur, Central University of Himachal Pradesh, India
   Suman Sharma, Central University of Himachal Pradesh, India
   Sahil Gautam, Central University of Himachal Pradesh, India

Tourism is booming around the world; Culture & heritage plays an important role in attracting millions of tourists to different destinations across the world. Cultural heritage tourism offers an opportunity to tourists to experience and understand different cultures in depth. Cultural Heritage tourism accounts for more than 40% of global international tourist arrivals. However, Cultural heritage tourism has both positives and negatives attached with it. The present chapter systematically reviews the existing literature with the aim to explain cultural heritage as an important component for tourism growth and also explain the concept of cultural heritage tourism and its components. This chapter identifies various positive & negative socio-cultural and economical aspects of cultural heritage tourism as well as how technology has helped destinations to increase tourist engagement, awareness and enhancing their experiences at the destination. The chapter also explains how cultural heritage can be used as a tourism product.

Chapter 11
Investigating the Effect Dynamic Interplay of Social Media Promotion on Tourist Revisiting Intention Through Tourist Satisfaction at Sepilok Orangutan 251
    Noor Fazliza Rasim, Universiti Malaysia Terengganu, Malaysia
    Zaliha Zainuddin, Universiti Malaysia Terengganu, Malaysia
    Sofea Cheah Azlan, Universiti Malaysia Terengganu, Malaysia
    Nurul Najwa Napatah, Universiti Malaysia Terengganu, Malaysia

This study investigates the dynamic interplay of social media promotion in shaping tourist attractions and impact of these factors on tourist satisfaction. A total of 231 respondents were participated and analyzed using SPSS-25. The result indicates that respondents' recognition of the center's marketing initiatives and their active use of social media are positively correlated. As a result, it is advised to strategically concentrate on enhancing the center's internet presence. This entails putting into practice more engaging and dynamic marketing efforts that correspond with the target audience's interests. The findings show the need to create a specialized media outlet that guarantees tourists learn everything to know about endangered species Orangutan and can be trusted to provide transparent information about the appropriate maintenance and adherence to international standards at the Sepilok Orangutan Rehabilitation Centre.

Chapter 12
Impact of Customers' Interpersonal Interactions in Social Commerce on Purchase Intention of Tourism Products and Services 277
    Md Shamim Hossain, Hajee Mohammad Danesh Science and
        Technology University, Bangladesh
    Rafi Ahmed Reza, Hajee Mohammad Danesh Science and Technology
        University, Bangladesh
    Md. Abdullah Al Noman, Hajee Mohammad Danesh Science and
        Technology University, Bangladesh

This study aims to determine the impact of customers' interpersonal interactions in social commerce on the purchase intention of tourism products and services.

Additionally, our research explores the influence of interpersonal interaction variables (perceived expertise, familiarity, and similarity) on the development of flow experience and its corresponding effects on customers' purchasing intentions of tourism products and services in the areas of social commerce, using the stimulus-organism-response paradigm. To test the structural model, the authors used a structural equation modeling technique. The study's primary data came from 391 Bangladeshi respondents who filled out questionnaires with seven points labelled "Likert type scale." The findings show that customers' interpersonal interactions have a positive impact on their perceived flow, which in turn has a positive impact on their intent to purchase tourism products and services. Theoretical consequences, practical suppositions, and possible research directions are all discussed based on the study results.

Chapter 13
Decision to Visit Ecotourism Among Generation Z: The Role of
Environment Sustainability and Social Sustainability 311
    Genoveva Genoveva, President University, Indonesia
    Tandi Gunadi, President University, Indonesia

Sustainability issues, related to the triple bottom line that occurred nowadays can affect the tourist's intention on visiting the ecotourism destination in Indonesia before it turns to visit decision-making. The researchers will choose generation Z who intend to visit ecotourism sites, such as Komodo National Park, Raja Ampat, Way Kambas, Kawah Ijen, Tanjung Puting and Gunung Leuser. However, in this study it was limited to visitors to Komodo National Park which is the most popular ecotourism in Indonesia and is protected by UNESCO. Enviromental sustainaibility and social sutanaibility are incorporated in this study in order to understand how they influence visit intention and visit decision. This research used a quantitative method using Smart PLS 3.0 (PLS-SEM) to analyze total 278 respondents from Generation Z in greater Jakarta. The results show that environmental sustainability and social sustainability developed by ecotourism positively affect tourist visit intention and also positive indirect effect on visit decision.

Chapter 14
Emerging Technologies in Metaverse Tourism: Opportunities and Challenges 333
    Nilanjan Ray, JIS University, India
    Tanmoy Majumder, JIS University, India
    Moumita Roy, JIS University, India

Artificial Intelligence (AI) in particular has revolutionised a number of industries, bringing concepts like the "sharing economy," "Internet of Things," and "Internet of People" to life. With chatbots and smart systems being used widely in travel agencies and airlines to improve consumer experiences, artificial intelligence (AI) has had a huge impact on the travel and tourism industry. According to projections, AI will keep advancing individualised solutions and completely changing the travel and tourism sector. This is part of a larger, continuous technological revolution that promises constant innovation and transformation. Information technology (IT) has also significantly changed how businesses operate internationally. The tourist sector is a prime example of how IT may improve communication with potential clients by using destination imagery. In the present market scenario, the tourism industry has also merged many parameters with the usage of information technology aiming to reduce the middlemen in marketing travel schemes to consumers.

Compilation of References 349

About the Contributors 411

Index 421

Preface

INTRODUCTION

It is with great enthusiasm that I present *Technological Innovation in Global Cultural Tourism*, a timely and essential contribution to the growing dialogue on the fusion of digital advancements with the ever-evolving field of cultural tourism. As global travelers seek more meaningful, immersive, and accessible experiences, technology has emerged as a powerful enabler—reshaping how we engage with heritage, traditions, and cultural identities around the world.

This volume brings together a rich tapestry of perspectives and research findings that reflect the dynamic interplay between technology and culture. In this digital age, cultural tourism is no longer confined to physical spaces. Innovations such as augmented reality, virtual tours, mobile applications, and big data analytics are creating new avenues for exploration and interpretation. These tools not only enhance visitor experiences but also play a critical role in the preservation and dissemination of cultural heritage. The integration of such technologies redefines not only how stories are told but also who gets to tell them and who gets to listen.

Our contributors—scholars, practitioners, and industry experts—have carefully examined a range of technologies and their applications across diverse cultural contexts. Through theoretical frameworks and empirical case studies, the chapters in this book highlight best practices, success stories, and critical evaluations of technology's role in transforming cultural tourism. Importantly, the book also considers the broader implications of this transformation—addressing vital concerns around authenticity, sustainability, equity, and ethics.

As we look ahead, emerging technologies such as artificial intelligence, wearable tech, and immersive media are poised to further revolutionize the cultural tourism landscape. This book offers forward-thinking insights into these developments, drawing on the knowledge and experiences of multiple stakeholders—from tourists and cultural custodians to developers, policymakers, and local communities. It is only through these collaborative lenses that we can fully grasp the opportunities and challenges in this evolving domain.

Technological Innovation in Global Cultural Tourism is intended for a broad audience—professionals and researchers across disciplines who are working to integrate technology into tourism, heritage management, and cultural development. It also serves as a valuable guide for decision-makers navigating the complex terrain of innovation, aiming to foster sustainable growth and cultural integrity through thoughtful technological adoption.

I hope this work sparks new ideas, encourages cross-sector collaborations, and ultimately contributes to a future where technology and culture enrich each other in meaningful and enduring ways.

ORGANIZATION OF THE BOOK

In Chapter 1, *Navigating the Dark Side of Tourism: Ethical Dilemmas, Impacts, and Cultural Reflections*, the authors take us on a reflective journey into the often-overlooked consequences of tourism. Through a narrative literature review, they expose the paradoxes at the heart of tourism—its economic allure often obscuring deep environmental, social, and cultural costs. This chapter urges a shift toward ethical frameworks that prioritize the integrity of host communities and challenge the commodification of culture.

Chapter 2, *Integrating Artificial Intelligence in Enhancing Cultural Tourism Experiences*, offers a forward-looking examination of how AI is revolutionizing the cultural tourism landscape. It explores cutting-edge applications—from AI-driven chatbots to dynamic translation tools—that enhance visitor interaction, inclusivity, and preservation efforts. The chapter demonstrates how technology can enrich cultural storytelling while advocating for responsible innovation.

In Chapter 3, *Ability of Virtual Tourism to Enhance Tourists' Engagement and Satisfaction in the Middle East: Moderating Role of Virtual Influencers*, a data-driven analysis uncovers the unique interplay between virtual experiences and consumer satisfaction. The study reveals how virtual influencers significantly elevate tourist engagement within virtual tourism platforms, offering insights from a broad Middle Eastern context. This chapter exemplifies the rise of digital personas in shaping modern tourism behavior.

Chapter 4, *Purchase Intention and Tourism Strategy in the Post-COVID-19 Era: Lessons and Perspectives from the Moroccan Experience*, delves into shifting consumer priorities in a post-pandemic world. Drawing on Morocco's evolving tourism strategies, the chapter illustrates how health consciousness, flexibility, and risk transparency have redefined travel decision-making. It offers valuable lessons on resilience, policy innovation, and trust-building in uncertain times.

Turning our focus to India, Chapter 5, *Exploring the Socio-Economic Effects of Rural Cultural Tourism: A Case Study of Shantiniketan, West Bengal*, examines tourism as both an economic catalyst and a cultural challenge. Through the lens of Shantiniketan, the chapter assesses how tourism drives local development while raising critical questions about equity, sustainability, and heritage preservation. It calls for policy mechanisms that empower communities and balance growth with cultural authenticity.

Chapter 6, *Investigating Sustainable Tourism in Indonesia: A Way Forward of the Tourism Industry*, connects national policy with global goals by aligning Indonesia's tourism agenda with the Sustainable Development Goals. This chapter outlines how the Sustainable Tourism Development (STDev) initiative and Tourism Observatories are paving the way for environmentally conscious, socially inclusive, and economically viable tourism practices, offering a blueprint for emerging economies.

In Chapter 7, *Tech Tales of Travel: The Confluence of Technology and Tourism Decision Making*, we see a comprehensive exploration of how modern technologies—from AI to social media—are reshaping tourist decision-making. Through quantitative analysis, the chapter confirms a robust link between digital tools and consumer confidence. It argues for ongoing innovation and ethical governance to sustain a tech-enabled tourism ecosystem.

Chapter 8, *Cultural Tourism in Digitalization Era: The Case of AR Glasses*, captures the immersive potential of augmented reality. Using the example of Pompeii's AR-guided experiences, the authors illustrate how digital tools can transform passive site visits into interactive journeys. This chapter champions experiential design and technology's role in revitalizing cultural engagement for the digital age.

Chapter 9, *The Use of Technology in Enhancing Pilgrimage Tourism Experiences and Hospitality Services*, explores how modern technological advancements can transform the traditionally spiritual and reflective domain of pilgrimage tourism. The authors provide a comprehensive overview of how digital tools, from online booking platforms to service personalization software, are reshaping the pilgrim's journey and the quality of hospitality services offered. Highlighting the underexplored intersection of technology and religious travel, this chapter makes a compelling case for further research in this niche yet impactful tourism segment.

Chapter 10, *Positive and Negative Aspects of Cultural Heritage Tourism: An Insight Story*, delves into the dual-edged nature of cultural heritage tourism. While this form of tourism plays a pivotal role in attracting global travelers and promoting cultural understanding, it also brings along various socio-cultural and economic implications. Drawing from a detailed literature review, the chapter highlights both the enriching and adverse effects of heritage tourism, while also reflecting on the role of technology in enriching tourist experiences and making heritage sites more accessible and engaging.

Chapter 11, *Investigating the Effect Dynamic Interplay of Social Media Promotion on Tourist Revisiting Intention through Tourist Satisfaction at Sepilok Orangutan*, offers a focused empirical analysis of how social media influences tourist satisfaction and revisit intentions, specifically in the context of the Sepilok Orangutan Rehabilitation Centre. Using quantitative methods, the study identifies a strong correlation between digital promotion strategies and tourist engagement, suggesting a need for robust online presence and transparent, informative content that fosters both awareness and trust in conservation-based tourism experiences.

Chapter 12, *Impact of Customers' Interpersonal Interactions in Social Commerce on Purchase Intention of Tourism Products and Services*, examines the powerful influence of social interactions within digital commerce environments on tourist purchasing behavior. By applying the stimulus-organism-response model, the authors investigate how factors such as perceived expertise, familiarity, and similarity within peer interactions contribute to flow experiences and ultimately drive purchase intentions. This study provides actionable insights for tourism marketers leveraging peer-to-peer engagement strategies in social commerce platforms.

Chapter 13, *Decision to Visit Ecotourism Among Generation Z: The Role of Environmental Sustainability and Social Sustainability*, addresses the growing influence of sustainability on the travel decisions of younger generations. Focusing on Generation Z travelers to Indonesia's UNESCO-protected Komodo National Park, the study reveals that both environmental and social sustainability significantly influence travel intentions and decisions. The findings underscore the increasing demand for ethically managed and eco-conscious travel offerings, particularly among youth demographics.

Lastly, Chapter 14, *Emerging Technologies in Metaverse Tourism: Opportunities and Challenges*, presents a forward-looking examination of how artificial intelligence and other emerging technologies are ushering in a new era of metaverse-based tourism. The chapter outlines the transformative role of AI in enhancing consumer experiences through personalization, automation, and intelligent service delivery, while also emphasizing the broader implications of IT in global tourism operations. This exploration of virtual tourism trends offers a valuable perspective on the future of travel in an increasingly digitized world.

CONCLUSION

As the chapters in this volume reveal, the tourism industry is undergoing a profound transformation driven by digital innovation, evolving traveler expectations, and a renewed global focus on sustainability and cultural preservation. From pilgrimage tourism enhanced by smart technologies to the immersive potential of the metaverse, each contribution in this collection presents a unique lens on how the sector is responding to new challenges and opportunities. The intersection of technology with cultural heritage, ecotourism, social media engagement, and social commerce illustrates a future where data-driven personalization, ethical responsibility, and meaningful experiences coexist.

This book aims not only to document these ongoing shifts but also to inspire further research, dialogue, and collaboration among academics, industry professionals, and policymakers. As tourism continues to serve as a powerful vehicle for economic development, cross-cultural understanding, and environmental stewardship, it is imperative that we critically assess both its impact and its potential. We hope the insights presented here will serve as a valuable resource for those seeking to shape a more resilient, inclusive, and forward-looking tourism landscape.

Acknowledgment

The process of crafting Technological Innovation in Global Cultural Tourism has been a rewarding experience, and we extend our heartfelt thanks to the numerous individuals and organisations whose support, knowledge, and motivation contributed to the realisation of this book.

We would like to express our heartfelt gratitude to the researchers, industry professionals, and cultural heritage experts who have kindly contributed their insights, case studies, and experiences. Your insights have been essential in crafting a thorough and progressive view on the impact of technology within cultural tourism.

We extend our gratitude to our academic mentors, colleagues, and peers for their invaluable feedback and intellectual engagement during the writing journey. Your insights and recommendations played a crucial role in enhancing our concepts and fortifying the content of the work.

We extend our heartfelt appreciation to the institutions and organisations that facilitated access to invaluable resources, data, and technological advancements in the realm of cultural tourism. Your groundbreaking contributions in this area consistently open up new avenues for eco-friendly and engaging travel experiences.

We extend our heartfelt thanks to our editors and publishing team for their patience, guidance, and steadfast support throughout this journey. Your knowledge and skills in advancing this project have been crucial.

We have made every effort to recognise all contributors, but we acknowledge that some names may have been unintentionally left out. We extend our sincere gratitude—your impact is truly valued.

This volume reflects the collective enthusiasm fuelling advancements in cultural tourism, and we aspire for it to be a valuable resource for those who care deeply about the evolution of travel and heritage.

Ahmad Albattat
Asia Pacific University of Technology & Innovation (APU), Malaysia

Introduction

In a time marked by swift technological progress and an escalating demand for meaningful cultural encounters, the convergence of innovation and international cultural tourism has emerged as increasingly essential. The digital revolution has reshaped how we explore, comprehend, and interact with global history, making cultural tourism more accessible, immersive, and sustainable than ever before.

The exploration of technological innovation in the realm of global cultural tourism delves into the significant effects that cutting-edge technologies—like artificial intelligence, virtual and augmented reality, blockchain, big data, and the Internet of Things—have on the landscape of cultural tourism. Technology enriches visitor experiences with virtual museum tours that go beyond geographical boundaries and AI-driven personalised travel suggestions, while also playing a crucial role in the preservation and promotion of cultural heritage.

This volume explores practical case studies, current trends, and future possibilities, providing valuable insights for industry professionals, government entities, academics, and travellers. This work explores the potential of digital technologies to improve sustainable tourism, support local communities, and safeguard delicate cultural sites, all while responding to the changing preferences of modern travellers.

Understanding the importance of technology in cultural tourism is crucial as we navigate a post-pandemic environment where digital and physical interactions converge. This volume serves as an extensive resource on the technologies driving this change, while also urging stakeholders to leverage these advancements to ensure that cultural tourism remains inclusive, educational, and enriching for generations to come.

We encourage you to explore the intriguing intersection of history and innovation, where the past meets the future and technology serves as a bridge among diverse civilisations.

Ahmad Albattat
Asia Pacific University of Technology & Innovation (APU), Malaysia

Chapter 1
Navigating the Dark Side of Tourism:
Ethical Dilemmas, Impacts, and Cultural Reflections – A Narrative Review

Priyanka Kanjilal
https://orcid.org/0009-0001-4598-8142
Asansol Engineering College, India

Nilanjan Ray
https://orcid.org/0000-0002-6109-6080
JIS University, India

Soumya Mukherjee
https://orcid.org/0000-0002-1464-4873
Swami Vivekananda University, India

Nirmal Chandra Roy
https://orcid.org/0000-0001-5863-0951
The University of Burdwan, India

ABSTRACT

This systematic literature review explores the shadows of tourism by examining its impact, ethical considerations, and cultural narratives through a critical lens. Tourism, while economically beneficial, often masks negative consequences, including environmental degradation, cultural commodification, and socio-economic inequalities. The review synthesizes research from various disciplines, focusing on how tourism can exploit local communities, exacerbate inequality, and contribute

DOI: 10.4018/979-8-3693-3196-5.ch001

to the erosion of cultural identity. It highlights ethical concerns surrounding issues like overtourism, sustainability, and the responsibilities of both tourists and industry stakeholders. The review also investigates the narratives constructed around tourism, where cultural traditions are often commercialized to cater to visitors, leading to questions about authenticity and appropriation.The review advocates for a paradigm shift in how tourism is approached, calling for policies that prioritize the well-being of host communities and respect for their cultural heritage, rather than purely economic gain.

INTRODUCTION

Lennon and Foley first presented the idea of dark tourism in their book "Dark Tourism: The Attraction of Death and Disaster." They noted that the goal of dark tourism is to honour horrific or sad events in human history and turn them into tourist attractions. Previously it is similar with the term as Heritage tourism which is a type of non-business travel in which visitors interact with a region's tangible and intangible cultural assets through experiences, purchases, and activities that help them feel more connected to the historical figures, artifacts, and locations they are visiting. Traveling to places connected to death, pain, tragedy, or extraordinary events is known as "dark tourism." Some of the places as castles and battlefields such as Culloden in Scotland and Bran Castle and Poienari Castle in Romania in india Port Blair Cellular Jail Jallianwala Bagh Roopkund Lake Kuldhara Shaniwar Wada are considered as a place for dark tourism. A type of tourism in which visitors visit locations linked to tragedy, death, (T. Johnston, P. Mandelartz Oxford (2016) According to studies on tourism (Zheng, Zhang, Qiu, Guo, & Zhang, 2020; Lacanienta, Ellis, Hill, Freeman, & Jiang, 2020), dark tourism has grown in popularity. As a matter of fact, dark tourism destinations frequently modify the brightness of lighting and the darkness of visual materials in order to achieve the desired results either by increasing environmental brightness, which inspires hope and triumph, or by decreasing environmental brightness, which stimulates psychological dark experience. It might facilitate traveller's transformational experiences. The dark tourism market is estimated to be valued at USD 31.86 Bn in 2024 and is expected to reach USD 38.13 Bn by 2031, growing at a compound annual growth rate (CAGR) of 2.6% from 2024 to 2031. somber ones (Growth trend & forecast 2024-2031). The individuals that were aware of dark tourism were notably younger and had higher levels of education(Millán et al.2019) .Young people are more open to trying new things and are aware of trends, thus dark tourism is both a niche industry and a trend in and of itself (José Magano, José A. Fraiz-Brea, and Ângela Leite 2022).There are a few studies revelled there are some influencing factors that act as important variables, positively and negatively affect dark tourism. High degree of darkness event impact attracts more tourist and experience of high or low negative emotion, promotion of that place and event(Rachael Ironside,2023). With the addition of symbolic elements to further bolster this idea, dark tourism has the potential to monetize and sell victims' agony. Dark tourism does, however, have certain advantages. The improvement of infrastructure can be sparked by visitors, who can also produce income, recovery, instruction, and remembering. The main component of dark tourism is understanding the tourist emotional reaction towards the places. Since travel is in some ways a self-organized activity, dark tourism has produced beneficial changes. After undergoing life-changing experiences, travellers are motivated to broaden their consciousness and look within for purpose (Sheldon, 2020) Dark tourism initiatives have been acknowledged for their ability to support peace and aid in the reconstruction of nations impacted by conflict through awareness-raising and education campaigns. (Dolnicar & McCabe, 2022) Dark tourism geographies face various trends and concerns related to axiological aspects, such as the absence of cultural humility, the impact of the 'digital turn,' and the blending of entertainment and education(Nitasha Tamar Sharma, Annaclaudia Martini,2024) According to Laing & Frost (2019), and Wight (2020), dark tourism invariably reflects how people negotiate and solidify their national, religious, ethnic, and political identities as well as how they view outgroups in each changing social setting. Concerns about ethics one question come to mind that Is visiting locations associated with suffering morally acceptable or not. As ethical standards differ across cultures and the diverse nature of the sector makes it difficult for the government to regulate tourism, leading to exploitation (K Garlick,2022) it has some positive way to look ethics of dark tourism is the past should not be forgotten but rather should be reemphasized without sensationalism or distortion. Dark tourist sites are significant monuments to humanity's ongoing inability to restrain its darkest excesses. Respecting historical settings and customs of the local community is one of the important components of dark tourism. Each location has deeply significant to the people who were personally impacted by emotionally and culturally. Visitors can guarantee that their presence at these locations positively influences the ongoing process of recollection and healing by honouring local customs and histories by respect local customs, act appropriately, abstain from repulsive behaviour.

OBJECTIVES OF STUDY

Investigate unproven theories, frameworks, and maybe unique techniques in order to offer a better understanding of the work that has to be done for future studies. The study does not provide formal hypotheses since the empirical evidence and theoretical reasoning are in conflict. However, put together a few study questions.

Q1. How the Dark Tourism is creating impact on tourism industry?
Q2. What are the motivating and challenging factors of Shadow of tourism?
Q3. How dark tourism made Ethical and cultural consideration?

According to the previously indicated theoretical framework, several problems—also referred to as questions—have been further investigated for this study. The influence of Dark tourism as a tool for influence tourism and its impact on the traditional tourism. motivating and challenging factors of Shadow of tourism were the key topics of discussion. Analysed the most recent research on the Dark Tourism by doing a thorough analysis of the literature. The guidelines set by Moher et al. (2009) for the Preferred Reporting Items for Systematic Reviews (PRISMA), a systematic review methodology was employed. This necessitated searching the database for pertinent papers by using keywords.

REVIEW PROCESS AND DATABASE SEARCH-

The study only considers empirical research that was done between 2020 and 2024 to ascertain the causes of the growing interest in dark tourism. Capturing the new frontiers in the field of study is the driving force for the concentration on contemporary publications. The number of Zen Z visitors to dark tourism destinations is rising, and the causes driving this expansion also have a significant beneficial influence on the socioeconomic development of the surrounding community. A thorough analysis of the literature was conducted to examine the most recent research on dark tourism. When it comes to review techniques, a systematic literature review (SLR) is thought to be the most scholarly and informative kind (Paul et al., 2021). SLR seeks to address a research topic, often pertaining to the current state of an area of study (Kraus et al., 2020). The secondary data collected from previous study related to dark tourism finds with the help of key words like Dark Tourism, Motivators, Impact, Ethics, and Cultural Narratives, Challenges, Economic effects. The previous data collected from the sources like Science Direct and Emerald insight, Google Scholer total no of data base found related with the above topic is 946.The Studies Included in the systematic review is 36

Figure 1. Database: Science direct and emerald insight, Google Scholar

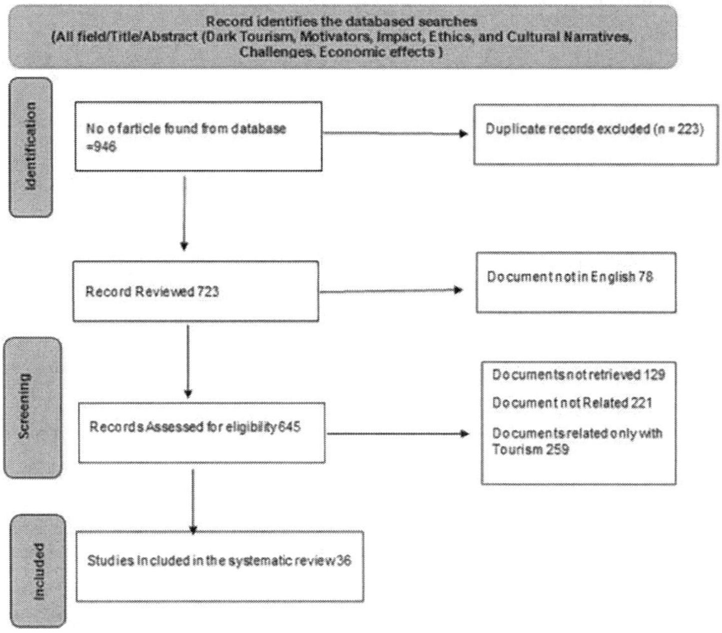

CASE STUDIES HIGHLIGHT THE SOCIOECONOMIC EFFECTS OF DARK TOURISM

Chernobyl Exclusion Zone, Ukraine

Context: A sizable exclusion zone was left behind after the 1986 Chernobyl nuclear accident; this area is now well-known for its dark tourist offerings.

Socio-Economic Impact

Economic: Chernobyl has witnessed an increase in tourists since being opened to the public in 2011, especially with the release of the HBO series "Chernobyl" in 2019. Local economies have benefited from this growth in tourism, guides, and hospitality services. Nearby towns like Slavutych and Pripyat have seen the emergence of small enterprises like hotels and restaurants.

Social: There are worries that the tragedy and the experiences of the survivors are being trivialized due to the increase of tourists. On the other hand, it has given some residents a means of telling their tales and keeping the occurrence in the public eye.

Challenges: A careful balance must be struck between protecting the tragedy's legacy and avoiding abuse or exploitation of the location.

Auschwitz-Birkenau Memorial and Museum, Poland

Context: During World War II, Auschwitz-Birkenau was a Nazi concentration and extermination camp; now, it is a monument and teaching facility. ·

Socio-Economic Impact

Economic: With over 2 million visitors a year, the site's tourist industry makes a substantial contribution to the local economy. This constant flow of visitors is advantageous to nearby companies including lodging facilities, dining establishments, and tour guides.

Social: Dark tourism in Auschwitz promotes a profound awareness of the horrors carried out during the Holocaust, which is a crucial educational function. The commercialization of such a hallowed place and how it ought to be portrayed to future generations, however, are still topics of discussion.

Cultural Sensitivity: With tight guidelines about visitor behaviour and a focus on historical knowledge rather than amusement, efforts are taken to guarantee that the place maintains its respect.

Ground Zero, New York City, USA

Context: The 9/11 Memorial and Museum serve as focal places of commemoration, and Ground Zero, the location of the terrorist attacks on September 11, 2001 in New York City, has grown to be a popular dark tourist destination.

Socio-Economic Impact

Economic: Lower Manhattan's economy has benefited greatly from the constant influx of tourists brought forth by the 9/11 Memorial. The retail, hotel, and real estate sectors have all prospered from the area's revitalization.

Social: Ground Zero is a place of communal grief and commemoration for a large number of Americans and foreign tourists. The museum is essential to teaching the next generation about what happened on 9/11 and what came after. It also gives victims' relatives and survivors a forum to talk about their experiences.

Ethical Concerns: Ground Zero, like other dark tourist destinations, presents ethical concerns regarding the monetization of tragedy. Local gift stores have come under fire for making money out of a site of great misery.

Robben Island, South Africa

Context: Nelson Mandela was one of the most well-known inmates of Robben Island, which served as a jail during South Africa's apartheid era. It is currently a well-liked location for dark tourism and a UNESCO World Heritage site.

Socio-Economic Impact

Economic: Robben Island boosts Cape Town's tourism business by drawing visitors from all over the world. The site's upkeep and the local economy are supported by the money made from ticket sales and guided tours.

Social: The location represents tenacity and the fight for liberation. It has an educational function by shedding light on the injustices of apartheid. As many of the tour guides were formerly incarcerated, they can provide guests first hand knowledge of the past.

Cultural Heritage: By keeping Robben Island a haunting tourist destination, South Africans are able to face their terrible history while also bringing attention to the effects of apartheid. But with efforts to commercialize increasing, there are questions about how to preserve the site originality.

The Killing Fields, Cambodia

Context: The Killing Fields are a group of locations in Cambodia where the Khmer Rouge dictatorship massacred and buried a great deal of people between 1975 and 1979.

Socio-economic Impact:

Economic: The Killing Fields and other sites, such as the Tuol Sleng Genocide Museum, have seen a rise in dark tourism, which has become a significant source of income for Cambodia's travel and tourist sector. The revenue received goes toward funding educational initiatives and site maintenance.

Social: These locations act as memorials for the genocide in Cambodia and offer information on the crimes and the significance of human rights consciousness. However, for many Cambodians, these locations are also a reminder of a sad past, and there is worry about whether the surge in tourism commodifies this misery.

Restoration and Preservation: Tourist-generated revenue has made it possible to preserve historical documents, mass graves, and human rights education in an effort to stop crimes in the future.

Pompeii, Italy

Context: In 79 AD, Mount Vesuvius erupted, destroying the ancient Roman city of Pompeii. Due of its devastating devastation, even if it does not entail human tragedy in the contemporary sense, it is frequently seen as a grim tourism destination.

Socio-economic Impact:

Economic: As one of Italy's most popular tourist destinations, Pompeii contributes significantly to the local economy. Because of the site's popularity, a strong tourism infrastructure has grown, encompassing lodging, transportation, and guided tours.
Social: Pompeii provides as a reminder of how human existence may be susceptible to the forces of nature, even as it lets tourists observe the destruction brought about by a natural calamity. It stimulates curiosity about archeology, history, and cultural preservation.
Conservation Concerns: Although Pompeii has seen an increase in revenue, the long-term viability of overseeing both tourists and archaeological research raises questions about the site's preservation.

Hiroshima Peace Memorial Park, Japan

Context: Located at the site of Hiroshima's atomic attack during World War II lies the Hiroshima Peace Memorial Park. The Hiroshima Peace Memorial Museum, the Atomic Bomb Dome, and a number of memorials honoring the dead are all located inside the park.

Socio-Economic Impact

Economic: To learn about the effects of nuclear warfare, Hiroshima has experienced a surge in both local and foreign tourists. The local economy has benefited from this, particularly in areas of lodging, dining, and cultural tourism.
Social: The Peace Memorial Park plays a vital role in advancing nuclear disarmament and world peace. Hibakusha, or survivors, use the site as a space for introspection and remembering. It also raises discussions about how these locations might strike a balance between the requirements of tourists and memorialization.
Global Impact: Hiroshima serves as a hub for global efforts to avert nuclear war, hosting regular gatherings and peace-promoting educational programs.

A REVIEW OF THEORETICAL AND EMPIRICAL CONTRIBUTIONS TO DARK TOURISM STUDIES

The current review amalgamates the highly relevant academic contributions made so far on the topic of dark tourism and makes an attempt to portray various learned theories as well as practices directed towards understanding this phenomenon. The following studies discuss several overriding issues examined in the field, particular attention being paid to such phenomena as the motivations of tourists and the relationship between culture and death.

Dark Tourist Spectrum (Raine, 2013)

Rachael Raine's study presents a new categorization of dark tourists according to their burial ground visitation motives. In conducting qualitative interviews at cemeteries located in London, Whitby, and Salford, Raine proposes the Dark Tourist Spectrum that ranges tourists who involve deeply themes of death and mortality from 'darkest' to 'lightest'. This research complements other studies on dark tourism in understanding how personal motivations contribute to the dark tourism experience in a new and fresh perspective classification system for research.

Diaspora Tourism and African Slavery (Otoo et al., 2021)

The author Felix Elvis Otoo and order investigate how diaspora tourism interacts with other forms of tourism heritage in respect of African slavery. Taking Ghana for instance, the authors study tourist types and motivations, such as concerns for heritage and historical consciousness, and their impact on the assessment of heritage sites. This research also underscored the impact that individuals and groups' recollections of the past have on the dynamics of diaspora tourism and why there are deeper implications in the issues of identity and tourism.

Eudaimonic vs. Hedonic Tourist Experiences (Lee & Jeong, 2019)

Wangoo Lee and Chul Jeong study the interaction of hedonistic (focused on pleasure) and eudaimonic (focused on meaning) aspects of tourism. The results show that, due to the inherent nature of entertaining definitions, entertainment it purposes does not always lead to eudaimonic outcomes. This research contributes to more detailed understanding of tourism in psychological terms, stressing that it is important to create an understanding of experience for tourists, especially for such types of tourism as dark tourism.

Thanatological Perspective on Dark Tourism (Stone & Sharpley)

Philip Stone and Richard Sharpley present a theoretical discussion of dark tourism through thanatology with a special emphasis on the demand for death-related experiences. They connect the societal perceptions of death to the phenomena of dark tourism. This framework positions dark tourism as an engagement strategy for individuals in dealing with the concept of death. This paper further enhances the understanding of the psychological aspect of the dark tourism.

Dark Tourism and Urban Sites (Lennon, 2020)

John J. Lennon's research gives accent to urban factor in the context of the dark tourism phenomenon. Referring to places connected with death, calamity, or catastrophes, Lennon points out that those places become of interest because of their past and emotional value. This article notes the urban aspect of dark tourism as occurring in the context of cities becoming primary hubs of the business of dark tourism and the experiences it offers.

Motivation Segmentation for Dark Tourism in Nepal (Min et al., 2021)

In their most recent work, Jihye Min and co. look into the reasons for dark tourism by investigating the case of earthquake memorials in Nepal. The research divides tourists according to their motives and relates these motives to the appended emotional and cognitive responses of the tourists after the visit. This research is important in illustrating the effects of different motivational factors on the experiences of dark tourists, and the relevant implications for the management and interpretation of these sites.

Taken together, these research efforts exhibit the expansion and richness of the dark tourism studies. They focus on many issues, ranging from tourists' motivation type's classification to the cultural and psychological theories of death tourism. There are many aspects that can be developed based on these approaches in the study of dark tourism, especially with regard to changing visitor profiles and the ethics of marketing death and disaster.

Theoretical and Empirical Approaches to Dark Tourism: A TCCM Analysis

Dark tourism, encompassing visits to sites associated with death, tragedy, and disaster, has gained substantial scholarly attention. To better understand the complexities of dark tourism, it is essential to explore the theoretical foundations, contextual settings, characteristics of tourism experiences, and the methodologies employed by researchers. The TCCM (Theory, Context, Characteristics, and Methodology) framework provides a comprehensive approach to categorizing and analyzing dark tourism studies. By applying this framework, we can systematically review and identify the diverse elements shaping dark tourism, shedding light on key trends and gaps in current research.

Table 1. TCCM (theory, context, characteristics, and methodology) analysis

Study	Theories	Contexts	Characteristics	Methodologies
Dark Tourist Spectrum (Raine, 2013)	Typology theory; spectrum model of dark tourist behavior.	Burial grounds (London, Whitby, and Salford in the UK).	Develops a spectrum of tourists ranging from "darkest" to "lightest" based on emotional and motivational engagement.	Qualitative research using semi-structured interviews; thematic analysis to create Dark Tourist Spectrum.
Diaspora Tourism and African Slavery (Otoo et al., 2021)	Diaspora and heritage tourism theories; collective memory and identity in tourism experiences.	Heritage sites in Ghana related to the transatlantic slave trade.	Focuses on how heritage and historical awareness shape tourist motivations, particularly those with ancestral connections.	Mixed-methods: quantitative surveys and qualitative interviews to assess tourist motivations and destination evaluations.
Eudaimonic vs. Hedonic Tourist Experiences (Lee & Jeong, 2019)	Psychological theories of well-being (hedonia and eudaimonia).	Tourist experiences (not specific to dark tourism).	Differentiates between hedonic (pleasure-driven) and eudemonic (meaning-driven) tourist experiences, showing they often overlap.	Quantitative research using surveys and structural equation modeling (SEM) to analyze relationships between variables.
Thanatological Perspective on Dark Tourism (Stone & Sharpley)	Thanatology (study of death and dying); cultural attitudes towards mortality and dark tourism.	Global focus, exploring various dark tourism sites.	Conceptualizes dark tourism demand as driven by societal attitudes toward mortality and the consumption of death-related tourism sites.	Conceptual paper based on literature review and theoretical framework development.

continued on following page

Table 1. Continued

Study	Theories	Contexts	Characteristics	Methodologies
Dark Tourism and Urban Sites (Lennon, 2020)	Urban tourism and heritage tourism theories; commodification of tragic sites in cities.	Urban contexts (Berlin, New York, Hiroshima).	Analyzes how cities incorporate dark tourism sites related to death, disaster, and tragedy, contributing to urban tourism growth.	Qualitative case study analysis using secondary data from tourism reports and statistics.
Motivation Segmentation for Dark Tourism in Nepal (Min et al., 2021)	Motivation and segmentation theory; visitor motivation analysis.	Earthquake memorials in Nepal (post-2015 earthquake sites).	Segments tourists based on motivations (e.g., education, remembrance), linking motivations to post-visit experiences.	Quantitative research using surveys and cluster analysis to segment tourists based on their motivations.

Using the TCCM framework to analyze dark tourism literature indicates the prolific development of several theoretical perspectives including, but not limited to, psychological health, the concept of the diaspora, and urban and heritage tourism. The examined materials are transnational and deal with specific tourist destinations such as sites of civilizations, urban tombs, and places of tragedy, with an emphasis on the transnationality of dark tourism. In addition, the tourism profile and the purpose of some of them are different. For example, some aim at finding meaning and history, while others wish to confront death or learn about different cultures. As for the methodology, the research has both quantitative and qualitative characteristics and provides a great understanding of dark tourists and the factors affecting them. This TCCM based analysis helps to understand the present research situation and its possible development such as the enhancement of emotional content and psychological aspects of dark tourism in practical studies.

FINDINGS AND CONCLUSION

Dark tourism has been a growing segment of the tourism industry, often linked to themes of tragedy and mystery. emphasize the role of dark tourism in cultural reflection and memory. societies remember and engage with their histories, particularly those marked by tragedy. Impact of dark tourism find differently positive and negative both influence how dark tourism is marketed and experienced in the future .one of the important motivator is Knowledge of dark tourism is linked to higher rumination on sadness, self-hatred, and hostility it is also found that Women and more educated individuals tend to know more about dark tourism .Participants who understand dark tourism are more likely to visit sites of tragedy and express a need to learn and understand Interestingly, those visiting tragic sites report higher levels of tourist wellbeing despite negative personality traits (José Magano,José Antonio Fraiz-Brea,Ângela Leite, 2022).Negative impact of inhibitors of Dark tourism are Facing down with death, mortality isolation, a person may experience depersonalization, in which they feel cut off from their ideas, feelings, sensations, or behaviours. Also some of experiencing pervasive sense of worry that something or someone evil is endangering the ideals, goals, or welfare of a group of people or a society. Traumatic event or experience memories can leave lasting, imperceptible scars. (V. Abraham et al. 2022). It has been discovered that visitor motives (including enthusiasm, relaxation, and curiosity) directly influence their behavioural intentions in a positive way. Importance of death as a primary motivator for tourist (Podoshen, J. S., & Anderson, A. R. (2020) The need for introspection on mortality, thrill-seeking, and curiosity are key aspects (Light, D. 2020) In specifically, the way that fear, empathy, and attraction interact to influence visitor behaviour(Buda, D. M. (2021) a want to engage with historical or cultural narratives, frequently emphasizing memorial and collective memory motivates tourist Yankholmes, A. K. B., & McKercher, B. (2021).As tourist are mostly connected with social media that's why Dark sites can pique people's curiosity and interest when they see them in the mainstream. Raine, R. (2022) The COVID-19 pandemic has given rise to new destinations for dark tourism, where travellers are drawn by a desire to learn about the pandemic's effects or to remember those who lost their lives. Zheng, Y., & Liu, X. (2023) Dark tourism commodifies tragedy by emphasizing the reasons for traveller's desire to interact with the worst facets of human experience and history. Stone, P. R., & Sharpley, R. (2023)

Some Demotivating factors which influence the Dark tourism. The moral conundrums that would put off prospective dark tourists. Significant demotivators are identified, including unease with the marketing of tragedy and concerns about voyeurism. Lennon, J. J., & Weber, K. (2020) the psychological cost of gloomy tourism. Unsettling or overpowering encounters may discourage traveller's from going to locations. Robb, E. M. (2021) Dark tourism participation may be hampered by social and psychological reasons such as peer pressure and cultural taboos, as well as by emotional emotions like dread and anxiety, which can result in apathy or deliberate avoidance. Johnston, T., & Mandich, G. (2021) Certain demographic groups may avoid visiting these locations due to unfavourable conceptions of dark tourism, such as the link with illness and the possibility of exploitation. Biran, A., & Hyde, K. F. (2022) The social stigma associated with dark tourism and how people's fears of being evaluated by others can discourage people from participating in this kind of travel. Podoshen, J. S., & Yan, Y. (2022). the moral concerns and ethical conundrums that might result from visiting locations connected to death and suffering, which motivate some travellers to steer clear of black tourism destinations. Light, D. (2023) Public health issues have proven to be a major turnoff for prospective dark tourists, especially considering the COVID-19 pandemic. Health concerns and fear of infection are cited as major demotivators. Zheng, Y., & Liu, X. (2023).

Cultural narratives are also relating with dark tourism. Visitors interact with locations that symbolize important historical or cultural tales, frequently pertaining to a country's identity or collective memory(Yankholmes, A. K. B., & McKercher, B. 2021) By using tales to reshape visitors' perceptions of historical events and their cultural relevance, dark tourism sites help to create and preserve cultural memory(Seaton, A. V., & Lennon, J. J. 2021) Cultural narratives are used by dark tourist destinations in hotly debated areas to deliver certain messages about memory, identity, and history(Ashworth, G. J., & Isaac, R. K. 2022) Storylines are designed to evoke strong feelings and cultural sensitivities in visitors, frequently presenting historical events in ways that are consistent with modern ideals (Sharpley, R., & Stone, P. R.2023) Stories are crafted to represent certain political or cultural objectives, and these stories influence how visitors perceive the past(Lennon, J. J. (2023). Folklore aids in the creation of a cultural identity following a calamity (Yoshida, K., & Bui, H. T. (2024). Summarising the motivating and demotivating factors of dark tourism indicating cultural taboos and emotional limitations are demotivating elements for dark tourism, but curiosity, cultural heritage, learning, emotional involvement, historical understanding, and media impact are driving factors.

FUTURE SCOPE

Future research is encouraged to look at how multiauthor collaboration affects knowledge creation and scientific advancement in general. Gaining more insight into these processes might help to improve our discipline's scientific foundation and encourage multidisciplinary collaboration. Future investigations into dark tourism should concentrate on developing strong theoretical foundations, comprehending the affective dimensions of visitor experiences, elucidating the nature and extent of dark tourism, and investigating novel approaches to promotion and administration. In addition, it's important to assess the sustainability and economic effects of dark tourism as well as the moral and ethical issues that surround it. These approaches will contribute to the development of the subject and make dark tourism a more logical and long-term part of the travel and tourist sector. need to prioritize comprehending visitors' experiences, broadening its purview beyond historical tourism, and filling in knowledge gaps in order to advance world peace. As it is found that very less research done on relationship between socio economic development and dark tourism, dark tourism play an important role in economic development in the local area required acceptability and support of the local community for the growth of dark tourism .The positive sentiments of inhabitants in Beichuan County, China, toward the growth of dark tourism, demonstrate that dark tourism may have a substantial beneficial economic impact on local communities. The effects on the environment, economy, and society were recognized by the locals, who also agreed that dark tourism had a good economic impact. There are several gap that can be minimise through future research concentrates in Several difficulties, such as a lack of theoretical frameworks, inadequate knowledge and education among tourist professionals, ethical issues, and unfavourable attitudes Dark tourism may grow if these problems are addressed and improvement in marketing techniques, ethical reflections, and education is also areas to be considered in future research

REFERENCES

Abraham, V., Pizam, A., & Medeiros, M. (2021). The impact of attitudes, motivational factors, and emotions on the image of a dark tourism site and the desire of the victims' descendants to visit it. *Journal of Heritage Tourism*, *17*(2), 264–282.

Abraham, V., Pizam, A., & Medeiros, M. (2022). The impact of attitudes, motivational factors, and emotions on the image of a dark tourism site and the desire of the victims' descendants to visit it. *Journal of Heritage Tourism*, *17*(3), 264–282. DOI: 10.1080/1743873X.2021.1955892

Applboim, T., & Poria, Y. (2020). Witnesses in uniform: Are Israeli defense forces officers in favor of their soldiers visiting Holocaust heritage sites in Poland? *Journal of Heritage Tourism*, *15*(4), 438–449. DOI: 10.1080/1743873X.2019.1666134

Auschwitz-Birkenau Memorial and Museum. (2021). Visitor numbers. https://auschwitz.org/en/museum/history-of-the-memorial/the-first-years-of-the-memorial/visitor-numbers (Accessed January 13, 2023).

Baloglu, S. (2000). A path analytic model of visitation intention involving information sources, socio-psychological motivations, and destination image. *Journal of Travel & Tourism Marketing*, *8*(3), 81–90. DOI: 10.1300/J073v08n03_05

Bauer, I. L. (2021). Death as attraction: The role of travel medicine and psychological travel health care in dark tourism. *Tropical Diseases, Travel Medicine and Vaccines*, *7*(1), 1–14. DOI: 10.1186/s40794-021-00149-z PMID: 34380578

Chen, S., & Xu, H. (2020). The moral gaze in commercialized dark tourism. *Current Issues in Tourism*, *24*(2), 1–20.

Christou, P. A. (2020). *Philosophies of hospitality and tourism: Giving and receiving*. Channel View Publications.

Das, J., & Chakraborty, S. (2021). Scope of dark tourism as a revival strategy for the industry: A study with special reference to Rajasthan. *Business Studies, XLII*(1 & 2).

Dhatrak, S. P. (2020). Dark tourism sites in India: A review. *Shanlax International Journal of Arts, Science and Humanities*, *8*(2).

Douglas, K. (2020). Youth, trauma and memorialisation: The selfie as witnessing. *Memory Studies*, *13*(3), 384–399. DOI: 10.1177/1750698017714838

Dresler, E. (2023). Multiplicity of moral emotions in educational dark tourism. *Tourism Management Perspectives*, *46*, 46. DOI: 10.1016/j.tmp.2023.101094

Fabros, M. G. M., Lopez, E. L. F., & Roma, M. N. (2023). Dark tourism in the Philippine context: Indicators, motivations, and spectrum. *Social Sciences & Humanities Open*, *7*(1), 100452. DOI: 10.1016/j.ssaho.2023.100452

Garlick, K. (2022). *Morbid curiosity: Exploring the ethics of dark tourism. West Chester University Digital Commons*. Doctoral Projects.

Hammoud, G., Refai, H., & Hammad, M. (2021). Using rumours and dark stories to promote tourism: Applied to Egyptian dark tourism sites. *Journal of Association of Arab Universities for Tourism and Hospitality*, *20*(1), 27–36. DOI: 10.21608/jaauth.2021.56728.1114

Iliev, D. (2021). Consumption, motivation and experience in dark tourism: A conceptual and critical analysis. *Tourism Geographies*, *23*(5), 963–984. DOI: 10.1080/14616688.2020.1722215

Jiang, Q., & McCabe, S. (2023). Exploring fundamental motives of tourists visiting dark tourism sites. *Asia Pacific Journal of Tourism Research*, *28*(6), 610–624. DOI: 10.1080/10941665.2023.2255313

Jordan, E. J., & Prayag, G. (2022). Residents' cognitive appraisals, emotions, and coping strategies at local dark tourism sites. *Journal of Travel Research*, *61*(4), 887–902. DOI: 10.1177/00472875211004761

Jureniene, V., & Radzevicius, M. (2022). Peculiarities of sustainable cultural development: A case of dark tourism in Lithuania. *Journal of Risk and Financial Management*, *15*(6), 264. DOI: 10.3390/jrfm15060264

Korstanje, M. E., & Seraphin, H. (2020). The dark tourist: Consuming dark spaces in the periphery. In Korstanje, M. E., & Seraphin, H. (Eds.), *Tourism, terrorism and security* (pp. 135–150). Emerald Publishing Limited. DOI: 10.1108/978-1-83867-905-720201009

Lacanienta, A., Ellis, G., Hill, B., Freeman, P., & Jiang, J. (2020). Provocation and related subjective experiences along the dark tourism spectrum. *Journal of Heritage Tourism*, *15*(6), 626–647. DOI: 10.1080/1743873X.2020.1739055

Lages, C. R., Perez-Vega, R., Kadić-Maglajlić, S., & Borghei-Razavi, N. (2023). A systematic review and bibliometric analysis of the dark side of customer behavior: An integrative customer incivility framework. *Journal of Business Research*, *161*, 113779. DOI: 10.1016/j.jbusres.2023.113779

Lee, W., & Jeong, C. (2019). Beyond the correlation between tourist eudaimonic and hedonic experiences: Necessary condition analysis. *Tourism Management*, *73*, 2182–2194.

Lee, W., & Jeong, C. (2020). Beyond the correlation between tourist eudaimonic and hedonic experiences: Necessary condition analysis. *Current Issues in Tourism*, *23*(18), 2182–2194. DOI: 10.1080/13683500.2019.1611747

Lennon, J. J., & Powell, R. (2018). Dark tourism and cities. *International Journal of Tourism Cities*, *4*(1), 1–3. DOI: 10.1108/IJTC-03-2018-086

Lewis, H., Schrier, T., & Xu, S. (2022). *Dark tourism: Motivations and visit intentions of tourists*. International Hospitality Review.

Light, D. (2017). Progress in dark tourism and thanatourism research: An uneasy relationship with heritage tourism. *Tourism Management*, *61*, 275–301. DOI: 10.1016/j.tourman.2017.01.011

Lin, Y. K., & Nawijn, J. (2020). The impact of travel motivation on emotions: A longitudinal study. *Journal of Destination Marketing & Management*, *16*, 16. DOI: 10.1016/j.jdmm.2019.05.006

Lv, X., Lu, R., Xu, S., Sun, J., & Yang, Y. (2022). Exploring visual embodiment effect in dark tourism: The influence of visual darkness on dark experience. *Tourism Management*, *89*, 89. DOI: 10.1016/j.tourman.2021.104438

Magano, J., Fraiz-Brea, J. A., & Ângela Leite, . (2023). Dark tourism, the Holocaust, and well-being: A systematic review. *Heliyon*, *9*(1), e13064. DOI: 10.1016/j.heliyon.2023.e13064 PMID: 36711286

Magano, J., Fraiz-Brea, J. A., & Leite, Â. (2022). Dark tourists: Profile, practices, motivations, and wellbeing to visit it. *International Journal of Environmental Research and Public Health*, *19*(19), 12100. DOI: 10.3390/ijerph191912100 PMID: 36231400

Magano, J., Fraiz-Brea, J. A., & Leite, Â. (2022). Dark tourists: Profile, practices, motivations and wellbeing. *International Journal of Environmental Research and Public Health*, *19*(19), 12100. DOI: 10.3390/ijerph191912100 PMID: 36231400

Min, J., Yang, K., & Thapa Magar, A. (2021). Dark tourism segmentation by tourists' motivations for visiting earthquake sites in Nepal: Implications for dark tourism. *Asia Pacific Journal of Tourism Research*, *26*(8), 866–878. DOI: 10.1080/10941665.2021.1925315

Mora, J. A., Nieto, A., & León-Gómez, A. (2023). A bibliometric analysis and systematic review of dark tourism: Trends, impact, and prospects. *Administrative Sciences*, *13*(11).

Nhlabathi, S. S., & Maharaj, B. (2020). The dark tourism discipline: A creative brand in a competitive academic environment? *Current Issues in Tourism*, *23*(19), 2428–2439. DOI: 10.1080/13683500.2019.1636770

Nørfelt, A., Kock, F., Karpen, I. O., & Josiassen, A. (2022). Pleasure through pain: An empirical examination of benign masochism in tourism. *Journal of Travel Research*.

Oren, G., Shani, A., & Poria, Y. (2021). Dialectical emotions in a dark heritage site: A study at the Auschwitz death camp. *Tourism Management*, *82*, 104194. DOI: 10.1016/j.tourman.2020.104194

Otoo, F. E., Kim, S. S., & King, B. E. M. (2021). African diaspora tourism: How motivations shape experiences. *Journal of Destination Marketing & Management*, *20*, 100565. DOI: 10.1016/j.jdmm.2021.100565

Page, M. J., Moher, D., Bossuyt, P. M., Boutron, I., Hoffmann, T. C., Mulrow, C. D., Shamseer, L., Tetzlaff, J. M., Akl, E. A., Brennan, S. E., Chou, R., Glanville, J., Grimshaw, J. M., Hróbjartsson, A., Lalu, M. M., Li, T., Loder, E. W., Mayo-Wilson, E., McDonald, S., & McKenzie, J. E. (2021). PRISMA 2020 explanation and elaboration: Updated guidance and exemplars for reporting systematic reviews. *British Medical Journal*, *372*, 160. DOI: 10.1136/bmj.n160 PMID: 33781993

Podoshen, J. S., Yan, G., Andrzejewski, S. A., Wallin, J., & Venkatesh, V. (2018). Dark tourism, abjection and blood: A festival context. *Tourism Management*, *64*, 346–356. DOI: 10.1016/j.tourman.2017.09.003

Prayag, G., Buda, D.-M., & Jordan, E. J. (2021). Mortality salience and meaning in life for residents visiting dark tourism sites. *Journal of Sustainable Tourism*, *29*(9), 1508–1528. DOI: 10.1080/09669582.2020.1823398

Qian, L., Guo, J., Qiu, H., Zheng, C., & Ren, L. (2023). Exploring destination image of dark tourism via analyzing user generated photos: A deep learning approach. *Tourism Management Perspectives*, *48*, 101147. DOI: 10.1016/j.tmp.2023.101147

Qian, L., Zheng, C., Wang, J., Pérez Sánchez, M. D. L. Á., Parra López, E., & Li, H. (2021). Dark tourism destinations: The relationships between tourists' on-site experience, destination image and behavioural intention. *Tourism Review*.

Raine, R. (2013). A dark tourist spectrum. *International Journal of Culture, Tourism and Hospitality Research*, *7*(3), 242–256. DOI: 10.1108/IJCTHR-05-2012-0037

Seaton, T. (2021). Remembrancing, remembrance gangs and co-opted encounters: Loading and reloading dark tourism experiences. In Sharpley, R. (Ed.), *Routledge handbook of the tourist experience* (pp. 328–350). Routledge. DOI: 10.4324/9781003219866-28

Seraphin, H., & Korstanje, M. E. (2021). Dark tourism tribes: Social capital as a variable. In Pforr, P., Dowling, R. K., & Volgger, M. (Eds.), *Consumer tribes in tourism: Contemporary perspectives on special-interest tourism* (pp. 83–99). Springer. DOI: 10.1007/978-981-15-7150-3_7

Shetty, P. (2020). Dark tourism in India. *International Journal of Disaster Recovery and Business Continuity*, *11*(1), 622–627.

Soulard, J., Stewart, W., Larson, M., & Samson, E. (2022). Dark tourism and social mobilization: Transforming travelers after visiting a Holocaust museum. *Journal of Travel Research*, *62*(4), 632–646.

Soulard, J., Stewart, W., Larson, M., & Samson, E. (2022). Dark tourism and social mobilization: Transforming travelers after visiting a Holocaust museum. *Journal of Travel Research*, *62*(4), 820–840. DOI: 10.1177/00472875221105871

Stone, P., & Sharpley, R. (2008). Consuming dark tourism: A thanatological perspective. *Annals of Tourism Research*, *35*(2), 574–595. DOI: 10.1016/j.annals.2008.02.003

Stone, P. R., & Morton, C. (2022). Portrayal of the female dead in dark tourism. *Annals of Tourism Research*, *97*, 103506. DOI: 10.1016/j.annals.2022.103506

Sun, J., & Lv, X. (2021). Feeling dark, seeing dark: Mind–body in dark tourism. *Annals of Tourism Research*, *86*, 103087. DOI: 10.1016/j.annals.2020.103087

Wight, A. C. (2020). Visitor perceptions of European Holocaust heritage: A social media analysis. *Tourism Management*, *81*, 104142. DOI: 10.1016/j.tourman.2020.104142

Zhang, Y. (2021). Unpacking visitors' experiences at dark tourism sites of natural disasters. *Tourism Management Perspectives*, *40*, 100880. DOI: 10.1016/j.tmp.2021.100880

Zhang, Y. (2022). Experiencing human identity at dark tourism sites of natural disasters. *Tourism Management*, *89*, 104451. DOI: 10.1016/j.tourman.2021.104451

Zhang, Y. (2022). Experiencing human identity at dark tourism sites of natural disasters. *Tourism Management*, *89*, 104451. DOI: 10.1016/j.tourman.2021.104451

ADDITIONAL READING

Azman, N., Valeri, M., Albattat, A., & Singh, A. (2025). Decoding Tourist Behavior in the Digital Era: Insights for Effective.

Biran, A., & Hyde, K. F. (2013). New perspectives on dark tourism. *International Journal of Culture, Tourism and Hospitality Research*, *7*(3), 191–198. DOI: 10.1108/IJCTHR-05-2013-0032

Magano, J., Fraiz-Brea, J. A., & Leite, Â. (2023). Dark tourism, the holocaust, and well-being: A systematic review. *Heliyon*, *9*(1), e13064. DOI: 10.1016/j.heliyon.2023.e13064 PMID: 36711286

Mora Forero, J. A., Nieto Mejia, A., & León-Gómez, A. (2023). A bibliometric analysis and systematic review of dark tourism: Trends, impact, and prospects. *Administrative Sciences*, *13*(11), 238. DOI: 10.3390/admsci13110238

Ray, N. (2014). Rural Tourism Issues And Challenges: A Case From Kamarpukur, India. *International Journal of Business Quantitative Economics and Applied Management Research*, *1*(4), 90–106.

Ray, N. (2015). Factors Influencing Tourists' Motivational Determinants for Promotion of Tourism Destination: An Empirical Assessment on Rural Tourism with Special Reference from Kamarpukur, West Bengal. In *Hospitality, Travel, and Tourism: Concepts, Methodologies, Tools, and Applications* (pp. 924-933). IGI Global.

Ray, N. (2017). Role of the marketing mix (7Ps) on the development of rural tourism: Evidence from Kamarpukur, West Bengal, India. In *Tourism Marketing* (pp. 173–186). Apple Academic Press. DOI: 10.1201/9781315365862-10

Ray, N., Das, S., Mutsuddi, I., Roy, M., & Majumder, T. (2025). Digital Technologies Shaping Tourist Behavior. In *Navigating AI and the Metaverse in Scientific Research* (pp. 501–520). IGI Global Scientific Publishing. DOI: 10.4018/979-8-3373-0340-6.ch024

Ray, N., Dash, D. K., Sengupta, P. P., & Ghosh, S. (2012). Rural tourism and it's impact on socioeconomic condition: Evidence from West Bengal, India. *Global Journal of Business Research*, *6*(2), 11–22.

Wang, J., & Luo, X. (2018). Resident perception of dark tourism impact: The case of Beichuan County, China. *Journal of Tourism and Cultural Change*, *16*(5), 463–481. DOI: 10.1080/14766825.2017.1345918

KEY TERMS AND DEFINITION

Dark Tourism: Travel to sites associated with death, tragedy, or suffering, such as battlefields, memorials, or disaster areas.

Dark Tourism Motive: The reasons or psychological drives behind why individuals visit places linked to death or disaster, such as curiosity, mourning, education, or thrill-seeking.

Dark Tourism Impact: The social, cultural, and emotional effects that visiting or promoting tragic sites can have on communities, visitors, and historical memory.

Cultural Narratives: Shared stories, traditions, and interpretations that shape how societies understand and communicate their history, identity, and values.

Economic Effects: The financial benefits or drawbacks dark tourism brings to local economies, including job creation, increased tourism revenue, or possible overdependence.

Chapter 2
Integrating Artificial Intelligence in Enhancing Cultural Tourism Experiences

Amrik Singh
https://orcid.org/0000-0003-3598-8787
Lovely Professional University, India

ABSTRACT

The rapid advancement of Artificial Intelligence (AI) is reshaping the cultural tourism sector, offering unprecedented opportunities to enhance visitor experiences and promote heritage preservation. This chapter explores the transformative role of AI in cultural tourism, focusing on its applications, benefits, and challenges. AI-powered tools such as virtual assistants, chatbots, and recommendation systems are revolutionizing how tourists interact with cultural sites by providing personalized and immersive experiences. The integration of machine learning and natural language processing allows for dynamic translation, real-time navigation, and context-aware storytelling, ensuring accessibility and engagement for diverse audiences. This chapter aims to conclude integrating AI into cultural tourism to create inclusive, sustainable, and enriched visitor experience.

INTRODUCTION

Cultural tourism, a sector deeply rooted in the appreciation of history, art, and heritage, has experienced significant transformation in recent years due to the integration of technological innovations. Among these advancements, Artificial In-

DOI: 10.4018/979-8-3693-3196-5.ch002

telligence (AI) has emerged as a pivotal force in redefining the way cultural tourism operates and engages with its audiences. By combining the power of machine learning, data analytics, and intelligent systems, AI is not only enhancing visitor experiences but also contributing to the sustainable management and preservation of cultural assets. Moreover, AI is instrumental in managing cultural tourism resources through predictive analytics, crowd management, and demand forecasting, thereby addressing sustainability concerns (Maheshwari et al., 2024; Sharma & Singh, 2024; Sharma & Singh, 2024a; Singh & Das, 2025; Singh & Hassan, 2024; Singh, 2024; Asplet & Cooper, 2000; Barney, 1991; Bounia et al., 2008; Bradford et al., 2008; Buhalis, & Yen, 2020; Buhalis, & Amaranggana, 2014; Christou, 2012; Davis, 1989; Dessylla, 2004; Dobrica, 2014; Edensor, 2001; Fuchs, 2014; Gholipour, 2014; Gretzel, 2011; Lavvas, 2001; MacDonald, & Joliffe, 2003). Case studies highlighting successful implementations of AI in museums, heritage sites, and cultural festivals will demonstrate its potential to bridge the gap between tradition and innovation. However, the adoption of AI also raises ethical and operational challenges, including data privacy, digital equity, and the risk of cultural homogenization. The appeal of cultural tourism lies in its ability to connect individuals with the tangible and intangible elements of a region's heritage. However, traditional approaches to cultural tourism often face challenges such as accessibility, engagement, and resource management. AI offers innovative solutions to these challenges by enabling personalized and immersive experiences that cater to the diverse needs and preferences of modern tourists. From AI-powered virtual assistants that provide real-time information to chatbots capable of offering multilingual support, the integration of AI technologies is revolutionizing the visitor journey. Beyond enhancing individual experiences, AI plays a crucial role in addressing the broader challenges of the cultural tourism sector. Predictive analytics and intelligent resource allocation systems empower cultural organizations to manage visitor flows, optimize operations, and forecast trends (Maheshwari et al., 2024; Sharma & Singh, 2024; Sharma & Singh, 2024a; Singh & Das, 2025; Singh & Hassan, 2024; Singh, 2024; Asplet & Cooper, 2000; Barney, 1991; Bounia et al., 2008; Bradford et al., 2008; Buhalis, & Yen, 2020; Buhalis, & Amaranggana, 2014; Christou, 2012; Davis, 1989; Dessylla, 2004; Dobrica, 2014; Edensor, 2001). These capabilities are particularly valuable in mitigating the environmental and social impacts of tourism, thereby aligning with sustainable development goals. However, the adoption of AI in cultural tourism is not without its complexities. Ethical considerations surrounding data privacy, digital equity, and cultural sensitivity require careful attention to ensure that AI applications respect and preserve the authenticity of cultural heritage. This chapter delves into the multifaceted role of AI in cultural tourism, exploring its benefits, challenges, and future potential. By examining case studies and emerging trends, the chapter aims to provide a comprehensive understanding of how AI can transform cultural tourism into a more accessible, sustainable, and enriched domain. Culture and tourism have always been inextricably linked. Cultural sights, attractions and events provide an important motivation for travel, and travel in itself generates culture. But it is only in recent decades that the link between culture and tourism has been more explicitly identified as a specific form of consumption: cultural tourism (Singh, 2024; Asplet & Cooper, 2000; Barney, 1991; Bounia et al., 2008; Bradford et al., 2008; Buhalis, & Yen, 2020; Buhalis, & Amaranggana, 2014;Christou, 2012; Davis, 1989; Dessylla, 2004; Dobrica, 2014; Edensor, 2001; Fuchs, 2014; Gholipour, 2014; Gretzel, 2011; Lavvas, 2001; MacDonald, & Joliffe, 2003). The emergence of cultural tourism as a social phenomenon and as an object of academic study can be traced back to the surge in post-World War 2 leisure travel. In Europe, travel helped to increase cultural understanding as well as rebuilding shattered economies. As incomes and consumption continued to rise in the 1960s and 1970s, so did international travel, and the consumption of culture. By the 1980s the flow of international tourists to major sites and attractions began to attract enough attention for the label 'cultural tourism' to be attached to an emerging niche market. Early academic studies of cultural tourism also surfaced at this time, and the World Tourism Organisation (WTO, as it was then) produced its first definition of the phenomenon. In the early 1990s the first estimate of the size of this 'new' market also emerged (at 37% of all international tourism) and were attributed to the WTO, even though Bywater (1993) comments that it was not clear how this estimate was derived. Interest in cultural tourism continued to grow throughout the 1980s and 1990s, driven by the 'heritage boom' (Hewison, 1987), the growth of international and domestic travel and the identification of cultural tourism as a 'good' form of tourism that would stimulate the economy and help conserve culture (Maheshwari et al., 2024; Sharma & Singh, 2024; Sharma & Singh, 2024a; Singh & Das, 2025; Singh & Hassan, 2024; Singh, 2024; Asplet & Cooper, 2000; Barney, 1991; Bounia et al., 2008; Bradford et al., 2008; Buhalis, & Yen, 2020; Buhalis, & Amaranggana, 2014;Christou, 2012; Davis, 1989MacDonald, & Joliffe, 2003). The beginning of the 1990s indicates a period of transformation of cultural tourism which, unlike the original orientation towards elite clientele, found a new opportunity for development in the orientation towards the mass market. Cultural tourism became a well-established phenomenon in many tourism destinations and was increasingly the target of academic research. The first textbooks on cultural tourism began to emerge ((Maheshwari et al., 2024; Sharma & Singh, 2024; Sharma & Singh, 2024a; Singh & Das, 2025; Singh & Hassan, 2024; Singh, 2024; Asplet & Cooper, 2000; Barney, 1991; Bounia et al., 2008) and a growing range of research papers appeared, linked to many different theoretical and methodological approaches (Maheshwari et al., 2024; Sharma & Singh, 2024; Sharma & Singh, 2024a; Singh & Das, 2025; Singh & Hassan, 2024; Singh, 2024; Asplet & Cooper, 2000; Barney, 1991).Growth in cultural tourism was also marked by fragmentation into a number of emerging niches, such as heritage tourism, arts tourism, gastronomic tourism, film tourism and creative tourism. Just as an expanding notion of culture had helped to stimulate the growth of cultural tourism in the 1990s, so the fragmentation of the cultural tourism concept itself helped to produce a surge in the proportion of publications dedicated to the field. Growth also brought its own challenges, and by 2013 Boniface was already signalling problems with the overcrowding of World Heritage Sites, a phenomenon that is now being linked with the idea of 'overtourism'. The problems being encountered with the conservation of tangible heritage and the growing desire of tourists for new experiences also helped to focus attention on the role of intangible heritage in tourism ((Maheshwari et al., 2024; Sharma & Singh, 2024; Sharma & Singh, 2024a; Christou, 2012; Davis, 1989; Dessylla, 2004; Dobrica, 2014; Edensor, 2001; Fuchs, 2014; Gholipour, 2014; Gretzel, 2011; Lavvas, 2001; MacDonald, & Joliffe, 2003)).Artificial Intelligence (AI) has become a transformative force in cultural tourism, reshaping the way destinations, institutions, and tourists interact. The integration of AI technologies in cultural tourism is crucial for the following reasons:

Enhanced Visitor Experiences

AI enables personalized and immersive experiences by analyzing visitor preferences and behavior. Tools such as AI-driven virtual assistants and chatbots provide real-time information, multilingual support, and tailored recommendations, ensuring a seamless and engaging visitor journey.

Improved Accessibility

AI-powered solutions make cultural tourism more inclusive. Features like automatic language translation, assistive technologies for differently-abled individuals, and virtual reality (VR) experiences allow a wider audience to explore cultural sites regardless of geographical or physical limitations.

Efficient Resource Management

AI assists in managing resources effectively by predicting visitor patterns, optimizing staff deployment, and automating routine operations. This is particularly beneficial for heritage sites that face challenges related to crowd management and conservation.

Sustainability and Conservation

AI plays a significant role in promoting sustainable tourism by monitoring and mitigating the environmental impacts of tourism activities. Predictive analytics can forecast visitor footfall and prevent over-tourism, while AI-driven monitoring systems ensure the preservation of fragile cultural assets.

Digital Storytelling and Interpretation

AI enhances storytelling through dynamic and interactive content delivery. By leveraging AI, cultural institutions can create engaging narratives using augmented reality (AR), virtual reality (VR), and other multimedia formats, offering tourists an enriched understanding of cultural heritage.

Cultural Heritage Preservation

AI supports the digital preservation of cultural assets through technologies like 3D scanning, modeling, and digital archiving. These efforts ensure that cultural artifacts and sites are safeguarded for future generations, even in the face of natural or human-induced threats.

Global Outreach and Marketing

AI-driven marketing strategies help cultural destinations reach a global audience. Advanced data analytics identify target demographics, optimize advertising campaigns, and enhance engagement through social media and other digital platforms.

Data-Driven Decision Making

AI enables cultural tourism organizations to make informed decisions based on data insights. From identifying emerging trends to analyzing visitor feedback, AI empowers stakeholders to adapt strategies for better outcomes.

Innovation in Cultural Events

AI facilitates the organization of cultural events by automating ticketing, providing real-time updates, and creating virtual event spaces. These innovations expand the reach of cultural festivals and exhibitions to a global audience.

Bridging Tradition and Modernity

AI acts as a bridge between traditional cultural practices and modern technological advancements. It ensures that cultural heritage remains relevant in a rapidly evolving digital landscape, fostering a deeper connection between the past and the present. In conclusion, AI is not merely a tool for enhancing operational efficiency but a catalyst for reimagining the cultural tourism experience. By leveraging its potential responsibly, cultural tourism can become more accessible, sustainable, and innovative while preserving the authenticity and integrity of cultural heritage.

TECHNOLOGY IN CULTURAL TOURISM

Tourism has long been acknowledged as a significant engine of economic growth and cultural interaction, with locations using their distinct charms to attract both local and international tourists. In the digital age, using technology in tourist marketing has become more important for improving visitor engagement and destination competitiveness (Maheshwari et al., 2024; Sharma & Singh, 2024; Sharma & Singh, 2024a; Singh & Das, 2025; Singh & Hassan, 2024; Singh, 2024; Asplet & Cooper, 2000; Barney, 1991; Bounia et al., 2008; Bradford et al., 2008; Buhalis, & Yen, 2020; Buhalis, & Amaranggana, 2014; Christou, 2012; Davis, 1989; Dessylla, 2004; Dobrica, 2014; Edensor, 2001; Fuchs, 2014; Gholipour, 2014; Gretzel, 2011; Lavvas, 2001; MacDonald, & Joliffe, 2003). Artificial intelligence (AI) and big data analytics have emerged as transformative tools for tourism stakeholders to fine-tune marketing tactics, tailor tourist experiences, and maximize resource allocation. Simultaneously, cultural heritage remains an important tourism component, providing the authenticity and feeling of place those modern visitors seek. Technology has become an indispensable component of cultural tourism, enhancing how heritage, traditions, and cultural experiences are shared and experienced globally.

Digital Accessibility and Inclusion

Virtual Reality (VR) and Augmented Reality (AR): VR and AR allow users to explore cultural sites, museums, and heritage landmarks from anywhere in the world, making experiences accessible to those who cannot visit in person.

Multilingual Support: AI-powered translation tools and voice guides make cultural content accessible to a diverse audience.

Enhanced Visitor Experience

Interactive Exhibits: Touchscreens, holograms, and smart exhibits bring history and culture to life in an engaging and immersive manner.

Mobile Applications: Dedicated apps provide audio guides, navigation, and real-time updates, enriching the on-site visitor experience.

Preservation of Cultural Heritage

3D Scanning and Modeling: Digital replicas of cultural artifacts and sites ensure preservation for future generations while allowing researchers and tourists to explore them virtually.

Digital Archiving: High-resolution imaging and cloud storage safeguard endangered artifacts and documents.

Smart Resource Management

Crowd Management Systems: IoT sensors and AI analyze visitor flow, ensuring better crowd control and reduced strain on cultural sites.

Sustainability Monitoring: Technology helps track environmental impacts and promotes sustainable tourism practices.

Education and Interpretation

Digital Storytelling: Multimedia technologies present cultural narratives in engaging formats like videos, animations, and interactive timelines.

Gamification: Games and quizzes based on cultural themes make learning about history and traditions fun and interactive.

Marketing and Global Outreach

Social Media Campaigns: Platforms like Instagram and TikTok amplify the visibility of cultural destinations, engaging younger audiences.

Targeted Advertising: Data analytics and AI-driven campaigns identify and reach potential cultural tourists effectively.

Cultural Events and Festivals

Virtual Events: Technology enables live streaming and virtual participation in cultural festivals, expanding their reach to global audiences.

Augmented Experiences: Digital projections, AR, and interactive installations elevate the appeal of events.

Personalization of Experiences

AI-Powered Recommendations: Machine learning algorithms tailor travel itineraries, suggesting cultural activities based on individual interests.

Wearable Technology: Devices like smart glasses or augmented reality headsets provide context-aware cultural insights during visits.

Bridging Past and Future

Blockchain for Authenticity: Blockchain ensures the authenticity and traceability of cultural artifacts and experiences.

Digital Twin Technology: Creating digital twins of cultural sites aids in restoration and visitor engagement.

CHALLENGES AND OPPORTUNITIES

While technology offers numerous benefits, it also presents challenges such as digital equity, data privacy, and ensuring that technological enhancements do not overshadow the authenticity of cultural experiences. Addressing these issues requires a balance between innovation and preserving cultural integrity. Technology is revolutionizing cultural tourism by making it more inclusive, engaging, and sustainable. By embracing innovation responsibly, cultural tourism stakeholders can offer enriched experiences while safeguarding heritage for future generations. Nowadays, cultural development is considered to be a matter of high priority for a modern state. Local cultural assets play a major role in the design and development of a successful and sustainable national cultural development policy (Sharma & Singh, 2024; Sharma & Singh, 2024a; Singh & Das, 2025; Singh & Hassan, 2024; Singh, 2024; Asplet & Cooper, 2000; Barney, 1991; Bounia et al., 2008; Bradford et al., 2008; Buhalis, & Yen, 2020; Buhalis, & Amaranggana, 2014;Christou, 2012; Davis, 1989; Dessylla, 2004; Dobrica, 2014; Edensor, 2001; Fuchs, 2014; Gholipour, 2014; Gretzel, 2011; Lavvas, 2001; MacDonald, & Joliffe, 2003). AI-driven customization, data analytics, and cultural authenticity help to boost tourist engagement and destination competitiveness. The study uses qualitative methodologies, including interviews with tourism stakeholders and content analysis, to identify significant themes such as AI-driven recommendation systems, data-driven decision-making, and cultural storytelling.

DIMENSIONS OF AI INCLUSION IN CULTURAL TOURISM

The integration of Artificial Intelligence (AI) into cultural tourism encompasses several interconnected dimensions, each contributing to a holistic transformation of the sector. These dimensions highlight the multifaceted impact of AI on cultural tourism, from visitor experiences to heritage preservation and sustainability.

Technological Dimension

- AI Technologies: Chatbots, virtual assistants, predictive analytics, machine learning, and recommendation systems are pivotal tools in cultural tourism.
- Applications: Enhancing digital interfaces, providing real-time information, and creating immersive experiences through AR/VR.
- Impact: Improves operational efficiency, fosters innovation, and ensures adaptability to changing technological trends.

Cultural Dimension

- Preservation: AI facilitates the digital archiving of artifacts, creating 3D models and virtual exhibitions.
- Storytelling: Enables dynamic and interactive storytelling that respects and highlights the uniqueness of local cultures.
- Impact: Strengthens the preservation of tangible and intangible cultural heritage while ensuring authenticity.

Social Dimension

- Accessibility: AI tools like language translation and assistive technologies make cultural tourism more inclusive.
- Engagement: Facilitates interaction and connection between diverse cultures through digital and virtual platforms.
- Impact: Promotes cultural exchange, inclusivity, and broader participation from underserved or remote audiences.

Economic Dimension

- Revenue Generation: AI-powered targeted marketing and dynamic pricing strategies boost profitability for cultural institutions.
- Cost Efficiency: Automation of routine tasks reduces operational costs and optimizes resource allocation.
- Impact: Drives economic growth in local communities and reinvestment in cultural tourism infrastructure.

Sustainability Dimension

- Resource Management: AI-driven crowd control and predictive analytics minimize over-tourism and environmental degradation.
- Conservation: Smart monitoring systems track and mitigate impacts on fragile heritage sites.
- Impact: Aligns cultural tourism with sustainable development goals, ensuring long-term viability.

Ethical Dimension

- Data Privacy: AI use raises concerns about the handling and security of visitor data.
- Cultural Sensitivity: Risks of cultural appropriation or homogenization require careful management.
- Impact: Ensures responsible AI deployment that respects user rights and cultural authenticity.

Educational Dimension

- Knowledge Sharing: AI enhances learning through gamified experiences, AR/VR-based storytelling, and interactive exhibits.
- Research: Provides insights into visitor behavior and emerging trends, enabling more effective cultural tourism strategies.
- Impact: Encourages cultural awareness and appreciation among diverse audiences.

Innovation Dimension

- Product Development: AI fosters the creation of new cultural tourism products, such as virtual tours and AI-guided itineraries.

- Technological Integration: Combines AI with other technologies like IoT, blockchain, and AR/VR for advanced applications.
- Impact: Drives continuous innovation, attracting tech-savvy tourists and investors.

Governance Dimension

- Policy Making: Data insights from AI help formulate effective policies for cultural tourism development and heritage protection.
- Collaboration: Encourages partnerships between governments, cultural institutions, and technology providers.
- Impact: Promotes strategic planning and collaboration for sustainable growth.

The inclusion of AI in cultural tourism spans multiple dimensions, each offering unique benefits and challenges. By addressing these dimensions comprehensively, stakeholders can leverage AI to enhance cultural tourism experiences while safeguarding heritage, fostering inclusivity, and promoting sustainability. Integrating artificial intelligence (AI) into cultural tourism offers numerous opportunities but also poses significant challenges. These challenges can be categorized into technological, ethical, cultural, and operational aspects:

Technological Challenges

- **Data Availability and Quality**: Cultural tourism often relies on diverse datasets such as historical records, cultural artifacts, and visitor preferences. Ensuring data accuracy and completeness can be difficult.
- **Infrastructure Gaps**: Many cultural tourism sites, especially in rural or developing regions, lack the technological infrastructure needed to support AI systems.
- **Interoperability**: Integrating AI with existing systems such as ticketing platforms, virtual tour software, or local guide services requires seamless compatibility.
- **Scalability**: AI applications may not scale well across varying sizes and types of cultural sites.

Ethical Concerns

- **Cultural Sensitivity**: AI applications must respect the unique traditions and cultural norms of the sites, avoiding misrepresentation or oversimplification of cultural heritage.

- **Bias and Stereotypes**: AI models trained on biased data may perpetuate stereotypes or misinterpret cultural significance.
- **Job Displacement**: Increased AI integration might reduce reliance on local tour guides and cultural interpreters, leading to employment concerns.

Cultural Challenges

- **Authenticity**: Over-reliance on AI-generated content, such as virtual tours or AR/VR experiences, may detract from the authentic experience of cultural tourism.
- **Community Acceptance**: Local communities might resist AI adoption due to fears of cultural dilution or lack of involvement in AI-based initiatives.
- **Globalization vs. Localization**: Balancing AI's globalized approach with the need for localized, culturally nuanced experiences is complex.

Operational Issues

- **Cost and Maintenance**: Implementing and maintaining AI solutions can be expensive, especially for smaller or underfunded cultural sites.
- **Skill Gaps**: Training staff to use AI tools effectively requires investment in education and capacity-building.
- **Cybersecurity**: Protecting sensitive visitor data and cultural heritage information from cyber threats is a significant concern.

Visitor Engagement Challenges

- **Over-Reliance on Technology**: Visitors may prioritize AI-driven experiences over human interaction, leading to a loss of personal connection.
- **Digital Divide**: Older visitors or those unfamiliar with technology may struggle to engage with AI-powered tools.

Regulatory and Legal Challenges

- **Copyright and Intellectual Property**: Using cultural artifacts in AI applications may involve legal complexities regarding ownership and usage rights.
- **Data Privacy**: Ensuring compliance with data protection laws (e.g., GDPR) when collecting and processing visitor data.

Sustainability Concerns

- **Environmental Impact**: AI systems, particularly those involving data centers or AR/VR applications, can have significant energy consumption, impacting environmental sustainability.
- **Overtourism**: AI-driven marketing campaigns might attract excessive visitors to fragile cultural sites, exacerbating conservation issues.

Strategies to Address Challenges

- Develop culturally sensitive AI models in collaboration with local experts and communities.
- Invest in digital infrastructure and provide training for stakeholders.
- Balance AI integration with authentic, human-led experiences to preserve cultural integrity.
- Implement robust legal and ethical guidelines for AI applications in cultural tourism.

AI holds immense potential to enhance cultural tourism, but its integration must be managed carefully to respect cultural heritage and provide meaningful, sustainable visitor experiences.

CONCLUSION

Tourism is a socio-economic phenomenon with important effects on human life and the national economies of the states. The journey, i.e. the movement of man from the place of permanent residence in another place, is the key element of tourism. Alongside the main ingredient is the incentive for vacations and recreation, a fundamental right of all people. As with other Greek destinations with a heavy reliance on a basic sun, sea and sand tourism model, Thessaly region is busy trying to diversify its tourism product. Cultural tourism is seen as one important means of achieving diversification. Nowadays, new cultural tourism is focused on the integration of production and consumption, and it creates linkages between suppliers and consumers. Instead of passive consumption, cultural tourists demonstrate a proactive approach to meeting their needs, wanting to actively participate in experiences while travelling. On the other side, suppliers focus their attention on the close interaction with consumers and co-creation of high-quality experiences. Indicate that AI-powered solutions considerably improve consumer experiences, and Big Data analytics boost strategic planning and market segmentation (Maheshwari et al., 2024; Sharma & Singh, 2024; Sharma & Singh, 2024a; Singh & Das, 2025; Singh & Hassan, 2024; Singh, 2024; Asplet & Cooper, 2000; Barney, 1991; Bounia et al., 2008; Bradford et al., 2008; Buhalis, & Yen, 2020; Buhalis, & Amaranggana, 2014;Christou, 2012; Davis, 1989; Dessylla, 2004; Dobrica, 2014; Edensor, 2001; Fuchs, 2014; Gholipour, 2014; Gretzel, 2011; Lavvas, 2001; MacDonald, & Joliffe, 2003). Furthermore, cultural heritage remains an important aspect in attracting tourists, with digital storytelling and immersive technology helping to preserve and promote Klaten's cultural treasures. AI-powered interactive experiences, such as augmented reality (AR) and virtual reality (VR), enhance visitor engagement, making cultural institutions more accessible and desirable. The study emphasizes the importance of predictive analytics in studying visitor behavior and customizing marketing techniques to enhance destination branding.Despite these benefits, issues such as technology infrastructure, data protection concerns, and the digital gap between enterprises remain. Addressing these issues needs collaboration among local governments, tourist stakeholders, and technology suppliers to promote inclusive and ethical AI deployment.

REFERENCES

Asplet, M., & Cooper, M. (2000). Cultural designs in New Zealand souvenir clothing: The question of authenticity. *Tourism Management*, *21*(3), 307–312. DOI: 10.1016/S0261-5177(99)00061-8

Bachleitner, R., & Zins, A. (1999). Cultural tourism in rural communities: The residents' perspective. *Journal of Business Research*, *44*(3), 199–209. DOI: 10.1016/S0148-2963(97)00201-4

Barney, J. (1991). Firm resources and sustained competitive advantage. *Journal of Management*, *17*(1), 99–120. DOI: 10.1177/014920639101700108

Bounia, A., Nikonanou, N., & Oikonomou, M. (2008). *Technology in the service of cultural heritage*. Kaleidoscope.

Bradford, G., Gary, M., & Wallach, G. (2000). *The politics of culture: Policy perspectives for individuals, institutions and communities*. New Press.

Buhalis, D., & Amaranggana, A. (2014). Smart tourism destinations. *Information and Communication Technologies in Tourism*, *2014*, 553–564.

Buhalis, D., & Yen, C. (2020). Smart tourism: AI, Big Data, and innovation. *Journal of Travel & Tourism Marketing*, *37*(1), 1–6.

Christou, L. (2012). Is it possible to combine mass tourism with alternative forms of tourism: The case of Spain, Greece, Slovenia and Croatia. *Journal of Business Administration Online*, *11*, 1.

Davis, F. D. (1989). Perceived usefulness, perceived ease of use, and user acceptance of information technology. *Management Information Systems Quarterly*, *13*(3), 319–340. DOI: 10.2307/249008

Dessylla, H. (2004). *Griekenland: Nieuwe Vormen Van Toerisme. Elke*. The Hellenic Center for Investment.

Dobrica, J. (2014). Cultural tourism in the context of relations between mass and alternative tourism. *Current Issues in Tourism*, *12*(1), 1–8.

Edensor, T. (2001). Performing tourism, staging tourism: (re)producing tourist space and practice. *Tourist Studies*, *1*(1), 59–81. DOI: 10.1177/146879760100100104

Fuchs, M., Höpken, W., & Lexhagen, M. (2014). Big Data analytics for knowledge generation in tourism destinations. *Journal of Destination Marketing & Management*, *3*(4), 198–209. DOI: 10.1016/j.jdmm.2014.08.002

Gholipour, H. F., & Tajaddini, R. (2014). Cultural dimensions and outbound tourism. *Annals of Tourism Research*, *49*(November), 203–205. DOI: 10.1016/j.annals.2014.08.006

Gretzel, U. (2011). Intelligent systems in tourism: A social science perspective. *Annals of Tourism Research*, *38*(3), 757–779. DOI: 10.1016/j.annals.2011.04.014

Lavvas, G. P. (2001). *Cultural heritage*. Department of Communication and Mass Media, University of Athens. (in Greek)

MacDonald, R., & Joliffe, L. (2003). Cultural rural tourism: Evidence from Canada. *Annals of Tourism Research*, *30*(2), 307–322. DOI: 10.1016/S0160-7383(02)00061-0

Maheshwari, N., Singh, V., Singh, A., & Ansari, A. I. (2024). Understanding Artificial Intelligence Adoption in Tourism Services and Marketing: Boon or Bane? In Nadda, V., Tyagi, P., Singh, A., & Singh, V. (Eds.), *AI Innovations in Service and Tourism Marketing* (pp. 359–374). IGI Global., DOI: 10.4018/979-8-3693-7909-7.ch018

Seaton, A. V. (2002). Tourism as metempsychosis and metensomatosis: The personae of eternal recurrence. In Dann, G. M. S. (Ed.), *The tourist as a metaphor of the social world* (pp. 135–168). CABI. DOI: 10.1079/9780851996066.0135

Sharma, M., & Singh, A. (2024). Embracing Technological Innovation: A Review of Hi-Tech Services in Hospitality Industry. *Evergreen*, *11*(4), 2818–2830. DOI: 10.5109/7326926

Sharma, R., & Singh, A. (2024a). Use of Digital Technology in Improving Quality Education: A Global Perspectives and Trends. In Nadda, V., Tyagi, P., Moniz Vieira, R., & Tyagi, P. (Eds.), *Implementing Sustainable Development Goals in the Service Sector* (pp. 14–26). IGI Global., DOI: 10.4018/979-8-3693-2065-5.ch002

Singh, A. (2024). Virtual Research Collaboration and Technology Application: Drivers, Motivations, and Constraints. In Chakraborty, S. (Ed.), *Challenges of Globalization and Inclusivity in Academic Research* (pp. 250–258). IGI Global., DOI: 10.4018/979-8-3693-1371-8.ch016

Singh, A., & Das, R. (2025). Women's Participation in Cultural Preservation and Commercialization of Rural Tourism: A Study on West Bengal. In Hassan, V. (Ed.), *Navigating Mass Tourism to Island Destinations: Preservation and Cultural Heritage Challenges* (pp. 313–340). IGI Global Scientific Publishing., DOI: 10.4018/979-8-3693-9107-5.ch012

Singh, A., & Hassan, S. C. (2024). Service Innovation Through Blockchain Technology in the Tourism and Hospitality Industry: Applications, Trends, and Benefits. In Singh, S. (Ed.), *Service Innovations in Tourism: Metaverse, Immersive Technologies, and Digital Twin* (pp. 205–214). IGI Global., DOI: 10.4018/979-8-3693-1103-5.ch010

Smith, M. K. (2003). *Issues in cultural tourism studies*. Routledge. DOI: 10.4324/9780203402825

Spilanis, G. (2000). Tourism and regional development. The case of the Aegean islands. In Tsartas, P. (Ed.), *Tourism development, multidisciplinary approaches*. Exantas.

Tsartas, P. (2003). Cultural tourism and regional development: Problems, possibilities, prospects. In Deffner, A., Konstandakopoulos, D., & Psycharis, Y. (Eds.), *Culture and regional economic development in Europe*. University of Thessaly Press.

Chapter 3
Ability of Virtual Tourism to Enhance Tourists' Engagement and Satisfaction in the Middle East:
Moderating Role of Virtual Influencers

Tareq Nael Hashem
https://orcid.org/0000-0001-9564-931X
Applied Science Private University, Jordan

Ahmad Albattat
Asia Pacific University of Technology and Innovation, Malaysia

Firas Alotoum
Applied Science Private University, Jordan

Hanan Suleiman
Talal Abu Ghazaleh University Collage for Innovations, Jordan

ABSTRACT

We aimed in current study to realize the hypothesis that virtual influencers moderate the relationship between virtual tourism (Interactivity, Realism, Multimedia Content, Social Interaction, Personalization, User-Friendly Interface) and tourists' engagement and satisfaction. For that reason, we have depended on quantitative methodology

DOI: 10.4018/979-8-3693-3196-5.ch003

through uploading a self-administered questionnaire online through Google Forms. Total of (968) customers from EMNA region, Gulf countries and Egypt responded to the questionnaire which enabled us to screen and analyze collected primary data through SPSS. Results indicated that acceptance of the main hypothesis as there appeared a moderating influence of virtual influencers on the relationship between virtual tourism and tourists' engagement and satisfaction as the incorporation of Virtual Influencers and Virtual Tourism variables led to a significant increase of 1.4% in the overall interpretation variable, as evidenced by the R2 value.

INTRODUCTION

The contemporary tourism field undergoes fundamental transformations using technology as well as artificial intelligence to improve operational efficiency and personalization of services alongside sustainable tourism practices. Online travel agencies (OTAs) team up with mobile apps to use AI-powered chatbots for providing 24/7 customer service that improves user experience. When running through big data analytics businesses achieve travel prediction and pricing adjustment systems to generate tailored marketing strategies for individual customers. Tourists gain confidence about their travel selection through virtual reality (VR) and augmented reality (AR) systems that permit virtual destination experiences before booking reservations. According to Bhardwaj et al. (2025), tourists experience simpler travel planning through customized recommendations provided by AI engines used by Airbnb and Booking.com as the systems track user behaviors. Technical developments lead to better efficiency for tourism providers in maintaining market competitiveness and improved satisfaction among their customers.

Grundner and Neuhofer (2021) argued that artificial intelligence produces substantial modifications to sustainability and destination management operations throughout the tourism industry. Through a partnership between IoT and AI the industry operates smart tourism programs to maintain resources better and reduce environmental impacts and visitor density by applying predictive analytics and real-time tracking systems. Organizations gain control of crowded tourist transport systems using AI while hotels implement automated sustainability practices to lower their power usage. Through machine learning algorithms business organizations analyze sentiment feedback from customers to detect service issues which help them maintain elevated service standards. AI language translation tools help international tourists to overcome communication challenges thus simplifying their travel experience. As AI continuously progresses it will develop superior sustainable travel features that will boost the tourism sector throughout its recovery from the global pandemic (Vărzaru et al., 2021; Al-Romeedy & Hashem, 2024).

From the above argument, it can be said that this current study aimed to examine the moderating influence of virtual influencers on the relationship between virtual tourism (Interactivity, Realism, Multimedia Content, Social Interaction, Personalization, User-Friendly Interface) and tourists' engagement and satisfaction.

LITERATURE REVIEW

Tourists Engagement

Calza et al. (2022) noted that digital technologies together with interactive platforms have dramatically upgraded tourist engagement which creates stronger bonds between visitors and travel locations. Social media proves essential for travelers because it enables them to provide real-time experience reports while receiving recommendations from other users through platforms including Instagram and TikTok and travel forums. Tourists actively participate longer at destinations by using gamification methods including reward-based apps and location-based challenges which provide virtual badges when visitors reach landmarks and reward-based apps which engage users for more extended periods. The use of augmented reality (AR) applications showing historical reenactments together with interactive city guide systems enables travelers to be deeply immersed in environmental and cultural contexts which results in superior educational value as well as memorability of their travel experiences. Tourism providers can develop interactive experiences through these instruments to exceed basic sightseeing activities which build visitor engagement for personal discovery during their travel journey (Wirentake and Arfani, 2024).

According to Singh et al. (2025), tourist engagement transforms through AI-powered experiences because these systems deliver customized solutions which reflect the individual behaviors of visitors. Tourism benefits from immediate personal suggestions about things to do and places to eat which come from chatbots and virtual assistants and from AI algorithms that generate customized travel plans using behavioral history and current performance data. Panigrahy and Verma (2025) noted that touristic software combines visitor surveys with sentiment detection to help locations improve their content and sustain visitor enthusiasm. Virtual and hybrid events which feature live-streamed tours or workshops allow tourists to maintain their destination connections even after completing their journeys through physical travel. Experiential and participatory tourism delivers multiple benefits because it enhances visitor satisfaction levels and creates destination enthusiasts who become authentic promoters of travel destinations. Technology will shape future tourist engagement through the development of comprehensive experiences which provide customized and emotionally and intellectually meaningful interactions for visitors (Jia et al., 2025).

Tourists Satisfaction

Damanik and Yusuf (2022) and Dorokhov et al. (2023) stated that in the tourism sector success directly correlates with the level of satisfaction that tourists experience regarding their expectations. Businesses use technological progress and data analysis tools to provide clients with individualized experiences and smooth interactions which improve their satisfaction levels. The pairing of AI recommendation technology with personalized recommendations delivers customized activities, lodging options, dining choices depending on preferences and service optimization is achieved through real-time feedback instruments (Saxena et al., 2024). Mobile applications which provide digital check-ins and keyless hotel entry as well as instant customer service increase both convenience and reduce customer friction. Tourism providers benefit from sentiment analysis which evaluates online assessments and social media feelings to detect customer issues as well as market trends to enhance their services ahead of time. The tourism industry can develop stress-free travel experiences through innovative solutions which will make visitors feel valued and lead them to wish for future travel (Maczynska, 2024).

Virtual Influencers

Ying (2024) and Góraj (2024) argued that computer-generated virtual influencers through artificial intelligence create lifelike avatars which market products and ideas on social media platforms for various brands. The advanced technologies of artificial intelligence (AI) and 3D modeling as well as motion capture enable the creation of digital beings which simulate human interactions with audiences. Kim and Yang (2023) noted that brands find virtual influencers more desirable than human influencers because they maintain full leadership over character depiction along with their messages and actions. Virtual influencers have become increasingly popular in recent times because young tech-focused audiences find novelty value in their futuristic presentation. Major brands use virtual influencers to connect with customers and create market trends for fashion and beauty as well as lifestyle choices (Zhao, 2022; Homsi, D., etal.,2022).

On the other hand, the academic field – Davlembayeva et al. (2025); Xin et al. (2024); Looi and Kahlor (2024) - examine virtual influencers through the technical combination of digital achievements and marketing approaches and psychological methods. Research teams examine consumer reactions towards virtual influencers by defining parameters through which they compare these influencers to human influencers within their fields of influence (Davlembayeva et al., 2025). Research indicates that audiences become curious about virtual influencers because of their digital origin although these viewers often question their authentic qualities because they recognize the artificial nature of these influencers. The growing presence of virtual influencers triggers multiple ethical problems in advertising because of the need to inform viewers about artificial nature and potential deceptive practices (Hewapathirana and Perera, 2024). Major scientific research must examine how consumer behavior evolves with rising virtual influencers along with the way influencer marketing changes and the social effects of merging real life with digital fictions. Marketing professionals along with policymakers need to grasp these ongoing dynamics because they apply to their tasks of managing digital communication (Varadarajan et al., 2022; Hashem etal.,2024).

Virtual Tourism

According to Van Nuenen and Scarles (2021), individuals now employ digital technologies to digitally experience travel environments including places of interest along with cultural features that replicate true destinations without actual physical attendance. The new method depends on virtual reality (VR) alongside augmented reality (AR) combined with 360-degree videos and interactive platforms which generate deep and interactive experiences. Godovykh et al. (2022) noted that the rise of virtual tourism became prominent over recent years because technology advances coincided with pandemic travel restrictions brought by COVID-19. This distinctive service enables people to explore distant locations as well as examine historical sites and observe upcoming vacation spots before arranging their final travel plans. Virtual tourism creates an interactive and real-life simulation through multimedia elements which provides users across various groups including adventurers and scholars with an electronic exploration replacement for physical touring (Samala et al., 2024).

Zhang et al. (2023) stated that virtual tourism exists as an academic discipline which merges fields between information technology and marketing together with psychology and cultural studies. Assessments of virtual tourism technology include its ability to boost operator interaction and personal fulfillment together with its usefulness for destination choices and its value in ecological tourism by cutting down transportation-related ecosystem damage. While scientific research investigates the cultural heritage preservation capability of virtual tourism through digital restorations of historical locations and threatened landmarks (Alrihani, 2022). Mazzetto (2024) argued that the industry still faces obstacles because it needs to protect digital reality authenticity while working through technology limitations and determining how virtual tourism impacts tourism business operations over time.

Virtual tourism research continues to expand because it offers valuable knowledge about combining its virtual assets with traditional tourism practices to develop promotional marketing strategies and educational programs for preserving cultural heritage (Nag and Mishra, 2024; Hashem & Suleiman,2025).

Interactivity

Virtual tourism functions on interactivity since it enables users to experience digital spaces by taking active control instead of watching them from afar. Virtual destinations become more accessible through hotspots that users can click and 360-degree viewing together with motion-based controls that detect hand movements. Users benefit from immersive experiences when virtual environments offer interactive elements like quizzes combined with gamified tours and decision-based storytelling options throughout virtual museums. People who can interact with their virtual environment experience a shift from passive viewing to active participation and they stay engaged longer (Weber-Sabil and Han, 2021).

Figure 1. Interactivity in virtual tourism

(Weber-Sabil and Han, 2021)

Realism

According to Weber-Sabil and Han (2021), believable virtual tourism experiences require realism to become effective in their delivery to users. Virtual environments render authentic real-life scenes through high-resolution 360 videos, detailed 3D computer models and spatial audio systems. Simulated wind sensations together with programmable lights that adapt autonomously to surrounding stimuli work to decrease distinctions between the artificial and real modes of travel. Truly realistic simulation techniques strengthen user presence so visitors develop the sense that they stand in the actual place. Travel destinations become more relatable when their original qualities are authentic leading people to visit in reality and honor cultural or natural heritage sites.

Figure 2. Concept of reality in virtual tourism

(Weber-Sabil and Han, 2021)

Multimedia Content

de Jesus Duenas-Garcia (2022) argued that virtual tourism becomes deeper and more attractive through the combination of various multimedia content which includes videos alongside audio narrations together with animations and infographics. A virtual tour of the Great Wall of China unites drone aerial views with historical dialogue and time sequence visuals and environmental sounds to develop multi-sensory exploration. Various media platforms integrated into content support multiple learning abilities of users through educational and entertaining content delivery. Virtual environments attract repeat visits through dynamic content changes that match seasonality or present events directly to maintain user engagement.

Social Interaction

Alcala et al. (2023) noted that the combination of social interaction produces united virtual tourist activities which build connections between participants. Real-time communication through integrated chat features as well as multiplayer exploration options let users chat with both their friends and new acquaintances. Users on VR-Chat alongside Meta Horizon Worlds can use digital avatar platforms to virtually travel to replicated worldwide landmarks with others at the same time. The platform offers two capabilities: first users can share their travel experiences and second, they can create joint virtual postcards that improve overall engagement. Online visits that combine adventure with social activities become more interesting and rewarding when they blend exploration with socialization.

Personalization

Virtual tourism becomes more satisfying to tourists through personalized services which customize their trip experiences based on individual preferences and behaviors to deliver more relevant and deepened engagement. Virtual tourism platforms match each user through data reviews of past travel activities combined with personal preferences or trip history to suggest tailored plans. The method directs visitors toward meaningful and interactive exploration so they remain more engaged and experience increased satisfaction because the content remains specific to each individual's personal preferences. This leads users to develop stronger emotional bonds with virtual environments which generates faithfulness toward the platform and leads to extended time on the platform (Trunfio et al., 2022).

User-Friendly Interface

A user-friendly interface in virtual tourism improves both tourist engagement and satisfaction since it enables easy movement while decreasing system confusion and enhancing the intuitive pleasure of using the system. Users experience enhanced content connection through interfaces which use clear layouts and responsive controls along with interactive features to make their exploration both simple and engaging. This flawless interaction drives user engagement by prompting extended duration and higher frequency of use because it delivers an agreeable experience which fulfills or surpasses user expectations and thereby increases both follow-up visits and favorable recommendations (Shamim et al., 2024).

Research Questions and Objectives

The main question of current study is the following:
What is the moderating influence of virtual influencers on the relationship between virtual tourism (Interactivity, Realism, Multimedia Content, Social Interaction, Personalization, User-Friendly Interface) and tourists' engagement and satisfaction?
Realizing such aim required to achieve the following objectives:

- Identify the concept of virtual influencers in the digital age
- Highlight the idea of virtual tourism
- Investigate how may virtual influencers have an impact on the relationship between virtual tourism (Interactivity, Realism, Multimedia Content, Social Interaction, Personalization, User-Friendly Interface) and tourists' engagement and satisfaction

Model and Hypotheses

In order to better understand the relationship between variables, we have developed a theoretical framework as in Figure 3 below:

Figure 3. Theoretical framework

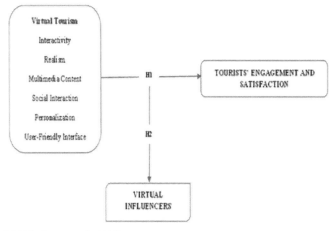

(Casillo et al. 2025; Omran et al., 2025)

From the above theoretical framework, we were able to extract the following set of hypotheses:

H1: Virtual tourism has an influence on tourists' engagement and satisfaction from perspective of online customers
H1.1: Interactivity has an influence on tourists' engagement and satisfaction from perspective of online customers
H1.2: Realism has an influence on tourists' engagement and satisfaction from perspective of online customers
H1.3: Multimedia Content has an influence on tourists' engagement and satisfaction from perspective of online customers
H1.4: Social Interaction has an influence on tourists' engagement and satisfaction from perspective of online customers
H1.5: Personalization has an influence on tourists' engagement and satisfaction from perspective of online customers
H1.6: User-Friendly Interface has an influence on tourists' engagement and satisfaction from perspective of online customers
H2: Virtual influencers moderate the relationship between virtual tourism and tourists' engagement and satisfaction from perspective of online customers

Underpinning Theory

The current study was carried out with the underpinning theory of '**Source Credibility Theory**' initially developed by Carl Hovland (Von Hohenberg and Guess, 2023). The theory demonstrates that source credibility defines how influential a particular source (virtual influencers) becomes in their interactions. The research assesses how virtual influencer credibility affects how virtual tourism attributes affect tourist engagement as well as satisfaction levels.

Theoretical and Practical Implications

We expected from the current study to have both theoretical and practical implications. From a theoretical perspective this research aims to broaden Source Credibility Theory through its analysis of virtual influencers since these are digital entities rather than human information sources. Research adds to the knowledge about virtual credibility functions and its modifying impact on virtual tourism attribute performance and user satisfaction. The research explores how trustworthiness along with expertise and reliability appear to non-human AI-driven sources.

From a practical perspective, this research discoveries enable tourism marketers and developers to create superior virtual tourism experiences by properly implementing virtual influencers. The research on virtual influencers demonstrates their ability to improve satisfaction alongside engagement so tourism marketers could implement them for virtual platform promotion and user experience customization and enhanced platform interaction. The adoption along with user retention improves as a result.

METHODOLOGY AND MATERIALS

Methodological Approach

We have chosen the quantitative methodology to be the main methodological approach in current study. It was found to be the most suitable as it can be applied on a larger sample size to collect primary data. This can of great help to generalize results.

Population and Sampling

The population of study consisted of customers from online sources. The tool of study was uploaded online through Google Forms in order to collect primary data from customers. After application process, we were able to collect primary data from (968) customers as a convenient sample.

Tool of Study

A questionnaire was designed in order to be the main instrument of study. The questionnaire consisted of three main sections as according to the following table 1.

Table 1. Questionnaire sections

Section	Content
Demographics	Age, gender, occupation, income, country of residence
Independent Variable	Virtual Tourism 40 Statements
Dependent Variable	Tourists' Engagement and Satisfaction 10 Statements
Moderating Variable	Virtual Influencers 8 Statements

Regarding validity, we have presented the questionnaire items before a group of scholars and academics in the field. All statements which scored 85% of arbitrators' approval were kept. The questionnaire in its final version consisted of (85) items.

Statistical Processing

Statistical package for social sciences (SPSS) was used in order to screen and analyze collected primary data. Dealing with demographic variables was done through frequencies and percentages. Regarding questionnaire items, we have used mean (μ) and standard deviation (σ) to check respondents' attitudes towards questionnaire items. As for hypotheses, the main hypothesis was tested using multiple regression, while sub-hypotheses were tested using linear regression. Checking reliability and consistency of study tool was done depending on testing its content using Cronbach's Alpha (α) as in equation 1. As in Table 2, all variables scored higher than 0.70, this meant that the questionnaire was reliable and consistent.

Equation 1. Cronbach's Alpha

$$\alpha = \frac{k}{k-1}\left(1 - \frac{\sum_{i=1}^{k}\sigma_{Y_i}^2}{\sigma_X^2}\right)$$

1. k*k*: The number of items in the scale or questionnaire.
2. σYi2*σYi*2: The variance of each individual item (Yi*Yi*).
3. σX2*σX*2: The variance of the total score (sum of all items).
4. ∑i=1kσYi2∑*i*=1*kσYi*2: The sum of the variances of all individual items.

Table 2. Alpha value

Variable	α
Interactivity	0.912
Interactivity	0.946
Multimedia Content	0.767
Social Interaction	0.863
Personalization	0.867
User-Friendly Interface	0.851
Tourists' Engagement And Satisfaction	0.893
Virtual Influencers	0.943

RESULTS AND DISCUSSION

Demographics Results

Table 3 below presented frequencies and percentages of demographics regarding respondents. It was noticed that majority of respondents were males forming 61.4% of total sample who held BA degree forming 63% of the sample. Table 3 also indicated that majority of respondents were employees forming 79.5% with an income that surpassed $2000 forming 45.5%. it was also noted that the majority of responses came from MENA region (Jordan, Syria, Lebanon, Palestine) forming 64.3%, while 21.9% from Gulf countries and 13.8% from Egypt.

Table 3. Demographics

	f	%
Gender		
Female	374	38.6
Male	594	61.4

continued on following page

Table 3. Continued

	f	%
Education		
BA	610	63.0
Diploma or less	10	1.0
PhD	241	24.9
MA	107	11.1
Occupation		
Business Owner	66	6.8
House wife	44	4.5
Retired	88	9.1
Employee	770	79.5
Income		
$1001-$1999	330	34.1
Less than $1000	198	20.5
More than $2000	440	45.5
Residence		
MENA (Jordan, Syria, Lebanon, Palestine)	622	64.3
Guld Countries	212	21.9
Egypt	134	13.8
Total	**968**	**100.0**

Questionnaire Analysis

As was mentioned before, mean (μ) and standard deviation (σ) were used to check respondents' attitudes regarding questionnaire items. Table 4 indicated that all items in the questionnaire were positively received as they all scored a mean that was higher than mean of scale 3.00.

Table 4. Questionnaire analysis

Statement	μ	σ
When I watch a virtual tourism ad, I feel like I'm part of the place.	3.436	.940
I interact with the ad and feel like the place is close to me.	3.455	1.019
I can access all the areas I want to visit.	3.440	1.096
I see all the features I'm interested in in the tourist destination I intend to visit.	3.568	1.048
I found no discrepancy between the content and the desires I had in mind when viewing it.	3.207	1.066
My interaction with the virtual environment was excellent, and I felt like I was part of the surrounding environment.	3.601	.960

continued on following page

Table 4. Continued

Statement	μ	σ
All the elements were attractive and eye-catching, and they were able to capture my attention significantly.	3.727	.965
Virtual tourism was able to meet some of my questions and expectations.	3.727	.950
Interactivity	**3.520**	**.793**
I didn't find any difference between the content and reality of the various tourist destinations.	2.930	1.403
There is a significant difference between virtual content and reality due to photographic tricks.	3.205	1.413
The spaces and views are deceptive in virtual tourism compared to reality, so I don't trust them.	3.296	1.447
Virtual tourism content may be close to reality, but it is completely inaccurate.	3.555	1.369
The content is true to reality, based on my personal experience.	2.961	1.367
I don't care about elaborate tourism advertisements that are far removed from the truth.	3.331	1.472
I believe that photography tricks have contributed to increasing profits for tourism organizations at the expense of the individual and their expectations.	3.456	1.442
Reality	**3.308**	**1.266**
The content may be similar, but it's not identical.	3.653	.884
Technology cannot convey the actual reality to the user.	3.296	1.179
I don't trust the content, but it may be slightly close to reality. I may leave room for surprises.	3.608	1.049
The content is usually very engaging and eye-catching.	4.008	.673
Multimedia content provides answers to questions and is not necessarily realistic.	3.699	.817
Multimedia content has increased my interest in many tourist destinations.	3.808	.891
I believe that multimedia content added value to my experience during the visit.	3.719	.757
I may have decided to visit a particular destination because of the virtual content presented to me.	3.566	1.010
Multimedia Content	**3.670**	**.567**
I share my virtual tourism experience with my friends and family.	3.565	.755
I post ratings and reviews on virtual content if I've actually visited a particular tourist destination.	3.656	1.003
I share my experience all the time to ensure others benefit from it.	3.588	1.011
Sharing my virtual tourism experience has improved my attitude toward tourism in general.	3.588	.917
I interact with users all the time, especially if we have common ground.	3.451	.968
Social Interaction	**3.570**	**.751**
The ads I receive are consistent with the information in my profile.	3.361	1.028
Most of the ads I find are for destinations I'd like to visit.	3.224	1.022
The same ads reach my close friends and those in my profile.	3.111	.912
I have no problems receiving ads because they all align with my interests and personality.	3.292	1.102
The nature of the content in the tourism ads is appropriate for my general taste.	3.497	.843
I often have to report ads for tourist destinations that don't suit my taste.	2.931	.941
I feel that the tourist destinations I receive ads for are very appropriate for the nature of the searches I usually conduct.	3.542	.944
Personalization	**3.280**	**.726**
I don't have to download a specific app. I browse ads easily.	3.431	1.056
The presentation and content are very convenient for me.	3.635	.958

continued on following page

Table 4. Continued

Statement	μ	σ
I can easily browse virtual tourism ads with my family.	3.749	.805
I find ads with virtual content presenting reality in a smooth and easy way.	3.567	.866
Augmented and virtual reality make it easy to view and interact with ads because they are fun and easy.	3.772	.673
User-Friendly Interface	**3.630**	**.701**
I always share ads with virtual content to spread knowledge.	3.136	1.199
I always share ads with virtual content to spread culture among my family and friends.	3.227	1.126
I always share ads with virtual content to spread joy. They're fun and entertaining.	3.159	1.224
I'm proud of the level of technological advancement in advertising that my country has achieved.	3.705	1.014
When making a decision, I have no problem booking a tourist destination with a company that implements virtual advertising.	3.409	.985
I am completely satisfied with the nature of the virtual ads I receive.	3.341	.928
I always try to review virtual content for any tourist destination I want to visit.	3.773	.951
I believe that technology has provided many services to the tourism sector in my country.	3.773	.974
The adoption of augmented and virtual reality is a very positive thing for attracting tourists to tourist destinations.	4.045	.563
I usually comment on and evaluate virtual ads even before I decide to use them, and this is a positive thing.	3.045	1.087
Tourists' Engagement And Satisfaction	**3.461**	**.729**
Virtual influencers increase my awareness of tourist destinations.	3.432	.654
I find that virtual influencers reflect my tourism experience in an inspiring and exciting way.	3.409	.651
Virtual influencers encourage me to explore and engage more with virtual destinations.	3.409	.651
Virtual influencers help guide me toward specific tourist experiences.	3.318	.595
It's good that the virtual influencer offers personalized recommendations that meet my expectations and interests.	3.386	.611
Most of the virtual influencers' content is engaging and I like it.	3.227	.635
I have no problem sharing their content on social media.	3.023	.754
I find the virtual influencers' content innovative and engaging.	3.386	.611
Virtual Influencers	**3.324**	**.547**

Multicolleniarity Test

The independent variables were evaluated for multicollinearity using Variance Inflation Factor (VIF) and Tolerance analysis. These calculations can be ascribed to the ensuing probable advancements. The data demonstrates the absence of multicollinearity, as indicated by all Variance Inflation Factor (VIF) values being below 10 and all Tolerance values exceeding 0.10 (Gujarati & Porter, 2009).

Table 5. Multicolleniarity test

variable	Tolerance	VIF
Interactivity	.493	2.030
Interactivity	.901	1.110
Multimedia Content	.634	1.578
Social Interaction	.390	2.562
Personalization	.319	3.136
User-Friendly Interface	.420	2.382

Hypotheses Testing

The first hypothesis was examined using Multiple Regression Analysis. It was demonstrated a robust positive correlation (r = 0.791) between the independent and dependent variables. The independent variables explain 64.5% of the overall variation in the dependent variable. F value was statistically significant at the 0.05 level, indicating that Virtual tourism has an influence on tourists' engagement and satisfaction from perspective of online customers.

Also the coefficients table 6 showed the following:

H1.1: Interactivity has an influence on tourists' engagement and satisfaction from perspective of online customers, since t- value is significant at 0.05 level.
H1.2: Realism has an influence on tourists' engagement and satisfaction from perspective of online customers
H1.3: Multimedia Content has an influence on tourists' engagement and satisfaction from perspective of online customers, since t- value is significant at 0.05 level.
H1.4: Social Interaction has an influence on tourists' engagement and satisfaction from perspective of online customers, since t- value is significant at 0.05 level.
H1.5: Personalization has an influence on tourists' engagement and satisfaction from perspective of online customers, since t- value is significant at 0.05 level.
H1.6: User-Friendly Interface has an influence on tourists' engagement and satisfaction from perspective of online customers, since t- value is significant at 0.05 level.

Table 6. H1 testing

	H1: Virtual tourism has an influence on tourists' engagement and satisfaction from perspective of online customers							
		Unstandardized Coefficients		Standardized Coefficients				
Model		B	Std. Error	Beta	t	Sig.	R	R Square
1	(Constant)	.126	.101		1.247	.213	.791[a]	.626
	Interactivity	.112	.026	.122	4.341	.000		
	Realism	.025	.012	.043	2.056	.040		
	Multimedia Content	.067	.032	.052	2.111	.035		
	Social Interaction	.259	.031	.267	8.449	.000		
	Personalization	.249	.035	.248	7.102	.000		
	User-Friendly Interface	.241	.032	.231	7.601	.000		

Regarding H2 (**Virtual influencers moderate the relationship between virtual tourism and tourists' engagement and satisfaction from perspective of online customers**). Table 7 illustrated a statistical association between virtual tourism and tourists' engagement and satisfaction, with a p-value of 0.000 ($R^2 = 0.493$). Following the integration of the Virtual Influencers in the next phase, we saw a significant rise in the overall interpretation variable, shown by an R2 value of 1%. The incorporation of Virtual Influencers and Virtual Tourism variables led to a significant increase of 1.4% in the overall interpretation variable, as evidenced by the R2 value. This indicated that Virtual influencers moderate the relationship between virtual tourism and tourists' engagement and satisfaction from perspective of online customers

Table 7. Sub-hypotheses testing

H2: Virtual influencers moderate the relationship between virtual tourism and tourists' engagement and satisfaction from perspective of online customers									
					Change Statistics				
Model	R	R Square	Adjusted R Square	Std. Error of the Estimate	R Square Change	F Change	df1	df2	Sig. F Change
1	.702[a]	.493	.493	.51909	.493	939.952	1	966	.000
2	.709[b]	.503	.502	.51436	.010	18.878	1	965	.000
3	.719[c]	.517	.515	.50733	.014	27.905	1	964	.000

ANOVA						
Model		Sum of Squares	df	Mean Square	F	Sig.
1	Regression	253.278	1	253.278	939.952	.000[b]
	Residual	260.297	966	.269		
	Total	513.575	967			

continued on following page

Table 7. Continued

						Change Statistics				
Model	R	R Square	Adjusted R Square	Std. Error of the Estimate		R Square Change	F Change	df1	df2	Sig. F Change

H2: Virtual influencers moderate the relationship between virtual tourism and tourists' engagement and satisfaction from perspective of online customers

Model										
2			Regression	258.273	2	129.136	488.114	.000c		
			Residual	255.302	965	.265				
			Total	513.575	967					
3			Regression	265.455	3	88.485	343.784	.000d		
			Residual	248.120	964	.257				
			Total	513.575	967					

a. Dependent Variable: TOURISTS' ENGAGEMENT AND SATISFACTION
b. Predictors: (Constant), ind
c. Predictors: (Constant), ind, Virtual Influencers
d. Predictors: (Constant), ind, Virtual Influencers, mod

Discussion

We hoped in the current study to examine the influence of virtual tourism (Interactivity, Realism, Multimedia Content, Social Interaction, Personalization, User-Friendly Interface) on satisfaction and engagement of tourists through the moderating role of virtual influencers. For that reason, we have developed a questionnaire that was uploaded online to gather primary data from 968 customers from regions including MENA, Gulf countries and Egypt. Through SPSS it was seen that study hypotheses were accepted and virtual influencers moderate the relationship between virtual tourism and tourists' engagement and satisfaction from perspective of online customers.

Among the chosen variables of virtual tourism (Interactivity, Realism, Multimedia Content, Social Interaction, Personalization, User-Friendly Interface), it was found that they all had a positive influence in increasing satisfaction and engagement of tourists. The highest of them appeared to be that social interaction scored the highest influence as tourist engagement levels together with satisfaction rates depend on social interaction experiences. This agreed with Weber-Sabil and Han (2021) who noted that a high significant t-value demonstrates that engagement benefits from features which include reviews together with forums and social media integration. Tour operators should promote both user submissions like customer reviews and travel blogs in addition to social sharing tools to enhance trust and social bonds among vacationers.

In the second rank came the variable of personalization as tourists' satisfaction and engagement levels get directly affected by personalized experiences. The computed t-value indicates that personalized recommendations deliver better satisfaction levels to users. AI-driven approaches in personalization offer customized travel itineraries alongside targeted offers which strengthen user experience and loyalty levels.

The third rank was scored by the variable of user friendly-interface as tourists' engagement and satisfaction get affected by how easily they can navigate the platform. The major significance of the t-value indicates that intuitive navigation combined with fast loading and mobile-friendliness leads to increased engagement. Shamim et al. (2024) agreed with the idea adding that the improvement of satisfaction rates demands that travel websites focus on designing user-friendly interfaces through simple menus alongside clear CTAs to reduce user complaints.

In the fourth rank came interactivity as the interactive property of a system positively affects traveler engagement levels and satisfaction ratings. Statistical evidence demonstrates that interactivity leads to better customer engagement and satisfaction because the t-value reaches the 0.05 significance threshold. Weber-Sabil and Han (2021) agreed on such resulting arguing that interactive features including virtual tours and chatbots and quizzes should be integrated by online travel platforms to boost user satisfaction and maintain tourist engagement.

In the final rank came variables of multimedia contents and realism respectively. Touristic multimedia content directly affects how travelers get involved and how content satisfies their needs during their stays. The significance of the t-value ($p < 0.05$) indicates that multimedia content such as videos and images and audio files improve both engagement and visitor satisfaction levels. Travel platforms should incorporate detailed multimedia elements (such as destination videos along with photo galleries) to boost presentation appeal as well as information processing efficiency. According to de Jesus Duenas-Garcia (2022), the realism of multimedia content creates positive effects on visitor engagement together with their satisfaction levels. The hypothesis is presented in the paper yet the essential t-value significance remains absent. Research findings that establish realism (through high-quality images and 360° videos along with VR experiences) as significant would probably increase trust and immersion levels. Travel websites should receive backing to create virtual hotel tours for enhancing both visitor engagement and satisfaction levels.

CONCLUSION AND RECOMMENDATIONS

Limitations of Study

Current study was limited to the following:

- The study faces limitations because it concentrates on Kuwaiti banking institutions and particular demographic characteristics that decrease the ability to generalize conclusions across other industries and regions. Virtual tourism together with influencers display unique characteristics that depend upon cultural backgrounds of users and specific conditions.
- Using self-reported data establishes limitations in study accuracy because participants might under or overstate their engagement levels through interviewer and recall biases. The obtained results may become less accurate because of this factor.

Future Research

Launching from reached results, discussion and conclusion, we recommend the following future research:

1. The influence of virtual influencers on different cultural settings requires further study through future research investigations. The study of Western and Middle Eastern countries would show how cultural backgrounds influence both the way people view virtual influencers and virtual tourism attributes.
2. Research conducted over multiple time periods would reveal the full evolution of relationships between virtual tourism attributes, virtual influencers and their effects on tourist outcomes. The effect of virtual influencers on consumers changes as they encounter virtual tourism experiences multiple times.

REFERENCES

Al-Romeedy, B. S., & Hashem, T. (2024). From Insight to Advantage: Harnessing the Potential of Marketing Intelligence Systems in Tourism. In *Marketing and Big Data Analytics in Tourism and Events* (pp. 80-98). IGI Global.

Alcala, K., D'Achille, A., & Bruckman, A. (2023). The Stage and the Theatre: AltspaceVR and its Relationship to Discord. *Proceedings of the ACM on Human-Computer Interaction, 7*(CSCW1), 1-21. DOI: 10.1145/3579529

Alrihani, N. (2022). *Interactive mixed reality experiences: integrated digital representations of tangible/intangible Cultural Heritage assets and immersive technology applications to improve heritage visitor experiences*. The University of Liverpool.

Bhardwaj, S., Sharma, I., Kaur, G., & Sharma, S. (2025). Personalization in Tourism Marketing Based on Leveraging User-Generated Content With AI Recommender Systems. In *Redefining Tourism With AI and the Metaverse* (pp. 317–346). IGI Global Scientific Publishing. DOI: 10.4018/979-8-3693-8482-4.ch010

Calza, F., Trunfio, M., Pasquinelli, C., Sorrentino, A., Campana, S., & Rossi, S. (2022). *Technology-driven innovation. Exploiting ICTs tools for digital engagement, smart experiences, and sustainability in tourism destinations. SLIOB*. Enzo Albano Edizioni Naples.

Casillo, M., Colace, F., Lorusso, A., Santaniello, D., & Valentino, C. (2025). Integrating Physical and Virtual Experiences in Cultural Tourism: An Adaptive Multimodal Recommender System. *IEEE Access : Practical Innovations, Open Solutions, 13*, 28353–28368. DOI: 10.1109/ACCESS.2025.3539205

Damanik, J., & Yusuf, M. (2022). Effects of perceived value, expectation, visitor management, and visitor satisfaction on revisit intention to Borobudur Temple, Indonesia. *Journal of Heritage Tourism, 17*(2), 174–189. DOI: 10.1080/1743873X.2021.1950164

Davlembayeva, D., Chari, S., & Papagiannidis, S. (2025). Virtual influencers in consumer behaviour: A social influence theory perspective. *British Journal of Management, 36*(1), 202–222. DOI: 10.1111/1467-8551.12839

Davlembayeva, D., Chari, S., & Papagiannidis, S. (2025). Virtual influencers in consumer behaviour: A social influence theory perspective. *British Journal of Management, 36*(1), 202–222. DOI: 10.1111/1467-8551.12839

de Jesus Duenas-Garcia, M. (2022). *Living in Borderlands. Archaeology and Meaningful Divulgation of the Northern Frontier of Mesoamerica*. University of California, Merced.

Dorokhov, O., Malyarets, L., Ukrainski, K., Petrova, M., Yevstrat, D., & Aliyeva, A. (2023). Consumer expectations and real experiences: Case of Ukrainian tourists in Turkey. *Access Journal*, *4*(1), 102–114. DOI: 10.46656/access.2023.4.1(8)

Godovykh, M., Baker, C., & Fyall, A. (2022). VR in tourism: A new call for virtual tourism experience amid and after the COVID-19 pandemic. *Tourism and Hospitality*, *3*(1), 265–275. DOI: 10.3390/tourhosp3010018

Góraj, K. (2024). The Impact of Computer-Generated Influencers on Social Media Advertising. *Social Communication*, *25*(1), 137–144. DOI: 10.57656/sc-2024-0014

Grundner, L., & Neuhofer, B. (2021). The bright and dark sides of artificial intelligence: A futures perspective on tourist destination experiences. *Journal of Destination Marketing & Management*, *19*, 100511. DOI: 10.1016/j.jdmm.2020.100511

Gujarati, D. N., & Porter, D. C. (2009). *Basic Econometrics* (5th ed.). McGraw Hill Inc.

Hashem, T., & Suleiman, H. (2025). *Promotion of Jordan's Golden Triangle via Recreational and Religious Tourism Marketing Strategies*. Tourism Ethics and Responsible Community Development, GoodFellow Publishers.

Hashem, T. N., Albattat, A., Valeri, M., & Sharma, A. (Eds.). (2024). *Marketing and Big Data Analytics in Tourism and Events*. IGI Global. DOI: 10.4018/979-8-3693-3310-5

Hewapathirana, I. U., & Perera, N. (2024). Navigating the age of AI influence: A systematic literature review of trust, engagement, efficacy and ethical concerns of virtual influencers in social media.

Homsi, D., Freihat, S. M. S. S., Hashem, T. N., & Alshayyab, A. A. (2022). Touristic marketing through blogging and vlogging; does it attract customers' trust? *Calitatea*, *23*(190), 170–178.

Jia, S., Chi, O. H., Martinez, S. D., & Lu, L. (2025). When "old" meets "new": Unlocking the future of innovative technology implementation in heritage tourism. *Journal of Hospitality & Tourism Research (Washington, D.C.)*, *49*(3), 640–661. DOI: 10.1177/10963480231205767

Kim, D., & Wang, Z. (2023). The ethics of virtuality: Navigating the complexities of human-like virtual influencers in the social media marketing realm. *Frontiers in Communication*, *8*, 1205610. DOI: 10.3389/fcomm.2023.1205610

Looi, J., & Kahlor, L. A. (2024). Artificial intelligence in influencer marketing: A mixed-method comparison of human and virtual influencers on Instagram. *Journal of Interactive Advertising*, *24*(2), 107–126. DOI: 10.1080/15252019.2024.2313721

Maczynska, P. (2024). Holistic Travel Wellness: Designing Wearable Technologies to Improve Long-Distance Flight Comfort.

Mazzetto, S. (2024). Integrating Emerging Technologies with Digital Twins for Heritage Building Conservation: An Interdisciplinary Approach with Expert Insights and Bibliometric Analysis. *Heritage*, *7*(11), 6432–6479. DOI: 10.3390/heritage7110300

Nag, A., & Mishra, S. (2024). Sustainable competitive advantage in heritage tourism: Leveraging cultural legacy in a data-driven world. []. Emerald Publishing Limited.]. *Review of Technologies and Disruptive Business Strategies*, *3*, 137–162. DOI: 10.1108/S2754-586520240000003008

Omran, W., Casais, B., & Ramos, R. F. (2025). Attributes of Virtual and Augmented Reality Tourism Mobile Applications Predicting Tourist Behavioral Engagement. *International Journal of Human-Computer Interaction*, •••, 1–14. DOI: 10.1080/10447318.2025.2470293

Panigrahy, A., & Verma, A. (2025). Tourist experiences: a systematic literature review of computer vision technologies in smart destination visits. *Journal of Tourism Futures*.

Samala, A. D., Ricci, M., Angel Rueda, C. J., Bojić, L., Ranuharja, F., & Agustiarmi, W. (2024). Exploring campus through web-based immersive adventures using virtual reality photography: A low-cost virtual tour experience. *International journal of online and biomedical engineering*, *20*(1).

Saxena, S. K., Gupta, V., & Kumar, S. (2024). Enhancing Guest Loyalty in the Hotel Industry Through Artificial Intelligence-Drive Personalization. In *New Technologies in Virtual and Hybrid Events* (pp. 335–350). IGI Global. DOI: 10.4018/979-8-3693-2272-7.ch017

Shamim, N., Gupta, S., & Shin, M. M. (2024). Evaluating user engagement via metaverse environment through immersive experience for travel and tourism websites. *International Journal of Contemporary Hospitality Management*.

Singh, B., Kaunert, C., & Lal, S. (2025). AI-Driven Solutions for Virtual Tourism: Balancing Visitor Experience and Ecosystem Conservation. In *Integrating Architecture and Design Into Sustainable Tourism Development* (pp. 21-40). IGI Global Scientific Publishing.

Trunfio, M., Jung, T., & Campana, S. (2022). Mixed reality experiences in museums: Exploring the impact of functional elements of the devices on visitors' immersive experiences and post-experience behaviours. *Information & Management*, *59*(8), 103698. DOI: 10.1016/j.im.2022.103698

Van Nuenen, T., & Scarles, C. (2021). Advancements in technology and digital media in tourism. *Tourist Studies*, *21*(1), 119–132. DOI: 10.1177/1468797621990410

Varadarajan, R., Welden, R. B., Arunachalam, S., Haenlein, M., & Gupta, S. (2022). Digital product innovations for the greater good and digital marketing innovations in communications and channels: Evolution, emerging issues, and future research directions. *International Journal of Research in Marketing*, *39*(2), 482–501. DOI: 10.1016/j.ijresmar.2021.09.002

Vărzaru, A. A., Bocean, C. G., & Cazacu, M. (2021). Rethinking tourism industry in pandemic COVID-19 period. *Sustainability (Basel)*, *13*(12), 6956. DOI: 10.3390/su13126956

Von Hohenberg, B. C., & Guess, A. M. (2023). When do sources persuade? The effect of source credibility on opinion change. *Journal of Experimental Political Science*, *10*(3), 328–342. DOI: 10.1017/XPS.2022.2

Weber-Sabil, J., & Han, D. I. D. (2021). Immersive Tourism-State of the Art of Immersive Tourism Realities through XR Technology.

Wirentake, M. P., & Arfani, S. (2024). *Exploring English through tourist attractions: Motivating students to speak*. Jakad Media Publishing.

Xin, B., Hao, Y., & Xie, L. (2024). Virtual influencers and corporate reputation: From marketing game to empirical analysis. *Journal of Research in Interactive Marketing*, *18*(5), 759–786. DOI: 10.1108/JRIM-10-2023-0330

Ying, C. W. (2024, July). Preliminary Exploration of Intelligent Virtual Avatars in the Virtual Influencer Industry. In *2024 IEEE 24th International Conference on Software Quality, Reliability, and Security Companion (QRS-C)* (pp. 1284-1291). IEEE. DOI: 10.1109/QRS-C63300.2024.00167

Zhang, S., Tan, Y., Zhong, Y., Yuan, J., & Ding, Y. (2023). Psychological recovery effects of 3D virtual tourism with real scenes—A comparative study. *Information Technology & Tourism*, *25*(1), 71–103. DOI: 10.1007/s40558-023-00246-z

Zhao, X. (2022). Virtual fashion influencers: towards a more sustainable consumer behaviour of generation Z?

Chapter 4
Purchase Intention and Tourism Strategy in the Post–COVID–19 Era:
Lessons and Perspectives From the Moroccan Experience

Badr Bentalha
https://orcid.org/0000-0003-1339-542X
National School of Business and Management, Sidi Mohammed Ben Abdellah University, Morocco

Ahmed Benjelloun
https://orcid.org/0009-0004-9673-2747
National School of Business and Management, Sidi Mohammed Ben Abdellah University, Morocco

Hajar Slimani
National School of Business and Management, Moulay Ismail University, Morocco

Bouteïna El Gharbaoui
National School of Business and Management, Moulay Ismail University, Morocco

ABSTRACT

The COVID-19 pandemic has had an unprecedented impact on the global tourism industry, including Morocco. This article examines purchase intentions and tourism strategies in the post-COVID-19 era, drawing lessons from the Moroccan tourism experience. The empirical study shows that tourists' intention to buy has changed

DOI: 10.4018/979-8-3693-3196-5.ch004

considerably as a result of the COVID-19 pandemic. Whereas price and destination used to be the decisive criteria, health concerns, social distancing, booking flexibility and safety now take priority. The research shows that tourists' purchasing intentions have changed considerably as a result of health concerns. he article concludes that post-COVID success will depend on agile, innovative strategies and strong public-private partnerships, as exemplified by Morocco. Tourist confidence will be crucial and will rely on transparent management of health risks. An analysis of decision-making criteria will enable us to identify the levers on which to act to win back the confidence of tourists in an uncertain health context.

INTRODUCTION

The coronavirus health crisis has taken a heavy toll on the tourism sector worldwide. In Morocco, this sector is considered to be among those most damaged by the closure of borders and the emergency measures put in place. The tourism sector, which accounts for 11% of Morocco's GDP, has been hard hit by the COVID-19 health crisis. With the closure of borders and travel restrictions, the number of foreign tourists to Morocco fell drastically in 2020, dropping by 78% compared to 2019. Having welcomed 13 million foreign visitors in 2019, Morocco received less than 3 million in 2020. This plummet is explained by the closure of international air links between March and June 2020 to stem the spread of the virus. Even after the resumption of flights, connections remain limited today due to the restrictions still in force in many countries. The absence of foreign tourists has forced many hotels, restaurants, travel agencies, and other tourist establishments to close temporarily or drastically reduce their activity, resulting in significant financial losses and mass lay-offs. In addition, almost all festivals and cultural events that usually attract international visitors had to be postponed or canceled.

The government has put in place strict sanitary measures in tourist establishments to reopen them quickly but safely. Morocco has also launched promotional campaigns targeting key tourist markets such as France, Spain, Germany, and the UK, using influencers and social networks to convey a positive image of Morocco. It also provided financial assistance to help struggling operators through the crisis. As soon as the borders are gradually reopened in 2021, Morocco has deployed an intense international promotional campaign to restore its image as a safe and attractive destination, and strategic partnerships with international tour operators. Entry conditions have been eased for vaccinated tourists. In 2023, the Kingdom will continue to invest massively in major structuring projects. The aim is to diversify the tourism offering to boost long-term recovery.

In the post-Covid context, tourists have become more cautious and demanding. They want health guarantees first and foremost. Their intention to buy will depend on the seriousness of the protocols put in place in hotels, restaurants, and tourist sites to prevent risks. Strict disinfection and social distancing procedures will reassure them. The financial dimension is also essential. After the economic crisis, many tourists have reduced travel budgets. Promotional offers or value-for-money holidays will influence their purchase intention. Lastly, post-crisis purchasing intentions are also dictated by flexibility. Tourists want to be able to easily cancel or postpone their bookings in the event of an epidemic rebound. Flexible cancellation and refund policies are therefore essential.

This article examines purchase intentions and tourism strategies in the post-COVID-19 era, drawing lessons from the Moroccan tourism experience. Tourism strategies need to adapt to this new tourism reality. Morocco was quick to introduce strict health protocols to reassure tourists. Promotion now targets national and regional tourism. New products emphasize outdoor experiences and connection with nature. Purchase intent is the motivation and willingness of tourists to buy a given tourism product. It is a key indicator for understanding the outlook for the tourism sector. The empirical study shows that tourists' intention to buy has changed considerably as a result of the COVID-19 pandemic. Whereas price and destination used to be the decisive criteria, health concerns, social distancing, booking flexibility and safety now take priority.

To answer our question, we will first take stock of the current situation of tourism worldwide and in Morocco, and then present the different scenarios proposed for revitalizing tourism. The second part will deal with the methodological choices made in our research, and we will conclude by presenting and discussing the results obtained from our empirical study.

1. THEORETICAL AND CONCEPTUAL FRAMEWORK

1.1. The State Of World and Moroccan Tourism

The global tourism boom has been a constant driver of global economic growth since the 1950s. Since then, international tourist arrivals have risen from 25 million to 450 million in 1990 and passed the billion mark in 2013, when the number of international tourists grew by 6% to reach 1.4 billion in 2015. In 2019, growth was 4% in both Europe and Africa and 3% in the Americas (UNWTO, 2019). This growth has been the result of the development of new technologies, the advent of low-cost airlines that have democratized travel, and the evolution over the last 3 decades of mass tourism by the middle classes of emerging and densely populated countries such as China and India. Digitization, new business models, more affordable travel, and societal changes have shaped this sector (Noor et al., 2012; Rosli et al., 2023). In terms of jobs according to a UNWTO report (2019), one in 10 jobs worldwide comes from tourism, if direct, indirect, and induced jobs are taken into account: 319 million people were employed by the sector in 2018. The World Travel & Tourism Council (WTTC) forecasts 421 million jobs in 2029.

In the face of COVID-19, 96% of the world's destinations impose travel restrictions. More specifically, total or partial closure of borders to tourists, restrictions on travel to specific destinations, total or partial suspension of flights, and various other measures, such as compulsory testing, quarantine or isolation, medical certificates, cancellation or suspension of visa issuance, etc (Alla et al., 2022). Global tourism growth is therefore compromised by the direct impact and collateral effects of the pandemic (Rosli & Zaki, 2022). The International Air Transport Association (IATA) has published an analysis indicating that the COVID-19 crisis has caused a drop in airline passenger ticket sales revenues of $314 billion in 2020, with domestic and international demand falling by around 48% compared with 2019. The two main factors behind this decline are the global financial crisis and travel restrictions that have penalized international travel (Lamsiah & Bentalha, 2022).

The tourism growth model has always considered international tourist arrivals as the main driver of development. Nevertheless, it has been heavily criticized during health and financial crises (Hall, 2019). The new forms of tourism that have emerged with the democratization of travel have led to the emergence of a phenomenon of tourist overexposure, over-tourism, and mass tourism (Fabry & Zeghni, 2017), with the tourism sector becoming both vector and victim of the pandemic. This volume-based tourism growth model is championed by major corporations as well as national tourism management organizations. Players have reacted to the pandemic by trying to reduce the negative impact by reducing the fleet for airlines (Simple Flying, 2020) or seeking to reinvent themselves by integrating digital into events (Slimani, 2020), without neglecting the contribution of states and governments and the important role played by subsidies and financial aid that enable the various players to survive in times of crisis (Fabry & Zeghni, 2017; Benjelloun et al., 2021). Given the scale of the current pandemic, rethinking tourism is a necessity, as returning to normal after the crisis without considering a new qualitative rather than quantitative growth model could be fatal (Shamim & Bentalha, 2023; Alla & Bentalha, 2024). The tourism model will have to be less based on international tourism and more oriented towards national and more environmentally-friendly types of tourism, despite consumer optimism that could be high at the end of the pandemic and all the efforts that could be undertaken by the various media.

The tourism situation in Morocco is close to that worldwide. The two years leading up to the COVID-19 crisis saw some recovery, with tourist arrivals up 8.3% and 10% in 2017. Indeed, Morocco welcomed a record number of tourists in 2018, some 12.3 million people. What's more, since 2017 the pace of growth in foreign tourist arrivals has outstripped that of Moroccan residents abroad, whereas until 2016 the opposite trend profile was generally observed. This growth also affected domestic tourism, thanks to improved connectivity and transport networks, as well as to various measures taken (Hussin et al., 2021). This aspect of domestic tourism has begun to stabilize the tourism sector's business cycle, acting as a buffer against negative shocks, particularly during periods when foreign tourist arrivals are falling. For this reason, it is imperative to remedy the problems that can hinder the development of tourism, especially in terms of accessibility and adaptation of the offer.

Like all countries facing this pandemic, Morocco is confronted with this crisis. Tourism, which underpins the country's economy and has over the past two decades been seen as the locomotive of socio-economic progress, has been paralyzed by the repercussions of the spread of the virus. In terms of numbers, 3,500 tourist accommodation businesses, 500 tourist catering businesses, 1,450 travel agencies, 1,500 tourist transport companies, and 1,500 car rental companies have been affected by the health crisis. After a 70% drop in arrivals, the number of tourism businesses closed reached 3,465, out of 3,989, or 87%, with only 520 open. This led to a drop in foreign currency tourism revenues. The drop in traffic due to the Coronavirus has already had, and will continue to have, a negative impact on air travel performance in general.

1.2. Scenarios for Morocco's Tourism Recovery

Morocco's strategic approach to developing the tourism sector aims to promote and revitalize this sector in this period of pandemic. This strategy has placed the concern for inter-regional imbalance at the heart of its concerns and has defined eight in the form of territorial units presenting a similar and unified offer (Hmioui et al., 2019). The emphasis was placed on rehabilitating the heritage of imperial cities and the development of urban spaces (Benjelloun, 2019; Meziane et al., 2025; Boudri et al., 2025). For local tourism, post-crisis recovery was timid (Beddaa & Bentalha, 2025). The international recommendations are summarized in three categories: crisis management and impact mitigation; recovery measures and accelerating recovery and preparing for the future (Table 1).

Table 1. Recommendations for tourism recovery after COVID-19

Recommendations	Axes
Crisis management and impact mitigation	■ Offer financial assistance and tax relief to help companies retain employees and keep businesses operating. Support independent workers and vulnerable groups who are most impacted. ■ Improve business cash flow by deferring taxes, fees, and other financial obligations. Provide loans, grants or other funding. ■ Adjust taxes, regulations, duties, and fees related to transport and tourism to ease the burden. Review policies to facilitate recovery. ■ Strengthen consumer rights, protections and confidence in travel safety and quality. ■ Promote skills training, especially digital skills, to equip workers to adapt and succeed. ■ Include tourism in economic stimulus and emergency relief packages at local, national, regional and global levels. ■ Develop crisis response plans and coordination mechanisms between public and private sectors. Strategize for long-term resilience.
Stimulus measures & accelerating recovery	■ Offer tax breaks, subsidies or other financial incentives to encourage tourism investment and sustain operations. ■ Adjust taxes, fees and regulations to ease the burden on tourism businesses. Streamline policies to facilitate travel. ■ Advance travel facilitation by improving visa processes, digitalizing procedures, and enhancing border crossings. ■ Promote skills training and job creation, with a focus on digital skills, to equip workers to adapt. ■ Incorporate sustainability and conservation into recovery plans and development. ■ Closely monitor traveler sentiment and behavior to respond quickly to changing demand. Restore traveler confidence and stimulate demand. ■ Increase marketing campaigns, events, conferences and meetings to attract visitors. ■ Invest in partnerships between government and private sector to align efforts. ■ Include tourism in national, regional and global economic revitalization programs and development aid.
Recovery in tourism	■ Diversify target markets, tourism offerings, and business models to mitigate risk. ■ Invest in market research and analytics to understand travelers. Accelerate digital transformation. ■ Strengthen tourism leadership, coordination and regulations across local, regional and national levels. ■ Prepare crisis management plans. Improve ability to withstand and recover from shocks. Integrate tourism into national emergency systems. ■ Invest in developing tourism talent and human capital through education, training and skills development. ■ Firmly establish sustainable tourism as a top national priority with policies and funding to support it. ■ Transition to a circular economy model that maximizes resources and minimizes waste. Align with and contribute to the UN Sustainable Development Goals.

Source: UNWTO, 2019

The coronavirus pandemic has brought about major changes in the short, medium, and long term. It is challenging to accurately evaluate which organizations and stakeholders should be responsible for implementing a strategic recovery plan for Moroccan tourism. Additionally, it is difficult to determine the extent of the pandemic's influence on Moroccan consumer behavior. However, developing and executing such a strategic recovery plan has become vital with the rise of digital technologies, innovations, and social media (Hmioui et al., 2017; Bentalha, 2025; Bentalha & Boukare, 2024; Boudri et al., 2024). On the other hand, the primary difficulties in deploying these plans into effective marketing and relaunch strategies stem from deficiencies in the knowledge, skills, and organizational capabilities within tourism companies and organizations (Bouhtati et al., 2023). The literature review we carried out showed that the strategy for revitalizing the tourism sector occupies a variety of statuses, depending on the way organizations and stakeholders perceive it. This enabled us to identify four approaches to providing the necessary answers to our problem.

1.3. Tourism Purchase Intent in the COVID-19 Era

Purchase intention in the tourism industry is a critical factor that determines consumers' likelihood to purchase travel services online. Understanding the factors that influence purchase intention can help businesses in the tourism sector develop effective marketing strategies and enhance customer satisfaction and loyalty.

Trust and perceived value are two significant factors that influence consumers' intention to purchase travel services online. Bonsón et al., (2015) indicate that trust plays a crucial role in shaping consumers' purchase intention. The study suggests that trust in online travel platforms is positively influenced by perceived value and assurance. The integration of trust antecedents, such as assurance, positively affects trust and subsequently enhances purchase intention in the context of online travel. Agag & El-Masry (2016) also emphasize the importance of trust in influencing consumers' intention to purchase travel online. Their study integrates the innovation diffusion theory and technology acceptance model (TAM) to examine the relationship between consumers' intention to participate in online travel communities and their intention to purchase travel online. The findings reveal that trust significantly mediates the relationship between the intention to participate in online travel communities and the intention to purchase travel online.

Satisfaction and loyalty are consequences of consumers' behavior that are influenced by the perceived value of a holiday experience. Lu & Chen (2021) suggest that motivation, involvement, and tourist knowledge act as antecedents to the perceived value of a holiday experience. These constructs significantly influence consumers' satisfaction and loyalty. Therefore, understanding and enhancing consumers' motivation, involvement, and tourist knowledge can positively impact purchase intention in the tourism industry (Padlee et al., 2019; Bentalha, 2023). Prebensen et al., (2014) also emphasize the role of experience value as an antecedent to satisfaction and loyalty. They argue that the perceived value of a travel experience can significantly influence consumers' satisfaction and loyalty. Therefore, marketers in the tourism industry should focus on creating unique and valuable experiences for consumers to enhance their satisfaction and foster loyalty.

Personal values play a significant role in shaping consumers' online purchase intention in the context of travel websites. Kumar et al., (2021) highlight the strong influence of personal values on online purchase intention. Their study indicates that consumers' values significantly affect their intention to purchase travel services online. Therefore, understanding consumers' values and aligning marketing strategies with these values can enhance purchase intention in the tourism industry.

According to a study by Chen et al (2021), tourist buying intentions have changed significantly since the Covid-19 pandemic. Fear of contracting the virus and health restrictions have created new expectations. According to Lee et al (2020), the primary concern of post-Covid tourists is now health safety. Their purchasing intentions will depend heavily on the hygiene measures implemented in tourist establishments such as hotels and restaurants (Hmioui et al., 2022). In addition, Chen et al. (2021) highlight the increased importance of price in purchase intention. As travel budgets have been impacted by the crisis, tourists are now looking for promotional offers and value-for-money holidays. What's more, booking flexibility influences purchase intentions (Roy et al., 2021). Tourists want to be able to easily postpone or cancel their trips in the event of an epidemic rebound. So, as Lee et al. (2020) summarize, the three keys to post-COVID tourism purchase intention are strict health standards, affordable prices, and flexibility. Destinations and tourism operators need to take these into account. Roy et al (2021) surveyed Indian tourists and confirmed the key role played by flexible cancellation and refund policies in purchase intentions.

While the existing literature provides valuable insights into the factors influencing purchase intention in tourism, there are still some knowledge gaps that need to be addressed. One potential research direction is to explore the impact of social media and online reviews on purchase intention. With the rise of social media platforms and the increasing reliance on online reviews, understanding how these factors influence consumers' purchase intention in the tourism industry can provide valuable insights for marketers. Additionally, further research could investigate the role of sustainability and environmentally responsible practices in shaping purchase intention in tourism (Bentalha, 2024). Rausch and Kopplin (2021) highlight the importance of sustainable clothing in influencing consumers' purchase intention and behavior. Exploring how sustainability-related factors influence purchase intention in other tourism sectors can help businesses develop more sustainable practices and attract environmentally conscious consumers (Bentalha, 2024). Another area for future research is the role of website quality, reputation, and perceived risk in shaping purchase intention in online shopping. Bentalha et al. (2020) et Qalati et al. (2021) suggest that these factors mediate and moderate the relationship between perceived service quality and purchase intention. Further investigation into the specific mechanisms through which these factors influence purchase intention can provide valuable insights for businesses in the tourism industry. In conclusion, understanding the factors that influence purchase intention in the tourism industry is crucial for businesses to develop effective marketing strategies and enhance customer satisfaction and loyalty. Trust, perceived value, satisfaction, loyalty, and personal values have been identified as significant factors influencing purchase intention. However, there are still knowledge gaps that need to be addressed, including the role of social media, sustainability, and website quality. Future research in these areas can provide valuable insights for marketers and contribute to the advancement of knowledge in the field of purchase intention in tourism.

2. RESEARCH METHODOLOGY

Since our research aims to explore and verify potential relationships between variables, developing a conceptual model is crucial. A conceptual model visually depicts hypothetical connections using a diagram. It illustrates the relationships between explanatory variables and the response variable under investigation. The conceptual model serves as a hypothesis-testing tool to elucidate the complex web of factors that may influence organizational resilience. The model provides a graphical display of our theoretical framework, guiding analysis to verify the significance, directionality, and magnitude of each relationship. Figure 1 shows the conceptual model we created based on hypothesized relationships for this study. The model provides a visual representation of the variables and their proposed interactions and correlations within the scope of our explanatory research.

Figure 1. Conceptual research model

Source: Personnal elaboration

After determining the key variables relevant to our study, we formulated specific research hypotheses about the potential relationships between these variables. Each hypothesis offers a testable statement about the suspected correlation or causal link between two or more variables under examination. Clearly defining these hypothetical relationships in advance allows us to structure our analysis to empirically investigate them. Our main research question is related to analyzing how the post-COVID-19 tourism strategy influences consumer purchase intention. To support this main question, we have identified five research hypotheses:

- H1: "Accessibility of information significantly influences purchase intention".
- H2: "The physical and scenic environment significantly influences purchase intention".
- H3" Price has a significant influence on purchase intention".
- H4" Information security significantly influences purchase intention".
- H5" Quality of service has a significant influence on intention to buy".

The criteria of verifiability, confirmability, and refutability of our conceptual model, derived from the literature, lead us to choose an adapted positioning with a hypothetico-deductive logic. In questioning the nature of reality and the status of knowledge, we take the view that reality exists, but that it can be adjusted to suit the context and the interpretations of the interviewees and respondents. Indeed, to test the effect of the COVID-19 pandemic in Morocco on the tourism sector, we need to take into account control variables to enrich and complete our knowledge of reality. The hypotheses thus adopted are part of the field but justified by the literature, which advocates our approach to scientific reasoning of a hypothetico-deductive type. At this stage, we need to familiarize ourselves with the research field, formulate our theoretical proposals, clarify the research problem, and specify the questions and items to be included in the final questionnaire.

3. RESULTS AND DISCUSSION

Once we had operationalized the variables in our study, we collected the data using a questionnaire that grouped all the statements and affirmations developed from the items that make up each variable. Respondents were asked to choose on a five-point Likert scale from "Poor" to "Excellent".

3.1. Testing the Validity And Reliability Of Study Variables

Once the study had been carried out, we carried out a simple data encoding procedure and collected all the responses in a database, to carry out statistical analyses and check that the questionnaires contained no incorrect or missing information. We then carried out statistical tests on the collected data. We analyzed variable validity by checking the Kaiser-Meyer-Olkin measure of sampling precision and Bartlett's test of sphericity. We then verified the consistency and internal reliability of the items making up each variable using Cronbach's alpha test. Table 2 summarizes the results of the principal component analysis (PCA).

Table 2. Results of validity and reliability tests on the "Tourism strategy" variable

Explanatory variable: Tourism strategy	Number of items before PCA	Number of items after PCA	KMO index	Bartlett's test	Restituted variance	Cronbach's Alpha
Information Accessibility	11	8	0,696	0,000	45,424%	0,817
Physical and scenic environment	13	6	0,702	0,000	39,027%	0,779
Pricing	3	3	0,672	0,000	64,554%	0,721
Safety	4	3	0,667	0,000	64,864%	0,783
Quality of service	8	8	0,791	0,000	43,109%	0,773

Source: Study results (SPSS V.26)

The "Tourism Strategy" dimension is represented by five variables: information accessibility, physical and scenic environment, price, safety, and service quality. After two iterations, the "Information accessibility" variable is represented by 8 items. The value of the KMO index (=0.696), which ensures sampling precision, is acceptable, while Bartlett's sphericity test gives a highly significant value (= 0.000). The calculation of Cronbach's alpha for the variable "Accessibility to information" gives satisfactory results for the assessment of reliability (α =0.817). The "Physical and scenic environment" variable is represented by 6 items. The value of the KMO index is 0.702, as is the Bartlett test (=0.000). Reliability analysis based on the 6 selected items yielded a satisfactory value for Cronbach's alpha (α =0.779), underlining the internal consistency between the selected items. For the three variables "Price", "Safety" and "Quality of service", the results of the first analysis yielded satisfactory and acceptable values for the KMO index, Bartlett's test, and Cronbach's alpha. The percentages of total variance show that the items selected for the five variables of the Tourism Strategy dimension make a strong contribution to the component selected in the PCA.

Analysis of the reliability of the "Purchase intention" variable by calculating Cronbach's alpha (Table 3) gives satisfactory results, underlining the internal consistency between the items selected for this variable (α =0.795).

Table 3. Validity and reliability test results for the "Purchase intention" variable

Variable to explain: Purchase intention	Number of items before PCA	Number of items after PCA	KMO index	Bartlett's test	Restituted variance	Cronbach's Alpha
Purchase intention	6	6	0,761	0,000	50,616%	0,795

Source: Study results (SPSS V.26)

While the validity analysis gives equally satisfactory results (KMO Index ≥ 0.70, Bartlett's Sphericity Test = 0.000). The percentage of variance restored indicates that the items selected make a strong contribution to the component retained in the PCA (50.616%).

3.2. Testing the Research Hypotheses

Testing the research hypotheses will enable us to confirm or refute each of the aforementioned hypotheses, and will also give us a clear picture of the link between the explanatory variables and the variable to be explained. This will be done primarily through the study of correlation, the aim of which is to measure the direction and strength of the relationship between the variables in the research model. This study is based on Pearson's correlation coefficient (r), which indicates the direction and strength of the relationship in the linear relationship used (Table 4). Bivariate correlation analysis is performed using SPPS (V26.0) statistical analysis software.

Table 4. Correlation test results for study variables

Items	Pearson's r correlation coefficient
Information accessibility and purchase intention	r = 0.594** (significant correlation at the 0.01 level (two-tailed))
Physical and scenic environment and purchase intention	r = 0.540** (significant correlation at the 0.01 level (two-tailed))
Price and purchase intention	r = 0.869** (significant correlation at the 0.01 level (two-tailed))

continued on following page

Table 4. Continued

Items	Pearson's r correlation coefficient
Safety and purchase intention	r = 0.871** (significant correlation at the 0.01 level (two-tailed))
Quality of service and intention to buy	r = 0.348* (significant correlation at the 0.05 level (two-tailed))

Source: Study results (SPSS V.26)

The results in Table 4 show that there is a significant positive correlation (0.594) between information accessibility and purchase intention among the Moroccan population. This result validates our first derived hypothesis (H1). The results also allow us to say that there is a significant average correlation (0.540) between physical and scenic environments and purchase intention. This allows us to conclude that the second derived hypothesis is validated. The results show, based on Pearson's r correlation coefficient (0.869), that there is a strong, significant, and positive relationship between price and purchase intention. These results allow us to validate this third-derived hypothesis (H3). The results also show, with a coefficient of (0.871), that there is a strong, significant, and positive relationship between safety and purchase intention. These results allow us to validate the third derived hypothesis (H4). Finally, the results of the bi-variate correlation analysis show a positive and significant mean intensity relationship (0.348) between service quality and purchase intention. We therefore validate our last derived hypothesis (H5).

Validation of the universal hypothesis is the result of combining the five derived hypotheses on tourism strategy determinants and purchase intention indicators. Table 5 summarizes the results of the hypothesis tests.

Table 5. Test results for the derived hypotheses and the research hypothesis of our study

Hypotheses	Hypothesis statements	Results	Meaning	Intensity
H1	Accessibility of information significantly influences purchase intention.	Validated	Positive	Medium
H2	The physical and scenic environment significantly influences purchase intention.	Validated	Positive	Medium
H3	Price has a significant influence on purchase intention.	Validated	Positive	Strong
H4	Safety has a significant influence on purchase intention.	Validated	Positive	Strong
H5	Quality of service has a significant influence on intention to buy.	Validated	Positive	Medium

Source: Study results (SPSS V.26)

Overall, the results are positive and validate the hypotheses formulated. All the variables tested (accessibility to information, physical environment, price, safety, and quality of service) have a positive and statistically significant influence on the purchase intention of consumers of tourist services. The strongest effects concern price and safety, showing that these are crucial determinants of purchase intention in this post-COVID-19 context. Accessibility to information and quality of service have moderate effects. Only the physical environment seems to have a limited effect on purchase intention.

These results confirm the importance of certain marketing and experiential levers (price, safety, information) in stimulating sales. They also give indications as to which areas should be strengthened as a priority (working on price and safety). Given that all our derived hypotheses have been validated, we can say that our universal hypothesis, based on the significant influence of the national tourism strategy on the purchase intention of Moroccan citizens, is accepted.).

Given that price and security have a strong positive influence on purchase intent, it is advisable to keep prices competitive and ensure a high level of security for customers. This could be achieved, for example, by providing a reinforced security service or clear guarantees in the event of a problem. Accessibility to information and quality of service have an average positive influence on purchase intention. It would therefore be worthwhile to improve these aspects, for example by providing more product information online or in-store, or by training staff more to offer better customer service. The physical and scenic environment also has a positive influence. Consider investing in in-store design and layout to create a more attractive atmosphere and stimulate purchases. Given the positive influence of all these factors, an overall strategy combining improvements in each of them could significantly increase customer purchase intent. Tests should be carried out to determine the most profitable investments. Finally, it would be interesting to replicate the study regularly to monitor the evolution of these influences over time and adapt the sales strategy accordingly. However, one limitation is that purchase intention does not always translate into actual purchase. This would need to be supplemented by a study of actual consumer behavior. Also, the results may not be generalizable to other contexts.

From a managerial point of view, the results clearly suggest that price and safety exert an overriding influence on the purchasing decision. This finding is not insignificant, and merits particular attention from managers. Indeed, in a market where consumer confidence can be fragile, investing in robust security protocols becomes not only a competitive advantage, but a strategic necessity. Companies would do well to communicate clearly about their guarantees, and put in place protection systems that are visible to their customers. At the same time, price sensitivity continues to be a determining factor, suggesting that an aggressive, or at least competitive, pricing strategy remains essential to boost sales. Information accessibility and service quality, meanwhile, exert a moderate but significant influence. This finding invites managers to rethink their information channels and staff training. Clear, accessible and relevant information can make all the difference in the consumer's buying journey. Likewise, attentive, personalized service provided by well-trained staff can turn a simple visit into a concrete purchase. These elements, although secondary to price and safety, are nonetheless significant levers for improving sales performance. The physical and scenic environment also appears to be a positive influencing factor. This dimension, often neglected in traditional economic analyses, deserves to be reconsidered. The layout of sales areas, the ambience created and the ergonomics of the customer journey are all elements that can, subtly but surely, influence the purchasing decision. Investing in the aesthetic and functional quality of sales outlets could therefore prove wise, particularly for sectors where the shopping experience is a differentiating factor.

In economic terms, these results call for a careful allocation of resources. Investments should first target the most influential factors - price and safety - before extending to secondary elements. A methodical approach, based on empirical tests, would enable us to identify the most profitable investments and optimize return on investment. For example, determining the balance point between price reduction and sales volume increase, or assessing the real impact of security measures on customer conversion. It should be noted, however, as the text rightly points out, that purchase intention does not systematically translate into actual purchase. This nuance is fundamental to economic analysis, as it highlights the potential gap between predictive models and commercial reality. Further research into actual consumer behavior would therefore be necessary to refine strategies and maximize investment efficiency. Finally, the question of the transferability of these results to other contexts remains open. Purchasing dynamics can vary significantly from one sector, culture or period to another. A regular, contextualized study of influencing factors is therefore essential as part of good management practice. This vigilance enables us to adapt our strategies to market trends and maintain their relevance in a constantly changing business environment.

CONCLUSION

In conclusion, Morocco, like other international destinations, particularly those around the Mediterranean, has suffered the negative effects of the COVID-19 crisis, due to the partial or total closure of borders, restrictions on certain destinations, and the obligation to undergo tests or quarantine on departure or arrival. In this sense, Morocco's tourism development model will have to be rethought. In the future, tourist destinations should also be promoted through social media and direct marketing actions to motivate Moroccan and foreign customers.

The article proposes a conceptual model linking travel purchase intention to several determinants. This model is empirically tested with a representative sample of potential tourists. The results validate several significant relationships in the model and show that purchase intention is primarily determined by destination confidence, perceived value, and attitudes toward travel. Based on these results, the article formulates managerial recommendations to stimulate purchase intention and boost tourism after the COVID-19 crisis. Recommended strategies include: building confidence through visible health and safety measures, actively promoting value and attractive offers, working on image, and changing negative attitudes linked to the crisis.

The article thus contributes to a better understanding of tourism purchasing intentions in a post-crisis context. The managerial implications provide concrete avenues for boosting demand. Methodologically, the conceptual model and empirical test approach provide solid, generalizable results. Nevertheless, the study is based solely on declared purchasing intentions. Intentions do not always translate into actual purchasing behavior. The conceptual model focuses on individual determinants of purchase intention. It does not take into account external factors such as the economic situation. The temporality of the study is limited to the immediate post-crisis period. Long-term trends in tourism behavior are not addressed. Finally, competitive aspects between destinations are not taken into account in the strategic recommendations. There are several possible extensions and perspectives to this work. Firstly, it is possible to complement the study of intentions with an analysis of actual travel purchasing behavior, by following a sample of tourists over time. Secondly, it is possible to extend the study to different countries and tourist contexts to increase the generalizability of the results, and to enrich the conceptual model by integrating external variables such as the economic situation or health measures. Finally, our study could be developed by adopting a longitudinal vision, studying the evolution of tourism intentions and behaviors over the long term post-crisis, or by cross-referencing the results with other academic work and managerial contributions on the subject.

REFERENCES

Agag, G., & El-Masry, A. A. (2016). Understanding consumer intention to participate in the online travel community and effects on consumer intention to purchase travel online and WOM: An integration of innovation diffusion theory and TAM with trust. *Computers in Human Behavior*, *60*, 97–111. DOI: 10.1016/j.chb.2016.02.038

Alla, L., Bentalha, B., & Bouhtati, N. (2022). Assessing supply chain performance in the covid 19 context: a prospective model. In 2022 14th International Colloquium of Logistics and Supply Chain Management (LOGISTIQUA) (pp. 1-6). IEEE. DOI: 10.1109/LOGISTIQUA55056.2022.9938083

Beddaa, M., & Bentalha, B. (2025). Optimizing Local Attractiveness Through Territorial Digital Communication. In Sustainable and Intelligent Territorial Marketing and Entrepreneurship (pp. 159-192). IGI Global.

Benjelloun, A. (2019). Le patrimoine culturel, levier d'attractivité pour la destination touristique «Fès». Revue du contrôle, de la comptabilité et de l'audit, 3(2).

Benjelloun, A., Kaddari, F., & El Gharbaoui, B. (2021). La pédagogie numérique comme solution à la continuité pédagogique en temps du COVID-19 (Cas des étudiants de la ville de Fès). *Alternatives Managériales Economiques*, *3*(1), 650–666.

Bentalha, B. (2023). Motivating Factors for Hotel Employees: A Fuzzy Logic Approach. In Strategic Human Resource Management in the Hospitality Industry: A Digitalized Economic Paradigm (pp. 159-178). IGI Global. DOI: 10.4018/978-1-6684-7494-5.ch008

Bentalha, B. (2024). Contribution des randonnées au développement d'un tourisme durable dans la région Fès Meknès. Numérisation et durabilité, Vers une économie responsable et innovante, 226-245.

Bentalha, B. (2024). Contribution des randonnées au développement d'un tourisme durable dans la région Fès Meknès. Numérisation et durabilité, Vers une économie responsable et innovante, 226-245.

Bentalha, B. (2025). Artificial Intelligence in B2B Sales: A Survey of Current Applications and Future Trends. AI, Economic Perspectives, and Firm Business Management, 143-164.

Bentalha, B., & Alla, L. (2024). Revealing the subtleties: The art of qualitative studies in science and management. In *Applying qualitative research methods to management science* (pp. 1–21). IGI Global. DOI: 10.4018/979-8-3693-5543-5.ch001

Bentalha, B., & Boukare, M. (2024). AI-Driven Territorial Intelligence: An Integrated Approach to Enhancing Digital Sovereignty. In Generative AI and Implications for Ethics, Security, and Data Management (pp. 231-261). IGI Global.

Bentalha, B., Hmioui, A., & Alla, L. (2020). La performance des entreprises de services: Un cadrage théorique d'un concept évolutif. *Alternatives Managériales Economiques*, *2*(1), 58–78.

Bonsón Ponte, E., Carvajal-Trujillo, E., & Escobar-Rodríguez, T.Bonsón. (2015). Influence of trust and perceived value on the intention to purchase travel online: Integrating the effects of assurance on trust antecedents. *Tourism Management*, *47*, 286–302. DOI: 10.1016/j.tourman.2014.10.009

Boudri, R., Bentalha, B., Andaloussi, O. B., & Abbass, Z. (2025). Leveraging the "Made in Morocco" Label for Smart Marketing and Sustainable Territorial Attractiveness. In Sustainable and Intelligent Territorial Marketing and Entrepreneurship (pp. 69-94). IGI Global.

Boudri, R., Bentalha, B., & Benjelloun, O. (2024). Phygital marketing and the pain of paying: An Amazon Go netnographic case study. In *AI and data engineering solutions for effective marketing* (pp. 348–363). IGI Global. DOI: 10.4018/979-8-3693-3172-9.ch017

Bouhtati, N., Alla, L., & Bentalha, B. (2023). Marketing Big Data Analytics and Customer Relationship Management: A Fuzzy Approach. In Integrating Intelligence and Sustainability in Supply Chains (pp. 75-86). IGI Global. DOI: 10.4018/979-8-3693-0225-5.ch004

Chen, Y., Ding, D., Meng, L., Li, X., & Zhang, S. (2021). Understanding consumers' purchase intention towards online paid courses. *Information Development*. Advance online publication. DOI: 10.1177/02666669211027206

Dash, G., Kiefer, K., & Paul, J. (2021, January). Kiefer, Kip., & Paul, J. (2021). Marketing-to-Millennials: Marketing 4.0, customer satisfaction and purchase intention. *Journal of Business Research*, *122*, 608–620. Advance online publication. DOI: 10.1016/j.jbusres.2020.10.016

Fabry, N., & Zeghni, S. (2017). "Le tourisme du futur: entre mobilité et proximité". inGerardin H. et Montalieu T. (éditeurs), Mobilités et soutenabilité du développement, Paris, Karthala, 2017

Flying, S. (2020). "United couldfollow American withearly 757 & 767 retirement". https://simpleflying.com/united-757-767-early-retirement/

Hall, C. M. (2019). Constructing sustainable tourism development: The 2030 agenda and the managerial ecology of sustainable tourism. *Journal of Sustainable Tourism*, *27*(7), 1044–1060. DOI: 10.1080/09669582.2018.1560456

Hmioui, A., Alla, L., & Bentalha, B. (2017). Pilotage de la touristicité territoriale au Maroc Proposition d'un indice de touriscticité pour la destination Fès. Entrepreneuriat, Innovation, Gouvernance et Développement territorial, 120-143.

Hmioui, A., Alla, L., & Bentalha, B. (2019). La performance touristique territoriale: Cas de la destination Fès. *Alternatives Managériales Economiques*, *1*(1), 3–21.

Hmioui, A., Alla, L., & Bentalha, B. (2022). Perception of sustainable tourism by international clients: Case of the visit to a hotel establishment. Reconfigurations du tourisme en contexte de la crise du Covid-19: Quelles démarches pour quelles résiliences au Maroc et ailleurs ?, 1 (1), pp.5-38

Hussin, N., Padlee, S. F., & Zulkiffli, S. N. A. (2021). Benefit Segmentation in Seaside Destination: A Domestic Tourism Perspective. *Estudios de Economía Aplicada*, *39*(10). Advance online publication. DOI: 10.25115/eea.v39i10.5341

Kumar, A., Prakash, G., & Kumar, G. (2021). Does environmentally responsible purchase intention matter for consumers? A predictive sustainable model developed through an empirical study. *Journal of Retailing and Consumer Services*, *58*, 102270. DOI: 10.1016/j.jretconser.2020.102270

Lamsiah, A., & Bentalha, B. (2022). Dakhla: A Growing Touristic Destination with a Diplomatic Sway. *Alternatives Managériales Economiques*, *1*, 94–115.

Lee, S., Han, H., Radic, A., & Tariq, B. (2020). Corporate social responsibility (CSR) as a customer satisfaction and retention strategy in the chain restaurant sector. *Journal of Hospitality and Tourism Management*, *45*, 348–358. DOI: 10.1016/j.jhtm.2020.09.002

Lu, B., & Chen, Z. (2021). Live streaming commerce and consumers' purchase intention: An uncertainty reduction perspective. *Information & Management*, *58*(7), 103509. DOI: 10.1016/j.im.2021.103509

Meziane, B., Alla, L., & Bentalha, B. (2025). Transformational Trends of Territorial Economic Intelligence Strategies in the Digital Era: A Systematic Theoretical Exploration. In Utilizing Technology to Manage Territories (pp. 455-490). IGI Global.

Mohseni, S., Jayashree, S., Rezaei, S., Kasim, A., & Okumus, F. (2018). Attracting tourists to travel companies' websites: The structural relationship between website brand, personal value, shopping experience, perceived risk and purchase intention. *Current Issues in Tourism*, *21*(6), 616–645. DOI: 10.1080/13683500.2016.1200539

Noor, N. M. M., lina Ahm, I. A., Ali, N. H., & Ismail, F. (2010). Intelligent decision support system for tourism destination choice: A preliminary study. In *2010 International Symposium on Information Technology* (Vol. 3, pp. 1357-1361). IEEE. DOI: 10.1109/ITSIM.2010.5561594

Padlee, S. F., Thaw, C. Y., & Zulkiffli, S. N. A. (2019). The relationship between service quality, customer satisfaction and behavioural intentions. *Tourism and Hospitality Management*, 25(1), 121–139. DOI: 10.20867/thm.25.1.9

Prebensen, N., Woo, E., & Uysal, M. S. (2014). Experience value: Antecedents and consequences. *Current Issues in Tourism*, 17(10), 910–928. DOI: 10.1080/13683500.2013.770451

Qalati, S. A., Vela, E. G., Li, W., Dakhan, S. A., Hong Thuy, T. T., & Merani, S. H. (2021). Effects of perceived service quality, website quality, and reputation on purchase intention: The mediating and moderating roles of trust and perceived risk in online shopping. *Cogent Business & Management*, 8(1), 1869363. Advance online publication. DOI: 10.1080/23311975.2020.1869363

Rausch, T. M., & Kopplin, C. S. (2021, January). Rausch, Theresa Maria., & Kopplin, C. (2021). Bridge the gap: Consumers' purchase intention and behavior regarding sustainable clothing. *Journal of Cleaner Production*, 278, 123882. Advance online publication. DOI: 10.1016/j.jclepro.2020.123882

Rosli, A. B. A., & Zaki, N. A. M. (2022). Understanding The Impacts Of Covid-19 Pandemic On Consumer Behaviour In Malaysia. TIJARI International Journal of Islamic Economics, Bussiness and Entrepreneurship, 2(4).

Rosli, N. A., Zainuddin, Z., Yusliza, M. Y., Muhammad, Z., & Saputra, J. (2023). Investigating the effect of destination image on revisit intention through tourist satisfaction in Laguna Redang Island Resort, Terengganu. *International Journal of Advanced and Applied Sciences*, 10(6), 17–27. DOI: 10.21833/ijaas.2023.06.003

Roy, G., Datta, B., Mukherjee, S., Basu, R., & Shrivastava, A. K. (2021). Effect of eWOM valence on purchase intention: The moderating role of product. *International Journal of Technology Marketing*, 15(2-3), 158–180. DOI: 10.1504/IJTMKT.2021.118201

Shamim, R., & Bentalha, B. (2023). Blockchain-Enabled Machine Learning Framework for Demand Forecasting in Supply Chain Management. In Integrating Intelligence and Sustainability in Supply Chains (pp. 28-48). IGI Global. DOI: 10.4018/979-8-3693-0225-5.ch002

Slimani, H. (2020). L'impact du facteur humain sur le développement de l'entreprise Touristique Cas: Les NTIC dans le secteur Touristique. *Revue Internationale des Sciences de Gestion*, *3*(2).

UNWTO. (2019), Faits saillants du tourisme, édition 2019, [On line], https://www.unwto.org/fr/publication/faits-saillants-du-tourisme-2019 (Consulted 11/01/2024)

Chapter 5
Exploring the Socio-Economic Effects of Rural Cultural Tourism:
A Case Study of Shantiniketan, West Bengal

Nilanjan Ray
https://orcid.org/0000-0002-6109-6080
JIS University, India

Tapas Kumar Chatterjee
https://orcid.org/0000-0001-5419-3045
IMT Nagpur, India

Indranil Bose
https://orcid.org/0009-0002-6025-2915
MIT University, Shillong, India

ABSTRACT

This study explores the diverse effects of rural cultural tourism on the socio-economic circumstances of local communities within the region. The objective of this research is to investigate the effects of tourism on the local economy, lifestyle, and socio-cultural dynamics within the host community in and around the tourist location. The results suggest that rural cultural tourism has propelled the advancement of infrastructure, bolstered local entrepreneurship, and attracted investment, consequently augmenting household incomes and alleviating poverty. Nevertheless, the research also emphasizes challenges, such as the imperative for sustainable tourism practices, equitable distribution of benefits, and the preservation of cultural integrity. The study

DOI: 10.4018/979-8-3693-3196-5.ch005

underscores the significance of community engagement, governmental support, and the establishment of effective policy frameworks in optimizing the beneficial impacts of rural cultural tourism while mitigating potential adverse effects.

INTRODUCTION

Cultural tourism possesses the potential to induce intricate transformations within our societal structure. This research examines the beneficial effects of rural tourism, functioning as a catalyst for the socio-economic upliftment of rural communities located in Shantiniketan, Birbhum districts of West Bengal, India. This region holds significant importance within the tourism industry of West Bengal. Tourism serves as a crucial driver in the evolution of a district and a state such as West Bengal, which is currently experiencing modern economic growth through a structural reconfiguration of its economic framework. In recent decades, rural tourism has emerged as a prominent focal point in contemporary tourism research. Rural tourism entails the exploration of rural environments and interaction with various rural elements, including art, culture, heritage, and traditional crafts. Shantiniketan differentiates itself within West Bengal as a center for a diverse array of rural cultural handicraft tourism offerings distributed throughout the district. Cultural tourism encompasses both overnight accommodations and day trips to rural areas, incorporating activities such as sightseeing, walking, cycling, and engagement in a plethora of countryside pursuits. The government of West Bengal has recognized the substantial potential embedded in rural tourism attractions, leading to the development of policy frameworks aimed at attracting both domestic and international tourists, as well as investors, to these sectors.

REDEFINING RURAL TOURISM: A NEW PERSPECTIVE

Rural tourism, once narrowly viewed as village-based and pastoral in nature, has experienced a significant conceptual evolution. Enhanced by global connectivity and shifting travel motivations, rural tourism now encompasses an expansive range of experiences that move beyond traditional perceptions of scenic landscapes and rustic charm. This broadened definition captures a hybrid of cultural immersion, sustainable practices, and experiential storytelling that appeals to modern travelers in search of authentic, meaningful connections. Defining "rural tourism" remains complex, requiring an integration of conventional understandings and emerging perspectives that reflect its multidimensional nature.

According to the United Nations World Tourism Organization (UNWTO, 2019), rural tourism refers to activities rooted in nature, agriculture, and rural cultural experiences that occur in non-urban settings characterized by low population density, agricultural land use, and traditional social structures. Scholars often conceptualize rural tourism as engaging rural life, arts, heritage, and local culture in a manner that brings economic and social benefits to communities while fostering direct interaction between residents and visitors (Naqshband, 1980). Furthermore, tourism experts highlight the ethical responsibility of protecting natural and cultural environments, a value central to rural tourism development.

The concept of Pro-Poor Tourism (PPT), as proposed by Brown and Hall (2008), aims to orient tourism benefits towards poverty reduction in rural areas, though this approach has faced critiques for its potential to perpetuate global inequalities if broader power dynamics are unaddressed (Harrison, 2008). Negi (1990) identifies several rural tourism attractions, including scenic rural landscapes, open space, tranquility, rural sports, ethnic traditions, and educational sites, emphasizing that rural tourism serves as a response to urban dwellers' desire for outdoor leisure and relaxation. Pilgrimage tourism has also been recognized as a form of rural tourism where visitors engage deeply with the spiritual heritage of rural sites (Turner, 1973).

Bramwell and Lane (1993) discuss the versatile nature of rural tourism, which spans farm holidays, nature-focused excursions, ecotourism, and heritage tourism. Rural tourism thus offers job creation, counters rural-urban migration, and fosters economic revitalization (Muthoo and Onul, 1996). Lane (1994) adds that rural tourism is inherently small-scale, embedded within traditional structures, and reflective of the intricate interplay between rural environments, local economies, histories, and cultural identities. This diverse framework includes activities from agri-tourism and green tourism to gastronomic and equestrian tourism, each facilitating immersive rural experiences where travelers participate in local practices and traditions (Sharpley and Sharpley, 1997).

The EU's LEADER program, among others, underscores rural tourism's emphasis on community-driven, localized tourism products. Here, rural tourism is not merely an industry but a "state of mind," defined by activities, settings, and experiences that resonate deeply with visitors seeking to understand rural life. Contemporary studies advocate for historical methodologies to deepen the understanding of tourism's evolution, with archival research revealing the socio-economic and cultural roots of tourism practices (Saarinen et al., 2017; Pirie, 2022).

Rural tourism increasingly embodies a responsible and sustainable model, offering visitors the chance to engage with rural communities that exhibit agricultural landscapes, traditional practices, and often face economic marginalization (Manaf et al., 2018; Situmorang et al., 2019). The COVID-19 pandemic has intensified the focus on sustainability in rural tourism, emphasizing the sector's resilience and its role in ecological conservation (Priatmoko et al., 2023). Recent academic literature explores rural tourism through themes of economic rejuvenation, environmental stewardship, local governance, and the intrinsic value of authentic experiences (Lane and Kastenholz, 2015). Additionally, recent discussions in rural tourism literature highlight resource management, climate change effects (Dashper, 2014; Ruiz-Real et al., 2021), and rural entrepreneurship, with a particular emphasis on sustainability, community empowerment, and cultural authenticity (Rosalina et al., 2021). In this broader and nuanced understanding, rural tourism is characterized by its rural locality, commitment to sustainable practices, small-scale operations, traditional underpinnings, and community-led development. Far from being monolithic, rural tourism reflects the rich diversity and complexity of rural landscapes, economies, and cultures, providing tourists with a unique portal to meaningful, place-based experiences that are thoughtfully managed and locally governed.

Table 1. Several cases from different countries perspectives

Reference	Country	Perspectives
Bramwell & Lane, 1993	**Italy**	Rural tourism in regions like Tuscany has revitalized local economies. It has encouraged the preservation of traditional agricultural practices and local cuisine while providing economic benefits through agritourism and cultural events
Singh, 2018	**India**	In rural Maharashtra, cultural tourism initiatives have improved local livelihoods by providing training in hospitality and guiding services. Community-based tourism has been instrumental in preserving local crafts and traditions, empowering women through employment opportunities
Koutsou, 2019	**Greece**	Rural cultural tourism in Greece has focused on sustainable practices, promoting local products and crafts. This has resulted in job creation and economic diversification in regions traditionally reliant on agriculture
Wamwara & Ndung'u, 2020	**Kenya**	In Kenya, rural cultural tourism has enhanced local communities' socio-economic conditions by providing alternative livelihoods to agriculture. Initiatives such as community-owned lodges and cultural experiences have improved income levels and fostered community development
Cáceres & Duran, 2021	**Peru**	The development of cultural tourism in rural areas, such as the Sacred Valley, has led to economic growth by providing opportunities for local artisans and promoting sustainable agricultural practices. This has encouraged cultural exchange and increased community pride
Smith & Watmough, 2019	**Canada**	Indigenous cultural tourism in rural Canada has empowered Indigenous communities economically and culturally. Through showcasing traditional practices, storytelling, and art, these communities have fostered cultural awareness and improved their socio-economic status

SURVEY OF LITERATURE

Rural cultural tourism possesses considerable potential to enhance the economic advancement of rural regions. As articulated by Lane (1994), rural tourism, encompassing cultural tourism, possesses the capacity to invigorate local economies by facilitating revenue generation through the direct expenditures of visitors, fostering employment opportunities, and endorsing the commercialization of regional products. Moreover, Richards (1996) highlights that cultural tourism can help diversify the economic base of rural communities, reducing their dependence on agriculture and other traditional industries.

The social and cultural impact of rural cultural tourism is complex. On one hand, it can help preserve and revitalize local traditions, customs, and cultural practices. Richards and Hall (2000) argue that tourism can play a crucial role in sustaining cultural heritage by providing financial resources for the preservation of historical sites and traditional practices.

However, the commercialization of culture can also lead to the erosion of authenticity. As stressed by Cohen (1988), there is a risk that cultural tourism might lead to the commodification of cultural practices, where traditions are altered or staged to meet tourists' expectations. This can lead to a loss of cultural identity and a disconnect between local communities and their heritage (Greenwood, 1977).

In an investigation conducted by Sharpley and Roberts (2004), it was determined that rural tourism has the potential to enhance household income levels and create novel employment prospects, particularly for women and youth who might otherwise migrate from rural locales in pursuit of economic opportunities. The advancement of rural cultural tourism may also catalyze the formation of small and medium-sized enterprises (SMEs), thereby promoting entrepreneurial endeavors and fostering innovative practices within rural economies (Liu, 2006). While anthropologists, such as Geertz (1973), articulate culture as encompassing a broad recognition of holistic attributes, emphasizing the entirety of the anthropogenic world—including material culture, cultivated landscapes, social institutions, alongside knowledge and meaning—this delineation indicates that culture encompasses historical contexts and traditions (heritage and history), creative expressions (artistic works, performances), as well as the lifestyle practices, customs, and habits of individuals. Although there is a prevailing consensus regarding the conceptualization of culture within numerous tourism discourses, the extent to which the term ought to be expanded to encompass all dimensions of quotidian existence remains a matter of contention.

Eagleton (2000: 32) posits that "it is hard to resist the conclusion that the word 'culture' is both too broad and too narrow to be greatly useful." Indeed, it proves to be a formidable challenge to delineate parameters surrounding the definitions of culture in the contemporary postmodern, globalized milieu, where culture could feasibly be construed as nearly any activity pertinent to the lives and lifestyles of human beings. Cultural tourism has emerged as a focal point of significance from a global perspective (OECD, 2009), yet it is evident that no characterization of cultural tourism can commence without a preliminary definition of culture, which surprisingly encompasses both global and local relevance. It may be represented in physical and material forms, whether tangible or intangible; as political and symbolic constructs, or as the everyday practices that manifest as a continuous and dynamic phenomenon. Furthermore, it is configured in diverse manners by the various stakeholders engaged directly or indirectly in the promotion and development of cultural tourism systems. Numerous scholars assert that culture epitomizes a comprehensive mode of existence for a community or social group, characterized by distinctive systems, forms of social engagement, and artistic, innovative, and creative outputs. Recently, one of the most salient trends emerging is the investigation of diverse market segments within the broader framework of cultural tourism.

The proliferation of cultural tourism has given rise to a diverse array of niche and sub-niche sectors, reflecting the multifaceted interests of contemporary tourists. These niches encompass arts tourism (Hughes, 2000), tourism on cultural heritage impact (Timothy, 2011), heritage tourism (Park, 2013), and World Heritage Sites (Leask and Fyall, 2006), each offering distinct opportunities for engagement with local and global heritage. Literary tourism (Robinson and Anderson, 2004), film tourism (Beeton, 2005), festival tourism (Picard and Robinson, 2006), indigenous tourism (Butler and Hinch, 1996, 2007), and creative tourism (Richards, 2001c, 2011, 2021) serve to exemplify the extensive scope of cultural tourism's allure, offering tourists profound, thematic experiences that encapsulate distinctive cultural, historical, and artistic dimensions. Shantiniketan, with its deep historical and cultural roots, holds a powerful position within this complex tourism landscape. It stands out as a compelling cultural tourism destination due to its rich and varied offerings across numerous cultural tourism niches. The destination's unique selling proposition is anchored in a diversified portfolio of tourism products, showcasing both depth and breadth in its cultural assets. Shantiniketan offers distinct product lines that vary in length, width, and depth, catering to a wide range of visitor interests and preferences, thus positioning itself as a cultural hub with both local and global significance. To ensure sustainable development and effective promotion of Shantiniketan as a premier cultural tourism destination, it is essential to prioritize impact assessments. Conducting comprehensive evaluations of the social, economic, and environmental impacts of tourism activities can guide responsible destination management, ensuring that Shantiniketan maintains its cultural integrity while supporting local communities. Recognized as an epicenter of the cultural heritage of undivided Bengal, Shantiniketan's influence extends globally, offering rich potential for heritage preservation, educational tourism, and immersive cultural experiences in an increasingly interconnected world.

Table 2. Select existing literature

Year	Authors	Implications
2022	Vyslobodska, Brychka, & Bulyk	In this scholarly article, the authors elucidate the distinctive characteristics associated with the diversification of agricultural producers' activities, particularly within the framework of rural tourism development, while underscoring the critical significance of green tourism in rural locales.
2023	Berondo	Cultural tourism in rural settings exerts a beneficial influence on socio-economic conditions by facilitating revenue generation, creating employment opportunities, and safeguarding traditional practices, thereby fostering community development and enriching the overall tourism experience.
2024	Akorio et.al	The phenomenon of rural tourism in Kalapatta Sub County, Uganda, exerts a substantial influence on socio-economic development through the mechanisms of income generation, the provision of employment opportunities, the enhancement of infrastructure, and the preservation of cultural heritage, albeit facing challenges such as environmental degradation and the inequitable distribution of benefits.
2024	Supera et.al	Rural tourism in Surigao del Norte, Philippines, exerts a predominantly favorable influence on economic, socio-cultural, and ecological capital. Nonetheless, it is imperative to address challenges pertaining to infrastructure, business support, environmental protection, and community participation in order to ensure the sustainability and inclusivity of the sector.

OBJECTIVES OF STUDY

Keeping in mind of above discussion following objectives are:

1. To ascertain the primary factors influencing the proliferation, advancement, and inception of cultural tourism within the state of West Bengal broadly, and specifically within the context of Shantiniketan.
2. To analyze the impact of cultural tourism on socio-economic condition in the study area

METHODOLOGY

In consideration of the aforementioned objectives, researchers gathered primary data through field surveys, face-to-face interactions, and observation methods. Additionally, secondary data was obtained from various journals, research articles, and websites affiliated with WBTDC. For the purpose of this current investigation, 230 participants were chosen using the convenience sampling technique to examine the impact of cultural tourism in Shantiniketan, located in Birbhum district. The fundamental assumption underlying factor analysis is that all variables within a specific group exhibit high levels of correlation with each other, while demonstrating relatively low correlations with variables in other groups.

Table 3. KMO and Bartlett's test

KMO Measure of Sampling Adequacy		0.871
Bartlett's Test of Sphericity	Approx. Chi-Square	806.782
	Df	35
	Significant	0.000

Table 4. Rotated component matrix

Rotated Component Matrix[a]	Component	
	1	2
Traditional Life	**0.611**	0.528
Education	**0.509**	0.464
Cultural Preservation	**0.522**	0.515
Quality life	**0.711**	0.227
Availability of Tourist police	0.350	**0.720**
Security Issue	0.115	**0.838**
Cultural Rural Tourism brings more Positive in social effect	**0.753**	0.124
Available of Civic Volunteers	0.229	**0.810**
Impact of local performing artists' community	0.113	**0.837**

Extraction Method: Principal Component Analysis.
Rotation Method: Varimax with Kaiser Normalization.
a. Rotation converged in 3 iterations.

Table 5. Total variance explained

Component	Initial Eigenvalues			Extraction Sums of Squared Loadings			Rotation Sums of Squared Loadings		
	Total	% of Variance	Cumulative %	Total	% of Variance	Cumulative %	Total	% of Variance	Cumulative %
1	4.752	52.804	52.804	4.752	52.804	52.804	3.343	37.140	37.140
2	1.091	11.008	63.812	1.091	11.008	63.812	2.400	26.672	63.812
3	.670	7.439	71.252						
4	.562	6.242	77.494						
5	.540	6.000	83.494						
6	.510	5.664	89.158						
7	.400	4.441	93.599						
8	.306	3.401	97.001						
9	.270	2.999	100.000						

Extraction Method: Principal Component Analysis.

Table 6. Prime factor identification

Factor	Factor Name	Parameters
Factor-I	Cultural Factors	Traditional Life
		Education
		Cultural Protection
		Quality life
		Availability of Tourist police
Factor-II	Host Community Factors	Security Issue
		Cultural Rural Tourism brings more Positive in social effect
		Available of Civic Volunteers
		Impact of local performing artists' community

Factor analysis gives us two factors (Cultural Factors and Host Community Factors) which has contributed to the growth of cultural tourism in the study area. In order to determine the overall impact of cultural tourism on socio-economic development in Shantiniketan, the following regression equation has been considered:

$$Y_i = \beta_0 + \beta_1 F_1 + \beta_2 F_2 + \varepsilon_i$$

where y_i is dependent variable (socio-economic impact in the study area) which is solely dependent on factor scores of (F_1) and (F_2).

Hypothesis:

The null hypothesis to be tested in the study is as follow:

H_0 = There is no significant impact of tourism on socio-economic condition in the study area (Shantiniketan)

ANALYSIS AND DISCUSSIONS

Multiple Linear Regression has been fitted using the two extracted factors to understand the impact of tourism on socio-economic condition in Shantiniketan. The findings from the regression analysis have been summarized below.

Table 7. Regression model

Multiple R			0.756			
R Square			0.689			
Adjusted R Square			0.712			
Standard Error			68.69			
Observations			385			
Durbin Watson (DW)			1.78			
ANOVA						
	df	SS	MS	F	Significance F	
Regression	2	859	429.5	123.56	0.0035	
Residual	198	689	3.47			
Total	385	1548				
		Coefficients	Standard Error	t-Statistics	P-value	VIF
Intercept		2.66	0.244	10.08	0.006	
F1		2.13	0.156	13.65	0.004	1.89
F2		1.21	0.235	5.149	0.002	1.96

The table presented delineates several key statistical metrics pertinent to the assessment of the predictive capability of the regression model employed in this study. The "R" column, which denotes the multiple correlation coefficient, provides a quantifiable measure of the degree of association between the independent variables and the dependent variable, reflecting the model's predictive accuracy. An R value of 0.756 indicates a commendable level of predictive ability, suggesting a strong correlation between the predictors and the outcome variable. Further elaborating on this, the column labeled "R Square" presents the R^2 value, which serves as the coefficient of determination. An R^2 value of 0.689 implies that the independent variables account for 68.9% of the variance observed in the dependent variable, thereby illustrating the extent to which the model elucidates the fluctuations within the dataset. The analysis of variance (ANOVA) framework introduces the F-ratio, a statistic employed to evaluate the overall adequacy of the regression model in relation to the dataset. The results, specifically denoted as $F(2, 198) = 123.56, p < 0.05$, indicate that the independent variables are statistically significant in predicting the dependent variable. This finding denotes a robust alignment of the regression model with the data, affirming its validity. Moreover, the specified regression equation pertaining to the economic status of local community residents within the research area underscores the model's application. Each t-value presented in the analysis reaches statistical significance at a 95% confidence level, reinforcing the reliability of the results. Consequently, the overall F-value also attains statistical significance, further corroborating the model's effectiveness. In conclusion, the regression analysis elucidates that both cultural elements and factors intrinsic to the host community significantly contribute to the holistic enhancement of the socio-economic status of residents in Shantiniketan. These findings underscore the importance of integrating cultural and community-related variables in economic assessments, thereby highlighting the multidimensional nature of socio-economic advancement in rural contexts.

ADDITIONAL FINDINGS

Upon exploring Shantiniketan, visitors engage in an educational experience regarding the artistry exhibited by local craftsmen. This particular experience engraves a profound impression on the minds of the visitors. The artisans in Shantiniketan additionally operate as entrepreneurs, simultaneously pursuing initiatives to promote their creations at regional fairs or markets. Functioning collaboratively as a cohesive unit, they present their unique designs while exchanging a variety of concepts and methods. Visitors acquire handicrafts during their stay in Shantiniketan for their family and friends, thus transporting these items back to their urban residences. This practice arises from the incorporation of such products into their urban lifestyles, thereby fostering a synthesis of urban and rural cultures. As a result, a network of cultural linkages between urban and rural environments is established. Occasionally, modern culture capitalizes on traditional heritage. The rural experience, encompassing activities such as cycling tours, treehouse adventures, yoga retreats, agritourism, horse-drawn carriage rides, and exploring craft markets, ranks as the second most favored option among respondents. Within the context of the marketing mix promotion, four essential components were identified. Among these factors, the Public Relations (PR) Cell receives the highest evaluation, whereas publications rank the lowest.

The respondents emphasize the critical importance of interpersonal relationships with local residents in promotional activities. Significantly, in Shantiniketan, Rabindra Bharati University and the West Bengal Tourism Development Corporation possess well-established PR Cells, as confirmed by the respondents. Fairs, trade exhibitions, and high-quality brochures are regarded as more impactful than publications by the respondents. This group asserts that fairs, trade exhibitions, and brochures exert a more considerable influence on their perceptions compared to any form of publication. Moreover, meticulously designed brochures, infused with comprehensive information about accommodations, pricing, itineraries, attractions, and additional services, are considered vital for tourists visiting Shantiniketan. These brochures should incorporate illustrations, maps, and visually appealing graphic designs on their covers and layouts. This study highlights the necessity of tourism education in motivating individuals to pursue entrepreneurial opportunities within the tourism industry. According to the findings, tourists are occasionally discouraged from engaging in indigenous activities such as birdwatching, fishing, and participating in seasonal fairs and festivals. Many tourists, predominantly from urban areas, contribute to the erosion of rural cultures, resulting in environmental degradation of the surrounding regions.

CONCLUSION & RECOMMENDATIONS

In cultural destinations, it is essential to enhance the convenience of services provided to tourists, particularly regarding comfort and accessibility. Efforts should be directed towards fostering travel trade partnerships by integrating marketing initiatives with tour operators, guides, and other stakeholders, while also incorporating new participants such as allied industries like international hotel chains, airlines, and credit card companies. The quality of budget accommodations and homestay facilities must be elevated to ensure a superior experience for tourists.

Consequently, local authorities, Public-Private Partnership initiatives, and government subsidies ought to prioritize infrastructure development to enhance service delivery. Protection of natural resources, local heritage, and the indigenous lifestyles of the local populace is vital. Fundamental infrastructures, including electricity, adequate drainage systems, roads, and hotels, should be consistently developed year-round. The implementation of a comprehensive marketing philosophy presents various advantages. Management must first ascertain the consumer needs—specifically, the requirements of tourists—pertaining to particular tourism products and services.

These offerings may encompass architectural resources, natural resources, cultural resources, culinary experiences, accessibility, accommodation, and transportation. The traditional marketing paradigm of producing goods and services for sale to consumers has become obsolete within the tourism industry. Marketing within the tourism sector is both a complex and demanding endeavor. The array of tourism products and services available in urban destinations is typically straightforward to access; however, in rural tourism contexts, satisfying consumer demands becomes a multifaceted challenge due to the varying needs, tasks, attitudes, expectations, and behavioral patterns of individuals.

REFERENCES

Akorio, F. A., Turyamureeba, S., Tugume, A., & Eze, V. H. U. (2024). Rural Tourism and Socio-Economic Development in Kalapatta Sub County Kabong District of Uganda. [JHASS]. *Journal of the Humanities and Social Sciences*, 6(1), 31–38. DOI: 10.36079/lamintang.jhass-0601.606

Beeton, S. (2005). *Film-Induced Tourism*. Channel View. DOI: 10.21832/9781845410162

Berondo, R. G. (2023). *The Impact of Socio–economic and Traditional Practices of the Local Folks in the Tourism Industry*. Cultural Landscapes Insights. DOI: 10.59762/cli901324531220231205131244

Blomstrom (1983). Strategic market planning in the hospitality industry. Educational Institute for the American Hotel and Motel Association, Michigan.

Bramwell, B., & Lane, B. (1993). Rural tourism and sustainable rural development. *Journal of Sustainable Tourism*, 1(1), 1–4. DOI: 10.1080/09669589309450696

Bramwell, B., & Lane, B. (1993). Rural tourism and sustainable rural development. *Journal of Sustainable Tourism*, 1(1), 1–4. DOI: 10.1080/09669589309450696

Brown, F., & Hall, D. (2008). Tourism and development in the global South: The issues. In Brown, F., & Hall, D. (Eds.), *Tourism and development in the Global South* (pp. 1–24). Routledge. DOI: 10.1080/01436590802105967

Butcher, J. (2001). 'Cultural baggage and cultural tourism', in Innovations in Cultural Tourism, Proceedings of the 5th ATLAS International Conference, Rethymnon, Crete, 1998, Tilburg: ATLAS, pp. 11–18.

Butler, R., & Hinch, T. (Eds.). (1996). *Tourism and Indigenous Peoples*. International Thomson Business Press.

Butler, R., & Hinch, T. (Eds.). (2007). *Tourism and Indigenous Peoples: Issues and Implications*. Butterworth-Heinemann. DOI: 10.4324/9780080553962

Cáceres, J. A., & Duran, J. (2021). The role of rural tourism in promoting sustainable development in Peru. *Tourism Management Perspectives*, 39, 100854.

Cohen, E. (1988). Authenticity and commoditization in tourism. *Annals of Tourism Research*, 15(3), 371–386. DOI: 10.1016/0160-7383(88)90028-X

Cooper, C. (1994). Tourism product life cycle. In Seaton, A. (Eds.), *Tourism: The state of the art* (pp. 340–346). J., Wiley.

Cooper, C., Fletcher, J., Gilbert, D., & Wanhill, S. (1993). *Turism Principles and Practice*. Pitman.

Dashper, K. (2014). Rural tourism: Opportunities and challenges. *Journal of Rural Studies*, *36*(1), 32–40.

Donnelly, J. H. J. (1976). Marketing intermediaries in channels of distribution for services. *Journal of Marketing*, *40*, 55–70.

Eagleton, T. (2000). *The Idea of Culture*. Blackwell.

Geertz, C. (1973). From the native's point of view: On the nature of anthropological understanding. In Rabinow, P., & Sullivan, W. M. (Eds.), *Interpretive social science: A reader* (pp. 225–241). University of California Press.

Greenwood, D. J. (1977). Culture by the pound: An anthropological perspective on tourism as cultural commodification. In Smith, V. L. (Ed.), *Hosts and Guests: The Anthropology of Tourism* (pp. 129–138). University of Pennsylvania Press.

Harrison, D. (2008). Pro-poor tourism: A critique. *Third World Quarterly*, *29*(5), 851–868. DOI: 10.1080/01436590802105983

Hughes, H. L. (2000). *Arts, Entertainment and Tourism*. Butterworth Heinemann.

Jolliffe, L., & McDonald, R. (2003). Cultural rural tourism: Evidence from Canada. *Annals of Tourism Research*, *30*(2), 282–301.

Karali, E., Das, S., & Roy, A. (2021). The impact of climate change on rural tourism: Adaptation strategies and sustainability. *Tourism Management Perspectives*, *40*(2), 100824.

Koutsou, S. (2019). The socio-economic impact of rural tourism in Greece: Opportunities and challenges. *International Journal of Tourism Research*, *21*(1), 30–40.

Kumar, D., Zulkifli, N., & Ray, N. (2023). Identifying Critical Factors for Sustainable Tourism and Local Community Development: Evidence from Select Destinations in Bangladesh. *ASEAN Journal on Hospitality and Tourism*, *21*(1), 124–135. DOI: 10.5614/ajht.2023.21.1.09

Lane, B. (1994). What is rural tourism? *Journal of Sustainable Tourism*, *2*(1-2), 7–21. DOI: 10.1080/09669589409510680

Lane, B. (1994). What is rural tourism? *Journal of Sustainable Tourism*, *2*(1-2), 7–21. DOI: 10.1080/09669589409510680

Lane, B., & Kastenholz, E. (2015). Rural tourism: The evolution of practice and research approaches – towards a new generation concept? *Journal of Sustainable Tourism, 23*(8-9), 1133–1156. DOI: 10.1080/09669582.2015.1083997

Leask, A., & Fyall, A. (Eds.). (2006). *Managing World Heritage Sites.* Butterworth-Heinemann. DOI: 10.4324/9780080461755

Lewis, RC (1980). Benefit segmentation for restaurant Advertisement. *Cornell HRA Quarterly,* 6-12

Lovelock & Wright. (1999). *Principals of Service Marketing and Management translated by AbolfazalTajzadeh.* Samt Publication.

Manaf, N. A., Situmorang, D. S., & Rosalina, M. (2018). Rural tourism entrepreneurship: Exploring the role of local communities. *International Journal of Tourism Research, 20*(6), 732–745.

Middleton, V. T. C. (1994). *Marketing in Travel and Tourism.* Butterworth-Heinemann.

Mill, R. C., & Morrison, A. M. (1992). *The Tourism System.*

Mill, R. C., & Mossison, A. M. (1992). *The Tourism System: An Introductory text* (2nd ed.). Prentice Hall.

Muthoo, A., & Onul, B. (1996). Rural tourism and its role in economic development. *Tourism Economics, 2*(4), 309–321.

Negi, J. (1990). Rural tourism in the Third World: Promises and problems. *Annals of Tourism Research, 17*(4), 476–484.

OECD. (2009). *The Impact of Tourism on Culture.* OECD.

Page, S., & Getz, D. (1997). The business of rural tourism: International perspectives. *Journal of Sustainable Tourism, 5*(1), 35–48.

Park, H. Y. (2013). *Heritage Tourism.* Routledge. DOI: 10.4324/9781315882093

Perreault, W.Jr, & McCarthy, J. E. (1999). *Basic Marketing—A Global Managerial Approach.* Irwin/McGraw Hill.

Priatmoko, S., Rosalina, M., & Situmorang, D. (2023). Post-Covid sustainability and rural tourism: A focus on new trends. *Journal of Sustainable Tourism, 31*(2), 239–256.

Ray N & Das D K (2011). 3Hs Tourism, An Alternative Approach of Developing Rural Tourism at Kamarpukur: An Empirical Study, South *Asian Journal of Tourism and Heritage Referred International Journal,* 4(2), India.

Ray N & Das D K, Ghosh S, Sengupta P P. (2012): Rural tourism and its Impact on Socio- Economic Condition: Evidence from West Bengal, India *Global Journal of Business Research* the IBFR, 6(2), Hilo, USA

Ray, N., Das, D. K., Sengupta, P. P., & Ghosh, S. (2011). Information Technology and Its Impact on Tourism: An Overview. In Khurana, R., Agrawal, R., & Debnath, C. (Eds.), *Computing Business Application and Legal Issues*. Excel Book Publication.

Renaghan, L. M., & Kay, M. Z. (1987). What meeting planners want: The conjoint-analysis approach. *The Cornell Hotel and Restaurant Administration Quarterly*, *28*(1), 66–76.

Richards, G. (1996). *Cultural Tourism in Europe*. CAB International.

Richards, G. (2001c) Creative Tourism as a Factor in Destination Development, ATLAS 10th Anniversary International Conference papers, 4–6 October, Dublin.

Richards, G. (2011). Creativity and tourism: The state of the art. *Annals of Tourism Research*, *38*(4), 1225–1253. DOI: 10.1016/j.annals.2011.07.008

Richards, G. (2013). Tourism development trajectories: From culture to creativity? In Smith, M. K., & Richards, G. (Eds.), *Routledge Handbook of Cultural Tourism* (pp. 297–303). Routledge.

Richards, G. (2021). Business Models for Creative Tourism. *Journal of Hospitality and Tourism*, *19*(1), 1–13.

Richards, G., & Hall, D. (2000). *Tourism and Sustainable Community Development*. Routledge.

Roberts, L., & Hall, D. (2001). Rural tourism and recreation: Principles to practice. *Tourism and Hospitality Management*, *7*(3), 212–218.

Robinson, M., & Andersen, H. (Eds.). (2004). *Literature and Tourism: Essays in the Reading and Writing of Tourism*. Thomson International.

Ruiz-Real, J. L.. (2021). Climate change and rural tourism: Challenges and opportunities. *Journal of Tourism Futures*, *7*(1), 24–37.

Saarinen, J.. (2017). Historical perspectives on rural tourism: Exploring the evolution of rural destinations. *Journal of Rural Tourism Studies*, *5*(3), 109–125.

Sesser, W. E., & Morgan, I. P. (1977). The Bermuda Triangle of food service chain. *The Cornell Hotel and Restaurant Administration Quarterly*, *17*(February), 56–61. DOI: 10.1177/001088047701700410

Sharpley, R., & Sharpley, J. (1997). Rural tourism: An introduction. *International Journal of Tourism Research*, *9*(4), 213–230.

Singh, R. (2018). Community-based tourism and its impact on rural development in India. *Journal of Tourism and Cultural Change*, *16*(1), 43–59.

Situmorang, D. S.. (2019). Rural tourism and local development: A community approach. *Tourism Review*, *74*(1), 90–104.

Smith, C., & Watmough, S. (2019). Indigenous cultural tourism in rural Canada: A case study of community empowerment. *Journal of Rural Studies*, *68*, 125–133.

Supera, M., Guerra, E., Villamar, E., & Saranza, C. (2024). Rural Tourism Development in the Philippines: Balancing Economic Growth with Ecological and Socio-Cultural Sustainability. *Journal of Economics. Finance and Management Studies.*, *7*(6), 3307–3322. DOI: 10.47191/jefms/v7-i6-25

Timothy, D. J. (2011). *Cultural Heritage and Tourism: An Introduction*. Channel View. DOI: 10.21832/9781845411787

Turner, V. (1973). The center out there: Pilgrim's goal in rural tourism. *Journal of Anthropological Research*, *29*(1), 137–151.

Vyslobodska, H., Brychka, B., & Bulyk, O. (2022). Rural tourism as an alternative direction of activity diversification of agricultural products producers. *Scientific Messenger of LNU of Veterinary Medicine and Biotechnologies.Series Economical Sciences*, *24*(99), 10–14.

Wamwara, H., & Ndung'u, N. (2020). The socio-economic impact of cultural tourism on local communities in Kenya. *African Journal of Hospitality, Tourism and Leisure*, *9*(1), 1–15.

Withiam, G. (1985). *Hotel companies aim for multiple markets: The current proliferation of brand names to an effort by hotels to become*. Cornell HRA Quarterly.

Yesawich, P. C. (1987). Hospitality Marketing for the'90s: Effective Marketing Research. *The Cornell Hotel and Restaurant Administration Quarterly*, *28*(1), 48–57.

Zeithaml, V., & Bitner, M. J. (1996). *Services Marketing*. McGraw-Hill.

Zeithaml, V. A. (1988). Consumer Perceptions of Price, Quality, and Value: A means-End Model and Synthesis of Evidence. *Journal of Marketing*, *52*(3), 2–22. DOI: 10.1177/002224298805200302

ADDITIONAL READING

Chatterjee, P., Chakrabortty, N., & Ghosh, S. (2024). Rural Tourism and Homestays in India: Impact on Local Economy, Culture and Ecology. *International Journal of Tourism & Hospitality Reviews*, *11*(2), 12–18. DOI: 10.18510/ijthr.2024.1122

Imam, A., Ray, N., & Patra, N. (2024). A Study on Factors Affecting Cold Supply Chain Performance in India. In *Information Logistics for Organizational Empowerment and Effective Supply Chain Management* (pp. 224–240). IGI Global Scientific Publishing.

Kumar, C. M., Sujatha, K., & Kumar, K. R. (2025). Rural Tourism in India: Constraints and Opportunities. In *Language and Cross-Cultural Communication in Travel and Tourism* (pp. 223-233). Apple Academic Press.

Nadotti, L., & Vannoni, V. (2019). Cultural and event tourism: an interpretative key for impact assessment. *Eastern journal of European studies, 10*(1), 115.

Ray, N., & Das, D. K. (2016). Relationship among influencing factors of tourism infrastructure: An empirical assessment at Kamarpukur, India. In *Handbook of Research on Chaos and Complexity Theory in the Social Sciences* (pp. 297–309). IGI Global. DOI: 10.4018/978-1-5225-0148-0.ch021

Ray, N., Das, D. K., Ghosh, S., & Sengupta, P. P. (2011). Rural Tourism and Its Impact on Socio- Economic Condition: A Case Study on Kamarpukur, In Global Conference on Business & Finance, Vol. 6, the IBFR, USA

KEY TERMS AND DEFINITIONS

Tourism: Tourism refers to the activities of people traveling to and staying in places outside their usual environment for leisure, business, or other purposes for not more than one consecutive year. It encompasses travel for recreation, relaxation, exploration, and cultural experiences, contributing significantly to the global economy and intercultural exchange.

Cultural Tourism: Cultural tourism involves traveling to experience the places, artifacts, and activities that authentically represent the stories, people, and past and present of a particular area. It includes visits to heritage sites, museums, art galleries, theaters, festivals, and other expressions of culture and tradition.

Socio-cultural Impact: Socio-cultural impact refers to the effect that tourism activities have on the social structures and cultural practices of a host community. These impacts can be positive, such as increased cultural exchange and preservation of traditions, or negative, such as cultural commodification, loss of authenticity, and social tensions.

Rural Tourism: Rural tourism is a form of tourism that takes place in non-urban areas, typically involving small-scale, community-driven activities that allow visitors to experience rural life, nature, agricultural practices, and local traditions. It supports sustainable development and often aims to benefit local economies without significantly altering rural environments.

Chapter 6
Investigating Sustainable Tourism in Indonesia:
A Way Forward for the Tourism Industry

Augustin Rina Herawati
Universitas Diponegoro, Indonesia

Nina Widowati Widowati
Universitas Diponegoro, Indonesia

Teuku Afrizal
Universitas Diponegoro, Indonesia

ABSTRACT

Sustainable tourism is a type of tourism that comprehensively considers its present and future economic, social, and environmental impacts while addressing the needs of visitors, industry, environment, and communities. Tourism plays a significant role in achieving three Sustainable Development Goals (SDGs). SDGs-8 focuses on creating conditions for quality jobs and promoting local culture and products, with sustainable tourism serving as a driver for these objectives. Goal 12 emphasizes the need for clean and environmentally friendly products, particularly in the context of tourism, to enhance the health of forests and oceans. Goal 14, addressing life below water, calls for careful management of global resources, with a specific focus on monitoring sustainable development impacts in tourism. The Sustainable Tourism Development (STDev) program in Indonesia prioritizes the implementation of Sustainable Tourism Observatories (STO) as a fundamental approach.

DOI: 10.4018/979-8-3693-3196-5.ch006

1. INTRODUCTION

Tourism has an important role in Indonesia's economy, serving as a leading economic sector amid globalization (Hadi et al., 2021). According to the United Nations World Tourism Organization (UNWTO), the global travel and tourism industry, encompassing related businesses like catering and cleaning, accounted for 9.8% of the total global gross domestic product in 2016 (UNWTO, 2017a). Additionally, it represented 7% of global trade and contributed to approximately 11% of the world's employment, both directly and indirectly, in the same year (UNWTO, 2017b; UNWTO, 2017a). However, the substantial economic contributions of tourism come with significant environmental repercussions (Pan et al., 2018). Global tourist trips, including those by same-day visitors, resulted in approximately 1302 million tons of CO_2 emissions in 2005, constituting 5% of the world's anthropogenic CO_2 emissions (Peters and Dubois, 2010; IPCC, 2007).

To address these environmental concerns and promote responsible tourism, the concept of sustainable tourism emerges as a viable solution. Sustainable tourism, as defined by the UNWTO, involves tourism activities that consider current and future economic, social, and environmental impacts. This approach aims to meet the needs of visitors, the industry, the environment, and local communities while safeguarding and enhancing future opportunities. Sustainable tourism focuses on three key aspects: environmental, economic, and socio-cultural (Hadi, 2021). In essence, it strives to minimize the negative impacts of current tourism activities and optimize positive effects for long-term sustainability (Weaver, 2006).

2. THE NOTION OF SUSTAINABLE TOURISM

Sustainable tourism serves as an approach to address issues arising from tourism activities. It aims to mitigate adverse effects by maximizing positive impacts. The ensuing definition provides further insight into the concept of sustainable tourism:

According to the World Tourism Council (UNWTO) in 2005, sustainable tourism is defined as tourism that comprehensively considers its present and future economic, social, and environmental impacts while addressing the needs of visitors, the industry, the environment, and host communities. This can be essentially translated as tourism that takes into account the current and future economic, social, and environmental consequences, while meeting the needs of visitors, industry, environment, and local communities. UNWTO emphasizes three integral elements that are inseparable from the concept of sustainable tourism:

- **Sustainable Economy**: Ensuring the welfare of different society strata and achieving superior cost-efficiency in all economic endeavors. The economic sector is crucial for a company's viability, operations, and long-term sustainability.
- **Social Sustainability**: Referring to the preservation of human rights and the promotion of equitable opportunities across all societies. The concept entails equitable distribution of advantages with a specific emphasis on alleviating poverty, prioritizing local communities, preserving and strengthening their support networks, recognizing and honoring cultural values, and refraining from any kind of exploitation.
- **Sustainable Environment**: Involving the conservation and effective management of resources, particularly those that are non-renewable or vital for human survival. Activities falling within this category encompass endeavors aimed at reducing air, land, and water contamination, while also preserving biodiversity and cultural heritage.

Damanik and Weber (2006) delineate the fundamental tenets of sustainable tourism, placing particular emphasis on the ecological, financial, and socio-cultural aspects of a tourist locale. To attain long-lasting sustainability, it is crucial to establish a well-established equilibrium among these three dimensions. The essential components of sustainable tourism development encompass:

- **Environmental Aspects**: Maximizing the utilization of environmental resources that are vital for the growth of tourism, maintaining ecological processes, and protecting the natural history and biodiversity within a tourist destination.
- **Economic Aspects**: Supporting sustainable economic activities is essential for ensuring long-term economic viability. This entails ensuring equitable socio-economic advantages for all parties involved, such as providing stable job possibilities, avenues for generating revenue (e.g., through entrepreneurial endeavors), and delivering social welfare programmers to local populations, so aiding in the alleviation of poverty.
- **Socio-Cultural Aspects**: When it comes to sustainable tourism, it is crucial to demonstrate reverence for the socio-cultural genuineness of local populations. This involves safeguarding the cultural and traditional heritage values that they have nurtured and promoting a stronger sense of tolerance and comprehension among other civilizations.

The Global Sustainable tourist Council (GSTC) is an autonomous international organization that is committed to developing and supervising worldwide benchmarks in the tourist industry. The objective is to increase awareness and promote the adoption of sustainable tourism principles among both public and private stakeholders. The GSTC states that in order to meet the criteria for sustainable tourism, destinations must embrace an interdisciplinary, holistic, and integrative approach that encompasses four main objectives:

- Exhibiting sustainable practices in managing destinations;
- Optimizing economic advantages for local communities while minimizing adverse effects;
- Maximizing benefits for society, visitors, and culture while minimizing detrimental impacts;
- Maximizing environmental benefits while minimizing negative consequences.

The GSTC has created an evaluation matrix or set of metrics for tourist destinations and the tourism industry to use sustainable tourism practices in acknowledged tourist regions. The Indonesian Ministry of Tourism has officially recognized and approved these guidelines, using them as the fundamental framework for creating regulations, such as Minister of Tourism Regulation No. 14 of 2016, which provides guidelines for Sustainable Tourism Destinations and assessment criteria for the Indonesia Sustainable Tourism Awards (ISTA).

According to Inskeep (1991), the objectives of sustainable tourism include the following elements:

- **Raising Awareness and Enhancing Understanding**: Advocating for a greater recognition and comprehension of the significant impact that tourism can have on both the environment and the economy.
- **Equitable Development**: Endeavoring to achieve a state of balanced and just development in all areas pertaining to tourism.
- **Improving Quality of Life**: Striving to enhance the overall well-being and satisfaction of the local community impacted by tourism operations.
- **Delivering High-Quality Visitor Experience**: Guaranteeing that visitors have a top-notch and gratifying experience during their interactions with the location.
- **Ensuring Environmental Conservation**: Maintaining and safeguarding the overall quality of the environment in the face of tourism-related activities.

Moreover, according to Inskeep (1991), the tourism business has a vital role in promoting sustainable tourism growth, and it is the private sector's duty to offer tourism products and services. Inskeep delineates numerous crucial measures that the sector might undertake to improve sustainable tourism:

- **Environmental Protection**: The act of reducing and eliminating pollution in order to prevent harm to the environment.
- **Resource Management**: Ensuring the responsible and long-term utilization of land, water, and forests in tourism operations.
- **Waste Reduction**: The act of reducing waste by implementing activities such as recycling, reusing, and following established waste management and disposal protocols.
- **Energy Conservation**: Implementing energy conservation measures, such as optimizing the use of solar energy, wind power, and other energy-efficient methods.
- **Environmental Risk Reduction**: The act of refraining from utilizing dangerous chemicals and areas in order to minimize potential harm to the environment.
- **Green Marketing**: Utilizing green marketing tactics to promote soft tourism and mitigate negative effects on the environment and culture.
- **Damage Mitigation**: The act of replacing and regenerating regions that have been negatively affected by environmental deterioration and compensating for any harmful consequences.
- **Information Provision**: Providing travelers with extensive and dependable information.
- **Incorporating Environmental Values**: Integrating environmental values into day-to-day operational management tasks.
- **Periodic Audits**: Conducting regular audits to evaluate environmental practices in business operations, such as monitoring water quality, managing energy use, and waste disposal.

The concepts of sustainable tourism in Indonesia have been acknowledged for more than thirty years, as demonstrated by the guidelines stated in Chapter II of Laws of The Republic of Indonesia Number 9 of 1990 regarding the development of tourism in Indonesia. Despite being recognized in global scientific forums and included in tourism management courses, a comprehensive national policy was not in place until 2016. The introduction of Regulation No. 14 (2016) by the Ministry of Tourism was a notable advancement, including instructions for the creation of sustainable tourism sites. Indonesia's implementation of this rule displays its dedication to fully harnessing the possibilities of tourism growth.

3. SUSTAINABLE TOURISM DEVELOPMENT GOALS

Tourism plays a significant role in achieving three Sustainable Development Goals (SDGs) – goals 8, 12, and 14. Goal 8 focuses on creating conditions for quality jobs and promoting local culture and products, with sustainable tourism serving as a driver for these objectives. Goal 12 emphasizes the need for clean and environmentally friendly products, particularly in the context of tourism, to enhance the health of forests and oceans. Indonesia, aiming to become a tourism leader, can influence other nations by showcasing sustainability practices. Goal 14, addressing life below water, calls for careful management of global resources, with a specific focus on monitoring sustainable development impacts in tourism. Indonesia employs various indexing references to monitor its tourism competitiveness and adherence to sustainability practices (Lemy et al., 2020).

3.1. Sustainable Tourism Development Program in Indonesia

The Sustainable Tourism Development Programmed in Indonesia is a proactive initiative aimed at addressing the issues arising from unregulated tourism expansion, which can have detrimental effects on tourist locations. According to Canavan (2014), sustainable tourism management is essential for addressing problems such as facility damage, resource depletion, and resident dissatisfaction (Lemy et al., 2020). In the last twenty years, there has been a growing emphasis on environmental sustainability and collaborative governance among tourist stakeholders in global tourism development. Sustainable tourism encompasses three essential elements: strategic long-term planning, active involvement of the entire community, and a commitment to environmental sustainability. Local governments have a crucial responsibility in educating and involving locals in these efforts (Lemy et al., 2020).

In order to promote sustainable tourism development, it is necessary to analyze and modify social practices, such as consumption habits, which are shaped by societal norms and technical infrastructures. The future sustainability of society relies heavily on implementing crucial societal and behavioral changes, which can be influenced by governance systems. Sustainable tourism is acknowledged as a means of facilitating communication, resolving conflicts, and negotiating amongst different stakeholders who hold varying interpretations and perspectives (Lemy et al., 2020).

Multiple studies highlight the significance of sustainable tourism as a subject of research, focusing on global concerns regarding sustainability. Liu (2003) and David (2011) argue that sustainability serves as a strategic approach to alleviate adverse effects of tourism and guarantee its long-term viability (Lemy et al., 2020). The shift in the approach to assessing success in sustainable tourism entails the utilization of more intricate indicators, which priorities factors such as travel quality, duration of stay, and responsible expenditure, rather than relying solely on conventional metrics like tourist numbers and spending amounts. Figure 1 depicts the interconnections between sustainable tourist development, the Sustainable tourist Organization (STO), and sustainable tourism certification within the context of Indonesia.

3.2. Sustainable Tourism Destination

The Sustainable Tourism Development Programmed in Indonesia delineates many methods and actions aimed at establishing sustainable tourism destinations. The major elements encompass governance systems aimed at maximising economic benefits, active community participation, and the industry's responsibilities in safeguarding cultural heritage and preserving the environment. Sustainable tourist destinations encompass three key dimensions: economy, community, and environment. These dimensions are evaluated using indicators such as income measures, social well-being, and climate change adaptation. The program's objective is to promote economic prosperity in communities by prioritizing self-sufficiency via the enhancement of skills and knowledge. Empowering communities include the selection of facilitators and local partners to expedite the implementation of sustainable strategies. The level of success can be determined by the community's preparedness to predict and address the impacts of climate change.

The active participation of both local inhabitants and tourists is essential, as their attitudes and behaviors have a significant influence on the successful implementation of sustainable tourism. The programmed consists of nine components, which encompass national guidelines, a platform for a sustainable tourism strategy, and the creation of a master plan. The program's success is enhanced by contracts with specific destinations, training for assessors, and training for facilitators and partners. Conferences, whether on an international or national scale, promote the exchange of knowledge and the spread of progress. Meanwhile, the government is developing prototypes of key destinations to serve as exemplary models of sustainability.

Figure 1. Sustainable tourism for development in Indonesia

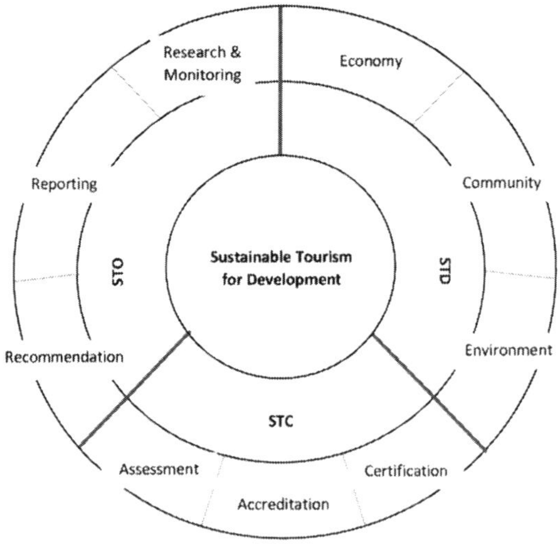

Source: Lemy et al., 2020

3.3. Sustainable Tourism Observatory

The Sustainable Tourism Development (STDev) programmed in Indonesia priorities the implementation of Sustainable Tourism Observatories (STO) as a fundamental approach. The approved sites are carefully selected based on their commitment to sustainable tourism principles, and the Monitoring Centre for Sustainable Tourism Observatories (MCSTO) is used to systematically monitor and evaluate their performance. Indonesia's MCSTO network, called Wonderful Indonesia STO, partners with regional governments, the Ministry of Tourism, and the United Nations World Tourism Organization (UNWTO) to strategize, oversee, and assess the execution of sustainable tourism.

The MCSTO primarily emphasizes three key areas: research and monitoring, reporting, and recommendation. Academic and research institutes function as Multi-Component Sustainable Transition Organizations (MCSTOs), engaging in field and action research to gather evidence on sustainable principles and tackle development concerns. The outcomes include updates on advancements and suggestions, which are disseminated via nationwide STO conventions. The primary objective of the STO programmed is to assess and evaluate various dimensions of the economy, society, and culture, with the ultimate goal of promoting national progress while upholding the ideals of sustainable development. The successful execution necessitates backing from diverse stakeholders, namely regional authorities and academic/research establishments. At present, there are five Multi-Country Sustainable Tourism Observatories (MCSTOs) in Indonesia that have been acknowledged by the United Nations World Tourism Organization (UNWTO), as indicated in Table 1.

Table 1. Indonesia monitoring center for STO

University	Location	Description
Bandung Institute of Technology (ITB)	West Java	• The Pangandaran Regency serves as the Sustainable Tourism Organization (STO), with a specific focus on implementing sustainable tourism practices in Batukaras Village, located in the Cijulang District. • This STO was formed through a collaboration between the Ministry of Tourism, Pangandaran Regency Government, and ITB, under the ITB Tourism Planning and Development Centre. • It has been a member of the International Network of Sustainable Tourism Observatories (INSTO) since September 2016.
Gadjah Mada University (UGM)	Yogyakarta	• Oversees the MCSTO in collaboration with Sleman Regency (2016), with a focus on Pulesari Tourism Village, Wonokerto, Turi. • Involves a partnership between the Ministry of Tourism, Sleman Regency, and UGM, with UGM's Postgraduate Programme supervising the MCSTO's operations. • Became a member of INSTO in September 2016.
University of Mataram (UNRAM)	Lombok, West Nusa Tenggara	• The STO in West Lombok Regency is responsible for managing operations in Sesaot and Senggigi Villages. • This STO was developed through a collaboration between the Ministry of Tourism, West Lombok Regency, and Unram, and is currently maintained by Unram Tourism Study Centre. • Joined INSTO as a member in September 2016.
Udayana University (UNUD)	Bali	• Sanur Village, situated in Denpasar, functions as the designated Special Tourism Office (STO). • The Ministry of Tourism and Unud collaborated to designate Sanur Village as the STO. • Sanur Village became a member of INSTO in October 2017.
University of Sumatera Utara (USU)	North Sumatra	• Oversees the Sustainable Tourism Organisation (STO) in Samosir Regency. • Created through a partnership between the Ministry of Tourism, four observatories, and USU as the central monitoring facility. • Received official recognition from the United Nations World Tourism Organisation (UNWTO) in October 2017 as a Monitoring Centre for Sustainable Tourism Organisations (MCSTO).

Source: The Ministry of Tourism of the Republic of Indonesia (2018).

3.4. Sustainable Tourism Certification

Indonesia's Sustainable Tourism Development (STDev) includes a plan that focuses on implementing a Sustainable Tourism Certification (STC) programmed. The purpose of this certification procedure is to evaluate and ascertain the sustainability standards and level of each destination, offering assurance to tourists and the general public on the destination's compliance with set quality criteria. Certification, as per Honey's (2008) definition, is conducting an audit and providing a written assurance that facilities, goods, processes, services, or management systems adhere to predetermined criteria (Lemy et al., 2020).

The purpose of certification in the tourism industry is to encourage the adoption of sustainable concepts and practices by all parties involved. Stakeholders, acknowledging the significance of sustainability, have dedicated their efforts to conceptualizing, quantifying, and establishing standardized sustainable practices throughout the years. The implementation of sustainable destination certification in Indonesia is in accordance with worldwide norms and initiatives, as noted by Honey (2008) ten years ago (Lemy et al., 2020). The objective of adopting sustainable destination certification in Indonesia is to attain exceptional standards in the tourism sector, satisfying the present requirements of tourists and communities while safeguarding the needs of future generations. The process might adhere to the principles specified in Regulation No. 14 (2016) issued by the Ministry of Tourism, which serves as a framework for the sustainable development of destinations.

The Sustainable Tourism Council (STC) in Indonesia fulfils eight objectives, which encompass the promotion of sustainable practices, the improvement of destination competitiveness, the reduction of carbon footprints, the creation of authentic experiences, and the dissemination of knowledge regarding environmental management. Essential metrics for implementing Sustainable Tourism Certification (STC) involve conducting pilot projects, which are assessments that provide a snapshot of the current situation, in various places such as Lombok, Wakatobi, Pangandaran, and Sleman. These exams evaluate the accuracy and consistency of certification tools. Another vital metric is the preparedness of the accrediting organization, which was previously overseen by the Ministry of Tourism and eventually transitioned to the Indonesia Sustainable Tourism Council. Assessments produce recommendations that are crucial for enhancing the performance of destinations in sustainable tourism.

4. ECOTOURISM

The notion of sustainability, specifically in the realm of tourist development, planning, and management, is frequently linked to phrases such as green tourism or ecotourism. Nevertheless, there has been persistent debate and discrepancies in the concept and implementation of ecotourism. The definition of ecotourism has been updated by the International Ecotourism Society (TIES) to encompass conscientious travel to natural regions, with the aim of preserving the environment, upholding the well-being of the local people, and incorporating interpretation and education (Wardana et al., 2021).

The objectives of ecotourism, according to EBSCO Sustainability Watch (2009), include increasing benefits for the environment, directing revenue towards conservation efforts, providing economic incentives for local communities, and promoting wildlife diversity (Wardana et al., 2021). Ecotourism also contributes to environmental education, awareness, and funding for conservation. Core criteria for ecotourism, as outlined by Fennel (2015), involve nature-based experiences, a conservation perspective, human sustainability through local participation, learning and education, and ethical behavior. The indicators of ecotourism, as defined by Ross and Wall (1999), include the preservation of the natural environment, generation of income, provision of education, promotion of high-quality tourism, and involvement of local communities.

4.1. Ecotourism and Village Tourism

Ecotourism, as defined by Nugroho (2011), involves professionally organized travel activities with elements of education, cultural heritage consideration, local community participation, and environmental conservation. It is characterized by efficient and lean operational services, with low visitor quantities in groups, high service quality, and added value. Consumers of ecotourism seek natural and cultural interaction, requiring service managers to provide safe and satisfying experiences while adhering to ecological standards (Zeppel, 2006).

The concept of village living is regarded as a deliberate attempt to achieve a harmonious equilibrium in life, while simultaneously promoting human values and promoting environmental progress in the context of economic development. Rural communities provide distinct encounters, contentment, rejuvenation, and chances to get knowledge about the preservation of the environment and culture (Nugroho et al., 2016). The demand for village tourism services is substantial, attracting both domestic and international tourists who are willing to undertake extensive journeys to remote areas such as Ngadas, Candirejo, Rajegwesi, Wanci, Komodo, Baluran National Park, Raja Ampat, and other exotic locations throughout the Indonesian Archipelago (Nugroho et al., 2018).

4.2. Ecotourism Destination

The development of ecotourism in Indonesia is intricately connected to the establishment and management of protected areas, such as wilderness areas (WA), natural conservation areas (NCA), and hunting parks. The Ministry of Forestry, which is in charge of identifying protected areas, has overseen the management of

414 sites spanning 23.1 million hectares. National parks account for 65 percent of the overall area (Rhee et al., 2004). The establishment of national parks entails the careful evaluation of factors such as significant landmarks, location, ecological system, unique plant and animal species, and employment responsibilities. The Ministry of Forestry has created 53 national parks, which are essential for overseeing protected areas and preserving biodiversity at both national and global levels (Rothberg, 1999). Ecotourism has experienced significant growth in Indonesian national parks, which actively promote and enable the development of ecotourism in nearby settlements.

Ecotourism services encompass not only national parks, but also encompass locations that possess cultural significance, wisdom, and natural balance. This, in turn, aids in the economic prosperity of communities. These ecotourism attractions are found in coastal ecosystems, seas, lands, protected areas, settlements, or regions having exceptional heritage values for future generations. Community organizations or people with expertise, experience, market information, and viable ecotourism destinations typically take the lead in promoting the growth of ecotourism beyond national parks. The favorable reaction from nearby communities yields social, economic, and environmental advantages, underscoring the obligation of all parties involved in guaranteeing the enduring viability of ecotourism endeavors in these regions (Nugroho et al., 2018).

5. THE LOCAL COMMUNITY INVOLVEMENT IN ECOTOURISM MANAGEMENT

Community participation in the administration of ecotourism involves different stages, such as planning, implementation, and utilization (Lukman, 2017). During the planning phase, community engagement entails endorsing tourism development proposals, actively contributing to the design plan process, and assuming responsibilities in planning socialization. The activities encompassed in this endeavor involve strategizing the transformation of local regions into ecotourism hubs, engaging in dialogues regarding conservation policies, tackling issues related to ecotourism, and establishing guidelines for visitors (Hijriati & Mardiana, 2014; Asriyani & Verheijen, 2020; Ayuningtyas & Dharmawan, 2011; Harahab & Setiawan, 2017).

During the execution stage, community involvement include the provision of human resources, cash, and materials for the growth of tourism. Localized, collaborative development methods of a smaller magnitude provide substantial involvement from the local population and mitigate the marginalization of communities. The activities carried out in this stage encompass the surveillance of ecotourism sites to deter disruptions, initiatives to restore forests, and the provision of community money for the purpose of development and upkeep. Local communities play an active role in the construction of infrastructure, conservation efforts, and the preservation of cultural assets (Muaz et al., 2017; Ayuningtyas & Dharmawan, 2011; Harahab & Setiawan, 2017; Hijriati & Mardiana, 2014; Ibrahim et al., 2019; Nuraini et al., 2019).

At the utilization level, the community experiences economic advantages by gaining employment opportunities and promoting businesses that are associated with tourism. Ecotourism generates economic benefits through several means such as providing housing, offering guided tours, renting out equipment, providing transportation services, offering culinary services, selling souvenirs, and showcasing cultural treasures. Employment prospects arise in diverse positions within the field of tourism management, hence supporting local micro, small, and medium firms. Conservation activities yield economic benefits through indirect means, including better prices for agricultural products and increased social and ecological contributions (Nuraini et al., 2019). Table 2 presents a comprehensive overview of the many types of local community participation in the administration of ecotourism in Indonesia. It highlights the diverse and valuable contributions made by these communities at different stages of the development process.

Table 2. The forms of local community involvement in ecotourism management in Indonesia

Planning	1. Addressing current ecotourism problems 2. Planning local area development into ecotourism destinations, including determining involved parties 3. Developing conservation methods/strategies based on local regulations 4. Establishing visiting rules/policies for tourists 5. Assessing people's perceptions of ecotourism benefits
Implementation	1. Maintaining order and safety in ecotourism environments 2. Supporting conservation through reforestation 3. Funding ecotourism development 4. Maintaining public infrastructure and cultural heritage objects around ecotourism areas
Utilization	**Direct Economic Benefits** 1. Providing tourism facilities/services: accommodation, transportation, culinary, tour guides, equipment rental, local handicrafts, photography, tour and cultural attractions packages 2. Employing local labor 3. Sharing profits from ecotourism management **Indirect Economic Benefits** Positive externalities from conservation activities and maintenance of village infrastructure (leading to better prices for local agricultural products) **Social Benefits** Increasing local community's capacity and contribution to conserving ecotourism areas and local culture

Source: Zakia, 2021

6. DEVELOPMENT PLANNING OF ECOTOURISM

During the implementation of the RPJMN (2015-2019) as outlined by Bappenas (2015), the focus was on promoting the growth of ecotourism by emphasizing the development of natural, cultural, and creative tourism. The policy is executed via the initiatives of biodiversity preservation (Ministry of Forestry), the enhancement of tourist sites (Ministry of Tourism), and the advancement of infrastructure (Ministry of Civil Work). The Ministry of Forestry establishes protected areas and national parks to facilitate the administration of environmental services and promote ecotourism. Annually, the Ministry of Tourism supports the growth of 16 domestic tourism attractions and 561 communities through the PNPM Mandiri programmed. The Ministry of Civil Work is constructing a port to facilitate the growth of marine and waterway ecotourism. Ecotourism development planning is executed with consideration for the economic, social, and environmental dimensions. Weaver (2002) presents the policy in a straightforward hierarchical structure as follows:

6.1. Macro or National Level

At the macro level of planning, the primary objective is to create a complete national institutional framework that promotes the growth of ecotourism. This framework encompasses national territories and takes into account global environmental concerns. The Government of Indonesia (GOI) has officially approved and implemented international agreements such as the Convention on Biodiversity, Wetland, and CITES. Crucial elements of macro-level policies encompass:

- **Establishment of National Institutions**: This entails the formation of a structured system that promotes collaboration with various entities at the ecosystem, local, and worldwide scales. Regulatory legislation aims to promote the growth of national parks, safeguard unexplored tribes, and conserve heritage places. The regulations delineate restrictions on quantity and total area, preservation of flora and fauna, execution of tasks and responsibilities, as well as coordination and methods for problem-solving.
- **Research and Development**: Research is essential for effective planning and management at both the local and ecosystem levels. Academic theory develops linkages between systems, clarifies the advantages and their allocation at the local and ecosystem levels. The results of research contribute to the formulation of legislative norms and methods for the management and development of national parks in Indonesia.
- **Technical and Financial Assistance**: This part seeks to promote economic expansion and bolster prosperity. The budget is allocated for the education

and training of personnel, marketing, and the improvement of infrastructure, including roads, bridges, telecommunications, electricity, and water supply. The Government of India (GOI) has a crucial role in the restoration of the environment, the reduction of poverty, and the provision of compensation for damages in the areas surrounding ecotourism sites.

Indonesia, known for its extensive cultural variety consisting of 17 thousand islands, 470 ethnic groups, 19 regions with customary law, and around 300 languages, possesses a valuable history that can be utilized for tourism (Nugroho et al., 2018). Utilizing the abundance of geographical and cultural resources can promote economic growth, increase the potential for tourism throughout the country, and strengthen Indonesia's national and geopolitical position (Nugroho & Dahuri, 2012).

Tourism is of utmost importance in Indonesia's economic, social, and environmental aspects. Within the realm of economics, the tourism industry plays a significant role in generating revenue from foreign currencies and stimulating economic activities at both the national and regional levels. From a social perspective, tourism has a crucial role in generating employment opportunities, cultivating a deep admiration for artistic endeavors, and nurturing a sense of pride in the customs and heritage, so enhancing the national identity. From an environmental perspective, tourism, namely ecotourism, highlights the distinctive natural components, such as plant and animal life, found on land, beaches, and in the oceans. It functions as a significant instrument for conserving the natural environment and traditional arts and culture.

The advancement of tourism, along with its accompanying industries, plays a crucial role in promoting national unity. Tourism villages can serve as cohesive elements throughout the geographical expanse of the Indonesian Archipelago. The government's role in safeguarding the well-being and social entitlements of rural residents enhances their prosperity, promoting inclusivity and favorable interactions that bolster the stability of the state and its governance (Nugroho & Dahuri, 2012).

6.2. Ecosystem Level

The scope of ecosystem area planning includes many regions such as river basins, mangroves, mountains, valleys, and other areas that are essential for the preservation of habitats and cultural heritage (Nugroho & Dahuri, 2012). These ecosystem zones may encompass one or more local groups, each providing components and interactions to maintain functional unity or regular life cycles. An ecosystem area's geographical boundaries can encompass a distinct zone, protected area, national park, or a specifically defined administrative region. Several crucial policies at the ecosystem level include:

- **Ecotourism Destination Management Vision**: Effective management of ecosystems necessitates a collective vision comprehended by all parties involved, exemplified by the preservation of coral reefs. The local populace or tour operators pledge to execute this vision by adopting predetermined management models, sanctioned by regulatory frameworks.
- **Collaboration and Synergy**: Enhancing regional development by promoting harmonious interactions with other sectors such as agriculture, forestry, and the fishing industry. The interconnections among different economic sectors play a crucial role in promoting overall economic expansion and enhancing the quality of life in these regions.
- **Integrated Area Management**: Entailing the establishment of trekking routes, territorial boundaries for ecosystems and watershed areas, and designated areas for habitat and cultural protection in order to promote an ecotourism region. The purpose of determining area borders is to mitigate the unauthorized transfer of costs or advantages. The meticulous implementation of area management is founded on agreements with stakeholders, with a focus on preserving tourism pathways and safeguarding areas at risk of extinction.

The implementation of ecosystem-level planning in Indonesia has been carried out through the enactment of Government Regulation No. 50 of 2010, which outlines the National Tourism Development Master Plan for the period of 2010-2025. The Ministry of Tourism has initiated the establishment of 50 National Tourism Destinations (NTD). The NTD idea corresponds to ecosystem or functional areas, and the Destination Management Organization (DMO) programmed has played a crucial role in promoting 15 NTDs. The aforementioned destinations encompass Sabang, Toba, Kota Tua, Pangandaran, Borobudur, Bromo-Tengger-Semeru, Batur, Rinjani, Flores, Tanjung Puting, Derawan, Toraja, Bunaken, Wakatobi, and Raja Ampat. DMO primarily emphasises the management of sustainable tourism destinations, encompassing the activities of planning, operating, and monitoring. The operation is carried out by a synchronized collaboration between the central and regional governments, involving local communities, travelers, and other stakeholders in the advancement of tourist regions (Nugroho et al., 2018).

6.3. Local Level

The core aspect of local-level planning centers on the local community, which includes individuals or groups who have a common interest in ecotourism. The borders are defined by the activities and economic pursuits of the indigenous community. This is applicable inside locations that are authorized by National Park administration, administrative or traditional regions, villages, indigenous villages, or local customs. The key issues in local-level policies are as outlined by Nugroho et al. (2018) as follows:

- **Participation**: Identifying the level of involvement from local residents and community members is a vital component of local planning. This helps determine the minimum number of people required and the degree to which stakeholders should be included, which in turn affects how benefits are distributed. Understanding and acknowledging the cultural values of a certain region is crucial for making significant contributions to the development of ecotourism services.
- **Empowerment**: The act of empowering local communities aims to stimulate the local economy, resulting in a multiplier effect. Emphasizing the involvement and engagement of the local community is crucial for the economic advancement of ecotourism services, as greater participation results in stronger motivations for environmental preservation.
- **Developing ecotourism destination areas**: Creating management plans that take into account the constraints of activities and business features, as well as the location and travel routes. Operators are motivated to deliver services based on the specific aspects of ecotourism when the area or place is specified.
- **Developing products and services supporting ecotourism conservation**: To promote ecotourism conservation, it is necessary to provide local communities with training in entrepreneurship, creativity, and leadership. This will help minimize their reliance on natural resources. Product and service innovations greatly enhance their worth, hence motivating environmental conservation endeavors.

Village-level planning centers around the empowerment, development, and management of ecotourism at the local level. Village tourism has the capacity to capitalize on the socio-cultural aspects, natural surroundings, and economic endeavors, thereby converting the village into a desirable tourist destination. The socio-cultural elements, encompassing housing, ethnic attire, gastronomic offers, arts, traditions, and values, enhance the community's value and profitability.

Natural resources such as mountains, beaches, lakes, oceans, valleys, and rivers provide prospects for exploration, sports, and adventure. Tourism benefits from the addition of economic potential, such as agribusiness, home industries, and other supporting sectors, which contribute value. The economic activity in the village is shaped by various elements, including demand and supply, internal and external forces, creation and innovation, leadership, organization, and the dynamics of village life. The tourism economic cluster arises as a result of these circumstances, tailored to the specific conditions of the community.

At the local level, multiple stakeholders, such as local inhabitants, operators, tourists, local government authorities, and national park officials, engage in interactions. Challenges develop as a result of obstacles in communication, problems in coordination, or discrepancies in comprehension regarding ecotourism, resulting in doubt regarding authority, rights, and obligations. Such circumstances can give rise to issues or disputes, hence jeopardising the preservation and long-term viability of managing ecotourism services (Nugroho & Negara, 2015).

7. DIGITALIZATION FOR SUSTAINABLE TOURISM

One of the fastest-growing frontiers in sustainable tourism is the use of digital technologies, often called "smart tourism" or "digitalization", to optimize resource use, manage visitor flows, personalize low-impact experiences, and improve monitoring and reporting. By utilizing big data, IoT sensors, AI-driven recommender systems, blockchain provenance tools, and mobile apps, destinations can both enhance tourist satisfaction and minimize environmental and socio-cultural pressures.

Digitalization transforms the static, infrastructure-heavy model of mass tourism into a dynamic, responsive ecosystem. Today's destinations face twin pressures: catering to growing traveller demand while preserving environments and cultural heritage. By tapping into real-time data streams (such as visitor footfall, energy and water consumption, and waste generation), destination managers can move beyond lagging annual reports toward immediate operational adjustments. For instance, when sensors detect overcrowding at a coastal heritage site, visitor flows can be rerouted via mobile alerts or timed ticketing, thereby mitigating erosion risks and ensuring a quality experience for all (Hicks, 2025). Likewise, monitoring energy and water metrics enables hotels and attractions to optimize resource use on the fly, reducing both costs and environmental impacts without sacrificing service levels.

Equally important, digitalization enables personalized, low-impact experiences that spread tourism's economic benefits more evenly. AI-powered recommendation engines synthesize variables such as CO_2e footprints, seasonality, and site popularity to sculpt bespoke itineraries that guide visitors toward under-utilized attractions or off-peak time slots. Early prototypes of these "green recommender systems" have demonstrated emission reductions, up to 25% per visitor, by gently nudging travelers away from congested hotspots toward equally compelling alternatives (Mullis, 2017). This alleviates pressure on icon sites while promoting regenerative tourism in lesser-known communities, amplifying local incomes and diversifying regional economies.

Finally, digital tools reinforce accountability through transparent sustainability metrics. In an era of rampant greenwashing, blockchain and distributed-ledger technologies offer immutable proof of environmental claims, from solar-powered resorts to certified low-emission transport partners. Platforms that publish verifiable carbon and waste data empower eco-conscious travelers to make informed choices and reward genuinely sustainable operators (You, 2025). Over time, this promotes a marketplace in which authentic sustainability becomes a competitive advantage rather than a marketing afterthought.

8. KEY TECHNOLOGIES AND THEIR APPLICATIONS

8.1. Smart Tourism Observatories (STO 2.0)

Next-generation STOs embed IoT sensors across key touchpoints, such as trailheads, beach entrances, heritage precincts, to collect continuous data on footfall, air quality, noise levels, and biodiversity indicators. These sensors feed into centralized dashboards, such as Indonesia's MCSTO network, enabling stakeholders to track ecosystem health in near real time and trigger automated management actions (e.g., temporary closures, capacity caps) when thresholds are breached (Fujimatsu et al., 2024). By extending observatory architectures to include predictive analytics—forecasting visitor surges based on weather and booking trends—destinations can shift from reactive to anticipatory management.

8.2. AI-Driven Recommender Systems

Composite sustainability indicators, including combining CO_2 emissions, crowd density, and local economic multipliers, serve as inputs for AI models that generate greener itineraries. A landmark trial in a European national park employed a prototype Travel Recommendation System (TRS) that achieved a 25% drop in per-visitor emissions by rerouting users toward lower-impact hiking circuits and eco-certified lodging (Mullis, 2017). Indonesian platforms can adopt similar frameworks, integrating local biodiversity data and community-run experiences to craft itineraries that maximize both environmental stewardship and economic inclusion.

8.3. Mobile Apps for Visitor Engagement

Smartphone applications offer powerful channels for passively reinforcing sustainable behaviors. Gamification mechanics, such as awarding points for recycling or using low-emission transport, can promote positive habits among tourists and residents alike. Real-time alerts on fragile ecosystems (e.g., coral reefs, bird nesting areas) not only educate but also reduce inadvertent damage by guiding visitors toward permissible zones (Reuters, 2024). Beyond consumer apps, back-end portals allow local guides and SMEs to update availability, post conservation alerts, and receive performance insights.

8.4. Virtual and Augmented Reality

Augmented reality (AR) and virtual reality (VR) experiences empower visitors to explore sensitive sites, such as coral atolls, cave sanctuaries, without physical intrusion. For example, a Cornell SC Johnson College study demonstrated that VR tours of coral-reef ecosystems can reduce on-site visitation pressure by up to 40%, while significantly enhancing environmental awareness and pro-conservation attitudes (Payton, 2025). AR overlays in heritage precincts can animate historical narratives, deepening engagement without the need for large tour groups that can accelerate wear on ancient masonry.

9. INTEGRATING DIGITALIZATION INTO EXISTING FRAMEWORKS

9.1. Regulatory Alignment

To fully utilize digital tools, Indonesia's tourism regulations, particularly Ministerial Regulation No. 14/2016 and the Indonesia Sustainable Tourism Awards criteria, should be updated to incorporate digital sustainability indicators. Metrics might include the share of certified businesses with real-time monitoring, the extent of data-driven visitor management plans, or the adoption rate of green-recommender APIs. Aligning local regulations with Global Sustainable Tourism Council standards will ensure consistency and facilitate cross-jurisdiction benchmarking.

9.2. Capacity Building

Many regional STO facilitators and destination managers lack the data-analytics and IoT-maintenance skills needed for sophisticated digital ecosystems. Partnerships between universities, technical institutes, and tech startups can deliver targeted training modules, covering everything from sensor calibration to dashboard visualization and AI model interpretation. The World Travel & Tourism Council advocates for blended learning programs that pair on-site workshops with online labs, ensuring both immediate and long-term capacity building.

9.3. Public–Private Collaboration

Telcos and fintech firms possess both the infrastructure and innovation capability to co-develop low-cost sensor networks and distributed-ledger platforms. China's "zero-waste" reward apps at major landmarks, where tourists earn digital tokens for sustainable actions, offer a template for similar schemes in Indonesia (You, 2025). Governments can incentivize participation through tax credits, data-sharing agreements, and pilot-project funding, accelerating deployment while maintaining public oversight.

10. INTEGRATING SMART FEATURES IN TRAVEL APPLICATIONS IN INDONESIA

10.1. Online Travel in Indonesia

Indonesia's digital travel ecosystem is dominated by a mix of global platforms and homegrown super apps, reflecting both international best practices and local innovation (Tan, 2024). According to 42matters data from October 2024, Google Earth leads with over 500 million downloads, followed by Grab (100 million+), Gojek (100 million+), and Traveloka (50 million+) among travel-related apps (See Table 3). Grab and Gojek, while primarily known for ride-hailing and food delivery, have evolved into super apps offering multi-modal transport and payments, making them critical gateways for travelers navigating Indonesia's archipelago (Sehyeon, 2024; Boxo, 2024). Traveloka and Agoda each boast 50 million+ downloads, establishing them as Indonesia's top two pure online travel agencies (OTAs) for flight and hotel bookings (See Figure 1) (GlobeNewswire, 2024). Tiket.com and RedDoorz, with 10 million+ downloads each, round out the local OTA market, catering to price-sensitive domestic tourists (GlobeNewswire, 2024).

Super apps like Gojek and Grab have built their massive user bases, over 180 million in Southeast Asia for Grab and more than 190 million for Gojek, to embed travel features directly into everyday services, from on-demand taxis to integrated e-wallet payments (Boxo, 2024; Bhimrajka, 2024). Their all-in-one nature reduces app fatigue and promotes a seamless traveler journey: booking a ride, ordering food near the hotel, and paying for attractions within a single interface. This integration model contrasts with traditional OTAs, which focus narrowly on accommodation and transport; as a result, Traveloka has expanded into fintech and lifestyle offerings to retain competitiveness.

Despite the super apps' breadth, specialized OTAs maintain strong brand awareness: a YouGov survey reports that 88% of Indonesians recognize Traveloka and 80% recognize Tiket.com, compared to 65% for Agoda and 49% for Booking.com (Tan, 2024). In web traffic terms, Similarweb data indicates Traveloka's top domains receive over 34 million visits monthly, underscoring its leadership in the online booking space (SimilarWeb, 2025). Regional market-intelligence firm Aggregate Intelligence ranks Traveloka as Asia's largest OTA by transaction volume, with a pre-IPO valuation of USD 3 billion and deep localization through e-wallet and partnership integrations (Aggregate Intelligence, 2024).

Macro-level market forecasts project that Indonesia's overall travel and tourism sector will grow from USD 3.49 billion in 2024 to USD 6.02 billion by 2035, driven largely by digital channels that now account for 38% of accommodation bookings via mobile apps (Market Research Future, 2025). As smartphone penetration approaches 80%, younger, tech-savvy travelers increasingly bypass traditional travel agents in favor of app-based bookings, reinforcing the need for OTAs and super apps to integrate smart features like real-time personalization and itinerary planners (Market Research Future, 2025)

In sum, Indonesia's online travel arena is defined by a synergy between super apps (Grab, Gojek) that offer end-to-end mobility and lifestyle services, and specialized OTAs (Traveloka, Tiket.com, Agoda) that lead in booking. Together, they form a fertile ground for deploying advanced digital tools, including AI-driven recommendations, real-time monitoring, and immersive AR, to elevate sustainable tourism and distribute its benefits more equitably across the archipelago.

Table 3. Most popular travel apps in Indonesia in October 2024 (42matters.com, 2024)

Application	Publisher	Downloads
Google Earth	Google LLC	500M+ Downloads
Grab – Taxi & Food Delivery	Grab Holdings	100M+ Downloads
Gojek – Food & Transportation	PT. GoTo Gojek Tokopedia Tbk.	100M+ Downloads
Traveloka: Book Hotel & Flight	Traveloka	50M+ Downloads
Agoda: Cheap Flights and Hotels	Agoda.com	50M+ Downloads
Tiket.com – Hotels and Flights	Tiket.com	10M+ Downloads
RedDoorz: Hotel Booking App	RedDoorz	10M+ Downloads
GoPartner	PT. GoTo Gojek Tokopedia Tbk	5M+ Downloads
ShopeeFood Driver	Shopee	1M+ Downloads
Bella Pro	Morada	1M+ Downloads

Figure 2. Most popular online travel agencies among consumers in Indonesia as of June 2023

Most Popular Online Travel Agencies among Consumers in Indonesia as of June 2023	
Traveloka	84.62%
Tiket.com	64.43%
Agoda	40.79%
Booking.com	33.64%
Pegipegi.com	28.16%
Trivago	15%
Airbnb	14.04%
Tripadvisor	11.68%
Nusatrip	7.02%
Skyscanner	6.44%
Expedia	4.95%
Others	1.12%

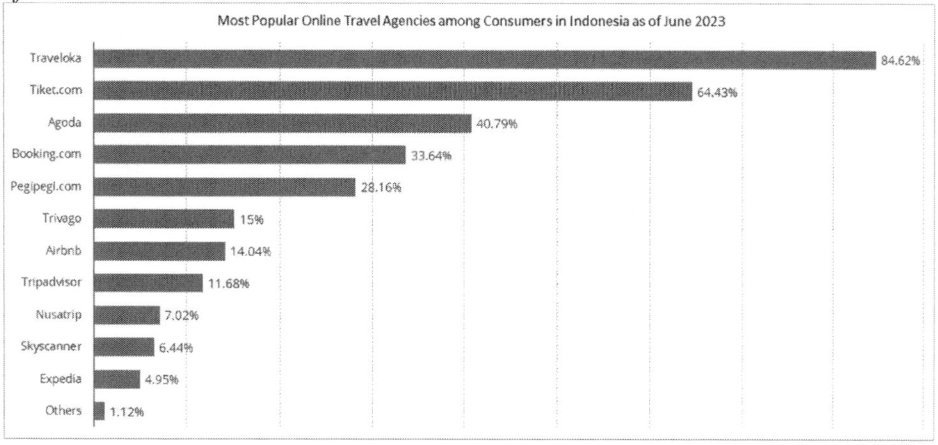

Source: Statista, 2024a

10.2 Real-Time Personalization and AI Recommendations

Real-time personalization and artificial intelligence (AI)-driven recommendations have become vital elements in enhancing the user experience within mobile travel applications (MTAs). According to Dorcic et al. (2019), personalization significantly impacts user engagement by providing tailored suggestions based on individual user data such as preferences, past behavior, and real-time context. For example, Hopper employs sophisticated AI algorithms to predict airfare prices and inform users of optimal booking times, significantly improving user satisfaction (Ho et al., 2021). Similarly, platforms like TripIt utilize user data to offer personalized itineraries and updates, demonstrating how AI can effectively meet individual travel needs (Sia et al., 2023). Traveloka, Indonesia's leading travel app, has yet to fully exploit AI's potential, primarily focusing on basic booking functionalities without extensive personalization (Chen & Tsai, 2019). Adopting advanced AI-driven personalization could enhance its competitive position against global leaders like Agoda and Booking.com (Statista, 2024a).

10.3 Geolocation and Context-Aware Services

Geolocation tracking and context-aware services have emerged as critical tools for enhancing traveler convenience and providing location-specific insights. According to Chen and Tsai (2019), real-time location-based services (LBS) enable travelers to access contextual information such as nearby attractions, traffic updates, and local services, thereby significantly improving navigational ease and overall trip satisfaction. Applications such as Japan Official Travel App and TripIt successfully integrate GPS and geolocation tracking, offering dynamic, real-time suggestions based on the traveler's location (Sia et al., 2023). However, despite the popularity of Indonesian apps like Traveloka, geolocation services remain underutilized, limiting their ability to provide context-specific, personalized experiences (42matters.com, 2024). Incorporating advanced geolocation capabilities could considerably enhance these platforms' appeal and usability.

10.4 Automated Itinerary Generation

Automated itinerary generation significantly enhances traveler convenience by allowing easy and efficient trip planning based on individual preferences, budget, and available time (Ho et al., 2021). Platforms like Planhop and KAYAK have successfully implemented itinerary planning features, demonstrating high user engagement due to streamlined and personalized trip management capabilities (Sia et al., 2023). Traveloka, despite its strong market presence, lacks comprehensive itinerary management, limiting its ability to offer a holistic travel planning experience (42matters.com, 2024). By adopting robust itinerary generation features, Traveloka could significantly improve its service offerings, making it competitive against international counterparts that excel in personalized travel management.

10.5 AR/VR for Pre-Visit Immersion

Augmented reality (AR) and virtual reality (VR) technologies offer significant potential to enhance user engagement by providing immersive pre-travel experiences (Kontogianni & Alepis, 2020). For example, apps such as Guides by Lonely Planet build AR to offer virtual tours and immersive content, significantly enriching the travel planning process and enhancing user engagement (Loureiro et al., 2020). Despite the growing global adoption of AR/VR, Indonesian travel applications like Traveloka and Tiket.com lag in implementing these immersive technologies (42matters.com, 2024). Addressing the technological and infrastructural challenges, such as bandwidth and device compatibility, could enable these platforms to capitalize on the substantial user engagement benefits offered by AR/VR technologies.

10.6 Data Privacy & Digital Literacy Challenges

While technological advancements in travel apps provide substantial user benefits, significant challenges related to data privacy and digital literacy remain prevalent in Indonesia (Sia et al., 2023). The adoption of advanced personalization features inherently requires extensive data collection, raising concerns around data privacy and security. Wang et al. (2016) emphasize the importance of balancing user convenience with privacy protection, highlighting the necessity of transparent data governance practices. Additionally, digital literacy levels among Indonesian users vary, influencing the effective utilization of sophisticated app features (Statista, 2024b). Implementing comprehensive user education initiatives and transparent privacy policies can mitigate these challenges, building user trust and promoting broader adoption of advanced travel app features.

11. EMBEDDING SMART CITY SOLUTIONS FOR SUSTAINABLE TOURISM

11.1. Smart Governance & Multi-Stakeholder Coordination

Smart governance, enabled through Information and Communication Technologies (ICT), facilitates efficient multi-stakeholder coordination in sustainable tourism development (Ivars-Baidal et al., 2023). Cities like Jakarta have implemented integrated platforms such as Jakarta Smart City (JSC), utilizing real-time data analytics for effective decision-making and responsive public service delivery (Soraya, 2015). Coordination among local governments, private sector entities, and tourism organizations through such platforms enhances visitor management, optimizes resource allocation, and promotes sustainable tourism practices (Fernández-Díaz et al., 2023).

11.2. Smart Environment & Real-Time Monitoring

Smart environmental monitoring, supported by IoT and real-time data analytics, significantly contributes to sustainable tourism by reducing environmental impacts and enhancing visitor experiences (Balletto et al., 2020). IoT-enabled sensors deployed across tourism destinations provide critical insights into environmental conditions, such as pollution levels and resource usage (Chung et al., 2019). Integrating these data streams into tourism applications allows for proactive management and timely interventions, ensuring the preservation of natural resources and maintaining the attractiveness of tourist locations.

11.3. Smart Mobility & Green Infrastructure

Smart mobility solutions, including integrated transportation platforms and green infrastructure, are crucial for sustainable urban tourism management (Amendola et al., 2022). Initiatives such as Jakarta's JAKLingko provide unified ticketing and real-time transport information, encouraging the use of public transportation and reducing private vehicle dependence (Chung et al., 2019). Additionally, integrating low-emission transport options and pedestrian-friendly infrastructure significantly contributes to reducing the environmental footprint of tourism activities.

11.4. Building Public Value and Inclusivity

Smart city solutions must prioritize inclusivity and public value creation to effectively support sustainable tourism (Fernández-Díaz et al., 2023). Ensuring digital accessibility, providing multilingual interfaces, and incorporating community participation into tourism planning enhances both resident and visitor experiences (Ivars-Baidal et al., 2023). Cities such as Yogyakarta have effectively implemented smart tourism initiatives with a strong focus on community involvement and public value creation, demonstrating the importance of inclusive smart city strategies (Faidat & Khozin, 2018).

11.5. Pilots, Standards, and the Muddling Through Approach

Adopting a pragmatic, incremental approach to integrating smart city technologies aligns with Lindblom's (1959) "muddling through" theory, highlighting gradual progress through iterative pilots and continuous refinement (Fernández-Díaz et al., 2023). Indonesian cities, such as Bandung and Surabaya, illustrate effective implementation through pilot projects that test and adapt innovative solutions before widespread adoption (Yusuf & Jumhur, 2018; Amalia et al., 2023). Establishing interoperability standards and best practices through pilot initiatives promotes broader technology adoption and sustainable tourism development.

12. POTENTIAL CHALLENGES AND MITIGATION

12.1 Digital Divide

Rural tourism sites, such as Java's agrarian homestays, often lack stable broadband or 4G coverage, rendering real-time apps unreliable. To bridge this gap, hybrid satellite-LTE networks and community mesh Wi-Fi systems can be deployed, backed by partial public subsidies. The OECD highlights such hybrid models as cost-effective for low-density regions, combining terrestrial and satellite backhaul to deliver ubiquitous connectivity (Srivastava, 2023).

12.2 Privacy & Data Security

Collection of granular location and behavior data must be governed by robust privacy frameworks. Adopting GDPR-style regulations, coupled with the EU's incoming Green Claims Directive, will protect user rights while ensuring data integrity. Transparent consent mechanisms, data-minimization practices, and open auditing of green credentials via blockchain will build traveler trust and safeguard against surveillance misuse (Hicks, 2025).

12.3 Technology Adoption Barriers

SMEs often face capital constraints that hinder adoption of sensors, analytics platforms, and blockchain systems. Targeted micro-grant programs, modeled on McKinsey & Company's SME Digitalization Playbook, can underwrite upfront hardware costs and provide stipends for training. Partnerships with NGOs and community organizations can extend support networks, ensuring widespread uptake.

13. IMPLICATIONS

13.1. Theoretical Implications

- **Integration of multi-level governance in sustainable tourism theory:** By examining Indonesia's Sustainable Tourism Development (STDev) program alongside the Monitoring Centre for Sustainable Tourism Observatories (MCSTO) network, this study shows how macro-, ecosystem-, and local-level governance interact in practice. It theorizes that sustainable tourism outcomes depend not only on balancing the three pillars (economic, socio-cultural, environmental), but on the dynamic coordination mechanisms (such as multi-stakeholder STO partnerships) that mediate between global standards (UNWTO, GSTC) and local implementation.
- **Advancing collaborative and community-centered tourism models:** The article synthesizes ecotourism and village tourism literatures to theorize a co-production model in which host communities, government bodies, and academics jointly design, monitor, and adapt tourism interventions. This contributes to governance theory by positioning community empowerment and

knowledge-sharing as core theoretical constructs that sustain long-term destination viability, rather than as peripheral add-on strategies.
- **Enriching sustainability metrics and certification theory:** By mapping Indonesia's adoption of GSTC destination criteria into Regulation No. 14/2016 and the Indonesia Sustainable Tourism Awards (ISTA), the study bridges certification theory and practical policy. It argues for a feedback loop between empirical observatory data and evolving metric design, suggesting that certification should be seen as a living system, continually refined through STO monitoring and academic research.

13.2. Practical Implications

- **Strengthen MCSTO capacity**: The Ministry of Tourism should allocate dedicated funding and technical support to existing MCSTOs, and consider expanding to under-represented regions, to ensure consistent data collection and policy feedback. Embedding a formal liaison unit within each regional government can institutionalize the multi-stakeholder governance model.
- **Iterative certification processes**: Incorporate real-time observatory findings into ISTA criteria revisions. This will help maintain alignment with global best practices and encourage destinations to pursue continuous improvement rather than one-off audits.
- **Adopt green management protocols**: Tour operators and accommodation providers should implement routine environmental audits (energy, water, waste) and integrate soft-tourism green marketing strategies to reduce their carbon footprint and appeal to increasingly sustainability-conscious travelers.
- **Capacity building in entrepreneurship**: Practical training programs (co-developed by universities and local NGOs) can enhance villagers' business skills, enabling them to innovate authentic products and services that reinforce conservation incentives (e.g., eco-guiding, handicrafts).
- **Participatory planning platforms**: Establish regular STO community forums where residents, assessors, and academics review observatory data together, co-design improvement plans, and monitor progress. This strengthens trust, aligns expectations, and embeds local knowledge in decision-making.
- **Tourism-linked value chains**: Encourage linkages between ecotourism operations and other rural industries (agriculture, handicrafts) to spread benefits beyond direct tourism services, thereby reducing economic vulnerability and reinforcing the multiplier effect of sustainable tourism development.

14. CONCLUSION

In conclusion, sustainable tourism in Indonesia is a multidimensional approach aimed at balancing economic growth, socio-cultural integrity, and environmental conservation. Recognized globally and increasingly embraced through comprehensive national policies such as Ministerial Regulation No. 14 of 2016, sustainable tourism development emphasizes responsible management practices and the active engagement of local communities. The Sustainable Tourism Development (STDev) program, notably through initiatives such as the Sustainable Tourism Observatories (STO) and the Monitoring Centre for Sustainable Tourism Observatories (MCSTO), illustrates Indonesia's commitment to systematically monitoring and optimizing tourism impacts.

Ecotourism further enriches Indonesia's tourism landscape by aligning tourism activities with environmental conservation and community participation. Indonesian national parks and village tourism projects serve as practical examples, emphasizing education, cultural preservation, and local economic empowerment. Such initiatives demonstrate how carefully planned ecotourism can generate tangible economic benefits while safeguarding ecological integrity and promoting community well-being.

The integration of digital technologies into sustainable tourism, through smart tourism observatories, AI-driven personalization, geolocation services, and immersive AR/VR applications, represents a transformative opportunity. These technologies enable real-time management, personalized experiences, and enhanced visitor engagement while ensuring minimal ecological disturbance. However, addressing the digital divide, ensuring data privacy, and overcoming technology adoption barriers remain critical challenges.

Furthermore, the concept of smart cities complements sustainable tourism by promoting efficient governance, smart mobility solutions, and real-time environmental monitoring. By integrating smart city infrastructure with tourism planning, Indonesia can achieve better resource management, reduce environmental impacts, and enhance visitor experiences. This alignment between tourism and urban management strategies emphasizes inclusivity, equitable economic distribution, and sustainability.

Finally, the continuous evolution of sustainable tourism certification frameworks and practices, supported by comprehensive stakeholder participation and capacity-building programs, is crucial for long-term success. The active involvement of local communities in planning, implementation, and benefit-sharing, along with iterative feedback mechanisms, ensures that sustainable tourism remains resilient, adaptive, and inclusive. As Indonesia advances its sustainable tourism agenda, promoting multi-level governance, strengthening technological infrastructures, and promoting collaborative community-centered approaches will be pivotal in achieving lasting sustainability and global competitiveness in the tourism sector.

REFERENCES

Amalia, D., Nesya, N., & Tyrta, M. (2023). Implementasi Kota Pintar (Smart City) Di Kota Surabaya. *Jurnal Birokrasi & Pemerintahan Daerah*, *5*(1), 57–63.

Amendola, C., La Bella, S., Joime, G. P., Frattale Mascioli, F. M., & Vito, P. (2022). An Integrated Methodology Model for Smart Mobility System Applied to Sustainable Tourism. *Administrative Sciences*, *12*(1), 40. Advance online publication. DOI: 10.3390/admsci12010040

Asriyani, H., & Verheijen, B. (2020). Protecting the Mbau Komodo in Riung, Flores: Local Adat, National Conservation and Ecotourism Developments. *Forest and Society*, *4*(1), 20–34. DOI: 10.24259/fs.v4i1.7465

Ayuningtyas, D. I., & Dharmawan, A. H. (2011). Dampak Ekowisata Terhadap Kondisi Sosio-Ekonomi Dan Sosio-Ekologi Masyarakat Di Taman Nasional Gunung Halimun Salak. *Sodality: Jurnal Transdisiplin Sosiologi, Komunikasi, Dan Ekologi Manusia*, *05*(03).

Balletto, G., Milesi, A., Ladu, M., & Borruso, G. (2020). A dashboard for supporting slow tourism in green infrastructures. A methodological proposal in Sardinia (Italy). *Sustainability (Basel)*, *12*(9), 3579. Advance online publication. DOI: 10.3390/su12093579

Bappenas. (2015). *Rencana Pembangunan Jangka Menengah Nasional (RPJMN) 2015-2019*. Perpres No 2 Tahun 2015. Jakarta: Bappenas.

Bhimrajka, A. (2024). *Battle of the Super Apps: Gojek vs. Grab – Who Comes Out on Top?* Miracuves: https://miracuves.com/battle-of-the-super-apps-gojek-vs-grab/ . Accessed on 10 May 2025.

Boxo. (2024). *15 Most Popular Super Apps in the World in 2024.* https://www.boxo.io/blog/most-popular-superapps-in-the-world. Accessed on 10 May 2025.

Chen, C. C., & Tsai, J. L. (2019). Determinants of behavioral intention to use the Personalized Location-based Mobile Tourism Application: An empirical study by integrating TAM with ISSM. *Future Generation Computer Systems*, *96*, 628–638. DOI: 10.1016/j.future.2017.02.028

Chung, N., Tyan, I., & Lee, S. J. (2019). Eco-innovative museums and visitors' perceptions of corporate social responsibility. *Sustainability (Basel)*, *11*(20), 1–16. DOI: 10.3390/su11205744

Damanik, J., & Helmut, F. W. (2006). *Perencanaan Ekowisata Dari Teori ke Aplikasi*. Andi Offset.

Dorcic, J., Komsic, J., & Markovic, S. (2019). Mobile technologies and applications towards smart tourism – state of the art. *Tourism Review*, *74*(1), 82–103. DOI: 10.1108/TR-07-2017-0121

Faidat, N., & Khozin, M. (2018). Analisa Strategi Pengembangan Kota Pintar (Smart City): Studi Kasus Kota Yogyakarta. *JIP (Jurnal Ilmu Pemerintahan). Kajian Ilmu Pemerintahan Dan Politik Daerah*, *3*(2), 171–180. DOI: 10.24905/jip.3.2.2018.171-180

Fennell, D. A. (2020). *Ecotourism*. Routledge. DOI: 10.4324/9780429346293

Fernández-Díaz, E., Jambrino-Maldonado, C., Iglesias-Sánchez, P. P., & de las Heras-Pedrosa, C. (2023). Digital accessibility of smart cities - tourism for all and reducing inequalities: Tourism Agenda 2030. *Tourism Review*, *78*(2), 361–380. DOI: 10.1108/TR-02-2022-0091

Fujimatsu, I., Levy, J., Park, J., & Waddelow, T. (2024). *An ecosystem approach to accelerating sustainable tourism*. Visa Economic Empowerment Institute.

Global sustainable Tourism Council. (2013). *GSTC Hotel & Tour Operator Criteria*. https://www.gstcouncil.org/gstc-criteria/gstc-industry-criteria/. Accessed on 27 December 2023.

Global Sustainable Tourism Council (GSTC). (2013). *GSTC Destination Criteria*. https://www.gstcouncil.org/gstc-criteria/gstc-destination-criteria/. Accessed on 27 December 2023.

GlobeNewswire. (2024). *Indonesia Ecommerce Market Databook 2024, Featuring Bukalapak, JD.id, Lazada, Shopee, Tokopedia, GoFood, GrabFood, Kulina, Wahyoo, Agoda, Bobobox, PegiPegi, Tiket and Traveloka*. https://www.globenewswire.com/de/news-release/2024/06/12/2897607/28124/en/Indonesia-Ecommerce-Market-Databook-2024-Featuring-Bukalapak-JD-id-Lazada-Shopee-Tokopedia-GoFood-GrabFood-Kulina-Wahyoo-Agoda-Bobobox-PegiPegi-Tiket-and-Traveloka.html. Accessed on 10 May 2025.

Hadi, C. E., Reinarto, R., & Rahadi, R. A. (2021). Conceptual Analysis of Sustainable Tourism Management in Indonesia. *JHTHEM*, *6*(23), 35–41. DOI: 10.35631/JTHEM.623004

Harahab, N., & Setiawan, S. (2017). Suitability Index Of Mangrove Ecotourism In Malang Regency. *Ecsofim: Journal of Economic and Social of Fisheries and Marine*, *04*(02), 153–165. DOI: 10.21776/ub.ecsofim.2017.004.02.05

Hicks, R. (2025). Post-*COVID boom in visitors sparks over-tourism fears in Asia.* Reuters: https://www.reuters.com/sustainability/land-use-biodiversity/post-covid-boom-visitors-sparks-over-tourism-fears-asia-2025-05-06. Accessed on 10 May 2025.

Hijriati, E., & Mardiana, R. (2014). Community Based Ecotourism influence the condition of Ecology, Social, and Economic Batusuhunan village, Sukabumi. Sodality: *Jurnal Sosiologi Pedesaan, 2*(3).

Ho, R. C., Amin, M., Ryu, K., & Ali, F. (2021). Integrative model for the adoption of tour itineraries from smart travel apps. *Journal of Hospitality and Tourism Technology, 12*(2).

Ibrahim, I., Zukhri, N., & Rendy, R. (2019). From Nature Tourism to Ecotourism: Assessing The Ecotourism Principles Fulfillment of Tourism Natural Areas In Bangka Belitung. *Society, 7*(2), 281–302. DOI: 10.33019/society.v7i2.111

Inskeep, E. (1991). *Tourism Planning: An Integrated and Sustainable Development Approach. VNR Tourism and Commercial Recreation Series.* Van Nostrad Reinhold.

Intelligence, A. (2024). *Who is the biggest OTA in Asia?* https://aggregateintelligence.com/who-is-the-biggest-ota-in-asia/. Accessed on 10 May 2025.

IPCC. (2007). IPCC Fourth Assessment Report: Climate change. In: Solomon, S., D, Q. (Eds.), *The Physical Science Basis.* Intergovernmental Panel on Climate Change. Cambridge.

Ivars-Baidal, J. A., Celdrán-Bernabeu, M. A., Femenia-Serra, F., Perles-Ribes, J. F., & Vera-Rebollo, J. F. (2023). Smart city and smart destination planning: Examining instruments and perceived impacts in Spain. *Cities (London, England), 137*(1), 104266. DOI: 10.1016/j.cities.2023.104266

Kontogianni, A., & Alepis, E. (2020). Smart tourism: State of the art and literature review for the last six years. *Array (New York, N.Y.), 6*(February), 100020. DOI: 10.1016/j.array.2020.100020

Lemy, D. M., Teguh, F., & Pramezwary, A. (2020). Tourism Development in Indonesia. *Establishment of Sustainable Strategies. Emerald Publishing Ltd, 11*, 91–108.

Loureiro, S. M. C., Guerreiro, J., & Ali, F. (2020). 20 years of research on virtual reality and augmented reality in tourism context: A text-mining approach. *Tourism Management, 77*(October 2019). DOI: 10.1016/j.tourman.2019.104028

Lukman, H. (2017). Partisipasi Masyarakat Dalam Pembangunan Desa Sukamerta Kecamatan Rawamerta Kabupaten Karawang. *Jurnal Politikom Indonesiana, 2*(2), 43–53.

Market Research Future. (2025). *Indonesia Travel and Tourism Market Overview Source*. https://www.marketresearchfuture.com/reports/indonesia-travel-and-tourism-market-44301. Accessed on 10 May 2025.

42. matters.com. (2024). *Most Popular Travel Apps: Indonesia*. https://42matters.com/most-popular-travel-apps-indonesia. Accessed on 10 May 2025.

Muaz, H., Rinekso, S. A., & Susilo, H. (2017). Potensi Daya Tarik Ekowisata Suaka Margasatwa Bukit Batu Kabupaten Bengkalis Provinsi Riau. *Jurnal Penelitian Sosial Dan Ekonomi Kehutanan, 14*(1), 39–56. DOI: 10.20886/jpsek.2017.14.1.39-56

Mullis, B. (2017). *The growth paradox: can tourism ever be sustainable?* World Economic Forum: https://www.weforum.org/stories/2017/08/the-growth-paradox-can-tourism-ever-be-sustainable/. Accessed on 10 May 2025.

Nugroho, I. (2011). *Ekowisata dan pembangunan berkelanjutan* (1st ed.). Pustaka Pelajar, Yogyakarta.

Nugroho, I., & Dahuri, I. (2012). *Pembangunan Wilayah: Perspektif ekonomi, sosial, dan lingkungan (second ed)*. Jakarta: LP3ES, Jakarta.

Nugroho, I., & Negara, P. D. (2015). *Pengembangan Desa Melalui: Dilengkapi dengan peraturan perundangan tentang pedoman pengembangan desa wisata*. Solo: Era Adicitra Intermedia.

Nugroho, I., Negara, P. D., & Yuniar, H. R. (2018). The Planning and The Development of The Ecotourism and Tourism Village in Indonesia: A Policy Review. *Journal of Socioeconomics and Development, 1*(1), 43–51. DOI: 10.31328/jsed.v1i1.532

Nugroho, I., Pramukanto, F. H., Negara, P. D., Purnomowati, W., & Wulandari, W. (2016). Promoting the Rural Development through the Ecotourism Activities in Indonesia. *American Journal of Tourism Management, 5*(1), 9–18.

Nuraini, Satria, A., & Sri, W. E. (2019). Mekanisme Akses Dan Kekuasaan Dalam Memperkuat Kinerja Institusi Pengelolaan Ekowisata Bahari. *Sodality: Jurnal Sosiologi Pedesaan,* 65–77.

Pan, S.-Y., Gao, M., Kim, H., Shah, K. J., Pei, S.-L., & Chiang, P.-C. (2018). Advances and Challenges in Sustainable Tourism toward a Green Economy. *The Science of the Total Environment, 635*, 452–469. DOI: 10.1016/j.scitotenv.2018.04.134 PMID: 29677671

Payton, B. (2025). *To the ends of the Earth: The Arctic's battle for sustainable tourism*. Reuters: https://www.reuters.com/sustainability/society-equity/ends-earth-arctics-battle-sustainable-tourism-2025-04-29/. Accessed on 10 May 2025.

Peeters, P., & Dubois, G. (2010). Tourism travel under climate change mitigation constraints. *Journal of Transport Geography*, *18*(3), 447–457. DOI: 10.1016/j.jtrangeo.2009.09.003

Reuters. (2024). *Driving sustainability in the critical world of digital infrastructure*. https://www.reuters.com/plus/acumen-stories/cop-28/eunetworks. Accessed on 10 May 2025.

Rhee, S., Kitchener, D., Brown, T., Merrill, R., Dilts, R., & Tighe, S., & USAID-Indonesia. (2004). (Submitted in). Report on Biodiversity and Tropical Forests in Indonesia. *Accordance with Foreign Assistance Act Sections*, *118/119*, 1–316.

Ross, S., & Wall, G. (1999). Ecotourism: Towards congruence between theory and practice. *Tourism Management*, *20*(1), 123–132. DOI: 10.1016/S0261-5177(98)00098-3

Rothberg, D. (1999). *Enhanced and Alternative Financing Mechanisms Strengthening National Park Management in Indonesia*.

Sehyeon, D. (2024). *Gojek, Indonesia's Super App Giant*. Medium: https://medium.com/%40davidsehyeonbaek/gojek-indonesias-super-app-giant-81283f63e3d5. Accessed on 10 May 2025.

Sia, P. Y. H., Saidin, S. S., & Iskandar, Y. H. P. (2023). Systematic review of mobile travel apps and their smart features and challenges. *Journal of Hospitality and Tourism Insights*, *6*(5), 2115–2138. DOI: 10.1108/JHTI-02-2022-0087

SimilarWeb. (2025). *Traveloka*. https://www.similarweb.com/company/traveloka.com/. Accessed on 10 May 2025.

Soraya, I. (2015). Faktor-Faktor yang Mempengaruhi Minat Masyarakat Jakarta dalam Mengakses Fortal Media Jakarta Smart City. *Jurnal Komunikasi*, *6*(1), 10–23.

Srivastava, R. (2023). *FEATURE-Bhutan seeks to balance economy and environment with tourist tax*. Reuters: https://www.reuters.com/article/markets/oil/feature-bhutan-seeks-to-balance-economy-and-environment-with-tourist-tax-idUSL8N3A93GD/. Accessed on 10 May 2025.

Statista. (2024a). *Most Popular Online Travel Agencies among Consumers in Indonesia as of June 2023*. https://www.statista.com/statistics/1200620/indonesia-most-used-online-travel-agencies/. Accessed on 10 May 2025.

Statista. (2024b). *Most preferred accommodation booking methods for year-end holiday travel in Indonesia as of November 2022.* https://www.statista.com/statistics/1379871/indonesia-preferred-accommodation-booking-methods/. Accessed on 10 May 2025.

Tan, S. (2024). *Indonesia: Which online travel agencies are best at turning awareness to purchase intent in Q1 2024?* YouGov: https://business.yougov.com/content/49688-indonesia-online-travel-agencies-best-at-turning-awareness-to-purchase-intent-q1-2024. Accessed on 10 May 2025.

UNWTO. (2005). *Making Tourism More Sustainable - A Guide for Policy Makers.* United Nations World Tourism Organization.

UNWTO. (2017a). *Discussion Paper on the Occasion of the International Year of Sustainable Tourism for Development 2017.* United Nations World Tourism Organization, Madrid, Spain, p. 84.

UNWTO. (2017b). *UNWTO Annual Report 2016.* World Tourism Organization.

Wang, T., Duong, T. D., & Chen, C. C. (2016). Intention to disclose personal information via mobile applications: A privacy calculus perspective. *International Journal of Information Management, 36*(4), 531–542. DOI: 10.1016/j.ijinfomgt.2016.03.003

Wardana, I.-M., Sukaatmadja, I.-P.-G., Ekawati, N.-W., Yasa, N.-N.-K., Astawa, I.-P., & Setini, M. (2021). Policy Models for Improving Ecotourism Performance to Build Quality Tourism Experience and Sustainable Tourism. *Management Science Letters, 11*, 595–608. DOI: 10.5267/j.msl.2020.9.007

Weaver, D. (2006). *Sustainable Tourism: Theory and Practice.* Elsevier Ltd.

You, X. (2025). *How renewable energy is helping China's tourism industry go green.* Reuters: https://www.reuters.com/sustainability/climate-energy/how-renewable-energy-is-helping-chinas-tourism-industry-go-green-2025-05-08/. Accessed on 10 May 2025.

Yusuf, R. M. S., & Jumhur, H. M. (2018). Penerapan E-Government Dalam Membangun Smart City Pada Kota Bandung Tahun 2018 E- Government Implementation in Building Smart City in Bandung 2018. *E-Proceeding of Management, 5*(3), 3126–3130.

Zakia. (2021). Ecotourism in Indonesia: Local Community Involvement and the Affecting Factors. *Journal of Governance and Public Policy, 8*(2), 93-105.

Zeppel, H. (2006). *Indigenous Ecotourism: Sustainable Development and Management.* CABI. DOI: 10.1079/9781845931247.0000

Chapter 7
Tech Tales of Travel:
The Confluence of Technology and Tourism Decision Making

Shubhra Mishra
Babu Banarasi Das University, India

Rinki Verma
Babu Banarasi Das University, India

ABSTRACT

The travel industry is going through an incredible era of innovation and change due to confluence of technology and tourism decision-making. This research explores the field of TechTales of Travel, with a particular emphasis on how tourism decision-making processes use Artificial Intelligence (AI), Big Data Analytics, Social Media/User-Generated Content, and Information and Communication Technology (ICT) infrastructure. Through surveys and multiple regression analysis conducted on a sample of 212 respondents involved in travel, the study explores how these technologies influence consumer perceptions and behaviours in trip planning. Findings reveal a significant positive relationship between technology integration and consumer decision-making, underscoring the importance of strategic technology utilization for enhancing travel experiences and meeting evolving customer expectations. The study emphasizes the need for continuous innovation, data-driven strategies, and ethical considerations to navigate the digital landscape effectively and ensure sustainable growth in the travel sector.

DOI: 10.4018/979-8-3693-3196-5.ch007

1. INTRODUCTION

"Tourism is a social, cultural and economic phenomenon which entails the movement of people to countries or places outside their usual environment for personal or business/professional purposes (World Tourism Organisation (UNWTO). These people are called visitors (which may be either tourists or excursionists; residents or non-residents) and tourism has to do with their activities, some of which involve tourism expenditure" (UNWTO). UNWTO data shows significant economic rebound in tourism, with international tourism receipts reaching USD 1.4 trillion in 2023, close to pre-pandemic levels. Strong demand, both domestic and international, has fuelled this recovery, leading to growth in receipts surpassing pre-pandemic levels in many destinations. UNWTO predicts a full recovery to pre-pandemic levels in 2024 with a 2% growth compared to 2019, contingent on the pace of recovery in Asia and economic/geopolitical risks (UNWTO, 2024).

The global tourism sector has changed tremendously in recent years, fuelled by fast technological advances. The advent of Tourism 4.0 and Smart Tourism has marked the beginning of a new age in which the incorporation of cutting-edge technology is reshaping conventional approaches to travel planning and decision-making (Rathore, 2020; Chen, 2020). This change is a major revolution altering the very nature of the tourist experience.

Artificial Intelligence (AI), Social Media & Content Marketing, Big Data Analytics, and advanced Digitalization or Information and Communication Technology (ICT) infrastructure converge together to create a new environment for the tourism industries (Kazak et al., 2020; Tham et al., 2019; de las Heras-Pedrosa et al., 2020; Cynthia et al., 2021).

When these pillars work together harmoniously, they provide unmatched possibilities to improve the effectiveness, customization, and overall experience in the travel industry. Technology is becoming more and more integrated into all aspects of the travel experience, from social media platforms influencing picking a destination to predictive AI algorithms directing itinerary planning to big data analytics creating customized recommendations. Customer online behavior may be analyzed utilizing non-traditional data sources like social networks by combining machine learning technologies like Natural Language Processing (NLP) with predictive analytics and deep learning algorithms (Kazak et al., 2020). Likewise, User contributions may rise if social media has an effect on content, and destinations will be able to leverage better their attractions—such as events, experiences, and icons—and elevate their reputation among travellers (de las Heras-Pedrosa et al., 2020).

Traditional consumer decision-making strategies are thus being replaced by data-driven approaches that make the most of these revolutionary technologies. The use of big data technology in smart tourism not only makes tourism management more proactive and effective in the use of tourism resources, but it also has the potential to boost consumer satisfaction with tourism services, which has enormous research potential and application opportunities (Chen, 2020). Digitalization is influencing the way travel is planned, as well as the exploration and promotion of new places, but it also impacts the travel experience (Cynthia et al., 2021).

This research investigates the integration levels within Tourism 4.0, examining how artificial intelligence (AI), social media, big data, and advanced ICT infrastructure shape tourist decisions. It aims to address concerns about changing decision-making dynamics in tourism and their impact on service efficiency. By analysing these elements and their interactions, this research provides insights into the transformative potential of new technologies in the travel industry, paving the way for a deeper understanding of opportunities in this era of tech tales of Travel.

The scope of the research includes an in-depth analysis of the tourist industry's integration of technology, such as Artificial Intelligence (AI), Big Data Analytics, Social Media/User-Generated Content, and Information and Communication Technology (ICT) infrastructure. The study specifically attempts to examine how these technology developments affect customer perception and decision-making in trip planning. While the study gives useful insights into the present status of technology integration in tourism, it also recognizes the changing nature of technology and its potential for future developments in moulding the travel experience.

2. THEORETICAL CONTRIBUTION AND PROPOSED MODEL

2.1 Tourism and Technology Integration- Concepts

While Smart Tourism emphasizes the use of data-driven solutions and smart infrastructure to improve destination management and visitor experiences, E-Tourism primarily focuses on the use of digital platforms and online resources to facilitate tourism activities and information distribution. Tourism 4.0 places an emphasis on the integration of advanced technologies across the entire travel ecosystem. In following paragraphs study will deliberate on the various types of terminology used in current scenario to understand the tourism and their behaviour.

2.1.1 Tourism 4.0

Tourism 4.0, rooted in Industry 4.0 dynamics, integrates technology into the tourism sector akin to digital systems. Its goal is to enhance tourism's value proposition by leveraging technologies like autonomous robots, virtual reality, and big data (Abdurakhmanova et al., 2022). The Industry 4.0 revolution is reshaping tourism systems to cater to tech-savvy consumers. Innovations such as Big Data, Automation, Virtual and Augmented Reality, Robotics, and ICT align perfectly with the Tourism 4.0 paradigm, facilitating significant transformations in the industry's design and operations (Bilotta et al., 2021). In Industry 4.0, virtualization, decentralization, real-time data gathering, and analysis capabilities, service orientation, modularity, and decentralization are common principles that support the development of a new tourism value ecosystem identified as Tourism 4.0 (Pencarelli, 2019).

The tourism industry has embraced Industry 4.0 technologies like the Internet of Things (IoT), artificial intelligence, big data analytics and virtual/augmented reality, giving rise to Tourism 4.0. Despite challenges, such as the potential blurring of technology and tourism experiences, these innovations offer opportunities to enhance tourist interactions (Stankov & Gretzel, 2020). Initially introduced in Portugal and adopted across Europe, Tourism 4.0 aims to improve operational efficiency, personalize experiences, and foster collaboration. To stay competitive, future industry professionals must develop expertise in Industry 4.0 including analytical thinking and big data management skills (Abdurakhmanova et al., 2022;Stankov & Gretzel, 2020).

Figure 1. Effect of human center design in shaping tourist experiences

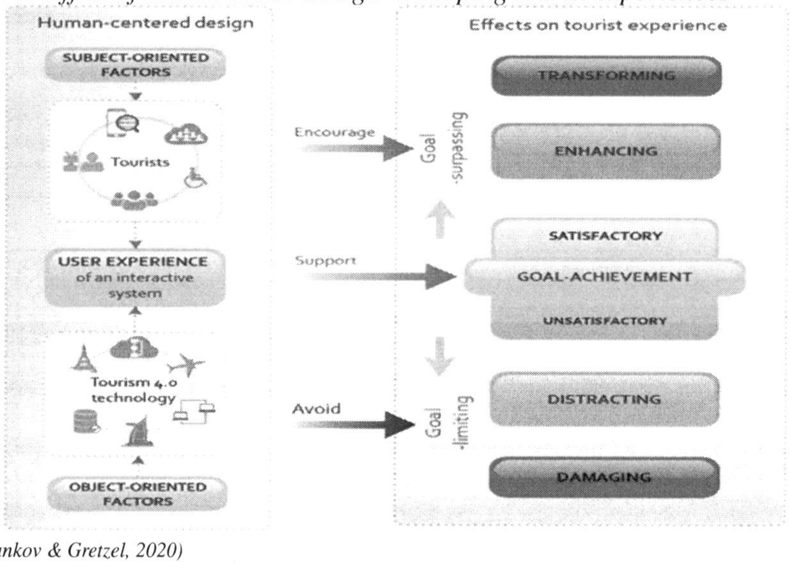

(Stankov & Gretzel, 2020)

In Tourism 4.0, technology-mediated tourist experiences offer both opportunities for surpassing goals and risks of limiting outcomes as shown in Figure 1. Interactive systems play a vital role in achieving system use goals and satisfying users, such as smartphones in tourism, despite occasional glitches. However, they can also lead to distractions or harm if they demand too much attention or cause environmental disruptions. It can also create added benefits and transformative effects by engaging users on different levels, enhancing the overall tourist experience (Stankov & Gretzel, 2020).

2.1.2 Smart Tourism

"Smart" has emerged as a broad phrase that encompasses technological, economic, and social developments brought about by inventions such as sensors, big data, and connection technologies such as IoT, RFID, and NFC (Gretzel et al., 2015). Within the travel sector, "smart" refers to more than just technology innovation; it also refers to a comprehensive strategy that combines cutting-edge technologies with sound economic and social principles to improve the traveller experience as a whole. To provide passengers with smarter travel destinations, services, and experiences, this all-encompassing mix makes use of technologies including mobile connection and IOT (Gretzel et al., 2015).

To fulfil tourists' demands for Smart Tourism Technology (STT) usage, destination marketers must prioritize three key elements: Interactivity, Personalization, and Informativeness (Jeong & Shin, 2019). Tourists expect personalized services throughout their journey, including pre-trip planning with real-time information, personalized experiences during the trip, and engagement after the trip for feedback and experience reliving (Buhalis & Amaranggana, 2014). Smart tourism encompasses various layers of smart components supported by Information and Communication Technologies (ICTs), as depicted in Figure 2.

Figure 2. Smart tourism constituents

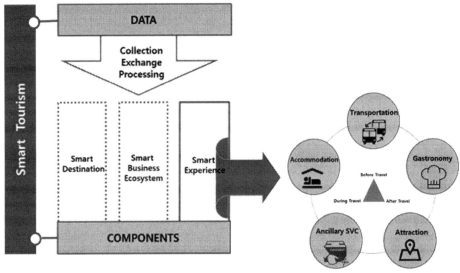

(Lee et al., 2020)

This updated model enhances the smart travel experience by incorporating new factors like gastronomy while streamlining less relevant ones(Lee et al., 2020). Travellers expect STTs(Smart Tourism Technology to deliver interactive features, personalized suggestions, and reliable trip information. For example, City Guide Apps for destinations like San Francisco should provide precise location details, real-time traffic updates, and trustworthy reviews, meeting tourists' specific needs. (Jeong & Shin, 2019) Smart Tourism Destinations aim to enhance the overall tourism experience by leveraging smart concepts such as real-time information, IoT for advanced customer service, and personalized services. These initiatives address common negative experiences like lost luggage, security concerns, delays, and subpar services (Buhalis & Amaranggana, 2014). The differences between smart tourism and e-tourism are outlined in Table 1 based on these descriptions and definitions. (Gretzel et al., 2015)

2.1.3 E-Tourism

Electronic tourism is use of digital technology, mostly via Internet, for travel-related tasks including itinerary planning, reservation, and information retrieval. It includes digital media such as travel review platforms, destination websites, and online travel firms. The advancement of ICT has revolutionized e-tourism, facilitating personalized experiences and online transactions. This evolution sustains the industry and improves living standards. Smart living is promoted through sustainable practices enabled by electronic tools (Rehman Khan et al., 2021). The widespread use of ICTs has directed to the integration of the digital and physical worlds. This integration is facilitated through the utilization of "smart key concepts," which include privacy protection and augmented reality. Therefore, Smart tourism emerges as a logical progression from e-tourism in this context (Hamid et al., 2021). Contextual suggestion systems, driven by IR and AI, help travellers plan strategically based on interests and context. Leveraging data from smart cities, these systems offer tailored recommendations, enhancing travel experiences and promoting sustainable lifestyles (Rehman Khan et al., 2021).

Table 1. Smart tourism vs. e-tourism (Gretzel et al., 2015)

	E-Tourism	Smart Tourism
Spare	digital	bridging digital & physical
Core Technology	websites	sensors & smartphones
Travel Phase	pre- & post-travel	during trip
Lifeblood	information	Big Data
Paradigm	interactivity	technology-mediated co-creation
Structure	value chain/intermediaries	ecosystem
Research	B2B, B2C, C2C	public-private-consumer collaboration

2.1.4 AI and Big Data

AI and Big Data technologies are transforming the way tourists plan, book, and enjoy their vacations. Personalized suggestions, that suggest travel destinations, lodging options, and activities based on historical behavior and personal interests, are powered by AI-driven algorithms.

a. Chatbots

The customer experience and service sector is one of the main areas where AI and Big Data impact tourism. Chatbots and virtual assistants with AI capabilities may instantly respond to inquiries from passengers in a customized manner, increasing consumer happiness and engagement. For instance, AI chatbots are used by hotels and airlines to manage reservations, offer travel advice, and respond to visitor questions, therefore increasing productivity and convenience for passengers.

Figure 3. Ask Diksha ChatBot by IRCTC

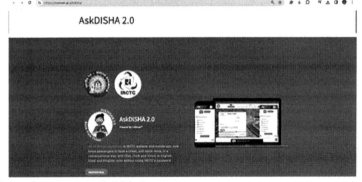

Image Source: https://corover.ai/askdisha/

The Indian Railway Catering and Tourism Corporation created the chatbot "Ask Disha" (Figure 3) to help people with tourism queries. The AI-driven chatbot works across many platforms, such as the Incredible India app and website, offering prompt and tailored replies to improve visitors' experiences. OYO Rooms, a prominent hotel chain in India, uses chatbots OYO YO! to handle customer inquiries, reservations, and complaints.

b. Dynamic Pricing Strategies

Indian airlines, like IndiGo and SpiceJet, use AI and big data to dynamically price their tickets. These technologies assist airlines in modifying ticket rates in response to variables such as variations in demand, seasonality, booking patterns, and pricing strategies of competitors. This enables airlines to maximize seat occupancy and provide competitive fares in order to maximize revenue.

c. Personalized Travel Recommendations

AI and Big Data analytics enable organizations to get important insights into their customers' preferences, behavior patterns, and trends. Businesses can identify new market trends, adjust their marketing plans, and provide passengers with individualized advice by evaluating enormous volumes of data. Big Data and AI are used by Indian travel websites like MakeMyTrip, Tripoto and Cleartrip to provide their customers with customized vacation suggestions. These services provide personalized recommendations for vacation locations, lodging options, activities, and packages based on user interests, booking history, and behaviour patterns. Additionally, artificial intelligence (AI) improves the travel experience by offering predictive information, such as weather forecasts, crowd projections at tourist destinations, and customized itineraries, guaranteeing a smoother and more comfortable journey.

2.1.5 Social Media/ User-Generated Content

Major platforms like Facebook, Instagram, and Twitter, serving as digital environments for communication and content sharing (Appel et al., 2019). Business executives and consultants are actively exploring ways to leverage social media platforms like Wikipedia, Second Life, YouTube and Twitter for profitable purposes. Social media encompasses a range of internet built applications, facilitating the exchange of User Generated Content (Kaplan & Haenlein, 2010).

Influencers and travel bloggers also contribute to promoting Indian tourism through their content. Additionally, user-generated content on platforms like TripAdvisor and Google Reviews influences tourists' decisions, with positive reviews attracting more visitors and negative feedback prompting alternative choices.

Positive reviews and recommendations can significantly boost a destination's popularity, as seen with popular tourist spots like Jaipur's Amer Fort and Goa's Baga Beach. Conversely, negative reviews can prompt travelers to explore alternative options or seek improvements in services.

Travel influencers are in high demand in persuading travellers to visit specific destinations or engage in particular activities, according to a report by ETHospitalityWorld.com. Statista indicates that India's influencer marketing segment was valued at INR 9 billion in 2021 and is projected to reach INR 22 billion by 2025. (*State of Travel Influencer Marketing, 2022*)

2.1.6 ICT and Digitalization Infrastructure

According to National Digital Tourism Mission Report by Digitalization in the tourism sector offers opportunities for enterprises to expand market reach, boost growth, enhance operational efficiencies, and gain a competitive edge. It enables the development of tailored products, improves destination connectivity, provides data for performance tracking, and enhances destination management. Long-term benefits include innovation and maintaining competitiveness in India's tourism sector.

Digital booking systems provide a hassle-free booking experience by streamlining the process of making reservations for travel, lodging, excursions, and activities. Additionally, improvements in digital infrastructure guarantee uninterrupted connectivity, enabling travellers to share their instances in real-time and access necessary services like mobile payments and online check-in, all of which improve their trips' overall effectiveness and security. Through Online Booking Platforms travelers plan their trips has been completely transformed by ICT. Booking flights, hotels, tours, and other transportation services has been revolutionized by online booking firms like MakeMyTrip, Yatra, and Cleartrip. Mobile Apps for Tourism now have fast access to information and services. These applications improve the trip experience by offering location-based and customized information.

Figure 4. Incredible India app by Ministry of Tourism

Image Source: https://play.google.com/store/apps/details?id=org.incredibleindia

Ministry of Tourism created the Incredible India App (Figure 4), which presents India as a holistic travel destination with an emphasis on spirituality, tradition, adventure, culture, yoga, wellness, and other aspects. It meets the needs of both local and foreign visitors, according to international standards and modern traveller preferences. The app includes features to assist travellers throughout their journey in India. Digital Marketing and Promotion tactics have changed as a result of digitalization and ICT tools. Digital marketing tools including social media, search engine optimization (SEO), and content marketing are used by tourism boards, hotels, tour operators, and local businesses to expand their worldwide reach.

The use of digital payment methods by travellers has made financial transactions easier. Examples of these systems include online payment gateways, UPI (Unified Payments Interface), and mobile wallets. Digital payment options provide travellers ease, security, and transparency whether making reservations, buying tickets, or paying for local businesses.

India's position in the Travel and Tourism Development Index (TTDI) in 2021, as reported by the World Economic Forum, was 54th. Additionally, the tourism sector made a significant contribution of approximately US$ 178 billion to India's GDP (World Economic Forum, 2023). As per IBEF's report on Growth of Tourism and Hospitality Industry, the coastal landscape of India, adorned with beautiful beaches, adds to its allure as a tourist destination. The travel market is projected to grow to

US$ 125 billion by FY2027, with an expected international tourist arrival of 30.5 million by 2028. (Hospitality Sector, Tourism in India IBEF)

The travel and tourism industry in India contributed Rs. 15.9 trillion (US$ 191.25 billion) to the country's GDP in 2022, according to World Travel and Tourism Council (WTTC). Furthermore, India's GDP from travel and tourism is predicted to increase at a rate of 7.8% per year on average during the following ten years. (WTTC Report, 2022)

Technology, including search engines, global distribution systems (GDS), and online travel agencies have driven growth in India's tourism sector. Cloud solutions and Software as a Service (SaaS) technologies have been pivotal for travel and hospitality companies. India's varied tourism offerings, such as spiritual tourism, attract both domestic and international travellers, supported by its competitive ranking of 34 in the Travel & Tourism Competitiveness Report 2019 (World Economic Forum, 2023).

According to the Ministry of Tourism, Foreign Tourist Arrivals (FTAs) in October 2023 reached 8, 11,411. The upcoming G-20 Presidency presents an exceptional opportunity for India's tourism sector to showcase its offerings and success stories globally. By 2028, the Indian tourism and hospitality industry is projected to earn US$ 50.9 billion in visitor exports, a significant increase from US$ 28.9 billion in 2018 (Figure 5). In line with this, the Tourism Ministry has launched the 'NamasteIndia' Campaign, aimed at encouraging international visitors to explore and experience India's rich cultural and tourism offerings. (Hospitality Sector, Tourism in India | IBEF)

Figure 5. Foreign tourists arriving in India

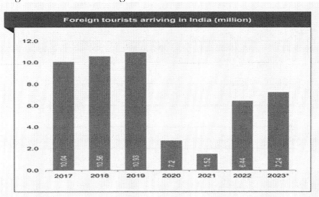

(Hospitality Sector, Tourism in India, IBEF)

The research gap identified in the study pertains to the scarcity of in-depth investigations regarding the collective influence of key technologies such as Artificial Intelligence (AI), Big Data Analytics, Social Media/User-Generated Content, and Information and Communication Technology (ICT) infrastructure in the tourism sector. Although numerous studies have delved into the impact of these technologies individually, there remains a notable dearth of research exploring their integrated effects on tourist experiences, decision-making processes, and overall service efficiency within the tourism industry.

This gap highlights the necessity for examining the synergistic integration of these technological components and its broader implications for augmenting customer satisfaction levels and enhancing the competitive edge of the tourism sector, especially in the context of the rapidly evolving landscape characterized by Tech Tales of Travel.

Technology integration is a key factor in how consumers make decisions and how tourists perceive travel in the modern travel environment. AI & Big Data, Social Media & User-Generated Content, and ICT & Digitalization Infrastructure are the three main independent variables included in the model suggested for this study. According to the model, in the modern travel setting, AI & Big Data, Social Media & User-Generated Content, and ICT & Digitalization Infrastructure have a significant influence on the dependent variables of consumer decision-making and their perceptions as shown in Figure 6.

These factors are crucial in determining how travel agencies communicate with customers and how the trip is perceived overall. Whereas social media and user-generated content (UGC) shape perceptions through reviews and suggestions, artificial intelligence (AI) and big data provide tailored recommendations and data-driven insights. ICT and digitalization infrastructure also provide convenient travel and uninterrupted communication. It is crucial to comprehend the connections between these independent factors as well as how they affect consumer behavior and perceptions when developing strategies to improve customer experiences and competitiveness in the ever-changing travel industry.

Figure 6. Proposed model I on association of various technology on consumer decision-making and tourists' perception

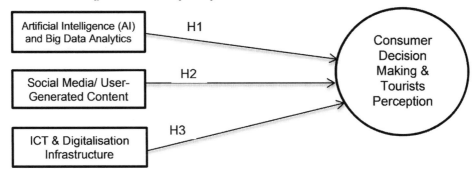

The Model I shown in Figure 6 lays the foundation for examining how the adoption of various technologies affects consumer decision-making and perception in the given context.

Figure 7. Proposed model II on technology integration effect on consumer decision-making and tourists' perception

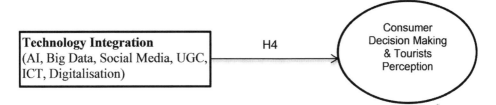

The proposed Model II in Figure 7 shows the combined effect of technology which includes AI, Big Data, Social Media, User-generated Content (UGC), Information technology and Digitalisation Infrastructure on Consumer decision making and their perception in tourism sector. Therefore, the suggested framework (refer Figure 6 and 7) summarises the association of variables using 4 hypotheses described in the study.

2.2 Hypothesis Development

2.2.1 AI and Big Data Analytics in Tourism Decision-Making

AI is an area that automates intelligent behavior. We can witness this behavior in all domains. K.R. Chowdhary gave a simple definition of intelligence in his book Fundamentals of Artificial Intelligence as, Perceive + Analyze + React (Chowdhary, 2020).

Studies show that AI-powered algorithms boost consumer happiness, optimize resource allocation, and make trip planning more efficient. Machine Learning (ML) is a technique of "learning" from experience (data) by identifying patterns in the data. According to Tom Mitchell machine learning is *"a computer program is said to learn from experience E with respect to some class of tasks T and performance measure P if its performance at tasks in T, as measured by P, improves with experience E"* (Mitchell, 1997). The COVID-19 pandemic has heightened the demand for social distancing, making AI devices valuable alternatives for human interaction, particularly in sectors like travel and tourism. (Chi et al., 2022)

Machine Learning (ML) algorithms, leveraging vast data sets, are powerful tools in pattern recognition and big data analysis. They have been applied in activity-travel behavior studies since the early '90s, initially with Artificial Neural Networks (ANN) used to model mode choice decisions (Koushik et al., 2020). In the tourism sector, personalized services are increasingly necessary due to diverse traveler preferences. Integrating big data and technologies is crucial for studying visitor preferences effectively (Pei & Zhang, 2021). Understanding travel decision-making is vital for enhancing transportation systems. Activity-based travel behaviour modelling, a significant aspect of transportation research, utilizes econometric and computational methods to delve into how people choose travel activities, aiding in developing more efficient transportation solutions. (Koushik et al., 2020) These systems, also known as intelligent travel agents or smart concierges, anticipate user needs and offer personalized recommendations automatically or on demand, enhancing the travel experience (Bulchand-Gidumal, 2020). Big data technology in tourism enhances resource utilization, fosters economic and social benefits, and promotes tourism development. (Chen, 2020). Big data revolutionizes the tourism industry by providing data-driven, real-time insights into traveler actions and behavior, improving decision-making processes. Its vast information availability enables swift adjustments to evolving passenger demands throughout the journey. Big data's predictive capabilities offer new avenues for increasing prospects, overall efficiency, and policymaking within the travel and tourism sector. (Padmaja et al., 2020)

The Internet of Things (IoT) is revolutionizing the tourism industry, leading to the emergence of "smart tourism." By integrating big data, blockchain, cloud computing, mobile communication, and artificial intelligence, IoT enhances the traveler experience. It has begun to influence customer satisfaction, reduce costs, and drive corporate profitability within this dynamic industry landscape (Verma et al., 2021).

Countries all around the world are using big data applications to study tourist flows and find substantial development prospects by using data created directly by passengers. As a result, big data is set to be extremely important in the future for both expanding economic sectors and social progress. (Padmaja et al., 2020)

H_1: AI & Big Data technologies have a significant impact on consumer decision-making.

2.2.2 Social Media/User-Generated Content in Tourism Decision-Making

Social media now has a big impact on tourism, influencing both pre- and post-trip planning and sharing. Travellers use social media to plan their schedule, get information, and get advice from reliable sources before leaving on a trip. (Oliveira et al., 2020)

Travellers often share their memorable travel experiences on social networking apps via mobile devices. This sharing behavior not only serves as a form of expression but also has the potential to inspire future trips among other travellers. Governments of tourist regions may create and enhance tourism goods and promote cultural sensitivity by learning what kinds of memorable tourism experiences encourage travellers to share via mobile social media while traveling (Wong et al, 2019).

Social media has transformed how tourists access and evaluate information about tourist products and destinations (Tsai et al., 2020). The concept of the use of social media from the consumer's perspective entails a focus on how consumers employ social media as a multifaceted communication tool for gathering information, sharing experiences, and evaluating travel organizations and destinations both before and after their trips (Chu et al., 2020). Travel vlogs also enhance a location's appeal and authenticity, shaping viewers' perceptions and sparking interest in visiting. With the rise of online video content, particularly travel vlogs, travellers seek real-life experiences and valuable insights before embarking on journeys, influencing their decisions and expectations significantly. (Abad & Borbon, 2021)

Social media has an influence on more than just trip planning; once a traveler has completed a journey, they may decide to share their experiences, which can impact other people's decisions to travel. Social media's dual function in the tourism industry highlights how crucial it is in influencing tourist behavior and location selections

(Oliveira et al., 2020). Influencers are becoming key players in modern marketing, acting as an extension of traditional word-of-mouth campaigns. Influencers affect consumers by raising brand awareness, showcasing expertise, building brand preference, and influencing purchase decisions. Effective influencer marketing hinges on selecting influencers who can provide tailored content to engage their audience effectively. (Chopra et al., 2020)

Travellers now easily share their experiences through text, photos, and real-time videos on social platforms, facilitating word-of-mouth communication (WOM). Both positive and negative e-WOM can influence consumer perceptions and decisions (Tsai et al., 2020). The usage of online user-generated content platforms can influence travelers' perceptions of destinations (Lam et al., 2020). Based on the given literature the following hypotheses are formulated:

H_2: Social Media User-Generated Content significantly shape impact on tourists' decision-making.

2.2.3 ICT & Digitalization Infrastructure in Tourism Decision-Making

Information and Communication Technologies (ICT) are integral to contemporary consumer cultures, offering diverse affordances like appraisal, planning, and socializing. Their widespread adoption has reshaped how consumers find information, make purchases, and engage with content. ICTs are particularly relevant in tourism, driven by the platform economy, offering numerous applications for travellers to navigate their experiences efficiently (Gössling, 2021). Destination platforms are vital for showcasing the brand and creating online experiences that attract potential tourists (Jiménez-Barreto et al., 2020). Before technological advancements that made it possible to book travel and tourism services online, the industry was dominated by travel agents, and making travel and tourism plans was extremely challenging for everyone else (Pillai & Sivathanu, 2020). The growth of tourism-related consumption in real-world and virtual environments has prompted the creation of new conceptual frameworks to explain how information and communication technologies (ICTs) are used in the tourism experience (Magasic et al., 2020).

GPS technology has greatly advanced mobility data collection, providing extensive spatio-temporal information about people's whereabouts and activities. This has revolutionized travel by offering real-time location details, enhancing safety, convenience, and exploration experiences for travellers globally (Nguyen et al., 2020). The evolution of technology in tourism can be seen in four stages: Opportunity (1985-1995) focused on connectivity and efficiency, Disruption (1996–2006) brought about online platforms and competition, Immersion (2007-2015) saw widespread smartphone use and data collection, and Usurpation (2016-2020, ongoing) signifies the dominance of global platforms in shaping consumer behaviour and preferences through real-time data analysis. (Gössling, 2021)

Websites and social media platforms may provide immersive and customized experiences with algorithmic and location-based services thanks to faster data transport (Magasic et al., 2020). Virtual Reality (VR) tourism, especially in the context of COVID-19 restrictions, offers significant advantages. With travel limitations due to lockdowns, VR technology provides an immersive experience without the need for physical travel, benefiting those unable to travel easily. It breaks the distance barrier by offering destination insights before travel decisions are made, revolutionizing the tourism experience (Lee & Kim, 2021).The tourism sector is undergoing digital transformations termed Tourism 4.0, aligning with Industry 4.0's technological advancements. Digitalization has profoundly changed travel behaviors, turning traditional tourists into digital travelers and smart tourists. This shift is driven by the digitalization of processes within the tourism value system, enabling real-time offers and bookings tailored to diverse tourist segments through websites and apps (Pencarelli, 2019). Based on the given information the following hypothesis is formulated:

> H3: ICT & Digitalization Infrastructure significantly contribute to positive perceptions among tourists.

2.2.4 Integration of All Technology and its Effect on Consumer Perception and Consumer Decision Making:

Tourism 4.0 technologies offer powerful capabilities that enhance interaction with systems and enrich the tourist experience, facilitating behavior change and long-term transformation. Prioritizing user experience is essential to designing technology that meets tourists' needs and preferences, creating engaging and enjoyable experiences that align with their goals (Stankov & Gretzel, 2020). The tourism industry is undergoing a transformative shift, driven by technological advancements that promise a brighter future amidst challenges like the COVID-19 pandemic. Recent progress in digital technologies has simplified destination exploration for users, prompting thorough research into their implications within the tourism sector. With digital tourism transcending borders and fostering international collaboration, it represents a promising avenue for industry growth and adaptation to the evolving landscape (Akhtar et al., 2021). The intangible aspects of travel make information search crucial for decision-making. Studying travel information search is vital for effective tourism marketing and management, considering the ongoing search for information during journeys and the challenge of comparing experiences. Modern technology enhances this process, making it more enjoyable, motivating, and personalized to individual preferences, leading to better decisions by travelers. (Xiang & Fesenmaier, 2022)

Based on the given information the following hypothesis is formulated:

H_4: There is a significant positive relationship between technology integration (combined effect of AI & Big Data, Social Media & User-Generated Content, and ICT & Digitalization Infrastructure) and Consumer Decision-Making and their Perception in travel planning.

3. RESEARCH DESIGN

The primary objectives of this study revolve around analysing the depth of technological integration within the tourism sector, specifically focusing on key components such as artificial intelligence (AI), social media platforms, big data analytics, and information and communication technology (ICT) infrastructure. Firstly, the study aims to meticulously examine how these technologies are integrated into various aspects of the tourism industry.

Secondly, it seeks to delve into the impact of this technological integration on the decision-making processes within tourism operations, elucidating how it influences strategic planning, resource allocation, and customer engagement. Lastly, the study endeavors to evaluate the overall effectiveness and efficiency of tourist services in the era of Tourism 4.0, emphasizing the role played by technology in enhancing customer experiences, streamlining operations, and driving innovation within the tourism landscape. Through these objectives, the study aims to provide valuable insights into the transformative potential of technology in shaping the future of the tourism industry. In this research, data collection relies on surveys administered to people who travel, gathering a comprehensive dataset enriched with demographic information and 5 pointer- Likert-scale responses. This includes responses from 'Strongly Disagree,' 'Disagree,' 'Neutral,' 'Agree' and 'Strongly Agree.' The structured survey design ensures that various perspectives are captured, offering a holistic understanding of the subject matter. Participants are selected based on their level of travel engagement, ensuring that the sample represents a diverse range of experiences and viewpoints. By employing this approach, the research aims to gather robust and representative data that can offer valuable insights into the dynamics of technology integration within the tourism sector. The questionnaire included 28 questions out of which 4 were about personal information and 8 were demography related. It was further divided into 4 constructs like AI & Big Data Analytics in Personalization, Social Media and User Generated Content, and ICT and Digitalization Infrastructure, and dependent variable, consumer decision-making and perception due to the impact of technology integration in Travel. Each of these items included 4 items.

For this research study, a total of 400 survey forms were distributed to individuals involved in the travel, aiming to understand the influence of technology integration on consumer decision-making and tourists' perceptions. Out of the distributed forms, 212 valid responses were received, resulting in a response rate of approximately 53%. This response rate signifies a significant engagement from the target population, providing a substantial dataset for analysis and offering valuable insights into the research questions and objectives.

Multiple regression analysis through SPSS 20 was used to find significant predictors, evaluate the overall model fit, and quantify the contribution of each independent variable (AI & Big Data, Social Media & UGC, ICT & Digitalization Infrastructure) to the dependent variables (consumer decision-making, tourists' perceptions).

4. RESEARCH METHODS, DATA ANALYSIS

The survey composed of demographic data such as age, gender, income level, educational background, employment status, travel frequency, and use of social media. These demographic factors are important as they can influence individuals' attitudes, preferences, and behaviors related to technology use in the travel context. (Ching-Fu et al., 2009). Data was collected from the sample size of 212 individuals (Table 3). Participants were selected based on their level of travel engagement, ensuring a varied mix of frequent travellers, occasional travellers, and different travel preferences (e.g., solo travellers, family travellers, group travellers). This approach helps in capturing diverse perspectives and experiences regarding technology integration in different travel scenarios. The sample includes participants from different age groups (e.g., Millennial, Gen X, Baby Boomers) to understand how generational differences may influence attitudes towards technology in travel. Using a convenience sample in this research the study offers practical advantages given the challenges associated with accessing the target population of travellers. Convenience sampling allows for the efficient collection of data from individuals who are readily available and willing to participate in the study. This approach is particularly useful when time and resources are limited, as it reduces the logistical complexities of recruiting participants from a diverse range of backgrounds and travel experiences.

Table 2. Demographic information

Demographic Data	N	%
Age		
· Under 18 years	4	1.89
· 18-24 years old	54	25.47
· 25-34 years old	114	53.77
· 35-44 years old	20	9.43
· 45-54 years old	12	5.66
· 55 or over	8	3.77
Gender		
· Male	112	52.83
· Female	100	47.17
· Other	0	0
Educational Background		
· Less than high school	2	0.94
· High school	12	5.66
· Intermediate	14	6.6
· Graduate	68	32.08
· Post Graduate	108	50.94
· Doctoral degree or higher	8	3.77
Employment Status		
· Freelancer	14	6.6
· Employed Full-Time	114	53.77
· Employed Part-Time	4	1.89
· Unemployed	22	10.38
· Student	56	26.42
· Retired	2	0.94
Travelling frequently		
· Never		
· Rarely (once a year or less)	44	20.75
· Occasionally (2-4 times a year)	118	55.66
· Frequently (5-9 times a year)	32	15.09
· Very frequently (10 times or more a year)	18	8.49
Social media Use		
· Yes	202	95.28
· No	10	4.72

continued on following page

Table 2. Continued

Demographic Data	N	%
Type of booking done for travel accommodations		
· Through online travel agencies (e.g., MakeMyTrip, Booking.com)	150	70.75
· Directly through the accommodation's website	44	20.75
· Through a travel agent	8	3.77
· Other	10	4.72
Type of research done for travel destinations and activities		
· Online search engines (e.g., Google, Bing)	146	68.86
· Social media platforms (e.g., Instagram, Facebook)	110	51.89
· Travel review websites (e.g., TripAdvisor, Yelp)	66	31.13
· Travel guidebooks	12	5.66
· Recommendations from friends/family	88	41.51
· Other	8	3.77
Type of travel engaged in		
· Leisure/vacation	158	74.53
· Business	30	14.15
· Adventure/exploration	98	46.23
· Cultural/heritage tourism	60	28.30
· Ecotourism/nature-based travel	40	18.87
· Wellness/spa retreats	12	5.66
· Volunteer/mission trips	4	1.89

4.1 Model Reliability and Validity

Pilot testing was used in this study to see whether the questionnaire design was effective and to find any potential problems or ambiguities in the survey items. For the pilot test, a small sample of individuals who matched the target demographic that is, travellers were chosen. In the preliminary testing stage, respondents were requested to finish the questionnaire and offer their opinions on the survey's overall experience, question relevancy, and clarity. This input was helpful in improving the survey instrument's readability and ensuring that the desired constructs were correctly captured. In this research, face validity is ensured through pilot testing to confirm that survey questions align with research objectives, while reliability is assessed using measures like Cronbach's alpha to ensure consistent and dependable results, enhancing the overall quality and trustworthiness of the data collected. The degree to which a measurement tool yields trustworthy and consistent data throughout time and under various situations is referred to as reliability. Cronbach's alpha (α) is a commonly used statistical indicator of internal consistency reliability (Taber, 2017). It measures the degree of correlation between items on a scale or a group of similar items.

Table 3. Reliability statistics

Cronbach's Alpha (α)	0.656
N Number of items	3

The scale or construct being tested in this research study has a Cronbach's alpha coefficient of 0.656 (Table 3). It implies that there is some correlation between the items on the scale, but that in order to improve the scale's dependability, more improvement or the addition of new items may be beneficial.

4.2. Data Analysis

Multiple regression analysis was used as statistical tool for examining the relationships between multiple independent variables and a dependent variable, such as consumer decision-making and tourists' perceptions in response to technology integration in the travel industry. This approach allows researchers to quantify the impact of each independent variable while controlling for other factors, providing insights into the relative importance of different technological aspects (Williams et al., 2013).

Table 4 depicts association between AI and Big Data Integration in Consumer Decision making and their perception in Travel and the p-value as 0.1% (<0.001) and the level of significance is 5% (Table 4). The p-value is less than the level of significance. The mean was found to be 14.87, and the standard deviation is 2.365. There's a Pearson correlation coefficient of 0.349 between Consumer Decision making and AI_BigData, indicating a positive correlation. The correlation is statistically significant ($p < 0.001$). The ANOVA table shows that the regression model is statistically significant ($p < 0.001$), indicating that there is a significant relationship between tourist decision-making and AI_BigData.

The regression equation is: ConsumerDM_Perception = 11.816 + 0.265 * AI_BigData

Table 4. Analysing the association between AI and Big Data Integration in consumer decision making and their perception in travel

Descriptive Statistics				
	Mean	Std. Deviation	N	
ConsumerDM_Perception	14.87	2.365	212	
AI_BigData	11.54	3.119	212	
Correlations				
			ConsumerDM_Perception	AI_BigData
Pearson Correlation	ConsumerDM_Perception		1.000	.349
	AI_BigData		.349	1.000
Sig. (1-tailed)	ConsumerDM_Perception		.	<.001
	AI_BigData		.000	.
N	ConsumerDM_Perception		212	212
	AI_BigData		212	212

ANOVA[a]						
Model		Sum of Squares	df	Mean Square	F	Sig.
1	Regression	143.670	1	143.670	29.104	<.001[b]
	Residual	1036.632	210	4.936		
	Total	1180.302	211			

a. Dependent Variable: ConsumerDM_Perception

b. Predictors: (Constant), AI_BigData

Coefficients[a]						
		Unstandardized Coefficients		Standardized Coefficients		
Model		B	Std. Error	Beta	t	Sig.
1	(Constant)	11.816	.586		20.163	<.001
	AI_BigData	.265	.049	.349	5.395	<.001

Coefficients[a]			
		95.0% Confidence Interval for B	
Model		Lower Bound	Upper Bound
1	(Constant)	10.660	12.971
	AI_BigData	.168	.361

a. Dependent Variable: ConsumerDM_Perception

Figure 8. Scatter diagram between AI and big data integration and consumer decision making and perception

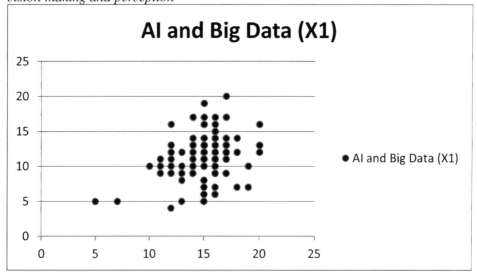

This equation suggests that for every one-unit increase in AI_BigData, Consumer decision making is expected to increase by 0.265 units. Both the constant term and the coefficient for AI_BigData are statistically significant ($p < 0.001$). The analysis indicates a positive and statistically significant relationship between Consumer decision-making and AI_Big Data, suggesting that as AI and Big Data increase, consumer perception of digital marketing in tourism industry (Figure8). Therefore, we accept the proposed hypothesis 1 (H_1) that AI & Big Data technologies significantly influence consumer decision-making in the travel industry.

The mean of consumer decision-making and Perception score is 14.87 with a standard deviation of 2.365, based on 212 observations. The mean SocialMedia_UGC (User-Generated Content) score is 12.92 with a standard deviation of 2.809, also based on 212 observations. There's a strong positive Pearson correlation coefficient of 0.578 between Consumer decision-making and Perception and SocialMedia_UGC. This correlation is statistically significant ($p < 0.001$), indicating a meaningful relationship between consumer perception of digital marketing and engagement with user-generated content on social media.

The ANOVA table suggests that the regression model is highly statistically significant ($p < 0.001$), indicating that there's a significant relationship between Consumer decision making and Social Media, UGC.

The regression equation is:

ConsumerDM_Perception = 8.586 + 0.486 * SocialMedia_UGC.

Both the constant term and the coefficient for SocialMedia_UGC are statistically significant (p < 0.001). In summary, the analysis indicates a strong positive relationship between Consume decision making and SocialMedia_UGC. Higher engagement with user-generated content on social media platforms is associated with more positive consumer perceptions of digital marketing.

4.2.1 Analysing The Association Between Social Media And User-Generated Content Integration In Consumer Decision Making And Their Perception in Travel

Table 5a. Descriptive statistics

	Mean	Std. Deviation	N
ConsumerDM_Perception	14.87	2.365	212
SocialMedia_UGC	12.92	2.809	212

Table 5b. Correlations

		ConsumerDM_Perception	SocialMedia_UGC
Pearson Correlation	ConsumerDM_Perception	1.000	.578
	SocialMedia_UGC	.578	1.000
Sig. (1-tailed)	ConsumerDM_Perception	.	<.001
	SocialMedia_UGC	.000	.
N	ConsumerDM_Perception	212	212
	SocialMedia_UGC	212	212

Table 5c. ANOVA[a]

Model		Sum of Squares	df	Mean Square	F	Sig.
1	Regression	393.812	1	393.812	105.151	<.001[b]
	Residual	786.490	210	3.745		
	Total	1180.302	211			

a. Dependent Variable: ConsumerDM_Perception
b. Predictors: (Constant), SocialMedia_UGC

Table 5d. Coefficients[a]

Model		Unstandardized Coefficients		Standardized Coefficients	t	Sig.
		B	Std. Error	Beta		
1	(Constant)	8.586	.627		13.696	<.001
	SocialMedia_UGC	.486	.047	.578	10.254	<.001

Table 5e. Coefficients[a]

Model		95.0% Confidence Interval for B	
		Lower Bound	Upper Bound
1	(Constant)	7.350	9.822
	SocialMedia_UGC	.393	.580

Figure 9. Scatter diagram between social media and UGC integration and consumer decision making and perception

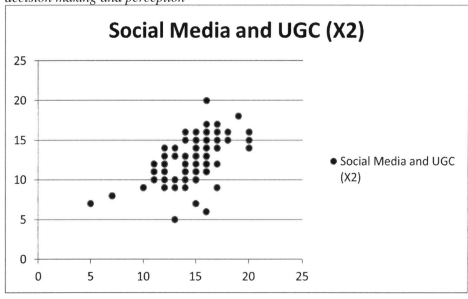

The p-value is 0.1% (<0.001) at significance level of 5% (Table 5). The p-value is less than the level of significance. Therefore, we accept the Hypothesis 2 that social media and user-generated content significantly influence consumer decision-making in the travel industry. There is a positive relationship between the variables social media and user-generated content integration in travel and consumer decision-making in the travel industry (Figure 9).

The association between ICT and Digitalization Integration in Consumer Decision making and their perception in Travel was analysed through correlation. The finding shows a strong positive Pearson correlation coefficient of 0.719 between Consumer Decision making and Perception and ICT and Digitalization. This correlation is statistically significant ($p < 0.001$), indicating a robust and meaningful relationship between consumer perception of digital marketing and their interaction with ICT in digital platforms. The ANOVA table 7 suggests that the regression model is highly statistically significant ($p < 0.001$), indicating that there's a significant relationship between between Consumer Decision making and Perception and ICT and Digitalization.

The regression equation is:

ConsumerDM_Perception = 4.200 + 0.689 * ICT_Digital

This equation suggests that for every one-unit increase in ICT consumer between Consumer Decision making is expected to increase by 0.689 units. Both the constant term and the coefficient for ICT_Digital are statistically significant ($p < 0.001$). In summary, the analysis indicates a strong positive relationship between ConsumerDM_Perception and ICT_Digital. Higher engagement with information and communication technology in digital platforms is associated with more positive consumer perceptions of use of digitialisation in tourism industry.

4.2.2 Analysing the association between ICT and Digitalization Integration in Consumer Decision making and their perception in Travel

Table 6a. Correlations

		ConsumerDM_Perception	ICT_Digital
Pearson Correlation	ConsumerDM_Perception	1.000	.719
	ICT_Digital	.719	1.000
Sig. (1-tailed)	ConsumerDM_Perception	.	<.001
	ICT_Digital	.000	.
N	ConsumerDM_Perception	212	212
	ICT_Digital	212	212

Table 6b. ANOVA[a]

Model		Sum of Squares	df	Mean Square	F	Sig.
1	Regression	610.199	1	610.199	224.770	<.001[b]
	Residual	570.103	210	2.715		
	Total	1180.302	211			

a. Dependent Variable: ConsumerDM_Perception
b. Predictors: (Constant), ICT_Digital

Table 6c. Coefficients[a]

Model		Unstandardized Coefficients		Standardized Coefficients	t	Sig.
		B	Std. Error	Beta		
1	(Constant)	4.200	.721		5.828	<.001
	ICT_Digital	.689	.046	.719	14.992	<.001

Table 6d. Coefficients[a]

Model		95.0% Confidence Interval for B	
		Lower Bound	Upper Bound
1	(Constant)	2.779	5.620
	ICT_Digital	.599	.780

a. Dependent Variable: ConsumerDM_Perception

Figure 10. Scatter diagram between ICT and digitalization integration and consumer decision making and perception

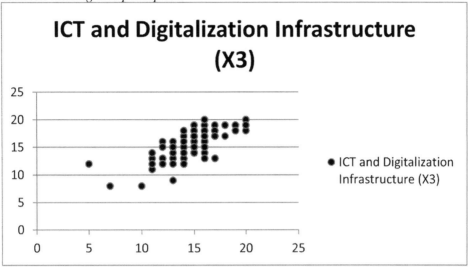

The p-value is 0.1% (<0.001) and the level of significance is 5% (Table 7). The p-value is less than the level of significance. Therefore, we accept hypothesis 3 that ICT & Digitalization Infrastructure have substantial impact on tourists' perceptions of convenience and modernity in the travel industry. There is a positive relationship between the variables ICT & Digitalization Infrastructure integration in travel and consumer decision-making in the travel industry (Figure 10).

The ANOVA results indicate that the regression model is highly statistically significant (p < 0.001), suggesting a significant relationship between Consumer Decision Making and all other variable of Technology Integration.

The p-value is 0.1% (<0.001) and the level of significance is 5% (Table 4). The p-value is less than the level of significance. Therefore, we accept Hypothesis 4 there is significant relationship between technology integration (combined effect of AI & Big Data, Social Media & User-Generated Content, and ICT & Digitalization Infrastructure) and Consumer Decision-Making and their Perception in travel planning (Figure 11). (Dahiru, 2011). Thus, accept the hypothesis 4 stating that there is positive relationship between the variables. Higher levels of technological integration are associated with more positive consumer perceptions of digital marketing.

4.2.3 Analysing the association between Technology Integration (combined effect of AI & Big Data, Social Media & User-Generated Content, and ICT & Digitalization Infrastructure) in Consumer Decision making and their perception in Travel

Table 7a. Correlations

		ConsumerDM_Perception	TechIntegration
Pearson Correlation	ConsumerDM_Perception	1.000	.691
	TechIntegration	.691	1.000
Sig. (1-tailed)	ConsumerDM_Perception	.	<.001
	TechIntegration	.000	.
N	ConsumerDM_Perception	212	212
	TechIntegration	212	212

Table 7b. ANOVA[a]

Model		Sum of Squares	df	Mean Square	F	Sig.
1	Regression	563.537	1	563.537	191.876	<.001[b]
	Residual	616.765	210	2.937		
	Total	1180.302	211			

a. Dependent Variable: ConsumerDM_Perception
b. Predictors: (Constant), TechIntegration

Table 7c. Coefficients[a]

Model		Unstandardized Coefficients		Standardized Coefficients	t	Sig.
		B	Std. Error	Beta		
1	(Constant)	4.813	.735		6.545	<.001
	TechIntegration	.252	.018	.691	13.852	<.001

Table 7d. Coefficients[a]

Model		95.0% Confidence Interval for B	
		Lower Bound	Upper Bound
1	(Constant)	3.363	6.263
	TechIntegration	.216	.288

a. Dependent Variable: ConsumerDM_Perception

Figure 11. Scatter diagram between technology integration and consumer decision making and perception

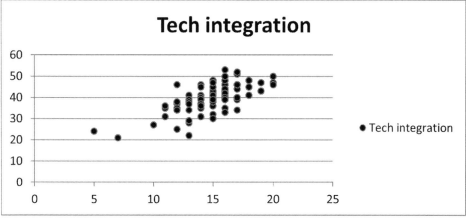

5. DISCUSSION

Figure 12. Scatter diagram between technology integration including AI & big data, social media & UGC and ICT & digitalisation infrastructure separately and consumer decision making and perception

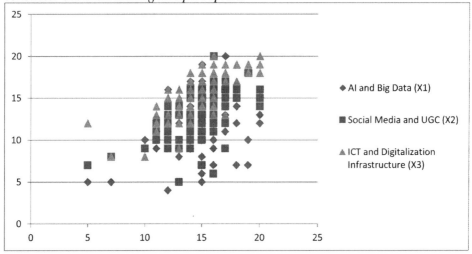

The analysis reveals compelling evidence to accept hypotheses for all four hypotheses tested. The p-values being less than the set significance level of 5% (<0.001) indicate a significant relationship between technology integration (AI & Big Data, Social Media & User-Generated Content, ICT & Digitalization Infrastructure) (Figure 12), and both consumer decision-making and tourists' perceptions in travel planning. Specifically, the alternate hypotheses are supported, indicating a positive relationship between these variables. This underscores the crucial role of advanced technologies in shaping consumer behaviors and perceptions within the travel industry, emphasizing the need for continued integration and strategic utilization of technology to enhance the overall travel experience and meet evolving customer expectations.

6. IMPLICATIONS AND RECOMMENDATIONS

This study investigates how consumer decision-making and visitors' impressions in the modern travel environment are affected by the significant effects of technology integration, including AI & Big Data, social media & user-generated content, and ICT & digitalization infrastructure. It makes use of multiple regression analysis to determine the relationships between these technology parameters and key travel industry outcomes.

The research contributes to theoretical knowledge by showing how technology integration significantly affects customer perceptions and decision-making in the travel sector. It adds to the collection of knowledge and encourages more research into the ways that technology is changing the travel industry. The findings help industry practitioners strategically use cutting-edge technologies like artificial intelligence (AI), big data, social media, and digital infrastructure to enhance consumer experiences, customize services, and make wise decisions. This may result in more innovation and competition in the travel industry.

The study emphasizes the benefits of technological integration in travel from a social perspective, such as enhanced convenience, sustainability, and economic expansion. It highlights how technology promotes connectedness, digital inclusion, and general well-being for tourists and industry participants. To enhance travel experiences and decision-making, industry stakeholders must integrate AI & Big Data, social media, and ICT infrastructure effectively. This requires continuous innovation, data-driven insights, and digital skills training. Collaborations with tech providers, user-centric design, and ethical data practices are crucial for building trust and competitiveness in the digital travel landscape.

7. CONCLUSION

The study concludes by highlighting the important influence of technology integration on consumer decision-making and travelers' impressions in the travel sector. This integration includes AI & Big Data, social media & user-generated content, and ICT & digitalization infrastructure. The significant correlations and regression results highlight the need to use advanced technology to improve customer experiences, personalize services, and drive innovation. These insights not only advance theoretical understanding but also provide industry practitioners with useful advice on how to strategically manage the rapidly changing digital ecosystem and efficiently cater to the shifting demands of contemporary visitors. To ensure sustainable development in the digital era and shape the future of the travel industry, it will be imperative to embrace continual innovation, data-driven initiatives, and ethical standards.

8. LIMITATIONS

The limited generalizability of the findings could result from the sample size and demographic representation, which may not adequately account for the wide variety of traveler opinions and actions. The use of convenience sampling in data gathering may introduce selection bias, since participants may not reflect the whole travel population. This could make it more difficult to extrapolate the findings to larger traveler segments.

Furthermore, the study may have missed additional important factors that might have an impact on customer perceptions and decision-making in the travel sector due to its concentration on certain technological integration components including social media, AI & Big Data, and ICT infrastructure.

The study did not account for external factors like economic upheavals, geopolitical developments, or cultural changes, which might have an independent impact on consumer behavior and views even in the absence of technological integration.

These limitations highlight the need for future research to use more rigorous sample methods, explore a broader range of technical characteristics, add objective measurements when appropriate, and account for external variables to improve the robustness and validity of the findings.

9. FUTURE SCOPE

There is a great deal of potential and possibility for future study in the area of technology integration and its effects on the tourism industry. Key areas of investigation include cross-cultural perspectives to understand global variations, longitudinal studies to track evolving trends, in-depth analyses of particular technologies like AI, Big Data, social media, and digital infrastructure, and studies into emerging technologies like VR, AR, and blockchain.

Furthermore, there is room to investigate ethical and sustainable issues, look at cooperative initiatives, and evaluate how technology may support resilient and responsible tourist activities. Future research may greatly improve consumer experiences, stimulate innovation, and influence the direction of the travel industry going forward on a worldwide basis by tackling these issues.

REFERENCES

Abad, P. E. S., & Borbon, N. M. D. (2021, October 1). Influence of travel vlog: Inputs for destination marketing model. *International Journal of Research Studies in Management*, *9*(3). Advance online publication. DOI: 10.5861/ijrsm.2021.m7729

Abdurakhmanova, G. K., Astanakulov, O. T., Goyipnazarov, S. B., & Irmatova, A. B. (2022, December 15). Tourism 4.0: Opportunities For Applying Industry 4.0 Technologies In Tourism. *Proceedings of the 6th International Conference on Future Networks & Distributed Systems.* DOI: 10.1145/3584202.3584208

Akhtar, N., Khan, N., Mahroof Khan, M., Ashraf, S., Hashmi, M. S., Khan, M. M., & Hishan, S. S. (2021, May 11). Post-COVID 19 Tourism: Will Digital Tourism Replace Mass Tourism? *Sustainability (Basel)*, *13*(10), 5352. DOI: 10.3390/su13105352

Android | Ministry of Tourism | Government of India. (n.d.). https://tourism.gov.in/important-links-latest-program-application-download/android

Appel, G., Grewal, L., Hadi, R., & Stephen, A. T. (2019, October 12). The future of social media in marketing. *Journal of the Academy of Marketing Science*, *48*(1), 79–95. DOI: 10.1007/s11747-019-00695-1 PMID: 32431463

Bilotta, E., Bertacchini, F., Gabriele, L., Giglio, S., Pantano, P. S., & Romita, T. (2021, November). Industry 4.0 technologies in tourism education: Nurturing students to think with technology. *Journal of Hospitality, Leisure, Sport and Tourism Education*, *29*, 100275. DOI: 10.1016/j.jhlste.2020.100275

Buhalis, D., & Amaranggana, A. (2014, December 27). Smart Tourism Destinations Enhancing Tourism Experience Through Personalisation of Services. *Information and Communication Technologies in Tourism*, *2015*, 377–389. DOI: 10.1007/978-3-319-14343-9_28

Bulchand-Gidumal, J. (2020). Impact of Artificial Intelligence in Travel, Tourism, and Hospitality. *Handbook of e-Tourism, 1–20.*https://doi.org/DOI: 10.1007/978-3-030-05324-6_110-1

Chen, N. (2020). Application of big data technology in smart Tourism. *Journal of Physics: Conference Series*, *1648*(4), 042101. Advance online publication. DOI: 10.1088/1742-6596/1648/4/042101

Chi, O. H., Gursoy, D., & Chi, C. G. (2022). Tourists' Attitudes toward the Use of Artificially Intelligent (AI) Devices in Tourism Service Delivery: Moderating Role of Service Value Seeking. *Journal of Travel Research*, *61*(1), 170–185. DOI: 10.1177/0047287520971054

Ching-Fu, C., & Wu, C. C. (2009). How motivations, constraints, and demographic factors predict seniors' overseas travel propensity. *Asia Pacific Management Review, 14*(3).

Chopra, A., Avhad, V., & Jaju, A. S. (2020, June 15). Influencer Marketing: An Exploratory Study to Identify Antecedents of Consumer Behavior of Millennial. *Business Perspectives and Research, 9*(1), 77–91. DOI: 10.1177/2278533720923486

Chowdhary, K. (2020, April 4). Fundamentals of Artificial Intelligence. *Springer Nature.* http://books.google.ie/books?id=8SfbDwAAQBAJ&printsec=frontcover&dq=Fundamentals+of+Artificial+Intelligence&hl=&cd=1&source=gbs_api

Chu, S. C., Deng, T., & Cheng, H. (2020, September 24). The role of social media advertising in hospitality, tourism and travel: A literature review and research agenda. *International Journal of Contemporary Hospitality Management, 32*(11), 3419–3438. DOI: 10.1108/IJCHM-05-2020-0480

Cynthia, M., Ingrid, P., & Alicia, Y. (2021). *Digitization trends in hospitality and tourism.* Smart Tourism., DOI: 10.54517/st.v2i2.1709

Dahiru, T. (2011, March 3). P-Value, a true test of statistical significance? a cautionary note. *Annals of Ibadan Postgraduate Medicine, 6*(1). Advance online publication. DOI: 10.4314/aipm.v6i1.64038 PMID: 25161440

De las Heras-Pedrosa, C., Millán-Celis, E., Iglesias-Sánchez, P. P., & Jambrino-Maldonado, C. (2020). Importance of Social Media in the Image Formation of Tourist Destinations from the Stakeholders' Perspective. *Sustainability (Basel), 12*(10), 4092. DOI: 10.3390/su12104092

Glossary of tourism terms | UNWTO. (n.d.). https://www.unwto.org/glossary-tourism-terms (Accessed: March 13, 2024)

Gössling, S. (2021, January 20). Tourism, technology and ICT: A critical review of affordances and concessions. *Journal of Sustainable Tourism, 29*(5), 733–750. DOI: 10.1080/09669582.2021.1873353

Gretzel, U., Sigala, M., Xiang, Z., & Koo, C. (2015, August 1). Smart tourism: Foundations and developments. *Electronic Markets, 25*(3), 179–188. DOI: 10.1007/s12525-015-0196-8

Hamid, R. A., Albahri, A., Alwan, J. K., Al-qaysi, Z., Albahri, O., Zaidan, A., Alnoor, A., Alamoodi, A., & Zaidan, B. (2021, February). How smart is e-tourism? A systematic review of smart tourism recommendation system applying data management. *Computer Science Review, 39*, 100337. DOI: 10.1016/j.cosrev.2020.100337

Hospitality Sector, Tourism In India | IBEF. India Brand Equity Foundation. https://www.ibef.org/industry/tourism-hospitality-india

International Tourism to Reach Pre-Pandemic Levels in 2024 https://www.unwto.org/news/international-tourism-to-reach-pre-pandemic-levels-in-2024#:~:text=International%20tourism%20hit%20US%241.4,earned%20by%20destinations%20in%202019. (Accessed: March 13, 2024)

Jeong, M., & Shin, H. H. (2019, November 8). Tourists' Experiences with Smart Tourism Technology at Smart Destinations and Their Behavior Intentions. *Journal of Travel Research*, *59*(8), 1464–1477. DOI: 10.1177/0047287519883034

Jiménez-Barreto, J., Rubio, N., Campo, S., & Molinillo, S. (2020, August). Linking the online destination brand experience and brand credibility with tourists' behavioral intentions toward a destination. *Tourism Management*, *79*, 104101. DOI: 10.1016/j.tourman.2020.104101

Kaplan, A. M., & Haenlein, M. (2010). Users of the world, unite! The challenges and opportunities of Social Media. *Business Horizons*, *53*(1), 59–68. DOI: 10.1016/j.bushor.2009.09.003

Kazak, A., Chetyrbok, P. V., & Oleinikov, N. N. (2020). Artificial intelligence in the tourism sphere. *IOP Conference Series. Earth and Environmental Science*, *421*(4), 042020. Advance online publication. DOI: 10.1088/1755-1315/421/4/042020

Koushik, A. N., Manoj, M., & Nezamuddin, N. (2020, January 7). Machine learning applications in activity-travel behaviour research: A review. *Transport Reviews*, *40*(3), 288–311. DOI: 10.1080/01441647.2019.1704307

Lam, J. M. S., Ismail, H., & Lee, S. (2020). From desktop to destination: User-generated content platforms, co-created online experiences, destination image and satisfaction. *Journal of Destination Marketing & Management*, *18*, 100490. DOI: 10.1016/j.jdmm.2020.100490

Lee, P., Hunter, W. C., & Chung, N. (2020, May 12). Smart Tourism City: Developments and Transformations. *Sustainability (Basel)*, *12*(10), 3958. DOI: 10.3390/su12103958

Lee, W. J., & Kim, Y. H. (2021, January 15). Does VR Tourism Enhance Users' Experience? *Sustainability (Basel)*, *13*(2), 806. DOI: 10.3390/su13020806

Magasic, M., & Gretzel, U. (2020). Travel connectivity. *Tourist Studies*, *146879761989934*(1), 3–26. Advance online publication. DOI: 10.1177/1468797619899343

Mardhiyah, D., Hartini, S., & Kristanto, D. (2020). An integrated model of the adoption of information technology in travel service. *International Journal of Innovation. Creativity and Change*, *11*(11), 283–299.

Mitchell, T. M. (1997, January 1). *Machine Learning*. http://books.google.ie/books?id=EoYBngEACAAJ&dq=machine+learning+by+Tom+Mitchell&hl=&cd=1&source=gbs_api

Nguyen, M. H., Armoogum, J., Madre, J. L., & Garcia, C. (2020, August). Reviewing trip purpose imputation in GPS-based travel surveys. [English Edition]. *Journal of Traffic and Transportation Engineering*, *7*(4), 395–412. DOI: 10.1016/j.jtte.2020.05.004

Oliveira, T., Araujo, B., & Tam, C. (2020, June). Why do people share their travel experiences on social media? *Tourism Management*, *78*, 104041. DOI: 10.1016/j.tourman.2019.104041 PMID: 32322615

Padmaja, N., Sudha, T., & Saurab, S. S. (2020). Application of Big Data in Forecasting the Travel Behaviour of International Tourists. *Learning and Analytics in Intelligent Systems*, *263–271*.https://doi.org/DOI: 10.1007/978-3-030-46943-6_30

Pei, Y., & Zhang, Y. (2021, April 1). A Study on the Integrated Development of Artificial Intelligence and Tourism from the Perspective of Smart Tourism. *Journal of Physics: Conference Series*, *1852*(3), 032016. DOI: 10.1088/1742-6596/1852/3/032016

Pencarelli, T. (2019, November 27). The digital revolution in the travel and tourism industry. *Information Technology & Tourism*, *22*(3), 455–476. DOI: 10.1007/s40558-019-00160-3

Pillai, R., & Sivathanu, B. (2020). Adoption of AI-based chatbots for hospitality and tourism. *International Journal of Contemporary Hospitality Management*, *ahead-of-print(ahead-of-print)*.https://doi.org/DOI: 10.1108/IJCHM-04-2020-0259

Rathore, S. (2020). Analyzing the influence of user-generated-content (UGC) on social media platforms in travel planning. https://doi.org/DOI: 10.5937/turizam24-24429

Rehman Khan, H. U., Lim, C. K., Ahmed, M. F., Tan, K. L., & Bin Mokhtar, M. (2021, July 21). Systematic Review of Contextual Suggestion and Recommendation Systems for Sustainable e-tourism. *Sustainability (Basel)*, *13*(15), 8141. DOI: 10.3390/su13158141

Report on National Digital Tourism Mission (NDTM) | Ministry of Tourism | Government of India. (n.d.). https://tourism.gov.in/whats-new/report-national-digital-tourism-mission-ndtm

Stankov, U., & Gretzel, U. (2020, July 25). Tourism 4.0 technologies and tourist experiences: A human-centered design perspective. *Information Technology & Tourism*, *22*(3), 477–488. DOI: 10.1007/s40558-020-00186-y

State of travel influencer marketing: Top 5 trends for travel influencers to keep in mind. (2022, November 16). ETHospitalityWorld.com. https://hospitality.economictimes.indiatimes.com/news/speaking-heads/state-of-travel-influencer-marketing-top-5-trends-for-travel-influencers-to-keep-in-mind/95547388#:~:text=Travel%20influencers%20are%20again%20being,INR%2022%20billion%20by%202025

Taber, K. S. (2017, June 7). The Use of Cronbach's Alpha When Developing and Reporting Research Instruments in Science Education. *Research in Science Education*, *48*(6), 1273–1296. DOI: 10.1007/s11165-016-9602-2

Team, C. (2018, September 28). *How airlines price their tickets; AI's role in optimising airline revenue management and ticketing - CRN - India*. CRN - India. https://www.crn.in/thought-leader/how-airlines-price-their-tickets-ais-role-in-optimising-airline-revenue-management-and-ticketing/

Tham, A., Mair, J., & Croy, G. (2019). Social media influence on tourists' destination choice: Importance of context. *Tourism Recreation Research*. Advance online publication. DOI: 10.1080/02508281.2019.1700655

Tsai, F. M., & Bui, T. D. (2020, March 1). Impact of word of mouth via social media on consumer intention to purchase cruise travel products. *Maritime Policy & Management*, *48*(2), 167–183. DOI: 10.1080/03088839.2020.1735655

Verma, A., Shukla, V. K., & Sharma, R. (2021, January 1). Convergence of IOT in Tourism Industry: A Pragmatic *Analysis. Journal of Physics: Conference Series*, *1714*(1), 012037. DOI: 10.1088/1742-6596/1714/1/012037

Williams, M. N., Grajales, C. A. G., & Kurkiewicz, D. (2013). Assumptions of Multiple Regression: Correcting Two Misconceptions. *Practical Assessment, Research & Evaluation*, *18*(11). http://pareonline.net/getvn.asp?v=18&n=11

Wong, J. W. C., Lai, I. K. W., & Tao, Z. (2019, August 1). Sharing memorable tourism experiences on mobile social media and how it influences further travel decisions. *Current Issues in Tourism*, *23*(14), 1773–1787. DOI: 10.1080/13683500.2019.1649372

World Economic Forum. (2023, October 9). *World Economic Forum.* https://www.weforum.org/publications/the-travel-tourism-competitiveness-report-2019/

World Travel & Tourism Council (WTTC) | Travel & Tourism Representative Council. (n.d.). World Travel & Tourism Council. https://wttc.org/news-article/india-travel-and-tourism-could-surpass-pre-pandemic-levels-by-the-end-of-2022

Xiang, Z., & Fesenmaier, D. R. (2022). Travel Information Search. *Handbook of E-Tourism*, 921–940. https://doi.org/DOI: 10.1007/978-3-030-48652-5_55

Chapter 8
Cultural Tourism in Digitalization Era:
The Case of AR Glasses

Mario Ossorio
University of Campania "Luigi Vanvitelli", Italy

ABSTRACT

The chapter illustrates the main charachteristics of cultural tourism, categories and preferences of cultural tourists and how digital technologies have improved internal processes of cultural tourism industry. The chapter also highlights the increasing role of the experience and the growing function of technologies as support for firms and travellers. Lastly, the chapter describes an immersive experience that tourists can live in Pompeii sites by using Augmented Reality glasses by AR Tour, through which they can walki through twenty must-see sites in the ancient Roman city.

INTRODUCTION

The impact of digitalization on various industries has significantly altered the socioeconomic landscape in which organizations operate to create and capture value. Digitalization enables individuals to better meet the needs and expectations of stakeholders. One of the key outcomes of digitalization is the emergence of new business models that are revolutionizing how organizations create value, leading to fresh business opportunities in multiple industries, particularly within the cultural sector. Cultural industry firms are increasingly recognizing the advantages of digital technologies for enhancing internal processes and meeting the demands of new markets. Simultaneously, digital companies are leveraging digital tools to enter the cultural services market with innovative business models. Within this framework,

DOI: 10.4018/979-8-3693-3196-5.ch008

cultural tourism demonstrates unique characteristics that make it a relevant subject for analyzing business model innovation.

The aim of this chapter is to analyse the role of digital technologies in cultural tourism industry.

Over the last eighty years, the tourism industry has increased worldwide, and, particularly, since the 1970s, it has become a relevant economic sector, growing at an exponential pace (Mak, 2008). Because of huge revenues generated, tourism represent a strategic cornerstone industry for an economy (Yan, Shah, Sharma, Chopra, Fareed, & Shahzad, 2022). Cultural tourism is defined as *"tangible and intangible attractions and products that represent material, intellectual, spiritual and emotional features of a society"* (United Nations World Tourism Organization, 2018), and represents a key part of tourism system (Hjalager, 2009). In 2020, an unforseen event, pandemic by COVID 19 immobilized most of the industries over the world generating devastating and still rising economic and operational externalities (Zopiatis, Pericleous, Theofanous, 2021), and stimulating an unprecedented proliferation of research on this topic (Sigala, 2020). Anyway, as other segments of tourism and hospitality industry, after COVID-19 pandemic times, cultural tourism has grown again at exponential rate.

This chapter aims to explore how over the last years digital platforms have supported the cultural tourist industry, by strenghtening sustainability and social responsibility practices.

The chapter is constituted in 4 sections. The first section explores the meaning of cultural tourism. Culture and tourism have been interconnected for centuries. Attending cultural activities, such as visiting museums and galleries, heritage sites, festivals and typical foods and drink tasting, is one of the main driver for travel, while travel in and of itself has also in turn affected culture through the development of travelling behaviour (Richards, 2018).

The second chapter illustrates the evolution of cultural tourist behaviors, the change in travellers needs and behaviors, the increasing role of the experience and the growing function of technologies as support for firms and travellers. The chapter also describes five categories of tourists considering the relevance of culture in the decision to visit a destination and the experience required.

The third section focuses on the relationship between digitalization and cultural tourism industry. Over the last decades, hi-tech industries have been generating a greater computer capacity and innovative technologies. The tourism industry represents an early adoptor of technologies by adopting computer reservation systems in 70s, distribution systems in 80s and the Internet in 90s (Qi, Buhalis and Law, 2008). Internet of things (IoT) (e.g.: Nadkarni and Teare., 2019), virtual reality (VR) (Kim et al., 2020), augmented reality (AR) (Nayyar et al., 2018), big data (Nadkarni and Teare, 2019), artificial intelligence (AI) and robotics (Kuo et al., 2017) represent the pillars of Industry 4.0 that have changed the dynamics charactherizing the cultural tourism industry. After the pandemic, the increased adoption of industry 4.0 technologies have generate a deep structural change that has accelerated digitalisation of cultural events (Statista, 2021).

The fourth section describes AR glasses that are created by AR Tour, a fledgling company that has been active in the primary archaeological locations of Campania for a number of years. Their advanced 3D reconstruction method accurately replicates historical sites using data from archaeological digs and scholarly research. These glasses are adopted inside Pompeii sites where they permit an immersive experience for tourists walking through twenty must-see sites in the ancient Roman city, which can be visited in about two total hours.

Concluding remarks section illustrates implications for managers and policy makers of the development of digital technologies for sustainable destinations.

1. CULTURAL TOURISM: EVOLUTION, CHARACTERISTICS AND DEFINITIONS

Culture and tourism have always been connected. For instance, cultural sites and events have pushed people to travel. Simultanously, people who travel increaes their cultural knowledge. Only in the last decades, the relationship between tourism and culture has been pointed out as a precse type of consumption: cultural tourism (Richards, 2018).

Cultural tourism has increasingly been considered as an autounomus form of tourism since 1980s. In fact, in that period the increasing rate of traveller interested in major sites and attraction stimulated great attention for cutural tourism considered then as an emerging niche market. Cultural tourism kept on growing throughout 80s and 90s mainly sustained by heritage boom (Hewison, 1987) and the concept that cultural tourism is considered as a "good" kind of tourism that supports economy and simultaneously preserves culture (Richards, 2001). During 1990s cultural tourism started a phase of transformation and more specifically changed by an elite clientele to a mass market, by affirming itself in many destinations and becoming the target of academic studies. The growth of research papers, along with several theoretical and methodological approaches, stimulated the fragmentation of the literature into a number of emerging streams such as heritage tourism, arts tourism, gastronomic tourism, film tourism and creative tourism.

The relevance of cultural tourism ha salso demonstrated by UNWTO Report on Tourism and Culture Synergies (2018), which estimated cultural tourism market was over 39% of all international tourism arrivals, or the equivalent of around 516 million international trips in 2017. Nevertheless, it is important to note that defining cultural tourism is a challenging task. There is no universal definition for cultural tourism, and many sources do not provide a clear description of the concept and the debate on the definition of cultural tourism is still open (Chen & Rahman, 2018). In the search for a comprehensive and exhaustive definition of cultural tourism, two prevailing orientations can be discerned by referencing the theoretical studies dedicated to this topic.

One perspective is more traditional, connecting cultural enjoyment with the heritage goods linked to it, reflecting the most profound and foundational aspects of this type of tourism. The other explores the meaning and features of cultural tourism through alternative, less conventional motivations and inspirations. Essentially, while the first approach focuses more on the object of enjoyment, the second directs its attention towards the modes and subjective motivations underlying it.

The first approach is represented by the definition of Origet de Cluzeau (1998) that emphasizes a fundamental element of cultural tourism: exploration and learning. This type of tourism is not limited to visiting places; it encourages travelers to immerse themselves in the cultural and historical heritage of a destination. In summary, cultural tourism, according to this definition, represents a form of travel that prioritizes the intensity of experiences and a deep understanding of diverse cultures, leading visitors to connect authentically with the places they visit.

The perspective opened by Amirou (2000) is entirely inverted, as he analyzes the relationship between tourism and culture, starting from the concept of "imaginary," which according to the author "helps to describe more simply the relationships between a subject and other sectors in which the activity of the spirit is exercised: art, thought, myth, religion, and tourism."

The viewpoint adopted attempts to provide a definition of cultural tourism and explain its components, starting not from the identification of the object, but from the intention with which subjects undertake cultural visits, in a perspective that we can describe as postmodern.

Reisinger (1994) points out that it offers an immersion in new and intense cultural experiences of an aesthetic, intellectual, emotional or psychological nature. By a different perspective, Silberberg (1995) states: "visits by persons from outside the host community motivated wholly or in part by interest in the historical, artistic, scientific or lifestyle/heritage offerings of a community, region or institution" (p. 362). Accordingly, cutural tourism can be considered as heritage tourism and art tourism (Richards, 2001). In this vein, cultural tourism takes into account museums, festivals, architecture, heritage, and tourist attractions related to food, language, and religion (Stylianou-Lambert, 2011). Therefore, establishing a connection with the local surroundings, including both the cultural and natural aspects, is essential in understanding the culture of the destination (Niemczyk, 2013). This caters to exploring unfamiliar places, their society, traditions, their passion for art, buildings, and the past, joining in cultural and artistic activities, reconnecting with one's origins, and connecting with the sacred; all while a traveler encounters the hospitality and cultural abundance of a specific destination.

Bonink (1992) identifies two approaches to defining cultural tourism: the "sites and monuments" approach, which focuses on the attractions visited by cultural tourists and sees culture as a product, and the "conceptual approach", which seeks to define cultural tourism qualitatively by examining the practices, experiences, and meanings of cultural tourists in contact with other places and cultures. McIntosh and Goeldner (1990) define cultural tourism as encompassing all aspects of travel that involve learning about the heritage, history, and contemporary ways of life of other cultures. In essence, cultural tourism offers cultural tourists the opportunity to explore and experience the processes and products of other cultures.

Initial conversations about cultural tourism also highlighted a distinction between 'general' and 'specific' cultural tourists. The former enjoy cultural experiences as part of a broader holiday, while the latter travel intentionally to immerse themselves in a particular aspect of the destination's culture (Richards 1996).

Identity is a crucial aspect of cultural tourism and tourism overall, with the focus on creating and reflecting identity becoming increasingly important (Mousavi et al., 2016). Both cultural tourists and hosts place high value on identity, with hosts seeking to showcase a distinctive identity to attract visitors and reap the benefits of tourism, while cultural tourists are drawn to unique local identities as part of their cultural consumption experience.

Experiences aimed to satisfy cultural needs and cultural attractions, such as cultural attractions, such as heritage sites, artistic and cultural manifestations, arts and drama are central points in the definition of Richards (1996). Therefore, the contemporary definition of cultural tourism is not limited to sites and monuments but encompasses ways of life, creativity and "everyday culture". In an effort to overview the different genres of cultural tourism, Nyemczyk (2013) outlines the following subcategories: cultural heritage tourism, museum tourism, industrial tourism, cultural events tourism, historical-military tourism, religious-pilgrimage tourism, and culinary tourism.

Stylianou-Lambert (2011) conducted a qualitative study on the various 'gazes' present in cultural tourism, revealing that tourists' perceptions of art museums vary significantly. These perceptions are shaped by diverse 'perceptual filters' that affect how they engage with their surroundings. This finding highlights the intricate nature of cultural tourism participation, suggesting that a multidisciplinary and multidimensional approach is necessary to fully understand its complexity.

2. CULTURAL TOURISTS BEHAVIORS AND PREFERENCES

Scholars point out that cultural tourism audience cannot be considered as an homogenous mass market (Richards, 1996; Guccio, Lisi, Mignosa & Rizzo, 2018). A cultural tourism offering varies greatly in the advantages it provides and the specific audience it caters to. This creates a diverse group of cultural travelers, forming a large-scale product that meets the needs of numerous people. Within this extensive product, there are numerous smaller offerings, each tailored to individual preferences and encompassing the entire range of material and service elements of the tourist experience (Nyemczyk, 2013). For instance, general cultural tourists consider cultural events or sites as a fraction of a broad travel experience, while for the specific ones, the main scope of the travel is to experience and value some traits of the culture of the place they visit. Under these circumstances, the features of physical setting would affect the kind of cultural consumption (Richards and van der Ark, 2013). The age also would influence cultural tourism behaviors. In this vein, younger visitors are more incline to appreciate contemporary art and modern architecture, while older ones would prefer traditional monuments and museums.

McKercher and Du Cros (2003) identify five types of tourists taking into account the relevance of culture in the decision to visit a destination and the experience required. More specifically, the purposeful tourist is someone who travels to a certain place specifically to gain knowledge about its culture, placing a high value on the information they receive. The incidental type, on the other hand, does not prioritize cultural activities when planning their trip but may still engage in them during their stay, attaching less importance to the cognitive aspect. The third category, which is characterized by serendipity, may not prioritize cultural activities when planning a trip, but they eagerly engage in such activities during their stay, leading to a high level of interest in cultural content. As for the fourth group, their approach to culture is casual and not a major factor in travel planning, resulting in a superficial experience with limited cognitive impact. The fifth and final element, sightseeing, involves a desire to learn about other cultures while visiting, but the focus is more on entertainment rather than in-depth exploration. The purposeful, the sightseeing and the serendipitous are seen as the primary cultural tourists thanks to their main motivator and decision on a destination basing on cultural values.

The initial distinction between general and specific cultural motivations remains apparent in contemporary motivational research. For instance, Galí-Espelt (2012) identifies two primary categories of cultural tourists: those whose primary motivation is cultural consumption and those for whom culture serves as a secondary motivation. She suggests categorizing these motivations based on the level of 'culturedness,' which is defined by the duration of the visit and a continuum from high to low cultural engagement.

3. DIGITAL TECHNOLOGIES AND CULTURAL TOURISM

Over the past few decades, the hi-tech industries have been increasing computer capacity and developing innovative technologies. The hospitality sector has been an early adopter of technology, incorporating computerized reservation systems in the 1970s, distribution systems in the 1980s, and the Internet in the 1990s (Buhalis and Law, 2008). Information and communication technologies (ICTs) have brought benefits to both travelers and businesses. Travelers can access information more easily and at a lower cost, allowing them to share knowledge (Mihajlovic, 2012). Companies have seen advantages such as reduced costs, increased revenue, simplified marketing research, and database development (Morrison et al., 1999). Industry 4.0 technologies such as Internet of Things (IoT), virtual reality (VR), augmented reality (AR), big data, artificial intelligence (AI), and robotics have transformed the hospitality industry. The adoption of these technologies has accelerated after the pandemic, leading to significant structural changes. In a recent literature review, El Archi et al. (2023) highlight digital technologies as key drivers of sustainable tourism development, offering new opportunities to enhance destination management, traveler experiences, and encourage sustainable behavior among tourists. Specifically, digital technologies have the potential to redefine how the tourism industry communicates and engages with tourists and stakeholders (Hays et al., 2013; Pencarelli, 2020).

According to this viewpoint, a interactive cultural tourism approach is better suited to modern social and economic systems that allow tourists to actively engage in leisure, cultural, and artistic activities, leading to a more genuine and authentic experience at the destination (Remoaldo et al., 2020). The focus on fully immersing oneself in the experience is a reaction to the overwhelming presence of mass cultural tourism, leading to a new type of tourist who actively participates in shaping their tourism activities throughout the entire experience (Remoaldo et a., 2017).

The emergence of digitalization has significantly influenced the growth of this innovative type of interactive and engaging cultural tourism, greatly impacting the customer experience. Various research has emphasized the positive effects of digital technologies on enhancing the appeal of cultural destinations through the sharing of information and collaborative value creation. (Porter and Heppelmann, 2014).

The "social web environment" has created new ways for tourists to engage, cooperate, and share experiences, ultimately promoting the dissemination of electronic word-of-mouth communication. This includes sharing opinions about destinations, services, and tourism companies (Volpentesta and Felicetti, 2012). In recent years, the increasing popularity of mobile app-based services has provided consumers with the chance to access timely, location-based, and relevant information services (Volpentesta et al., 2017).

Because of app-based services, travelers have the chance to obtain thorough and accurate information at the moment and place they are deciding on their tourism activities. However, the effectiveness of providing this information is limited, as it does not take into account changes in the tourist's circumstances unless the consumer actively participates in requesting and customizing services (Ribeiro et al., 2018).

4. VISIT POMPEI THROUGH AR GLASSES

Thanks to 3D reconstruction and Augmented Reality, it is really possible to travel back in time, discovering the digitally reconstructed ruins of Pompeii and presented in the form of immersive scenarios.

With AR Glasses, special visors that allow you to see the real world augmented with virtual content, the enjoyment of cultural heritage occurs in an experiential way, through languages made of sounds and graphical reconstructions. It will therefore be more immediate and enjoyable, especially for children, teenagers, and non-experts.

AR glasses are produced by AR Tour, a young start-up that has been operating in the main archaeological sites of Campania for several years. The scientific 3D reconstruction process implemented is able to reproduce the ancient archaeological structure to scale, based on documentation from archaeological excavations and historical studies.

One of the historical sites travellers can visit by using AR glasses is Pompei.

Pompei History

Pompeii, unlike other cities in Campania that were mostly founded by Greek colonists, was built by the Oscans, probably around the 9th-8th century B.C., although the currently available evidence does not date back further than the 6th century. The city developed on lava terraces formed many centuries earlier. It provided an important natural defense against the threat of invasions from neighboring peoples. The city was under Etruscan control for nearly fifty years (until 474 B.C.), when they occupied part of the inland Campania. Shortly after, it returned to Greek influence. It then became part of the Samnite expansion area (5th century), under which it experienced significant growth, forming the historical center whose remains can still be seen today. This can be identified in part by the ancient boundary wall, the architecture of various houses (characterized by a Tuscan atrium), the public buildings of the Triangular Forum, and the Temple of Apollo in the Civic Forum.

Meanwhile, Rome had begun its gradual advance into southern Italy and had started to overcome the resistance of the Italic peoples. Consequently, the Samnites were also forced to submit to the City, but only after three long and bitter wars, the last of which was fought between 298 and 290 B.C. Following the conquest of Campania, Pompeii also came under Roman dominion, becoming an "ally," a status that allowed for the maintenance of relative local autonomy. From that moment, its history became closely intertwined with that of the City, and only during the Social War waged by the Italic peoples in a last attempt to defend their freedom did it ally with the insurrectionary movement (91 B.C.). However, in 89 B.C. it was besieged by Sulla, stormed, and thus brought back under Roman control. In 80 B.C. it became a Roman colony under the name Colonia Cornelia Veneria Pompeii. As in the past, Pompeii continued to expand and develop in every sector, particularly in the economic one, greatly benefitting from its fertile hinterland and advantageous position. All activities related to trade and maritime traffic experienced a period of growth.

The life and splendor of Pompeii were destined to come to an end. It was August 24th in the year 79 A.D. A heavy rain of ash, pumice, and lava from the volcano began to pour down on the city and the nearby Herculaneum and Stabiae. Everything was buried under a thick layer of volcanic material to a depth of several meters. The inhabitants, most of whom fled towards the coast, were suffocated by the fumes of gases, while others met their death in their own homes.

Tour in Pompeii With AR Glasses

The tour in Pompeii selects around twenty must-see sites in the ancient Roman city, which can be visited in about two total hours. You can then continue to explore the city on your own. After a short briefing and the delivery of the Augmented Reality glasses, we start the walking tour inside the Pompeii site: from one attraction to another we walk without putting on the glasses, and the tour assistant is happy to answer all our questions in the meantime. It is important to remember that the person accompanying visitors on this tour is not a qualified tour guide. They can satisfy some of your curiosities, but their main role is to assist you with the use of the glasses. Once the point of interest is reached, they activate the visors of all participants from their smartphone: the immersive representation of the reconstruction is accompanied by an audio guide to aid understanding.

The audio guide is available in Italian, English, French, German, and Spanish.

The AR Glasses weigh only 100 grams and do not cause any nausea! They can also be used by children aged eight and up.

The archaeological excavations of Pompeii cover a very large area (about 66 hectares of which approximately 50 have been excavated). With the AR tour, it is possible to visit some of the most iconic and representative remains of the ancient Roman city.

The Quadriportico and the Grand Theater

Among these are the Quadriportico, the vast space where spectators could linger during the intervals of the adjacent Grand Theater performances. Later, this building changed its use, becoming a barracks for gladiators.

The Grand Theater welcomes us with its imposing staircase: it is still used for performances and concerts, and we imagine it crowded with people sitting on the steps of the cavea.

The Thermopolium and the Bakery

Along the Via dell'Abbondanza, it is exciting to discover what was in fact one of the many shops selling street food in Pompeii, the thermopolium of Vetutius Placidus. Staying on the food theme, another stop is at the bakery of Popidio, where the large ovens still tell of ancient aromas.

The Stabian Baths

The Stabian Baths were a place where citizens dedicated themselves to relaxation, conversing amicably about politics, theater, philosophy, and perhaps women. By the way, they also had their SPA, obviously smaller and less comfortable than those of their husbands! It is completely exposed the system of interstices which, placed under the floor, allowed the hot air produced in the furnace to circulate and heat the rooms. Thanks to AR, we can see the reconstruction of the floor on which the guests walked.

To date, over 30,000 tourists have taken advantage of the hi-tech glasses equipped with Augmented Reality to enhance the quality of their visit.

AR-Tour has as clients the main tour operators with whom it has defined agreements to offer the rental service of 3D glasses (AR Glasses) to groups of visitors accompanied by a tour guide. In this way, the service is integrated within a comprehensive package offered directly by the Tour Operator. The B2B sales component therefore represents an important element of AR-Tour's development.

The company's ambition, however, is to also be able to provide significant direct B2C sales with services bookable through a web portal and targeting a young audience in particular.

CONCLUSIONS

In recent years, Industry 4.0 technologies like the Internet of Things (IoT), virtual reality (VR), augmented reality (AR), big data, artificial intelligence (AI), and robotics have fundamentally transformed the tourism sector, imbuing cultural tourism with fresh significance and value. Some Industry 4.0 technologies are already being applied in the tourism sector. Big Data, for example, allows for the rapid collection and analysis of large volumes of data from multiple sources (internet, social networks, apps), surpassing the limits of traditional statistical information on which geographic analyses still rely. Robotics, along with artificial intelligence, are finding space in the hospitality sector, albeit with design and functionality characteristics different from industrial production. Augmented Reality is being used in communication and the enjoyment of cultural assets, thanks in particular to the widespread adoption of mobile technologies. There are now numerous experiences of using digital technologies in the tourist enjoyment of cultural heritage, in cities, museums, and archaeological sites. It is an immersive experience that gives the tourist the impression of being in front of a unique object and "enhances" interaction with the real world, providing information that cannot be perceived through the senses.

Managers of cultural sites and destinations should increase the adoption of mobile technologies given their powerful and consistent instrument capable of maximizing the appeal of destinations, involving, and keeping the interest of cultural tourists.

REFERENCES

Amirou, R. (2000). *Imaginaire du tourisme culturel*. Puf.

Bonink, C. (1992). Cultural tourism development and government policy. *Unpublished ma dissertation). Rijksuniversiteit, Utrecht, The Netherlands*.

Buhalis, D., & Law, R. (2008). Progress in information technology and tourism management: 20 years on and 10 years after the Internet—The state of eTourism research. *Tourism Management, 29*(4), 609–623. DOI: 10.1016/j.tourman.2008.01.005

Chen, H., & Rahman, I. (2018). Cultural tourism: An analysis of engagement, cultural contact, memorable tourism experience and destination loyalty. *Tourism Management Perspectives, 26*, 153–163. DOI: 10.1016/j.tmp.2017.10.006

El Archi, Y., Benbba, B., Nizamatdinova, Z., Issakov, Y., Vargáné, G. I., & Dávid, L. D. (2023). Systematic Literature Review Analysing Smart Tourism Destinations in Context of Sustainable Development: Current Applications and Future Directions. *Sustainability (Basel), 15*(6), 5086. DOI: 10.3390/su15065086

Galí-Espelt, N. (2012). Identifying cultural tourism: A theoretical methodological proposal. *Journal of Heritage Tourism, 7*(1), 45–58. DOI: 10.1080/1743873X.2011.632480

Guccio, C., Lisi, D., Mignosa, A., & Rizzo, I. (2018). Does cultural heritage monetary value have an impact on visits? An assessment using official Italian data. *Tourism Economics, 24*(3), 297–318. DOI: 10.1177/1354816618758729

Hays, S., Page, S. J., & Buhalis, D. (2013). Social Media as a Destination Marketing Tool: Its Use by National Tourism Organisations. *Current Issues in Tourism, 16*(3), 211–239. DOI: 10.1080/13683500.2012.662215

Hewison, R. (1987). *The Heritage Industry: Britain in a Climate of Decline* (1st ed.). Routledge.

Hjalager, A. M. (2010). A review of innovation research in tourism. *Tourism Management, 31*(1), 1–12. DOI: 10.1016/j.tourman.2009.08.012

Kim, M. J., Lee, C. K., & Jung, T. (2020). Exploring consumer behavior in virtual reality tourism using an extended stimulus-organism-response model. *Journal of Travel Research, 59*(1), 69–89. DOI: 10.1177/0047287518818915

Kuo, C. M., Chen, L. C., & Tseng, C. Y. (2017). Investigating an innovative service with hospitality robots. *International Journal of Contemporary Hospitality Management, 29*(5), 1305–1321. DOI: 10.1108/IJCHM-08-2015-0414

Mak, J. (2008). *Developing a dream destination: Tourism and tourism policy planning in Hawaii*. University of Hawaii Press. DOI: 10.21313/hawaii/9780824832438.001.0001

McIntosh, R., & Goeldner, C. (1990). *Tourism: Principles, Practices, Philosophies* (6th ed.). John Wiley & Sons, Inc.

McKercher, B., & Du Cros, H. (2003). Testing a cultural tourism typology. *International Journal of Tourism Research*, 5(1), 45–58. DOI: 10.1002/jtr.417

Mihajlovic, I. (2012). The impact of information and communication technology (ICT) as a key factor of tourism development on the role of Croatian travel agencies. *International Journal of Business and Social Science*, 3(24).

Morrison, A. M., Taylor, S., Morrison, A. J., & Morrison, A. D. (1999). Marketing small hotels on the World Wide Web. *Information Technology & Tourism*, 2(2), 97–113.

Mousavi, S. S., Doratli, N., Mousavi, S. N., & Moradiahari, F. (2016, December). Defining cultural tourism. In *International Conference on Civil, Architecture and Sustainable Development* (Vol. 1, No. 2, pp. 70-75).

Nadkarni, S., & Teare, R. (2019). Reflections on the theme issue outcomes: Expo 2020: what will be the impact on Dubai? *Worldwide Hospitality and Tourism Themes*, 11(3), 346–350. DOI: 10.1108/WHATT-03-2019-0013

Nayyar, A., Mahapatra, B., Le, D., & Suseendran, G. (2018). Virtual Reality (VR) & Augmented Reality (AR) technologies for tourism and hospitality industry. *International journal of engineering & technology*, 7(2.21), 156-160.

Niemczyk, A. (2013). Cultural tourists: "An attempt to classify them". *Tourism Management Perspectives*, 5, 24–30. DOI: 10.1016/j.tmp.2012.09.006

Origet de Cluzeau, C. (1998). *Le Tourisme Culturel*. Puf.

Pencarelli, T. (2020). The Digital Revolution in the Travel and Tourism Industry. *Information Technology & Tourism*, 22(3), 455–476. DOI: 10.1007/s40558-019-00160-3

Porter, M. E., & Heppelmann, J. E. (2014). How smart, connected products are transforming competition. *Harvard Business Review*, 92(11), 64–88.

Qi, S., Law, R., & Buhalis, D. (2008). Usability of Chinese destination management organization websites. *Journal of Travel & Tourism Marketing*, 25(2), 182–198. DOI: 10.1080/10548400802402933

Reisinger, Y. (1994). Tourist—Host contact as a part of cultural tourism. *World Leisure & Recreation*, *36*(2), 24–28. DOI: 10.1080/10261133.1994.9673910

Remoaldo, P., Freitas, I., Matos, O., Lopes, H., Silva, S., Fernández, M. D. S., & Ribeiro, V. (2017). The planning of tourism on rural areas: The stakeholders' perceptions of the Boticas municipality (northeastern Portugal). *European Countryside*, *9*(3), 504–525. DOI: 10.1515/euco-2017-0030

Remoaldo, P., Serra, J., Marujo, N., Alves, J., Gonçalves, A., Cabeça, S., & Duxbury, N. (2020). Profiling the participants in creative tourism activities: Case studies from small and medium sized cities and rural areas from Continental Portugal. *Tourism Management Perspectives*, *36*, 100746. DOI: 10.1016/j.tmp.2020.100746 PMID: 32953432

Ribeiro, M. A., Woosnam, K. M., Pinto, P., & Silva, J. A. (2018). Tourists' destination loyalty through emotional solidarity with residents: An integrative moderated mediation model. *Journal of Travel Research*, *57*(3), 279–295. DOI: 10.1177/0047287517699089

Richards, G. (2001). *Cultural attractions and European tourism*. CABI. DOI: 10.1079/9780851994406.0000

Richards, G. (2018). Cultural tourism: A review of recent research and trends. *Journal of Hospitality and Tourism Management*, *36*, 12–21. DOI: 10.1016/j.jhtm.2018.03.005

Richards, G., & van der Ark, L. A. (2013). Dimensions of cultural consumption among tourists: Multiple correspondence analysis. *Tourism Management*, *37*, 71–76. DOI: 10.1016/j.tourman.2013.01.007

Sigala, M. (2020). Tourism and COVID-19: Impacts and implications for advancing and resetting industry and research. *Journal of Business Research*, *117*, 312–321. DOI: 10.1016/j.jbusres.2020.06.015 PMID: 32546875

Silberberg, T. (1995). Cultural tourism and business opportunities for museums and heritage sites. *Tourism Management*, *16*(5), 361–365. DOI: 10.1016/0261-5177(95)00039-Q

Stylianou-Lambert, T. (2011). Gazing from home: Cultural tourism and art museums. *Annals of Tourism Research*, *38*(2), 403–421. DOI: 10.1016/j.annals.2010.09.001

UNWTO. (2018). *Report on tourism and culture synergies*. UNWTO.

Volpentesta, A. P., & Felicetti, A. M. (2012). Identifying opinion leaders in time-dependent commercial social networks. In *Collaborative Networks in the Internet of Services: 13th IFIP WG 5.5 Working Conference on Virtual Enterprises, PRO-VE 2012, Bournemouth, UK, October 1-3, 2012.* [Springer Berlin Heidelberg.]. *Proceedings, 13,* 571–581.

Volpentesta, A. P., Felicetti, A. M., & Ammirato, S. (2017). Intelligent food information provision to consumers in an internet of food era. In *Collaboration in a Data-Rich World: 18th IFIP WG 5.5 Working Conference on Virtual Enterprises, PRO-VE 2017, Vicenza, Italy, September 18-20, 2017* [Springer International Publishing.]. *Proceedings, 18,* 725–736.

Yan, Y., Shah, M. I., Sharma, G. D., Chopra, R., Fareed, Z., & Shahzad, U. (2022). Can tourism sustain itself through the pandemic: Nexus between tourism, COVID-19 cases and air quality spread in the 'Pineapple State' Hawaii. *Current Issues in Tourism, 25*(3), 421–440. DOI: 10.1080/13683500.2021.1965553

Zopiatis, A., Pericleous, K., & Theofanous, Y. (2021). COVID-19 and hospitality and tourism research: An integrative review. *Journal of Hospitality and Tourism Management, 48,* 275–279. DOI: 10.1016/j.jhtm.2021.07.002

Chapter 9
The Use of Technology in Enhancing Pilgrimage Tourism Experiences and Hospitality Services

Md Shamim Hossain
https://orcid.org/0000-0003-1645-7470
Hajee Mohammad Danesh Science and Technology University, Bangladesh

ABSTRACT

This paper investigates how technology can be utilized to enhance pilgrimage tourism and hospitality services. The article gives an overview of technology use in the pilgrimage tourism business, with a focus on technology's role in improving pilgrim experiences and the quality of hospitality services provided by hotels, restaurants, and other service providers. The report underlines the benefits of integrating technology in pilgrimage tourism, such as greater efficiency, convenience, and service personalization. Overall, the assessment shows how technology has the potential to dramatically improve the experiences and services supplied in the pilgrimage tourism business, as well as the need for future research to fully fulfill that potential. There hasn't been a lot of research done on pilgrimage tourism, and the current study focused on the potential use of technology to improve pilgrimage tourism experiences and hospitality services.

DOI: 10.4018/979-8-3693-3196-5.ch009

INTRODUCTION

Pilgrimages were among the first forms of tourism mobility to appear thousands of years ago. Its importance has waned in recent decades as other tourism segments have grown in prominence. Despite the fact that modern tourism is a relatively new phenomenon, its roots are clearly rooted in the age-old practice of pilgrimage (Collins-Kreiner, 2020). Pilgrimage is commonly characterized as a physical visit to a place made to pray, practice various religious rituals, and spiritually purify and/or enlighten (Gunlu & Okumus, 2010). Pilgrimage tourism is a type of travel that has been around for hundreds of years. Each year, millions of people go on pilgrimages to holy sites and take part in religious ceremonies (Ozturk et al., 2022). Pilgrimage tourism is a way to experience cultural, historical, and natural wonders, as well as social interactions with local people and spiritual fulfillment. The United Nations World Tourism Organization has declared 2017 the International Year of Sustainable Tourism for Development, with a focus on pilgrimage tourism as one of the key drivers of sustainable tourism (UNESCO, 2017).

Technology has revolutionized the travel and tourism industries in recent years, opening up new avenues for improving the experiences and services available to travelers (Buhalis, 2020). The application of technology has been especially essential in pilgrimage tourism (Rahman et al., 2022), as tourists are frequently looking for methods to enhance their experiences and make their journeys more meaningful. However, the impact of technology on pilgrimage tourism has gotten little attention in the academic literature, and a thorough evaluation of the available studies in this area is required.

The goal of this review article is to look at how technology can be used to improve pilgrimage tourism and hospitality services. The paper will provide an overview of the current state of technology use in the pilgrimage tourism business, with a particular emphasis on the role of technology in improving pilgrim experiences and the quality of hospitality services provided by hotels, restaurants, and other service providers. The paper will also emphasize the advantages of adopting technology in pilgrimage tourism, such as greater efficiency, convenience, and service personalization. Furthermore, the presentation will explore the obstacles and limitations of using technology in pilgrimage tourism, as well as make recommendations for future research in this area.

Overall, this review article gives a thorough look at how technology can be used to improve the experiences of pilgrims and the hospitality services they receive. The review article shows how technology could be used to make pilgrimage tourism experiences and services much better, and it makes suggestions for more research in this area. The results of this review study are important for both practitioners and researchers in the field of pilgrimage tourism. They can help guide the development of technology-based solutions that can help pilgrims have more meaningful and memorable experiences. In addition to its historical roots, pilgrimage tourism remains a vibrant and significant aspect of the travel landscape, attracting millions of people annually to sacred sites worldwide. The enduring appeal of pilgrimage lies in its multifaceted nature, encompassing cultural, historical, and spiritual dimensions. Participants embark on these journeys not only to witness awe-inspiring landmarks but also to engage in religious ceremonies, fostering a deep connection with their faith and fellow pilgrims (Ozturk et al., 2022). Despite the timeless allure of pilgrimage, its prominence has somewhat diminished in recent decades amidst the surge of other tourism segments. However, the United Nations World Tourism Organization's designation of 2017 as the International Year of Sustainable Tourism for Development underscored the enduring importance of pilgrimage tourism as a key driver of sustainable tourism (UNESCO, 2017). This recognition positions pilgrimage tourism at the intersection of tradition and innovation, paving the way for a contemporary reevaluation of its significance and potential enhancements through the integration of technology. As we delve into the exploration of technological advancements in pilgrimage tourism, we aim to unravel the ways in which modern tools and innovations can further enrich and elevate the pilgrimage experience, aligning it with the evolving needs and expectations of today's travelers.

PILGRIMAGE TOURISM

Pilgrimage tourism is a form of travel that has a long and rich history, dating back to ancient times when people would travel to sacred places to seek spiritual fulfillment, heal physical ailments, or offer supplication for personal or community issues (Timothy and Olsen, 2006). One of the earliest recorded forms of pilgrimage can be traced back to the ancient Greeks, who would travel to the sanctuary of Delphi to seek advice and guidance from the Oracle (Morgan and Morgan, 1990). Similarly, the ancient Romans would make pilgrimages to the shrines of their gods, and the early Christians would travel to the Holy Land to visit the places where Jesus lived and died (Hunt 1984). With the emergence of the Catholic Church and the growth of devotion to saints during the Middle Ages, the concept of pilgrimage gained broad popularity in Europe. The city of Rome, which was regarded to be the center of the Christian world and the home of the Pope at the time, was the most popular pilgrimage destination (Reader, 2007). Pilgrims would travel from all over

Europe to visit the city and pay tribute to the many shrines and basilicas dedicated to the saints.

In the centuries that followed, pilgrimage grew in popularity, and new pilgrimage destinations arose throughout Europe, including Santiago de Compostela in Spain, which became one of the world's most prominent pilgrimage sites (Pack, 2010). The Camino de Santiago, or pilgrimage to Santiago de Compostela, drew millions of pilgrims from all over Europe and was regarded as one of the great spiritual journeys of the Middle Ages. Pilgrimage tourism is also essential in many non-European cultures, such as Islamic and Hindu traditions. The Hajj, or pilgrimage to Mecca, is one of Islam's five pillars and is expected of every able-bodied Muslim once in their lifetime (Rowley and El-Hamdan, 1978; Luz, 2020). Similarly, the Kumbh Mela, a Hindu pilgrimage to one of India's four sacred rivers, gathers millions of people each year and is regarded as one of the world's greatest gatherings of humanity.

As researchers began to study modern conceptions of pilgrimage in the context of spiritual rather than religious reasons and activities in the 2000s, the definition of pilgrimage came to encompass both traditional religious and modern secular excursions. According to increasing study, a huge number of travelers desire a variety of experiences, such as enlightenment, education, enhanced spiritual and physical well-being, and challenge. Scholars have created new understanding regarding secular pilgrimage destinations and secular components of pilgrimage studies during this time period (Hyde and Harman, 2011). Pilgrimage tourism has grown in popularity in recent years as individuals want to reconnect with their spiritual and cultural pasts, as well as to feel the sense of community and connectivity that can be experienced on a pilgrimage journey (Handriana et al., 2022). Pilgrimages can now be found all over the world, from Catholic saints' shrines in Europe to Buddhist monks' temples in Asia to sacred indigenous places in North America. The history of pilgrimage tourism is vast and varied, and it demonstrates the continuing human need to connect with the sacred and find spiritual fulfillment. Pilgrimages have evolved and altered over the years, responding to the requirements and conditions of many cultures and societies, but the underlying objectives for the pilgrimage journey have remained consistent (Rinschede, 1992; Luz, 2020). The pilgrimage journey has continued to inspire and captivate people from all walks of life and from all areas of the world, whether inspired by a desire for spiritual growth, the search for physical healing, or the yearning for community and connection.

BENEFITS OF TECHNOLOGY ADOPTION IN PILGRIMAGE TOURISM

Pilgrimage tourism holds significant cultural, religious, and spiritual value for individuals around the world (Collins-Kreiner, 2020; Štefko et al., 2015). In recent years, the adoption of technology has revolutionized the way pilgrims engage with pilgrimage sites, enhancing their overall experience (Gazzaz and Mohamed, 2022; Hindersah et al., 2021). This article explores the benefits of technology adoption in pilgrimage tourism, highlighting how technological advancements have transformed accessibility, cultural preservation, information and education, navigation, community engagement, and augmented experiences.

Enhanced Accessibility: One of the key benefits of technology adoption in pilgrimage tourism is enhanced accessibility. Geographical barriers that once limited pilgrims' access to sacred sites have been overcome through the use of virtual reality (VR) and augmented reality (AR) experiences. These technologies enable virtual visits, allowing individuals to experience the pilgrimage journey and connect with sacred sites remotely. Virtual tours, interactive rituals, and 360-degree views provide a sense of presence and allow pilgrims to engage with the spirituality and cultural significance of the pilgrimage destination.

Cultural Preservation: Technology plays a vital role in the preservation and conservation of cultural heritage associated with pilgrimage sites. Through digitization efforts, artifacts, rituals, and historical information are safeguarded and made accessible to a wider audience. Digital archives preserve cultural traditions, rituals, and narratives, ensuring their longevity and creating opportunities for educational exploration. Pilgrims can now access detailed information about the cultural significance of pilgrimage sites, fostering a deeper understanding and appreciation of the heritage associated with these locations.

Improved Information and Education: Technology adoption in pilgrimage tourism has significantly improved the availability and dissemination of information. Mobile applications and online platforms provide comprehensive and up-to-date details about pilgrimage sites, including historical backgrounds, cultural practices, religious rituals, and local customs. Pilgrims can access interactive maps, audio guides, and multimedia content that enhance their knowledge and understanding. This abundance of information enriches the educational aspect of the pilgrimage experience, empowering pilgrims with a deeper connection to the spirituality and history of the site.

Enhanced Navigation and Wayfinding: Navigating pilgrimage routes can often be challenging, especially in unfamiliar surroundings. Technology-driven solutions have addressed this issue by providing precise navigation tools. Mobile apps equipped with real-time directions, maps, and location-based services assist pilgrims in efficiently following the pilgrimage route. These tools also help pilgrims locate essential facilities such as restrooms, accommodations, and dining options along the way, ensuring a smoother and more convenient journey.

Community Engagement: Technology facilitates connections and community engagement among pilgrims. Social media platforms and online communities create virtual spaces for pilgrims to share their experiences, exchange stories, and connect with like-minded individuals. Pilgrims can seek advice, offer support, and establish meaningful connections with fellow travelers. This sense of community enhances the pilgrimage experience by fostering a sense of belonging, camaraderie, and shared spiritual journeys.

Augmented Experiences and Education: The adoption of technology, particularly virtual and augmented reality, provides immersive and educational experiences for pilgrims. Virtual representations of sacred locations and augmented reality overlays offer interactive exploration and learning opportunities. Pilgrims can engage with historical reenactments, visualizations of ancient structures, and interactive displays that enrich their understanding of the pilgrimage site. These augmented experiences enhance the overall journey, creating memorable and transformative encounters with the spiritual and cultural aspects of the pilgrimage destination.

The benefits of technology adoption in pilgrimage tourism are numerous and diverse (Nandasena et al., 2022) (presented in Table 1). From enhanced accessibility and cultural preservation to improved information and education, navigation, community engagement, and augmented experiences, technology has revolutionized the way pilgrims engage with sacred sites. As technology continues to advance, pilgrimage tourism will witness further enhancements, offering pilgrims even greater opportunities for spiritual, cultural, and educational exploration. Embracing technology in pilgrimage tourism not only enriches the individual pilgrim experience but also contributes to the preservation and promotion of cultural heritage for future generations.

Table 1. Benefits of technology adoption in pilgrimage tourism

Technological Advancements	Impacts	Examples
Enhanced Accessibility	- Overcoming geographical barriers for remote access to pilgrimage sites.	- Virtual reality (VR) and augmented reality (AR) experiences allowing virtual visits to sacred sites.
Cultural Preservation	- Conservation and digitization of cultural heritage associated with pilgrimage sites.	- Digitized archives of artifacts, rituals, and historical information for preservation and wider dissemination.
Improved Information and Education	- Comprehensive and up-to-date information about pilgrimage sites.	- Mobile apps providing details on historical significance, cultural practices, religious rituals, and local customs.
Enhanced Navigation and Wayfinding	- Precise navigation tools for efficient pilgrimage route guidance.	- Mobile apps with real-time directions, maps, and location-based services.
Community Engagement	- Facilitating connections and community engagement among pilgrims.	- Social media platforms and online communities for sharing experiences and connecting with like-minded individuals.
Augmented Experiences and Education	- Immersive educational experiences through virtual and augmented reality.	- Virtual representations of sacred locations, enabling interactive exploration and learning.

THE USE OF TECHNOLOGY IN PILGRIMAGE TOURISM

Because of significant improvements in information and communication technology (ICT), the core of tourism and travel behaviors have altered in recent decades (Saluveer et al., 2020). The use of technology to improve pilgrimage tourist experiences and hospitality services has gotten a lot of attention in recent years. The use of technology in the pilgrimage tourism experience has the potential to significantly improve pilgrims' overall experience and to generate new possibilities for hospitality operators to better satisfy pilgrims' requirements. The use of technology in pilgrimage tourism has been an emerging research area in recent years, with a growing number of studies (De Ascaniis et al. 2018; Farooq and Altintas, 2022; Amaro et al., 2021) exploring the potential benefits and challenges of technology use in this context. This literature review aims to provide a comprehensive overview of the existing research in this area, highlighting the key findings and providing insights into the role of technology in enhancing pilgrimage tourism experiences and hospitality services.

Mobile apps for tourism (Hamouda, 2022; Hussein and Ahmed, 2022) have been studied. However, no study has looked into pilgrimage mobile apps. Although, the use of mobile applications and other digital tools is one of the most important ways that technology may improve pilgrimage tourism experiences (Khan and Shambour, 2018). Pilgrims can use mobile applications to get real-time information about their route, such as the history and significance of pilgrimage sites, directions to the next waypoint, and suggestions for local hospitality providers. A smartphone app, for example, may give a step-by-step guide for the Camino de Santiago, including maps, explanations of historical and cultural attractions, and restaurant, hotel, and other hospitality provider suggestions. Mobile applications and other digital tools, in addition to giving information and direction, may help pilgrims develop a sense of community and connection. An app, for example, may contain features like chat rooms, forums, and social media, allowing pilgrims to share their stories and interact with other visitors. This sense of camaraderie is especially crucial for single pilgrims, who may feel isolated and detached during their journey.

Technology can also be employed to improve pilgrims' safety and security during their journey (Zhan and Ning, 2021). GPS monitoring (D'Antonio et al., 2022), real-time communication (Hassannia et al., 2019), and emergency response systems (Liu and Wang, 2019), for example, can be used to monitor pilgrims' safety and wellness and to respond rapidly in the case of an emergency. This can help guarantee that pilgrimage tourism is a safe and joyful experience for all participants. In addition to benefits for pilgrims, using technology in pilgrimage tourism may assist local communities. For example, technology may be leveraged to provide new opportunities for local businesses, such as the development of smartphone applications and other digital tools to enhance pilgrimage tourism. Technology may also be used to encourage sustainable tourist practices, such as lowering the environmental impact of pilgrimage tourism and supporting local economies via the use of locally sourced products and services.

Moreover, technology has been used in a variety of ways to enhance the experiences of pilgrims, including providing information and guidance, facilitating communication and social interaction, and enhancing the spiritual and cultural aspects of the pilgrimage experience (De Ascaniis et al. 2018). For example, mobile applications have been developed to provide pilgrims (Doush et al. 2015) with information about the pilgrimage destination, including details on the history, culture, and religious significance of the site, as well as practical information such as maps (Parady et al., 2023), travel directions, and accommodation options (Canturk et al., 2023). In addition, technology has been used to create virtual tours and augmented reality experiences (Nautiyal and Polus, 2022) that allow pilgrims to immerse themselves in the pilgrimage destination, even if they are not able to physically visit the site. Consequently, virtual and augmented reality technologies are another way that technology might improve pilgrimage tourism experiences. Virtual reality may be utilized to create immersive and interactive experiences that allow pilgrims to explore and engage with pilgrimage destinations in novel and fascinating ways. A virtual reality tour of the Vatican, for example, may allow travelers to see the museums, basilicas, and other key places without having to physically visit the Vatican City. The use of augmented reality technologies can also improve the pilgrimage experience. For example, while travelers tour pilgrimage locations, an augmented reality app may offer historical and cultural facts. This might contain information about the site's history and significance, as well as recommendations for local lodging and other surrounding activities.

Furthermore, technology has been utilized to improve the quality of hospitality services in a variety of ways (Li et al., 2021), including online booking and payment systems, customer relationship management tools, and management information systems (Salameh et al., 2022). For example, online booking systems have been developed to allow pilgrims to book accommodation, travel arrangements, and other services easily and conveniently, while customer relationship management tools have been used to manage customer data and interactions, allowing service providers to better understand their customers' needs and preferences.

Also, technology may also be utilized to improve the quality of hospitality services by providing hospitality professionals with real-time feedback and information (Hossain and Rahman, 2022; Li et al., 2021). A smartphone app, for example, might allow pilgrims to score and evaluate their interactions with local hotels, restaurants, and other hospitality providers, offering vital input to the providers and assisting them in improving their services. Smart home technology (Ferreira et al., 2023) is another way that technology may improve hospitality services. Smart home systems, for example, may be used to automate many of the activities connected with maintaining a hotel or guesthouse, such as regulating the temperature, lighting, and other environmental elements, as well as ensuring that visitors have access to amenities like Wi-Fi and television.

Gamification (Wei et al., 2023) and storytelling (Kemp et al., 2023) are two more ways that technology might improve pilgrimage tourism. The application of game design concepts in non-gaming environments, such as tourism, to promote engagement and motivation is known as "gamification" (Abou-Shouk and Soliman 2021) Gamification could be used in the context of pilgrimage tourism to give pilgrims more interesting and dynamic experiences. For example, challenges, awards, and leaderboards could be added to the pilgrimage route. This may make the pilgrimage experience more joyful and memorable, as well as encourage pilgrims to interact more profoundly with the pilgrimage sites' history, culture, and spirituality. Another area where technology may improve pilgrimage tourism experiences is storytelling (Su et al., 2020). Technology can be used to create immersive and interactive narrative experiences that let pilgrims learn about the history, culture, and spirituality of pilgrimage sites in a new and interesting way. A virtual reality or augmented reality program, for example, may be used to bring stories and legends connected with a pilgrimage site to life, allowing pilgrims to experience the location in a fresh and meaningful way.

Although the Use of Technology in Enhancing Pilgrimage Tourism Experiences and Hospitality Services has not yet been investigated, the current investigations identified some potential uses, benefits, and challenges of various technologies in the context of pilgrimage tourism based on the above discussions (presented in Table 2)

Table 2. Potential uses, benefits, and challenges of various technologies in the context of pilgrimage tourism

Technology	Use in Pilgrimage Tourism	Key Benefits	Challenges
Mobile Apps	Information and guidance, community and social interaction, safety and security	Real-time information and directions, sense of community and connection, improved safety and security	Lack of standardized information, limited local content, privacy and security concerns
Virtual Reality	Immersive and interactive experiences	Enhanced cultural and spiritual experience, improved access to pilgrimage destinations	High cost of VR hardware, limited VR content, difficulty in accessing VR technology
Augmented Reality	Providing historical and cultural information	Improved cultural and historical experience, enhanced exploration of pilgrimage destinations	Limited AR content, compatibility issues with different devices
Online Booking and Payment Systems	Convenient booking and payment of services	Ease of use, improved efficiency and customer satisfaction	Privacy and security concerns, compatibility issues with different payment systems
Customer Relationship Management Tools	Management of customer data and interactions	Improved understanding of customer needs and preferences, improved service quality	Limited access to customer data, high cost of CRM systems, privacy and security concerns
Management Information Systems	Real-time feedback and information for hospitality providers	Improved service quality, better decision-making based on data analysis	Limited access to data, high cost of MIS systems, compatibility issues with different platforms
Smart Home Technology	Automation of hotel and guesthouse activities	Improved efficiency and convenience, improved service quality	High cost of smart home systems, compatibility issues with different devices, privacy and security concerns
GPS Monitoring	Monitoring pilgrims' safety and wellness, responding rapidly in case of an emergency	Improved safety and security during the journey	Dependency on functioning GPS technology and internet connectivity, potential for privacy concerns
Gamification and Storytelling	Enhancing the cultural and spiritual aspects of the pilgrimage experience	Interactive and engaging experience, increased motivation and engagement	Potential for limited appeal, dependency on functioning technology and internet connectivity

Given the rapid advancements in Information and Communication Technology (ICT), there has been a transformative shift in the core behaviors of tourism and travel over the past few decades (Saluveer et al., 2020). In response to this, the intersection of technology with pilgrimage tourism has become a focal point, drawing considerable attention in recent years. This intersection holds the promise of not only enhancing the overall pilgrimage experience for travelers but also creating new avenues for hospitality operators to better cater to the specific needs of pilgrims. The convergence of technology and pilgrimage tourism has emerged as a burgeoning area of research, evident in the increasing number of studies exploring the potential benefits and challenges of technology use in this context (De Ascaniis et al., 2018; Farooq and Altintas, 2022; Amaro et al., 2021). This literature review seeks to offer a comprehensive overview of the existing research landscape in this domain, shedding light on key findings and providing insights into the pivotal role of technology in elevating both pilgrimage tourism experiences and the quality of associated hospitality services.

In an era marked by digital transformation, the pilgrimage experience has undergone significant changes, with advancements such as interactive touchscreens, artificial intelligence, and mobile applications reshaping how pilgrims engage with sacred sites (Rahman et al., 2022; Gazzaz & Mohamed, 2022). These technological interventions not only enhance accessibility and provide personalized guidance but also revolutionize hospitality services. Mobile applications facilitate real-time information, seamless bookings, and improved communication between pilgrims and service providers, elevating the overall standard of hospitality (Hossain & Rahman, 2022; Hamouda, 2022). However, the manuscript also recognizes challenges such as the need to balance tradition with innovation and address cybersecurity concerns (Wei et al., 2023). By navigating these complexities, the paper contributes to a nuanced understanding of the impact and potential of technology in shaping pilgrimage tourism experiences and services (Nandasena et al., 2022).

CONCLUSION

Despite the scarcity of studies on the use of technology to improve pilgrimage tourist experiences and hospitality services, current investigations have discovered several possible uses, advantages, and limitations of various technologies in this context. These potential uses and benefits include the use of augmented reality and virtual reality to provide tourists with immersive experiences, the use of social media to promote pilgrimage destinations and engage with tourists, and the use of mobile applications to provide tourists with information, maps, and other services. However, issues like privacy concerns, the expense of technological installation, and a lack of infrastructure in specific locations must all be taken into account. While the use of technology in pilgrimage tourism has enormous promise, it is evident that considerable study and preparation must be given to its implementation in order to maximize its benefits and minimize its obstacles.

The application of technology in pilgrimage tourism is a complicated and multifaceted topic that has the ability to improve the whole experience of pilgrimage tourism while also taking into account the cultural and spiritual value of pilgrimage sites. Multiple stakeholders, including government agencies, pilgrimage site administrators, hotel providers, and technology businesses, must collaborate and coordinate for successful technology integration in pilgrimage tourism. Each of these stakeholders plays a vital role in ensuring that technology is used in ways that promote pilgrimage tourism's aims and ideals. There is also a need to investigate the particular ways in which technology may be utilized to improve the pilgrimage tourism experience, such as enhancing accessibility and navigation, giving tailored suggestions and itineraries, and expediting the booking and check-in processes. There is also a need to better understand the influence of technology on pilgrimage sites, especially its impact on cultural heritage and spiritual value. Finally, the ethical issues of using technology in pilgrimage tourism must be considered. The use of technology at pilgrimage sites, for example, may raise concerns about privacy and security, as well as the possibility of commercialization and commodification of spiritual experiences. It is critical for stakeholders to carefully explore these problems and devise methods to guarantee that technology is utilized in a manner that respects the cultural and spiritual value of pilgrimage sites.

APPLICATIONS

Practical Applications of the Study

The current study has several practical applications. Firstly, this study provides valuable insights for pilgrimage site administrators and service providers. By understanding the potential benefits and challenges of technology integration, administrators can make informed decisions on adopting tools such as mobile applications, virtual reality experiences, and online booking systems. This knowledge equips them to enhance the overall pilgrimage experience, making it more accessible and engaging for participants. Secondly, this study offers guidance to technology developers and innovators seeking to create solutions tailored to pilgrimage tourism. Understanding the specific needs of pilgrims, such as real-time information, interactive maps, and immersive experiences, enables developers to design applications that align with these requirements. This, in turn, contributes to the successful implementation of technology in the pilgrimage context. Thirdly, pilgrimage organizers can leverage the findings to strategize community-building initiatives. Social media platforms and online communities can be harnessed to create a sense of shared experience among pilgrims. This study emphasizes the importance of technology in fostering connections, and organizers can use this information to strengthen the community aspect of pilgrimage journeys. Fourthly, hospitality service providers can benefit from the insights on technology's impact on the quality of services. The study emphasizes the role of online booking systems, customer relationship management tools, and real-time feedback mechanisms. Service providers can adapt their offerings to align with these technological advancements, ensuring a seamless and satisfying experience for pilgrims. Fifthly, government agencies involved in tourism regulation can use this study to develop policies that support responsible technology integration in pilgrimage tourism. Addressing concerns such as privacy, cybersecurity, and cultural sensitivity, regulators can create frameworks that encourage the ethical use of technology while preserving the sacred nature of pilgrimage sites. Lastly, researchers and academicians can build upon the gaps identified in this study to further explore the nuanced relationship between technology and pilgrimage tourism. Future research can delve into specific technologies, their cultural implications, and the long-term effects on pilgrim experiences. This study, therefore, serves as a foundation for continued academic inquiry in this evolving field.

In summary, this study has several practical applications, ranging from informing administrators and developers to guiding organizers, service providers, government agencies, and researchers in their respective roles within the pilgrimage tourism ecosystem.

Theoretical and Policy Implications

The study holds significant theoretical and policy implications, contributing to tourism theory by offering insights into the intricate relationship between technology and pilgrimage tourism. In terms of theoretical applications, this research advances our understanding of tourism dynamics, innovation adoption, and cultural preservation. It sheds light on how technological advancements can be assimilated into traditional and culturally rich contexts, providing theoretical frameworks for the responsible integration of technology in pilgrimage experiences. Furthermore, the study aligns with innovation and diffusion theories, offering a case study on the adoption of technology within a sacred and culturally significant domain. Culturally, the research contributes to the field by exploring the delicate balance between preserving cultural heritage and embracing technological progress.

In terms of policy applications, the findings of this study are pivotal for guiding policymakers. The insights can inform the development of technology integration policies, ensuring that advancements enhance visitor experiences without compromising cultural values. Policymakers can use these recommendations to formulate strategies for sustainable tourism practices, aligning pilgrimage tourism with broader environmental conservation goals. Moreover, the study highlights the importance of digital preservation policies, providing guidance for governments and heritage organizations to support digitization efforts for cultural artifacts and rituals. Policies encouraging community engagement through technology-mediated platforms can also be developed, fostering connections among pilgrims. Additionally, ethical guidelines are crucial, and policymakers can draw from this research to establish codes of conduct addressing privacy concerns and ensuring technology respects the spiritual and cultural values of pilgrimage sites. In essence, the study's theoretical and policy applications provide a comprehensive foundation for navigating the intricate intersection of pilgrimage tourism and technology.

LIMITATIONS AND FUTURE RESEARCH DIRECTIONS

Despite the valuable contributions of this study, certain limitations warrant acknowledgment, and avenues for future research emerge. Firstly, the research primarily focuses on the potential benefits and challenges associated with the use of technology in pilgrimage tourism, and while it hints at privacy concerns, a more in-depth exploration of ethical considerations surrounding technology implementation is needed. Future research could delve into the nuanced ethical dimensions, examining issues of cultural commodification, privacy infringements, and the impact on the spiritual sanctity of pilgrimage sites.

Secondly, the study lacks a comprehensive analysis of the varying levels of technological infrastructure across pilgrimage destinations. Considering the potential discrepancies in access to and adoption of technology in different regions, future research could undertake a more granular examination of these differences. This could involve a comparative analysis of pilgrimage sites in technologically advanced regions versus those facing infrastructure challenges. Another limitation lies in the predominantly positive tone regarding the benefits of technology adoption. Future research should adopt a more critical lens, exploring potential drawbacks and unintended consequences associated with the integration of technology in pilgrimage tourism. Understanding the negative aspects, such as over-reliance on digital platforms or cultural dilution, would provide a more balanced perspective. Furthermore, the current study is situated within a specific time frame, and the rapid evolution of technology implies that new innovations may emerge. Future research should strive to keep pace with technological advancements, providing ongoing insights into the ever-changing landscape of pilgrimage tourism. Addressing these limitations and pursuing these future research directions will contribute to a more nuanced and comprehensive understanding of the intricate relationship between technology and pilgrimage tourism.

REFERENCES

Abou-Shouk, M., & Soliman, M. (2021). The impact of gamification adoption intention on brand awareness and loyalty in tourism: The mediating effect of customer engagement. *Journal of Destination Marketing & Management, 20*, 100559. Advance online publication. DOI: 10.1016/j.jdmm.2021.100559

Amaro, S., Barroco, C., & Fonseca, P. (2021). The use of information and communication technologies in religious tourism. In *The Routledge Handbook of Religious and Spiritual Tourism* (pp. 372–384). Routledge. DOI: 10.4324/9780429201011-31

Buhalis, D. (2020). Technology in tourism-from information communication technologies to eTourism and smart tourism towards ambient intelligence tourism: A perspective article. *Tourism Review, 75*(1), 267–272. DOI: 10.1108/TR-06-2019-0258

Canturk, D., Karagoz, P., Kim, S. W., & Toroslu, I. H. (2023). Trust-aware location recommendation in location-based social networks: A graph-based approach. *Expert Systems with Applications, 213*, 119048. DOI: 10.1016/j.eswa.2022.119048

Collins-Kreiner, N. (2020). Pilgrimage tourism-past, present and future rejuvenation: A perspective article. *Tourism Review, 75*(1), 145–148. DOI: 10.1108/TR-04-2019-0130

D'Antonio, A., Monz, C. A., Crabb, B., Baggio, J. A., & Howe, P. D. (2022). Proof of concept study using GPS-based tracking data to build agent-based models of visitors' off-trail behavior in nature-based tourism settings. *Applied Geography (Sevenoaks, England), 147*, 102771. DOI: 10.1016/j.apgeog.2022.102771

De Ascaniis, S., Mutangala, M.-M., & Cantoni, L. (2018). ICTs in the tourism experience at religious heritage sites: A review of the literature and an investigation of pilgrims' experiences at the sanctuary of Loreto (Italy). Church. *Communication and Culture, 3*(3), 310–334. DOI: 10.1080/23753234.2018.1544835

Doush, I. A., Alshattnawi, S., & Barhoush, M. (2015). Non-visual navigation interface for completing tasks with a predefined order using mobile phone: A case study of pilgrimage. *International Journal of Mobile Network Design and Innovation, 6*(1), 1. DOI: 10.1504/IJMNDI.2015.069207

Farooq, M., & Altintas, V. (2022). Role of Technology on Religious Tourism in Turkey. In Ramos, C., Quinteiro, S., & Gonçalves, A. (Eds.), *ICT as Innovator Between Tourism and Culture* (pp. 67–80). IGI Global., DOI: 10.4018/978-1-7998-8165-0.ch005

Ferreira, L., Oliveira, T., & Neves, C. (2023). Consumer's intention to use and recommend smart home technologies: The role of environmental awareness. *Energy, 263*, 125814. DOI: 10.1016/j.energy.2022.125814

Gazzaz, O. B., & Mohamed, H. S. (2022). Patterns of Touch Screen Technology Use in Religious Tourism and Pilgrimage. *International Journal of Customer Relationship Marketing and Management, 13*(1), 1–21. DOI: 10.4018/IJCRMM.300830

Gunlu, E., & Okumus, F. (2010). The Hajj experience of Turkish female pilgrim. *Tourism in the Muslim World Bridging Tourism Theory and Practice, 2*, 223–236.

Hamouda, M. (2022). Mobile Applications in Tourism. *International Journal of Technology and Human Interaction, 18*(1), 1–13. DOI: 10.4018/IJTHI.293198

Handriana, T., Yulianti, P., & Kurniawati, M. (2020). Exploration of pilgrimage tourism in Indonesia. *Journal of Islamic Marketing, 11*(3), 783–795. DOI: 10.1108/JIMA-10-2018-0188

Hassannia, R., Barenji, A. V., Li, Z., & Alipour, H. (2019). Web-based recommendation system for smart tourism: Multiagent technology. *Sustainability (Basel), 11*(2), 323. Advance online publication. DOI: 10.3390/su11020323

Hindersah, H., Agustina, I. H., & Chofyan, I. (2021). The spiritual path of pilgrimage tourism for sustainable development: Case-desa Astana-Cirebon, Indonesia. *International Journal of Sustainable Development and Planning, 16*(4), 751–758. DOI: 10.18280/ijsdp.160415

Hossain, M. S., & Rahman, M. F. (2022). Detection of potential customers' empathy behavior towards customers' reviews. *Journal of Retailing and Consumer Services, 65*, 102881. Advance online publication. DOI: 10.1016/j.jretconser.2021.102881

Hunt, E. D. (1984). Travel, tourism and piety in the Roman Empire: A context for the beginnings of Christian pilgrimage. *Echos du monde classique. Échos du Monde Classique, 28*(3), 391–417.

Hussein, S., & Ahmed, E. (2022). Mobile Application for Tourism. *International Journal of Customer Relationship Marketing and Management, 13*(1), 1–29. DOI: 10.4018/IJCRMM.290415

Hyde, K. F., & Harman, S. (2011). Motives for a secular pilgrimage to the gallipoli battlefields. *Tourism Management, 32*(6), 1343–1351. DOI: 10.1016/j.tourman.2011.01.008

Kemp, A., Gravios, R., Syrdal, H., & McDougal, E. (2023). Storytelling is not just for marketing: Cultivating a storytelling culture throughout the organization. *Business Horizons*, *66*(3), 313–324. Advance online publication. DOI: 10.1016/j.bushor.2023.01.008

Khan, E. A., & Shambour, M. K. Y. (2018, January 1). An analytical study of mobile applications for Hajj and Umrah services. *Applied Computing and Informatics*. Elsevier B.V. DOI: 10.1016/j.aci.2017.05.004

Li, M., Yin, D., Qiu, H., & Bai, B. (2021). A systematic review of AI technology-based service encounters: Implications for hospitality and tourism operations. *International Journal of Hospitality Management*, *95*, 102930. Advance online publication. DOI: 10.1016/j.ijhm.2021.102930

Liu, Z., & Wang, C. (2019). Design of traffic emergency response system based on internet of things and data mining in emergencies. *IEEE Access : Practical Innovations, Open Solutions*, *7*, 113950–113962. DOI: 10.1109/ACCESS.2019.2934979

Luz, N. (2020). Pilgrimage and religious tourism in Islam. *Annals of Tourism Research*, *82*, 102915. DOI: 10.1016/j.annals.2020.102915

Morgan, C., & Morgan, D. C. (1990). *Athletes and oracles: The transformation of Olympia and Delphi in the eighth century BC*. Cambridge University Press.

Nandasena, R., Morrison, A. M., & Coca-Stefaniak, J. A. (2022). Transformational tourism – a systematic literature review and research agenda. *Journal of Tourism Futures*, *8*(3), 282–297. DOI: 10.1108/JTF-02-2022-0038

Nautiyal, R., & Polus, R. (2022). Virtual tours as a solidarity tourism product? *Annals of Tourism Research Empirical Insights*, *3*(2), 100066. DOI: 10.1016/j.annale.2022.100066

Ozturk, I., Aslan, A., & Altinoz, B. (2022). Investigating the nexus between CO2 emissions, economic growth, energy consumption and pilgrimage tourism in Saudi Arabia. *Ekonomska Istrazivanja*, *35*(1), 3083–3098. DOI: 10.1080/1331677X.2021.1985577

Pack, S. D. (2010). Revival of the Pilgrimage to Santiago de Compostela: The Politics of Religious, National, and European Patrimony, 1879–1988. *The Journal of Modern History*, *82*(2), 335–367. DOI: 10.1086/651613

Parady, G., Suzuki, K., Oyama, Y., & Chikaraishi, M. (2023). Activity detection with google maps location history data: Factors affecting joint activity detection probability and its potential application on real social networks. *Travel Behaviour & Society*, *30*, 344–357. DOI: 10.1016/j.tbs.2022.10.010

Rahman, M. K., Akter, S., Hossain, M. M., & Hassan, A. (2022). Pilgrimage and Halal Tourism Event: Application of Technology. In *Technology Application in Tourism Fairs, Festivals and Events in Asia* (pp. 63–75). Springer Nature. https://doi.org/DOI: 10.1007/978-981-16-8070-0_4

Rahman, M. K., Akter, S., Hossain, M. M., & Hassan, A. (2022). Pilgrimage and Halal Tourism Event: Application of Technology. In Hassan, A. (Ed.), *Technology Application in Tourism Fairs, Festivals and Events in Asia*. Springer., DOI: 10.1007/978-981-16-8070-0_4

Reader, I. (2007). Pilgrimage growth in the modern world: Meanings and implications. *Religion*, *37*(3), 210–229. DOI: 10.1016/j.religion.2007.06.009

Rinschede, G. (1992). Forms of religious tourism. *Annals of Tourism Research*, *19*(1), 51–67. DOI: 10.1016/0160-7383(92)90106-Y

Rowley, G., & El-Hamdan, S. A. S. (1978). The Pilgrimage to Mecca: An Explanatory and Predictive Model. Environment and Planning A. *Environment & Planning A*, *10*(9), 1053–1071. DOI: 10.1068/a101053 PMID: 12262752

Salameh, A. A., Al Mamun, A., Hayat, N., & Ali, M. H. (2022). Modelling the significance of website quality and online reviews to predict the intention and usage of online hotel booking platforms. *Heliyon*, *8*(9), e10735. DOI: 10.1016/j.heliyon.2022.e10735 PMID: 36177224

Saluveer, E., Raun, J., Tiru, M., Altin, L., Kroon, J., Snitsarenko, T., Aasa, A., & Silm, S. (2020). Methodological framework for producing national tourism statistics from mobile positioning data. *Annals of Tourism Research*, *81*, 102895. Advance online publication. DOI: 10.1016/j.annals.2020.102895

Štefko, R., Kiráľová, A., & Mudrík, M. (2015). Strategic Marketing Communication in Pilgrimage Tourism. *Procedia: Social and Behavioral Sciences*, *175*, 423–430. DOI: 10.1016/j.sbspro.2015.01.1219

Su, L., Cheng, J., & Swanson, S. R. (2020). The impact of tourism activity type on emotion and storytelling: The moderating roles of travel companion presence and relative ability. *Tourism Management*, *81*, 104138. DOI: 10.1016/j.tourman.2020.104138

Timothy, D. J., & Olsen, D. H. (Eds.). (2006). *Tourism, Religion and Spiritual Journeys*. Routledge. DOI: 10.4324/9780203001073

UNESCO. (2017), "UNESCO and the International Year of Sustainable Tourism", *UNESCO*, 16 January, available at: https://en.unesco.org/iyst4d (accessed 5 February 2023).

Wei, Z., Zhang, J., Huang, X., & Qiu, H. (2023). Can gamification improve the virtual reality tourism experience? Analyzing the mediating role of tourism fatigue. *Tourism Management*, *96*, 104715. DOI: 10.1016/j.tourman.2022.104715

Zhan, L., & Ning, K. (2021). Minority Tourist Information Service and Sustainable Development of Tourism under the Background of Smart City. *Mobile Information Systems*, *2021*, 1–14. Advance online publication. DOI: 10.1155/2021/6547186

Chapter 10
Positive and Negative Aspects of Cultural Heritage Tourism:
An Insight Story

Rohit Thakur
https://orcid.org/0009-0009-2804-1211
Central University of Himachal Pradesh, India

Suman Sharma
Central University of Himachal Pradesh, India

Sahil Gautam
Central University of Himachal Pradesh, India

ABSTRACT

Tourism is booming around the world; Culture & heritage plays an important role in attracting millions of tourists to different destinations across the world. Cultural heritage tourism offers an opportunity to tourists to experience and understand different cultures in depth. Cultural Heritage tourism accounts for more than 40% of global international tourist arrivals. However, Cultural heritage tourism has both positives and negatives attached with it. The present chapter systematically reviews the existing literature with the aim to explain cultural heritage as an important component for tourism growth and also explain the concept of cultural heritage tourism and its components. This chapter identifies various positive & negative socio-cultural and economical aspects of cultural heritage tourism as well as how technology has helped destinations to increase tourist engagement, awareness and enhancing their experiences at the destination. The chapter also explains how cultural heritage can be used as a tourism product.

DOI: 10.4018/979-8-3693-3196-5.ch010

INTRODUCTION

Tourism industry is one of the most important industries across the world, contributing to the socio-economic growth of communities around the world. Tourism industry is having a great impact on different societies (Archer et al., 1998). The tourism sector makes up 10% of the world's GDP. (Neto, 2003). In a variety of tourist places, the tourism industry has given local residents chances for employment and self-employment. In 2022, there were about 917 million tourists who visited foreign countries. Following the Covid-19 outbreak, tourism has proven to be a stimulus for socioeconomic growth and development. (Li et al., 2022). Tourism as an activity has been changing in the last couple of decades due to social and technological change. Destinations around the world are focusing on accessible and affordable tourism for all, so that more and more economic development can be accelerated. Destinations have started to know their potential and have been successful in identifying their available resources which has helped them to create tourism products (Williams, 1998). There are various forms of tourism such as cultural heritage tourism, ecotourism, adventure tourism, religious tourism, rural tourism, gastronomy tourism, wine tourism, health & wellness tourism etc which are focus areas for many destinations around the world (Paresishvili et al., 2017). Among these forms of tourism, cultural heritage tourism is an important form of tourism which many destinations have successfully used as their USP for attracting more and more visitors each year. Due to change in society, technology and work life of people around the world, there is a shift from recreation to self-discovery that has led to emergence of niche markets in the tourism industry like adventure tourism, religious tourism, rural tourism, ecotourism, food tourism, wellness tourism, sustainable tourism, educational tourism, wine tourism. Amongst these one of the fastest growing forms of tourism is cultural heritage tourism (Craik, 2002).

MEANING OF CULTURE AND HERITAGE

Culture defines the identities of different communities around the world. Culture in simple words means people's behaviour, thought process, belief system, values that are passed by the previous generations through a formal or informal way (Throsby, 2001). In material aspects culture includes different elements like architecture, music, art, literature, philosophy and religion (Green, 1997). Culture also includes different customs and traditions followed by a particular community. Culture is mainly divided into two different types one is the material culture that includes architecture, goods, trade, technology and instruments, on the other hand second is the non-material culture which includes values, myths, beliefs, rituals, art forms, legends etc (Dant, 1999). Both material and non-material culture have a direct link between them, they have a great impact on each other. Different communities follow different cultures in all parts of the world. India is one the oldest communities in the world, which makes Indian culture very ancient and diverse. Culture is the soul of every nation, it defines the future of a particular society. In simple terms culture can be defined as "way of life" that includes the way people dress up, the food people eat, the way people practise religion, the customs & rituals people follow and the language people speak (Eliot, 2010). There are different elements attached with culture which include festivals, food, customs, rituals, traditions, languages, music, dance, art & architecture. On the other hand, Heritage refers to the culture which is passed by the ancestors to their next generations, which includes architecture, food, rites & rituals, customs, languages, art & craft, traditions, literature (Loulanski, 2006).

CULTURAL HERITAGE TOURISM

Cultural heritage tourism is one of the most important forms of tourism in the present times. Travellers from all parts of the world are interested in experiencing and learning about new culture and heritage (McKercher, 2002). Culture heritage tourism means travelling to new places which are important to a particular community, that showcase their lifestyle and cultural identity. Culture heritage tourism includes visiting historical buildings, monuments, temples, museums etc, participation in different fairs & festivals, tasting and cooking new food and indulging in various art forms (Richards, 2007). Most countries around the world have enormous cultural resources which are having cultural significance to their societies. Cultural heritage resources include architecture, music, dance, handicrafts, rituals & customs, food and festivals. There are thousands of important cultural heritage sites around the world, people around the world have different eating habits which is a sign that there are variety of food & beverages available at different sites, different communities around the world have different belief system, they follow different religion, they have different customs & rituals, communities are involved in different types of art forms (Timothy, 2011). Many festivals are celebrated around the year in different parts of the world. Due to the presence of different communities around the world, there is a difference of culture everywhere. Every country in the world has one or other cultural heritage resource that can be used as a unique product to attract more and more visitors to their destination. Cultural heritage destinations attract a particular segment of tourists having a keen interest in culture & heritage which makes them different from other tourists, such tourists can be called as CHT tourists (Weng, et al., 2019). People around the world, respective of their country, state, district or region are associated with different customs, rituals, languages, eating habits which makes them unique in their lifestyle and culture. Experiences from forefathers, teachings and history makes every society culturally different from each other.

COMPONENTS OF CULTURAL HERITAGE TOURISM

Tangible Cultural Heritage

Tangible cultural heritage includes objects which are significant and associated with history, architecture, archaeology and past generations. It includes temples, monuments, historic places, indigenous food, paintings, handicrafts and artefacts (Pai, 2014). Tangible cultural heritage is very important and worth preservation for the upcoming generations.

Temples, Monuments and Buildings

Most of the temples, monuments and buildings that have survived around the world are religious and cultural heritage in nature (Meskell, 2002). There are numerous temples, monuments and buildings located in all parts of the world which are associated with different religions, histories and communities. There are thousands of world heritage sites around the world under UNESCO (United Nations Educational, Scientific and Cultural Organization and more than 3000 sites under ASI (Archaeological Survey of India) in all parts of India. (Chalana, & Sprague, 2013). These sites are important for various communities, as they have cultural significance for different nations and the communities living there. These sites are tangible in nature and hence part of tangible cultural heritage. Millions of tourists from all parts of the world travel to these sites for pilgrimage, education and experiencing culture every year.

Handicrafts and Handlooms

Handicrafts are one of the main elements which reflect on the history and culture of communities in all parts of the world. There are thousands of handicrafts & handlooms made around the world (Tripathi et al., 2022). Ranging from metal craft, copper craft, wooden work, glass work, pottery, terracotta, bamboo craft, jute work, leather craft, bidriware, textiles, shawls etc. Handicrafts and handlooms act as souvenirs that are shopped by the tourists visiting different tourist's destinations.

Paintings

Painting is a form of art, usually drawn on a canvas, paper or cardboard. These paintings portray certain stories, scenes or characters. Paintings are also an important part of cultural heritage; people have been making different styles of paintings in different countries of the world depicting a particular community's culture (Myers, 2002). Paintings are also shopped as souvenirs by the tourists who visit to different locations around the world.

Literature

Literature is an important element of culture. It is an art of writing with the help of words. A particular community or nation's culture and its civilization is introduced through literature. Literature helps a particular community in growth and development and also shapes the younger generations. Literature can be called the soul of culture, as it defines the path for a particular society (Adler, 1998). Literature defines the religious practices, norms, rituals and values of a particular community.

Intangible Cultural Heritage

Cultural heritage is also intangible in nature, intangible cultural heritage includes values, oral traditions, social practices, rites & rituals, performing arts, knowledge & expressions which are inherited by our forefathers and are further passed to the next upcoming generations (Petrillo, 2019). Intangible cultural heritage does not have a physical appearance. There are 678 intangible cultural heritage elements under the UNESCO list in the world (Su et al., 2019).

Performing Arts

The world is a complete powerhouse of various forms of art, out of which performing arts is one of the significant forms of art that includes folk theatre, folk dance and folk music (Beeman, 1993). Performing arts can be seen at various festivals around the world, which represents the local culture of different communities at different regions in all parts of the world. There are hundreds of folk dances and various plays, skits and Naukad Natak performed at various stages during different festivals across the world. Performing arts mainly exhibit the rich history and cultural significance of a particular region.

Food

Food is another important part of culture, associated with different nations and communities. Food is tangible in nature; but it is considered as an important intangible cultural heritage practice. There are a variety of foods available around the globe which vary from place to place on the basis of geography, climatic conditions and availability of ecological resources (Timothy & Ron, 2013). Food is also an important element of culture, as food tells about the story of a particular community or region.

Folklore

Folklore is a set of stories associated with local traditions and beliefs of a particular region. Folklore has been an integral part of many communities for ages. There are a range of cultures, languages and religions across the world which have a complete package of short stories and tales associated with mythology and history (Bascom, 1965). Folklore and folktales are passed from one generation to the next generation which helps to create a bond between communities and preserve traditional values in the society. Traditional stories definitely represent different cultures around the world.

Oral Traditions

It is a type of communication between humans wherein different cultural ideas, art, and knowledge is shared, received and preserved through oral communication from one generation to another generation. Oral traditions mainly include chanting, riddles, poetry, songs and folktales. Knowledge is shared through communication only; no writing is done (Tonkin, 1995). Oral traditions shape and represent both culture and community.

Rites and Rituals

Rites are a set of formal rules and ceremonies which occur at a place on a specified time and day, mostly in a religious and sacred scenario, whereas Rituals are well established norms and customs followed by a particular community (Kurtz, 2015). Different societies perform different rites & rituals in their daily lives, which are part of their culture and traditions. Rites and rituals portray knowledge and information about different cultures and the people who participate. People from different communities and backgrounds participate in different rites and rituals to fulfil their commitment in their social lives.

Fairs and Festivals

Fairs & festivals are important components of different cultures of the world. Communities around the world celebrate different fairs and festivals throughout the year in different regions of the world. People showcase their culture and traditions during various fairs and festivals which reflects the unique cultures of the world. Fairs and festivals showcase the meaningful identities and rich customs of communities which are based on legends, history, rituals, traditions and seasons (Derrett, 2003). These celebrations also denote dedication, beliefs, power, peace, art, music, dance, food, rituals and humanity messages.

WHO IS A CULTURAL HERITAGE TOURIST?

Cultural heritage tourists are mainly focusing on investigation, research and experiencing different cultures and heritage (Nguyen & Cheung, 2014). The main motive of a cultural heritage tourist is to experience new culture by visiting different cultural and historical tourist attractions and also participate in various cultural activities (McKercher, 2002). Cultural heritage tourists are well educated and have a good experience and wish to stay for longer durations at a single destination.

CULTURE AND HERITAGE AS A TOURISM PRODUCT

Tourists travelling from different parts of the world have different motivations and desires which differ from one another, some travel for unique experiences, indigenous culture, food, architecture, fairs, festivals which serve as a tourist attraction for them. When we see cultural heritage as part of tourism, cultural heritage is ancient, rich and unique, portraying the legacy of forefathers that have survived for a long period of time (Edgell Sr, 2019). Cultural heritage of a destination represents the social values, identity and self-esteem of various communities of the world. Culture heritage is a fruit for most tourists who are interested in gaining new knowledge and experiences. Culture heritage of a destination provides an understanding to the tourists about the history and present culture and heritage of that destination, which creates a certain type of curiosity and influences the tourists to a great extent (McKercher & Du Cros, 2002). Cultural heritage tourism provides a platform and opportunity to visitors to understand, respect and learn about various cultures. Cultural heritage tourism can be used as a tool for promoting peace and harmony amongst different communities of the world (D'Amore, 1988). Due to changing environment and tourism trends globally new markets have started to emerge. From traditional leisure travel there is shift into new markets wherein tourists are more attracted towards new forms of tourism like cultural heritage tourism, adventure tourism, rural tourism, eco-tourism, wine tourism and gastronomy tourism. Destinations around the world have started to focus on adding cultural heritage oriented products along with tour packages and tourism activities. Every year visitors are travelling to different destinations around the world and who have keen interest in history, culture and heritage of such destinations. Getting unique and authentic experiences is the main motivation for travel. Such change in tourist motivation, behaviour and preference have started to promote cultural heritage tourism destinations in all parts of the world. The increasing demand for cultural heritage products have started to create business and job opportunities for local communities at different destinations and have led to generate socio-economic benefits for the local economy. Cultural heritage tourists mainly have a high level of education and awareness as well as a good amount of disposable income and cultural heritage tourism destinations mostly attract these tourists with high income and education, which have started to create high income benefits for the local communities at different cultural heritage destinations. Global cultural heritage tourism market is estimated at 556.96 billion USD in the year 2021 and is expected to grow at an annual (CAGR) 3.8% from the year 2022 to 2030 (UNWTO) This growth is driven by the various programmes and initiatives of different governments in all parts of the world for the promotion of cultural heritage tourism based products. In the year 2018 the United Nations declared the European year of Cultural heritage, which encouraged various stakeholders to develop more sustainable tourism products and promote sustainable tourism. Visitors in all parts of the world are seeking out both tangible cultural heritage and intangible culture heritage during their visits to different tourist destinations. Such destinations also offer an opportunity for the tourists to learn about cultural heritage, spirituality and knowledge about the history of these destinations. Constant efforts are also made by various governments to encourage and promote cultural heritage markets, which have a great influence on the global cultural heritage tourism market growth. Over the past years, there is a growth in the global cultural heritage market as tourists are participating and keen to know about different cultural heritage products. About 40% of global tourism accounts to cultural heritage tourism according to the United Nations World tourism organization. Global tourism industry is continuously changing because of the change in lifestyle of consumers, increase in digital innovation and flourishing cultures in all parts of the world. However, this trend of digital innovation and transformation in the tourism industry will also facilitate and help the tourism industry to grow in all its dimensions along with cultural heritage tourism. Use of ICT and virtual reality technology is expected to enhance consumer experiences and gain popularity in the coming times. Governments around the world are also making efforts and have started initiatives to promote technology advancements for the growth of cultural heritage tourism and other areas of the tourism sector. For example, the Ministry of Tourism, Government of India have started its two programmes for the improvement of the tourism sector in India namely, Prasad (Pilgrimage Rejuvenation and Spiritual Augmentation Drive) for growth of pilgrimage and cultural heritage tourism sites and Swadesh Darshan for theme based tourism circuits development in different regions of the country with the help of digital innovation and ICT (Munjal, 2021). In the year September 2020, Amazon launched a virtual tour experience platform which provides a virtual tour to far off cultural sites like temples, monuments and palaces. In July 2020 the Stanford library and the Council on Library and Information Resources launched a digital library of the Middle East for the general public, which offers the cultural legacy of North America and Middle East which is expected to increase tourist interest in cultural heritage tourism and attract more and more tourists to North America and Middle East. In the Pandemic times virtual tours are gaining popularity and creating a new trend in the travel and tourism industry. By creating innovative and attractive cultural heritage tourism products more and more visitors can be attracted and unique experiences can be offered to tourists. Destinations around the world should emphasise on identifying the resources, planning and promotion, both tangible and intangible cultural heritage elements like food, art & craft, architecture, music, dances, customs, rituals and festivals can be used for the growth of cultural heritage markets.

POSITIVE AND NEGATIVE ASPECTS OF CULTURAL HERITAGE TOURISM

There are many positive effects of culture heritage tourism on a destination like economic growth of locals, improvement in the standard of living, employment opportunities, business opportunities etc. On the other hand, it also brings negative effects on the destination, local community and the environment.

Positive Aspects of CHT

Protection of Local Cultural Heritage

Culture heritage tourism helps in the development of tourism destinations and attractions. With the starting of tourism activities at a destination, the government and the stakeholders start to focus on preservation and conservation of their local culture (Li, et al., 2020). The local culture of a destination acts as a tourism product for the tourists and offers them different experiences and satisfaction. The culture of a destination is one of the most important attributes which attracts or motivates a tourist to visit a destination (Farmaki, 2012). Culture of a destination includes different elements like art, architecture, handicrafts, food, music, dance etc. Tourism encourages different stakeholders to participate in conservation of local culture. Tourism brings revenues for the preservation and conservation of cultural heritage (Aas, et al., 2005). Tourism also creates opportunities for both the local residents and the tourists to share their culture with each other and understand other cultures as well. Culture heritage tourism also strengthens the cultural values and helps in keeping the local art & craft, traditions and values intact. Culture heritage tourism also empowers the local communities so that they can feel proud about it (Cole, 2006). With increase in tourist footfall at a destination and increasing local involvement in tourism activities the local community starts to preserve their culture and offer that culture in its purest form to the tourist, for instance food establishments like restaurants, cafes, dhabas, coffee shops and food stalls starts to sell to include local indigenous food into their menu, different accommodation units organise local folk music and dance performances for the tourists, people open their heritage houses for the tourists, local handicrafts & handlooms are offered to sell to the tourists at different tourist places at a destination. All these activities to a greater extent helps in the preservation of cultural heritage of a region. It can be rightly stated that tourism helps in the protection and preservation of local culture in all parts of the world. Certainly, communities have started to understand the value of their culture.

Revive Local Art Forms

Culture heritage tourism is associated with the cultural heritage of a destination. There are many indigenous art forms which have started to vanish in the era of globalisation, which is a major concern for various communities around the world (Kumaj, 2010). This extinction of local art forms has affected locals to a great extent, as they have started to lose their identity. There are thousands of different art forms at various destinations around the world which are vanishing with time. Culture Heritage tourism have created opportunities for local communities involved in making different art forms and have also empowered local artisans to enhance their art (Giampiccoli & Kalis, 2012). Tourism activities at different destinations in all parts of the world have also provided financial support and economic benefits. For instance, In Himachal Pradesh till the late 1980s the local weavers and artisans were suffering from low demand and lack of financial assistance from the outside, with the coming of tourism in the different parts of the state, suddenly there is an increase in the demand of local handlooms and handicrafts. Handlooms like Kullui Caps, Kullui shawls, Chamba ka Rumal, Chamba ki Thal are high in demand amongst the tourists. Most tourists visiting Himachal Pradesh love to buy these handlooms & handicrafts as souvenirs. The increasing demand of Himachali handlooms and handicrafts has helped the local artisans and weavers to gain economic benefits and business opportunities from tourism and also has helped in reviving local art forms to a great level. Another art form which is revived is the local folk dance and music. Most of the hotels and tourist sites in all destinations around the world have started to organise cultural performances for the tourists visiting their destination. These cultural shows have given a new spark to folk music and dance. Which have helped locals to continue and learn their traditions associated with folk dance and music.

Promotion of Cultural Heritage

Culture heritage tourism emphasis on cultural heritage of a destination. There are millions of tourists visiting various destinations around the world in search of knowledge and gain unique experiences from their travels. Every destination has a cultural value attached to the place, which is offered to the tourists visiting such destinations. The experiences and knowledge gained by the tourists from the destination is shared by them through various platforms like internet, social media platforms, print media, blogs and word of mouth with their friends, family and others which helps in promotion of the cultural heritage of the destination (Tham et al.,2013). In a world where people are connected with each other through the internet, user generated content plays an important role in marketing and promotion of the cultural heritage of the destination. A lot of travel bloggers are travelling to various destination in all parts of the world, where they indulge in tourism activities and experience cultural heritage of destination where they experience architecture through visiting different monuments, temples and buildings, by participating in culinary classes and eating different food, participation in different fairs and festivals, shopping different handicrafts and handlooms, witness different types of cultural shows portraying folk dance and music which is shared with large audience through their blogs on social media and internet (Tussyadiah & Fesenmaier, 2008). This content on the internet motivates and attracts a large number of travellers to a new destination, in search of authentic experience and knowledge. Further it helps in promotion of the destinations and forms a desire and image in the minds of the travellers.

Create Job Opportunities

Tourism is an important industry, it creates millions of job opportunities across the world, 10% of the global jobs are linked with the travel and tourism industry, Pre-pandemic one out of every four jobs created globally was created in the tourism sector (Sofronov, 2018). As per the data of WTTC (World Travel and Tourism Council) tourism industry created 107 million direct jobs and supported 234 million jobs in the year 2015 and is expected to create 126 million jobs by the end of

2030. It is expected that tourism destinations in the G20 countries like India, China, Mexico and South Africa will grow at a very fast pace. Tourism destinations in non G20 countries like Tanzania, Zambia, Myanmar, Kyrgyzstan and Vietnam will see slowest growth in the tourism sector. Tourism sector provides different types of jobs across the travel industry. There are multiple sectors which are linked directly and indirectly with the travel industry to provide different products and services for the tourists which can create unique experiences to the tourists. Tourism and travel industry includes transportation, accommodation, food and beverage services, banking, entertainment and other travel intermediaries. These allied sectors create millions of direct and indirect jobs for the local community at every tourism destination. Tourism industry forms a value chain which is very vast and creates employment opportunities for all types of people which are not necessarily linked with the tourism industry. According to a UNWTO report, every one job creates about one and half indirect (additional) jobs associated with the tourism industry. Tourism industry creates employment opportunities in hotels, resorts, travel agencies, transportation companies, restaurants, cafes, shopping malls, local markets, souvenir shops, confectionary shops. Tourism is a highly labour intensive industry. Every tourism unit carries different suppliers for the better operations, which include food and beverage suppliers, accounting services, manufacturers, marketing agencies, souvenir producers and companies providing tourist activities like adventure companies, entertainment providers, local farmers, self-help groups etc. Tourism industry creates opportunities for all and has great power to generate employment, they may not be directly linked to tourism, but are important for the success of tourism whether it is a person working in a hotel, a waiter in a restaurant, a taxi or auto driver, a person running his stall, a person selling flowers, a tour guide, a photographer, a shopkeeper selling different products like local handlooms at a tourism destination (Mill, 1990). Hence such jobs are considered as an important part of the tourism and travel sector.

Create Business Opportunity

Tourism industry is one of the most important industries for the economic growth of nations across the world. Tourism industry consists of many small enterprises which are flexible in terms of change and expansion. Small scale businesses are very important for tourism growth as they support the economic development of local residents at the destination (Dahles, 2002). Tourism activities at a destination creates various opportunities for businesses ideas to grow both online and offline. Tourism creates different opportunities for business at destinations like lodging business, transport business, tour guiding services, photography services, event organisers, food & beverage services etc (Swarbrooke & Horner, 2001). Many small and medium businesses have grown at various destinations due to increasing tourist movements. Tourism provides an opportunity and encourages the local community to participate in tourism activities and start their own businesses and support their local economy. Tourism has boosted the local economies, developed infrastructure, helped in cultural exchange and created many jobs at various destinations across the world which have resulted in flourishing and growth of many businesses across various tourism destinations in the world. Tourism growth also plays an important role in infrastructure development which helps in growth of tourism businesses (Lordkipanidze et al., 2005). Increasing tourist demand for different products and services have also created opportunities for new businesses to grow at various destinations. Tourism plays a vital role in creating business opportunities and successfully running them.

Poverty Alleviation

Tourism is a major industry for many countries in the world for their economic growth and development. Tourism has turned out to be a key element for many nations, as tourism has the power to bring foreign exchange which can help in alleviating poverty in all parts of the world. Over the last three decades' global tourist movement has grown 54% which is more than 700 million tourists. It is expected to grow at 5 to 6% annually with a higher speed by the year 2030. The global tourism receipts amounted to more than 1 trillion USD. According to the UNWTO (United Nations World Tourism Organization) tourism can play a significant role in poverty alleviation, creating economic value to cultural heritage, generating forex reserves and protecting the natural environment. Tourism activities in different destinations across the world have shown significant economic growth and have helped communities to come out of poverty. Tourism has been a successful measure for poverty alleviation and has helped in creation of new businesses and job opportunities which have improved the standard of living of local residents especially in many developing countries in the world (Goodwin,1998). Tourism provides opportunities for the poor sections of the society which help them to grab opportunities for jobs and starting new businesses which helps them in their economic growth.

Improve Standard of Living

Tourism industry is creating economic benefits in all destinations around the world (Hojeghan & Esfangareh, 2011). With involvement of locals in the tourism activities, local resident's earnings have started to increase, which have helped in the improvement of their standard of living. Tourism has led to creation of jobs and business opportunities for the local residents in destinations around the world which creates the multiplier effect which leads to great economic impacts and increases the disposable income of the local community (Crompton,1995). Increased income and employment helps the local residents to improve their lifestyle, education needs, housing needs, medical needs, nutritional needs, household furniture etc. Due to tourism activities there is a huge impact on the local economy. The increasing number of jobs created through tourism activities help the locals to be economically independent. Jobs like restaurant vendors, café vendors, souvenir traders, food stalls, parking attendants, tourism information officers, tour guides, photographers, travel agents, hotel employees are created through tourism which helps the locals to earn their living and improve their standard of living. Due to tourism development at a destination different small, medium and large business opportunities are created for the local resident which further helps in creating new jobs for the local community and increase economic growth of the local resident. The effect of the money spent by the tourists at a destination leads to an economic impact on the local population which helps them to earn a healthy income and also earn a good amount of profits which can support them in raising their standard of life. Tourism creates a good number of jobs at a destination ranging from low level wages to high paying professional positions (Choy,1995). Tourism helps the people to increase their income level and improve their living standards further, especially in the rural and semi-urban destinations.

Improvement in Public Facilities

Tourism industry is one of the most important industries in the world and is growing at a very fast pace in the present times. It is contributing to the economic growth and GDP of different countries in the world (Bhatia, 2002). Tourism activities at a new destination brings economic prosperity which leads to infrastructure development in that destination. The growing infrastructure includes road network, rail network, airports, water systems, parks, healthcare facilities, gardens, art galleries, museums, convention centres, public toilets, shopping malls, water management facilities, signage, waste management facilities and recreational facilities as these facilities are important for the growth and development of tourism at a destination. (Sumb, 2020). Governments also start to invest in the development of infrastructure which is helpful in the growth of the tourism sector and for the local residents. The number of tourist's footfall and the involvement of local residents in the tourism activities plays an important role in the growth and development of public infrastructure at a destination, which can support the tourism sector and local residents as a whole. The public infrastructure plays an important role in the visitor's experience and the level of satisfaction gained. The infrastructure growth at a destination due to tourism also helps in boosting the local economy and creating opportunities for jobs and business for the local residents of the destination.

Strengthen Social Values

Different destinations around the world have their rich culture and traditions, which is the real identity and wealth of the local communities. Tourism brings people from all corners of the world to a destination where the local communities and the visitors get a chance to interact and share knowledge about their cultures and values (Richards, 2007). Tourists understand and learn about the lifestyle of the local community. Tourism helps to enrich and broaden horizons of both the visitors and local residents. Which helps in strengthening the social values and respect for each other. Tourism has a great socio-cultural impact on communities and visitors in all parts of the world (Hausmann, 2007). Tourism also creates economic opportunities for the local residents of a destination and also uplift the quality of life and work as a power to support the host communities. Tourism not only creates jobs rather creates opportunities for the last person in a society especially the local women in the rural areas. Tourism also creates awareness about the local cultural heritage and fosters a sense of pride amongst the host communities.

Improvement in Institutional Infrastructure

Tourism is a global phenomenon, which has created awareness amongst the local residents at destinations around the world. Local residents have started to involve themselves in various professions like artisans and handicraft businesses for their economic gains. With increasing tourism activities, the number of participants have started to increase, which have led to creation of new institutions for training and education at various destinations (Abisuga-Oyekunle, 2017). Tourism has also helped destinations in keeping the traditional knowledge and local culture alive. Communities around the world have successfully revived their culture and heritage, because of tourism growth in their areas. Communities have come forward and joined hands to protect their traditional institution and restore them. There are various organisations who have successfully saved their institutions and their traditional art. Tourism has helped various communities around the world to keep their traditions alive and use them for entrepreneurship development and earn their livelihood from it. With the continuous innovation in the field of science and technology, communities have also started to promote and market their products across the world with the help of internet, print media and other social media platforms.

Negative Aspects of CHT

Increase in Property Prices

Tourism activities around the world are growing at a very high speed. Due to improvement in technology and globalisation there is an increase in infrastructure development in both urban areas and rural areas which have led to increase in the prices of property like land and building. With an increase in the tourist movement the demand for land use has increased. There is an increase in the infrastructure development like roads, rail networks, airports, accommodation units, shopping malls, hospitals and other institutions, which is a major reason for the increasing prices of property. Tourism has led to increase the possibilities of rent, houses and other existing buildings are converted into rentals. Tourism has also attracted and encouraged huge investments in different destinations both urban and rural that has increased the property prices. Farm lands are being used for construction of different infrastructure projects (Gant, 2016).

Increase in Cost of Services

Tourism industry is creating both business and employment opportunities for local residents of destinations around the world. There are different businesses associated with the tourism industry like the accommodation sector, transportation sector, travel agencies, restaurants, cafes, souvenir shops, medical units, entertainment sectors and other allied businesses. Due to new tax policies of the governments around the world the tax burden has increased on various businesses associated with the tourism industry (Timothy & Teye, 2009). The increased taxes have increased the cost of various goods and services provided by these businesses. For instance, there is an increase in the cost of accommodation units, increasing taxes have also increased the cost of transportation like cost of air travel. Due to increasing tax rates in destinations around the world there is an increase in the cost of services for the tourists and have made tourism an expensive activity in destinations around the world (Oklevik et al., 2019). Moreover, high taxes have also led to increase in the prices of tour packages and other associated services.

Difference of Opinions

Tourism at various destinations around the world provides an opportunity to both local residents and tourists from different cultural backgrounds to interact with each other. Tourism brings communities together and values each other's culture. On the other hand, tourism sometimes creates differences of opinions amongst both the local resident and the tourists because of their different culture like religion, language, belief, traditions etc (McKercher & Du Cros, 2002). Since both of them have a different mind-set and a separate cultural background they misunderstand or mislead each other which creates difference of opinions amongst them.

Overcrowding

Tourism industry is one of the fastest growing industries in the world. Destinations around the world are attracting millions of tourists each year (Pattullo, 2005). The increasing tourist movement of tourists to these destinations leads to over tourism or mass tourism, In other word the problem of overcrowding (Milano et al.,2019). There are tourist places which attract everyone and tourists wish to visit such places because they are famous. Overcrowding brings economic benefits to the local economy of the destination but on the other hand it brings negative impacts on the environment and distress to the residents of these destinations. (Wang et al., 2020). Over tourism creates more and more demand for available resources at the destinations, which start to harm both the natural as well as cultural environment of the destination. Over tourism also causes severe pollution at tourist places. Overcrowding at destinations also leads to conflicts between local residents and tourists at times which also creates chances for crime at tourist destinations. Overcrowding also affects the natural scenery of tourist destinations.

Convergence of Culture

Cultural tourism is one the most popular forms of tourism in the present times, Cultural tourism accounts to about 40% of international tourist flows across the world (Richards, 2007). Majority of cultural tourist consumption includes visiting cultural heritage attractions and sites. Due to increasing tourist flow, there is a great exchange of culture between the host population and the tourists, which creates an interest in the mind of both the tourist as well as the local residents. This increasing interest in different cultures leads to convergence of culture (Richards, 2014). The tourist slowly starts to adopt the culture of the local residents at times, on the other hand the local population also gets influenced by the outside culture or the culture of the tourists visiting and slowly adopts it. Convergence of culture is a major challenge for societies around the world as it creates a hybrid culture which loses its unique essence and identity.

Hybrid Culture

Tourism activities at destinations across the world sometimes create pseudo-events, which have no link to the culture of the destination and are meaningless (Richards, 2001). A different type of culture is presented to the tourists which is artificial and has nothing to do with the local communities and doesn't represent the actual real culture of the destination. There is no authenticity in the culture showcased to the tourists. A new form of culture is created which can be called a hybrid culture (Sanyal, 2005). For instance, sometimes locals tend to borrow different elements and add them into their food, dance, music, architecture etc. Local residents involved in tourism activities enjoy and feel happy about the economic benefits and improvement in standard of living due to tourism activities without thinking of cultural degradation and cultural loss.

Overpricing

Tourism brings opportunities for new businesses to grow at a destination. The local residents of the destination get access to new products and services which are available in the global markets (Goodwin, 1998). Due to globalisation, tourism destinations have access to various products and services from big brands with premium quality and high prices. The increasing tourist arrivals at a destination increases the demand for both premium products and services as well as the products and services of daily use. The increasing demand leads to increase in the prices of the goods and services which allows the sellers to increase the prices of the products and services (Buhalis, 2000). At times the sellers start charging extra or over prices for the same products and services due the high demand. Over pricing has become a major issue especially at the mass tourism and far fledged destinations (Cooper & Jackson, 1989). High demand or limited access to various products and services gives an opportunity to the sellers to sell their products and services in whatever prices they wish to sell and earn maximum profits. Over pricing has turned out to be a major problem for both tourists and especially for the local population.

Commodification

Selling the culture like a commodity for economic gain has become a trend in most of the cultural tourism destinations across the world (Richards, 2000). The local population involved in the tourism activities sometimes sell their culture as a product to meet the expectations and demands of the tourist and gain profit out of it. The local population in different time frames sell their religious rituals and ethnic customs and tradition to fulfil the demands of the tourist and earn profits from it, which is a perfect example of commodification (Su, 2011).

TECHNOLOGICAL INTEGRATION IN CULTURAL HERITAGE TOURISM IN PRESENT TIMES

The increasing prevalence of technological integration in cultural tourism has revolutionized people's engagement with and experiences of cultural heritage and locations. The following are some ways that technology is improving cultural tourism:

Use of Mobile Apps

For cultural travellers, mobile applications provide individualized and engaging experiences. These applications can offer tailored tours, interactive maps, and audio guides, letting travellers explore locations at their own leisure and learning pertinent details about the local way of life and history (Fang et al., 2017).

Using Digital Storytelling

Credits to technology, rich, interactive digital storytelling experiences that vividly depict cultural narratives can be produced. Travelers can experience a destination's history, art, and customs in novel ways by means of multimedia presentations, interactive displays, and digital installations (Navarrete, 2019).

Use of QR Codes and Near Field Communication (NFC) Technology

With just a code scan or smartphone tap, visitors can obtain more information about cultural landmarks thanks to QR codes and NFC technology. This offers a smooth and practical means of gaining access to pertinent content, including multimedia, interactive experiences, and historical data.

Use of Augmented Reality (AR) and Virtual Reality (VR)

These technologies let travellers immerse themselves in historical or cultural contexts while traveling or in the comfort of their own homes. For instance, museums can provide interactive and instructive virtual reality tours of their exhibits or historical locations.

Social Media and User-Generated Content

Sharing experiences and promoting cultural tourism are made easier with the help of social media platforms. Visitors can exchange images, videos, and evaluations about cultural sites, which can have an impact (Cuomo et al., 2021).

Use of Big Data and Analytics

By utilizing big data and analytics, tourism firms can learn more about the habits, interests, and patterns of their visitors. Destinations may better cater their products and marketing methods to the needs of cultural tourists by understanding the interests and motivations of their visitors.

Interactive Displays and Installations

By promoting active participation and investigation, interactive displays and installations raise visitor engagement. Touch-screen displays, immersive multimedia experiences, and interactive art installations are a few examples of these that allow visitors to engage in fresh and imaginative ways with cultural items and narratives (Danyun & Jiun, 2016).

Putting all things together, the use of technology in cultural heritage tourism enhances the experience of tourists, promotes cultural awareness, and helps to protect and promote cultural assets. Destinations can reach a wider audience and stay relevant in an increasingly digital world by embracing technology.

ROLE OF TECHNOLOGY IN CULTURAL HERITAGE TOURISM DEVELOPMENT

Technology plays an important and varied role in cultural heritage tourism, improving visitor experiences in many areas and aiding in the promotion and protection of cultural heritage. Technology affects cultural heritage tourism in the following significant ways:

Accessibility

Thanks to technological advancements, individuals with impairments and those unable to visit in person can now have greater access to cultural heritage locations and items. People can explore cultural heritage from anywhere in the globe with the use of virtual tours, augmented reality apps, and online exhibitions.

Education and Interpretation

Through interactive exhibitions, multimedia presentations, and mobile applications, technology makes educational encounters at cultural heritage sites easier (Pallud, 2017). To enhance their comprehension and admiration of historical sites, visitors can obtain comprehensive details regarding historical backgrounds, archaeological discoveries, and cultural importance.

Sustainability

Through the facilitation of sustainable development, conservation, and monitoring techniques, technology can support the sustainable management of cultural heritage tourism. Planning for the sustainable development of tourism infrastructure, managing visitor flows, and reducing environmental consequences are all made possible by geographic information systems (GIS), remote sensing, and data analytics.

Marketing and Promotion

Thanks to digital technologies, travel destinations may successfully sell and promote tourism experiences that incorporate cultural heritage. The showcasing of cultural assets, events, and activities through websites, mobile applications, virtual tours, and social media platforms reaches a wide range of prospective tourists and improves destination branding and visibility.

Preservation

By scanning and recording objects, monuments, and historical locations, digital technologies are essential to the preservation of cultural heritage. By using methods like photogrammetry and 3D scanning, cultural heritage can be preserved for future generations and shielded from degradation, natural disasters, and human threats (Dhonju et al., 2017).

Improved Visitor Experience

By providing immersive and interactive features, technology improves the visitor experience at cultural heritage sites. Visitors are drawn into gripping stories and given insights into the importance of cultural heritage through audio guides, multimedia exhibits, and virtual reality experiences, all of which contribute to the creation of unforgettable and significant experiences.

Community Interaction

Technology encourages participation in cultural heritage tourism efforts and community interaction. Through social media campaigns, online platforms, and crowdsourcing initiatives, local communities are empowered to share information, customs, and tales with a worldwide audience, aiding in the preservation and promotion of their cultural heritage (Giaccardi, 2012).

Therefore, technology is essential to cultural heritage tourism because it increases the accessibility, interest, and sustainability of cultural heritage. Destinations may ensure that their cultural heritage treasures are preserved, interpreted, and promoted for the benefit of both current and future generations of tourists by utilizing digital tools and advances.

ROLE OF TECHNOLOGY IN TRANSFORMING VISITOR EXPERIENCES, PRESERVATION AND COMMUNITY ENGAGEMENT IN CULTURAL HERITAGE TOURISM

Today, technology in various areas of cultural heritage tourism have transformed visitor experiences, preservation initiatives and community engagement in many ways

Experiences of Visitors

Personalization

Thanks to technology, visitors can have experiences that are customized to their interests and choices. Using interactive kiosks or smartphone apps, visitors can personalize their tours and access multimedia and pertinent information.

Interactivity

Visitors are immersed in immersive storytelling and hands-on learning through interactive displays, augmented reality (AR), and virtual reality (VR) experiences, which improves their comprehension and enjoyment of cultural heritage places.

Accessibility

Cultural heritage is now more accessible to a wider range of audiences, including those who are unable to attend in person and those with impairments, thanks to digital tools and online platforms. Heritage sites can be explored remotely with the use of audio guides, 360-degree movies, and virtual tours.

Community Involvement

Crowdsourcing and Citizen Science

Digital platforms facilitate crowdsourcing programs in which volunteers and members of the local community assist in the protection of cultural heritage. Citizen science initiatives encourage a sense of ownership and stewardship among community members by involving the public in data collecting, documentation, and monitoring.

Online Outreach

Cultural groups and communities can share their legacy with a global audience through social media, websites, and virtual events. To promote respect and knowledge of different cultures, online storytelling, digital exhibitions, and virtual tours highlight regional customs, traditions, and cultural practices.

Preservation Measures

Digitization

With the aid of cutting-edge imaging technologies like photogrammetry and 3D scanning, cultural items, monuments, and locations can be more easily digitized and preserved. Digital copies guarantee the preservation of historical artefacts and offer priceless resources for study and instruction.

Monitoring and Conservation

To help identify hazards like erosion, pollution, or unlawful operations, remote sensing, GIS, and data analytics are used in the monitoring and management of cultural heritage assets. This data-driven strategy guarantees the long-term viability of heritage assets and aids in conservation efforts.

SUMMARY

The concepts of culture & heritage and cultural heritage tourism are explained in this chapter. The destination's cultural legacy is a major factor in the creation of tourism goods that are sold to visitors as unique selling items (Hughes & Carlsen, 2010). Tourists are drawn to a destination by its cultural legacy. The research elucidates the notion of cultural heritage tourism as a significant form of tourism, contributing to 40% of foreign visitor arrivals at most global sites (Timothy, 2011). Additionally, the idea of a cultural heritage tourist is defined, emphasizing the traits of this type of traveller. In order to draw large numbers of visitors and revitalize their cultural legacy, the majority of tourist places worldwide have recognized the value of their cultural heritage and effectively incorporated it into their tourism offerings. Numerous locations have benefited from the rise in cultural heritage tourism in terms of safeguarding and maintaining their cultural heritage. Both the advantages and disadvantages of tourism related to cultural heritage have been emphasized. The benefits of cultural heritage tourism include strengthening societal values, reviving local artistic expressions, protecting and promoting local cultural assets and generating commercial & job opportunities (Zhuang, 2019). However, there are drawbacks to cultural heritage tourism as well. These include the convergence of cultures, crowding, commodification of cultures, development of hybrid cultures, overpricing, and the emergence of divergent viewpoints between visitors and locals (Richards, 2015). Many destinations have successfully incorporated technology to increase tourist engagement, awareness and enhancing their experiences at the destination through different means like mobile apps, virtual reality, digital storytelling, social media, user generated content and big data (Neuburger et al., 2018) Technological growth has also helped in educating tourist, enhancing their experience, increasing accessibility, community interaction, promotion & preservation of cultural heritage and facilitate sustainable development.

REFERENCES

Aas, C., Ladkin, A., & Fletcher, J. (2005). Stakeholder collaboration and heritage management. *Annals of Tourism Research*, *32*(1), 28–48. DOI: 10.1016/j.annals.2004.04.005

Abisuga-Oyekunle, O. A., & Fillis, I. R. (2017). The role of handicraft microenterprises as a catalyst for youth employment. *Creative Industries Journal*, *10*(1), 59–74. DOI: 10.1080/17510694.2016.1247628

Adler, P. (1998). Beyond cultural identity: Reflections on multiculturalism. *Basic concepts of intercultural communication: Selected readings*, 225-245.

Archer, B., Cooper, C., & Ruhanen, L. (1998). The positive and negative impacts of tourism. *Global tourism*, *2*, 63-81.

Bascom, W. (1965). The forms of folklore: Prose narratives. *Journal of American Folklore*, *78*(307), 3–20. DOI: 10.2307/538099

Beeman, W. O. (1993). The anthropology of theater and spectacle. *Annual Review of Anthropology*, *22*(1), 369–393. DOI: 10.1146/annurev.an.22.100193.002101

Bhatia, A. K. (2002). *Tourism development: Principles and practices*. Sterling Publishers Pvt. Ltd.

Buhalis, D. (2000). Marketing the competitive destination of the future. *Tourism Management*, *21*(1), 97–116. DOI: 10.1016/S0261-5177(99)00095-3

Chalana, M., & Sprague, T. S. (2013). Beyond Le Corbusier and the modernist city: Reframing Chandigarh's 'World Heritage' legacy. *Planning Perspectives*, *28*(2), 199–222. DOI: 10.1080/02665433.2013.737709

Choy, D. J. (1995). The quality of tourism employment. *Tourism Management*, *16*(2), 129–137. DOI: 10.1016/0261-5177(94)00023-4

Cole, S. (2006). Cultural tourism, community participation and empowerment. *Cultural tourism in a changing world: Politics, participation and (re)presentation*, 89-103.

Cooper, C., & Jackson, S. (1989). Destination life cycle: The Isle of Man case study. *Annals of Tourism Research*, *16*(3), 377–398. DOI: 10.1016/0160-7383(89)90051-0

Craik, J. (2002). The culture of tourism. In *Touring cultures* (pp. 123–146). Routledge.

Crompton, J. L. (1995). Economic impact analysis of sports facilities and events: Eleven sources of misapplication. *Journal of Sport Management*, *9*(1), 14–35. DOI: 10.1123/jsm.9.1.14

Cuomo, M. T., Tortora, D., Foroudi, P., Giordano, A., Festa, G., & Metallo, G. (2021). Digital transformation and tourist experience co-design: Big social data for planning cultural tourism. *Technological Forecasting and Social Change*, *162*, 120345. DOI: 10.1016/j.techfore.2020.120345

D'Amore, L. J. (1988). Tourism—A vital force for peace. *Tourism Management*, *9*(2), 151–154. DOI: 10.1016/0261-5177(88)90025-8

Dahles, H. (2002). Tourism, small enterprises and community development. In *Tourism and sustainable community development* (pp. 172–187). Routledge.

Dant, T. (1999). *Material culture in the social world*. McGraw-Hill Education.

Danyun, L., & Jiun, C. Y. (2016, October). Historical cultural art heritage come alive: Interactive design in Taiwan palace museum as a case study. In *2016 22nd International Conference on Virtual System & Multimedia (VSMM)* (pp. 1-8). IEEE.

Derrett, R. (2003). Festivals & regional destinations: How festivals demonstrate a sense of community & place. *Rural Society*, *13*(1), 35–53. DOI: 10.5172/rsj.351.13.1.35

Dhonju, H. K., Xiao, W., Sarhosis, V., Mills, J. P., Wilkinson, S., Wang, Z., Thapa, L., & Panday, U. S. (2017). Feasibility study of low-cost image-based heritage documentation in Nepal. *The International Archives of the Photogrammetry, Remote Sensing and Spatial Information Sciences*, *42*(W3), 237–242. DOI: 10.5194/isprs-archives-XLII-2-W3-237-2017

Edgell, D. L.Sr. (2019). *Managing sustainable tourism: A legacy for the future*. Routledge.

Eliot, T. S. (2010). *Notes towards the Definition of Culture*. Faber & Faber.

Fang, J., Zhao, Z., Wen, C., & Wang, R. (2017). Design and performance attributes driving mobile travel application engagement. *International Journal of Information Management*, *37*(4), 269–283. DOI: 10.1016/j.ijinfomgt.2017.03.003

Farmaki, A. (2012). An exploration of tourist motivation in rural settings: The case of Troodos, Cyprus. *Tourism Management Perspectives*, *2*, 72–78. DOI: 10.1016/j.tmp.2012.03.007

Gant, A. C. (2016). Holiday rentals: The new gentrification battlefront. *Sociological Research Online*, *21*(3), 112–120. DOI: 10.5153/sro.4071

Giaccardi, E. (2012). *Heritage and social media: Understanding heritage in a participatory culture*. Routledge. DOI: 10.4324/9780203112984

Giampiccoli, A., & Kalis, J. H. (2012). Tourism, food, and culture: Community-based tourism, local food, and community development in m pondoland. *Culture, Agriculture, Food and Environment*, *34*(2), 101–123. DOI: 10.1111/j.2153-9561.2012.01071.x

Goodwin, H. (1998, October). Sustainable tourism and poverty elimination. In *DFID/DETR Workshop on Sustainable Tourism and Poverty* (Vol. 13). London: Department for International Development.

Green, T. A. (Ed.). (1997). *Folklore: an encyclopedia of beliefs, customs, tales, music, and art* (Vol. 1). Abc-clio. DOI: 10.5040/9798216190714

Hausmann, A. (2007). Cultural tourism: Marketing challenges and opportunities for German cultural heritage. *International Journal of Heritage Studies*, *13*(2), 170–184. DOI: 10.1080/13527250601121351

Hodder, I. (1994). The interpretation of documents and material culture. *Sage biographical research, 1*, 393-402.

Hojeghan, S. B., & Esfangareh, A. N. (2011). Digital economy and tourism impacts, influences and challenges. *Procedia: Social and Behavioral Sciences*, *19*, 308–316. DOI: 10.1016/j.sbspro.2011.05.136

Hughes, M., & Carlsen, J. (2010). The business of cultural heritage tourism: Critical success factors. *Journal of Heritage Tourism*, *5*(1), 17–32. DOI: 10.1080/17438730903469805

Kumaj Jena, P. (2010). Indian handicrafts in globalization times: An analysis of global-local dynamics. *Interdisciplinary Description of Complex Systems: INDECS*, *8*(2), 119–137.

Kurtz, L. R. (2015). *Gods in the global village: the world's religions in sociological perspective*. Sage Publications.

Li, Y., Lau, C., & Su, P. (2020). Heritage tourism stakeholder conflict: A case of a World Heritage Site in China. *Journal of Tourism and Cultural Change*, *18*(3), 267–287. DOI: 10.1080/14766825.2020.1722141

Li, Z., Wang, D., Abbas, J., Hassan, S., & Mubeen, R. (2022). Tourists' health risk threats amid COVID-19 era: Role of technology innovation, Transformation, and recovery implications for sustainable tourism. *Frontiers in Psychology*, *12*, 769175. DOI: 10.3389/fpsyg.2021.769175 PMID: 35465147

Lordkipanidze, M., Brezet, H., & Backman, M. (2005). The entrepreneurship factor in sustainable tourism development. *Journal of Cleaner Production*, *13*(8), 787–798. DOI: 10.1016/j.jclepro.2004.02.043

Loulanski, T. (2006). Revising the concept for cultural heritage: The argument for a functional approach. *International Journal of Cultural Property*, *13*(2), 207–233. DOI: 10.1017/S0940739106060085

McKercher, B. (2002). Towards a classification of cultural tourists. *International Journal of Tourism Research*, *4*(1), 29–38. DOI: 10.1002/jtr.346

McKercher, B., & Du Cros, H. (2002). *Cultural tourism: The partnership between tourism and cultural heritage management*. Routledge.

Mele, C. (2000). *Selling the lower east side: Culture, real estate, and resistance in New York City* (Vol. 5). U of Minnesota Press.

Meskell, L. (2002). Negative heritage and past mastering in archaeology. *Anthropological Quarterly*, *75*(3), 557–574. DOI: 10.1353/anq.2002.0050

Milano, C., Novelli, M., & Cheer, J. M. (2019). Overtourism and tourismphobia: A journey through four decades of tourism development, planning and local concerns. *Tourism Planning & Development*, *16*(4), 353–357. DOI: 10.1080/21568316.2019.1599604

Mill, R. C. (1990). *Tourism: The international business*. Prentice Hall.

Munjal, P. G. (2021). Charting the role of digital platforms for cultural heritage tourism in India. *Worldwide Hospitality and Tourism Themes*, *13*(2), 186–198. DOI: 10.1108/WHATT-10-2020-0126

Myers, F. R. (2002). *Painting culture: the making of an aboriginal high art*. Duke University Press.

Navarrete, T. (2019). Digital heritage tourism: Innovations in museums. *World Leisure Journal*, *61*(3), 200–214. DOI: 10.1080/16078055.2019.1639920

Neto, F. (2003, August). A new approach to sustainable tourism development: Moving beyond environmental protection. [). Oxford, UK: Blackwell Publishing Ltd.]. *Natural Resources Forum*, *27*(3), 212–222. DOI: 10.1111/1477-8947.00056

Nguyen, T. H. H., & Cheung, C. (2014). The classification of heritage tourists: A case of Hue city, Vietnam. *Journal of Heritage Tourism*, *9*(1), 35–50. DOI: 10.1080/1743873X.2013.818677

Oklevik, O., Gössling, S., Hall, C. M., Steen Jacobsen, J. K., Grøtte, I. P., & McCabe, S. (2019).

Oklevik, O., Gössling, S., Hall, C. M., Steen Jacobsen, J. K., Grøtte, I. P., & McCabe, S. (2019, December 02). Overtourism, optimisation, and destination performance indicators: A case study of activities in Fjord Norway. *Journal of Sustainable Tourism, 27*(12), 1804–1824. DOI: 10.1080/09669582.2018.1533020

Pai, H. I. (2014). *Heritage management in Korea and Japan: The politics of antiquity and identity*. University of Washington Press. DOI: 10.1515/9780295804835

Pallud, J. (2017). Impact of interactive technologies on stimulating learning experiences in a museum. *Information & Management, 54*(4), 465–478. DOI: 10.1016/j.im.2016.10.004

Paresishvili, O., Kvaratskhelia, L., & Mirzaeva, V. (2017). Rural tourism as a promising trend of small business in Georgia: Topicality, capabilities, peculiarities. *Annals of Agrarian Science, 15*(3), 344–348. DOI: 10.1016/j.aasci.2017.07.008

Petrillo, P. L. (Ed.). (2019). *The Legal Protection of the Intangible Cultural Heritage: A Comparative Perspective*. Springer. DOI: 10.1007/978-3-319-72983-1

Richards, G. (2001). The development of cultural tourism in Europe. In *Cultural attractions and European tourism* (pp. 3–29). Cabi Publishing. DOI: 10.1079/9780851994406.0003

Richards, G. (2001). The experience industry and the creation of attractions. In *Cultural attractions and European tourism* (pp. 55–69). Cabi Publishing. DOI: 10.1079/9780851994406.0055

Richards, G. (2007). *Globalisation, localisation and cultural tourism. Destinations revisited. Perspectives on developing and managing tourist areas*. ATLAS Reflections.

Richards, G. (Ed.). (2007). *Cultural tourism: Global and local perspectives*. Psychology Press.

Richards, G. (2014). *Tourism trends: The convergence of culture and tourism*. Academy for Leisure NHTV University of Applied Sciences.

Richards, G. (2015). Evolving gastronomic experiences: From food to foodies to foodscapes. *Journal of Gastronomy and Tourism, 1*(1), 5–17. DOI: 10.3727/216929715X14298190828796

Sanyal, B. (2005). Hybrid planning cultures: The search for the global cultural commons. In *Comparative planning cultures* (pp. 27–50). Routledge.

Sofronov, B. (2018). The development of the travel and tourism industry in the world. *Annals of Spiru Haret University.Economic Series*, *18*(4), 123–137.

Su, X. (2011). Commodification and the selling of ethnic music to tourists. *Geoforum*, *42*(4), 496–505. DOI: 10.1016/j.geoforum.2011.03.006

Su, X., Li, X., & Kang, Y. (2019). A bibliometric analysis of research on intangible cultural heritage using CiteSpace. *SAGE Open*, *9*(2), 2158244019840119. DOI: 10.1177/2158244019840119

Swarbrooke, J., & Horner, S. (2001). *Business travel and tourism*. Routledge. DOI: 10.1016/B978-0-7506-4392-4.50012-4

Tham, A., Croy, G., & Mair, J. (2013). Social media in destination choice: Distinctive electronic word-of-mouth dimensions. *Journal of Travel & Tourism Marketing*, *30*(1-2), 144–155. DOI: 10.1080/10548408.2013.751272

Throsby, D. (2001). *Economics and culture*. Cambridge university press.

Timothy, D., & Teye, V. (2009). *Tourism and the lodging sector*. Routledge.

Timothy, D. J. (2011). *Cultural heritage and tourism: An introduction* (Vol. 4). Channel View Publications. DOI: 10.21832/9781845411787

Timothy, D. J., & Ron, A. S. (2013). Heritage cuisines, regional identity and sustainable tourism. In *Sustainable Culinary Systems* (pp. 275–290). Routledge.

Tonkin, E. (1995). *Narrating our pasts: The social construction of oral history* (No. 22). Cambridge university press.

Tripathi, R., Tripathi, M. A., & Rawat, A. (2022). Performance of women artisans as entrepreneurs in ODOP in Uttar Pradesh to boost economy: Strategies and away towards global handicraft index for small business. *Academy of Marketing Studies Journal*, *26*(1), 1–19.

Tussyadiah, I. P., & Fesenmaier, D. R. (2008). Marketing places through first-person stories—An analysis of Pennsylvania roadtripper blog. *Journal of Travel & Tourism Marketing*, *25*(3-4), 299–311. DOI: 10.1080/10548400802508358

Wang, J., Huang, X., Gong, Z., & Cao, K. (2020). Dynamic assessment of tourism carrying capacity and its impacts on tourism economic growth in urban tourism destinations in China. *Journal of Destination Marketing & Management*, *15*, 100383. DOI: 10.1016/j.jdmm.2019.100383

Weng, L., He, B. J., Liu, L., Li, C., & Zhang, X. (2019). Sustainability assessment of cultural heritage tourism: Case study of pingyao ancient city in China. *Sustainability (Basel)*, *11*(5), 1392. DOI: 10.3390/su11051392

Williams, S. (1998). *Tourism geography*. Psychology Press.

Zhuang, X., Yao, Y., & Li, J. (2019). Sociocultural impacts of tourism on residents of world cultural heritage sites in China. *Sustainability (Basel)*, *11*(3), 840. DOI: 10.3390/su11030840

Chapter 11
Investigating the Effect Dynamic Interplay of Social Media Promotion on Tourist Revisiting Intention Through Tourist Satisfaction at Sepilok Orangutan

Noor Fazliza Rasim
Universiti Malaysia Terengganu, Malaysia

Zaliha Zainuddin
Universiti Malaysia Terengganu, Malaysia

Sofea Cheah Azlan
Universiti Malaysia Terengganu, Malaysia

Nurul Najwa Napatah
Universiti Malaysia Terengganu, Malaysia

ABSTRACT

This study investigates the dynamic interplay of social media promotion in shaping tourist attractions and impact of these factors on tourist satisfaction. A total of 231 respondents were participated and analyzed using SPSS-25. The result indicates that respondents' recognition of the center's marketing initiatives and their active

DOI: 10.4018/979-8-3693-3196-5.ch011

use of social media are positively correlated. As a result, it is advised to strategically concentrate on enhancing the center's internet presence. This entails putting into practice more engaging and dynamic marketing efforts that correspond with the target audience's interests. The findings show the need to create a specialized media outlet that guarantees tourists learn everything to know about endangered species Orangutan and can be trusted to provide transparent information about the appropriate maintenance and adherence to international standards at the Sepilok Orangutan Rehabilitation Centre.

INTRODUCTION

The Sepilok Orangutan Rehabilitation Centre is a globally renowned destination that is dedicated to the rescue, rehabilitation, and conservation of orphaned and injured orangutans. It is a flagship conservation initiative in Sandakan, Sabah and provides visitors with a unique opportunity to witness the remarkable efforts made to safeguard this endangered species and promote environmental awareness (Sabah Tourism, 2023; Sepilok Orangutan Rehabilitation Centre, n.d.). Concerns have been expressed about Sepilok's management practices, including claimed scandals involving orangutan conservation species, as noted by Friends of the Orangutan (2019). There are saying of how the International Union for Conservation of Nature's (IUCN) Best Practice Guidelines for Great Ape Tourism are allegedly violated, there is a perceived lack of priority given to the safety endangered orangutan species, and how the facility permits public interaction with the animals in violation of these guidelines. These are the main reasons for the objections.

The significance of media influences, and social influences in supporting a destination's success in the modern tourism landscape has been widely acknowledged (Buhalis & Law, 2008; Kim, Vogt, & Knutson, 2015). The previously mentioned variables hold significant influence over tourists' perceptions and are vital for promotion of the destination, involvement, and overall visitor satisfaction. As such, they are essential for destinations to maintain their competitiveness and growth in the global tourism industry. In 2020, the tourism industry are going back to taken by government to restore the economy of tourism sector in Malaysia after the past Covid-19. Ferrarese (2023) reported on Al-Jazeera news, Malaysia's first flotation therapy centre owned by Arthur Wilkinson has faced risk of close down for nearly two years without tourists. Float For Health, a coastal township located in Tanjung Tokong, northeastern side of Penang Island, forced to be fully shut down due to the border restriction introduced during Covid-19. Not long before the reopened of country's border in April, Malaysia has cancel several restrictions such as PCR-test and vaccination in August. The increase of travel arrival may influenced by travel behaviour and preferences of different market segments that manipulating interest in tourism sector. Travel behaviour changes impacted from the result of the travel's bans and boarder closures, from various country lead to decline in the international travel (Gossling et al., 2020). Gossling et al., (2020) also proposed pandemic lead to increase of tourism's opportunities in road trips and ecotourism. The trips by road and nature-based tourism were much more preferred during pandemic due to restrictions on air travel and there is a need for physical distance. Nowadays, Malaysia still in struggling tourism economic industry, where the needs to compete with other countries in Southeast Asean increase. Indeed, the action should taken in all angle just to determine the opportunities and threat with strategic management implemented in every root of tourism development in Malaysia.

A comprehensive understanding of the complexity of visitor satisfaction at the Sepilok Orangutan Rehabilitation Centre requires an acknowledgement of the study's limitations. While immediate enjoyment is the main priority right now, it's important to be aware that long-term effects could be overlooked and include continued participation in the Sepilok's conservation efforts. By focusing solely on short-term satisfaction, there is a danger of overlooking the long-term effects that visitors' experiences may have on their future dedication with and support for conservation activities. In this environment, it becomes vital to examine media and social influences. According to Buhalis and Law (2008), these factors have a significant impact on how visitors perceive their immediate experiences as well as how likely they are to return. The ability of media to leave a lasting impression and the influence of social interactions on the choices made by tourists are essential elements that require close examination. In order to develop tactics that effectively support the conservation objectives of the Sepilok Orangutan Rehabilitation Centre, it is essential to comprehend how these effects interact and contribute to the overall happiness of tourists.

Finally, this study has provided useful insights into the complex dynamics of tourist satisfaction at the Sepilok Orangutan Rehabilitation Centre, with a focus on the interplay between media influences, social factors, and visitor experiences. It is imperative to recognize the inherent limits of this research, though. First off, the research was done in a constrained amount of time, which might have hampered the scope and depth of data that was gathered. The shortened time period might not fully represent the range of seasonal differences in visitor pleasure and behaviour. Second, a thorough grasp of the many visitor viewpoints may be hampered by bias introduced by the study's dependence on participant feedback on limited perceptions. Thirdly, the study used mostly quantitative data collection techniques, which may have obscured subtle qualitative insights that would have contributed to a deeper comprehension of visitor experiences and perspectives. In the end, the study was limited by research resources, which affected the breadth and depth of data gathering and analysis.

Study Background

The study aims to comprehend the variables affecting tourists' intentions the variables affecting tourists' intentions to return to Sabah, Malaysia's Sepilok Rehabilitation Centre. Renowned for its tourist destinations like Gunung Kinabalu, Sabah is a country with enormous tourism potential. Located in Sandakan, Sabah, the Sepilok Rehabilitation Centre is well-known for its Eco-tourism offerings. It is close to several popular tourist destinations, including Turtle Islands Park, the Kinabatangan River, and Gomantong Caves.

The study looks at outside variables that affect traveller choices, with a focus on media coverage, marketing campaigns, and recommendations from friends and family, or socials' circle. Cohen's typologies divide traveller into two groups: institutionalized (individual mass tourists, organized mass tourism) and non-institutionalized (drifter, adventurer). Recognizing these typologies makes it easier to categories outside factors and successfully promote the Sepilok Rehabilitation Centre. This study shows how to market the Sepilok Orangutan Rehabilitation Centre to both institutionalized and non-institutionalized tourists by taking media and social issues into account. As is well knowledge, each category in Cohen's typology has unique requirements to meet changing consumer desires and emerging travel patterns. According to Gossling et al. (2020), ecotourism has increased as a result of the pandemic. For a result, Sepilok ought to take advantage of this chance by utilizing social and media influences to mould traveller preferences and increase destination appeal in line with the quickly changing tourist scene.

There isn't much research on the Sepilok Orang Utan Rehabilitation Centre, despite being a popular destination. It was founded in 1964 and functions as a rehabilitation and conservation facility for sun bears, gibbons, and orangutans. The center's rehabilitation of more than 800 orangutans demonstrates its dedication to primate behaviour and ecology study as well as conservation (Yap et al., 2019). Its efforts have grown to include visitor education programmed and partnerships with nearby communities to raise knowledge of sustainable forest management.

Despite obstacles including illegal wildlife trading and deforestation, the Sepilok Rehabilitation Centre is essential to the preservation of endangered species. In addition to addressing conservation challenges, its establishment supports its objectives by promoting tourism and earning revenue. The centre is a major draw for traveller interested in Sabah's ecotourism and wildlife protection despite the challenges posed by globalization.

Problem Statement

In the context of promoting and maintaining tourism at the Sepilok Orangutan Rehabilitation Centre, the study addresses a number of important issues. The primary issues include a lack of enthusiasm among the locals, which could harm the destination's overall success. Furthermore, the study looks into how unclear delivery messages affect species conservation at Sepilok, especially with regard to orangutans. It lead to another critical issue is the need for a deliberate media strategy to promote the destination and its initial function establishment. In addition, the study explores the possibility of misrepresenting information on orangutan conservation efforts between WWF and Sepilok, highlighting the necessity of precise and unambiguous communication in order to improve visitors' overall pleasure and experience. All of the issues that have been noted help to achieve the main objective of comprehending and enhancing visitor satisfaction, which in turn affects the likelihood that visitors will decide to return to the Sepilok Orangutan Rehabilitation Centre.

Research Objective

Research Objective 1: To explore the interplay between Media influences and social influences on tourist attractions.
Research Objective 2: To determine the cumulative impact of media and social influences on tourist satisfaction.
Research Objective 3: To identify the strategies enhancement of tourist satisfaction to obtain intention to re-visit satisfaction to obtain intention to re-visit.

Research Question

Research Question 1: How do media influence and social influence shape the tourists' satisfaction?
Research Question 2: What is the cumulative impact of media influences and social influences to increase tourists' satisfaction?
Research Question 3: What specific strategies can be implemented to enhance tourist satisfaction, and how it can help increase intention to revisit?

Significance of Research

The study is to educate people about the importance of comprehending external factors impacting tourist attractiveness and satisfaction in order to aid in the development of the Sepilok Rehabilitation Centre. In view of the economic hardships Malaysia faced during the Covid-19 pandemic, necessity for Malaysia—and the Sepilok Orang Utans Rehabilitation Centre in particular—to become more competitive in the Southeast Asian market. The research highlights how external factors, such as travel demand and the effects of endemic Covid-19, have the potential to have a major impact on tourism arrivals, revenue production, and employment prospects for local populations.

Furthermore, the study emphasizes how important media is in influencing attitudes and marketing strategies in the travel and tourism sector, particularly social media platforms. With an anticipated 4.41 billion social media users by 2025 (Dixon, 2023), the study highlights both the advantages and disadvantages of media's influence on travel destinations. In example, the Sepilok Orang Utans Rehabilitation Centre can profit from using media influences to create marketing programmed that are specifically tailored to the interests and behaviour of their target audience.

The study also emphasizes how important personal opinions are in influencing how people perceive and feel about tourist places. Visitors to the Sepilok Orang Utans Rehabilitation Centre provide a variety of input, which highlights the necessity for the centre to handle customer feedback well in order to improve visitor happiness. The study highlights how important it is to comprehend and take into account different points of view in order to provide a favourable impression of the location and raise overall consumer satisfaction.

Research Limitation

The research primarily uses surveys to acquire quantitative data, which are then analysed using either online or in-person methods at the Sepilok Orang Utans Rehabilitation Centre. This approach was selected because it is simple to convert into the Statistical Package for the Social Science (SPSS), a programme that is frequently used in a variety of industries, including retail, government, healthcare, market research, and education, for the analysis of statistical data. Because of its effectiveness in data analysis and Orang Utans Rehabilitation Centre perceive their experiences and level of satisfaction.

Resources are limited, which limits the research, especially since there aren't many studies on the Sepilok Orang Utans Rehabilitation Centre. Information collecting presents difficulties because the official Sepilok blogs and a few guest blogs are the main sources of information. There has been little research on external determinants in the tourism sector; most studies have concentrated on broad industry issues rather than the particular combination of external determinants, visitor satisfaction, and intention to return, as this study on the Sepilok Orang Utans Rehabilitation Centre explores.

Summary

The objective of this research is to create a thorough theoretical framework for destination attachment framework for destination attachment that takes into account external determinants and modifies the relationship with visitor satisfaction. Destination managers may find the theoretical groundwork presented here useful in developing measurement tools at the construct and indicator levels. Five components are included in the model: perceptions of the visitors of media and social influence, intention to return, and tourist satisfaction. The components, features, and aspects impacting visitors' perceptions of media, social, satisfaction, and intention to return are all analysed in this study. Indeed, the suggested model can be modified to gauge patron loyalty in a number of tourism-related industries.

LITERATURE REVIEW

Media Influences

Influences of media is giving the most impacts on behaviour, individuals' beliefs, attitudes, and what is normal and acceptable behaviour. From the research conducted by Dill (2019), media role models significantly effect on behaviour especially among young people. According to Buhalis and Foerste (2015) social media affects the travel and tourism sector. It looks at how social media sites like Facebook, Instagram, and Twitter affect traveller decisions about where to go and their overall experiences as tourists, highlighting how social media influences traveller perceptions and decision-making in an shifting tourism industry. According to Javed et al. (2020), Cohen gave a meaningful explanation of social media by outlining its key features and analyzing thirty distinct interpretations of the term. According to Zeng and Gerritsen (2014), user-generated content of media can also be produced and shaped. Through influences of media to cultural trends, it effect on promotion of consumer products and lifestyles. The media itself is a platform which can help building a demand for certain products, services, and experiences, that shape the customer choices and preferences. A study shown the popularity of social media platforms such as Instagram lead to arise of influence culture and influence customer preferences and purchasing behaviour (Khamis et al., 2017).

Social Influences

This is one of the most significant influence to individuals' behaviour, values, and attitudes. This critical roles used to influence individuals' opinion on particular issues. As consequence of endemic Covid-19, social distance can have a substantial impact on how individuals perceive and evaluate leisure and vacation activities such as hiking, outdoor activities, and nature-based tourism, as well as personal services such as spas, eating, and concierge services (Sigala, 2020). According to Josiassen and Assaf (2013), the varied excursions correspond with different levels of social prominence, and certain travel plans are socially prominent, which means that relatives and friends are often aware of the specifics of the itinerary, including the location and departure time. This related to how social environment can be a tools to increase the awareness towards destination. A theory in social support says that a person would comfortably do something with enough social support from their friends and family members (Berkman et al., 2000). This means positive feedback from social circle can influence the expectation and satisfaction for destination core product. This is because the social support from positive surrounding would definitely bring impact towards the individuals' decision, based on their recommendations. Social capital theory from Lin (1999) says individuals' social networks bring access to worth resources, precisely in information and advice. The individuals are more likely seeking advice and opinion life choices from their friends and relatives. They will consider very much views from friends and family on certain options, and satisfy with their choices when they got proper recognition from their social support. Indeed, individuals will more likely comfortable to depend on their social influences to enlist destination options demand and build expectations.

Tourists Satisfaction

Tourist satisfaction is an important aspect in the tourism industry. It defined as overall evaluation of tourist's experience from the expectations and perceptions of the destination (Meng et al., 2008). It affecting every decision making from tourists either they will revisit the destination and have recommendation on it. The tourism industry are much dependent on tourist satisfaction to maintain relevant on their performance. It is a key factor to success in tourism industry to attract more visitors exactly from positive word-of-mouth recommendations (Chen, et al., 2016). There are several factors to influence tourist satisfaction such as quality of service, destination image, and worth of money (Chen et al., 2016). A study by Kozak and Rimmington (2000) found on significant predictors in tourist satisfaction for service quality and destination image. It continue with a study showed that service quality, value for money, and destination attractiveness primarily influence the tourist satisfaction

(Chen et al., 2016). Tourist satisfaction usually utilized in tourism research as stated by Meng et al., (2008). Then, it would be better if a good combination of method are used to make sure the data are valid and reliable.

Intention To Revisit

Intention to re-visit theme in research has been used before by Kim et. al., (2003) talking about how the factors of push and pull can bring the intention to revisit national parks in Korea. Significantly, various activities listed under these factors can influenced the revisit intention to the same destination. As one of behavioral destination would come up with their concept of destination intentions, it may depends on what the destination would come up with their concept of destination image (Chen & Tsai, 2007). While, the intention to revisit may empowered with the policy makers implementation in National Sustainable Goal (Gebara & Laurent, 2023). These variables itself needed the elements of sustainable to attract tourists as the main functions of the destination is related to ecotourism. Therefore, it is crucial to understand the roles of each factors that may bring out the intention to revisit among visitors.

Conceptual Framework

Figure 1. Conceptual framework of research

H1: Media influences and social influences positively impact towards tourist satisfaction.
H2: Tourist satisfaction positively impacts towards intention to re-visit.

METHODOLOGY

Study Design

The study focuses on two independent variables media influences and social influences. With tourist satisfaction acting as a moderator, the goal is to evaluate the influence of these factors on the intention to return to the Sepilok Orang Utan Rehabilitation Centre. The Statistical Package for Social Science (SPSS), renowned for its user-friendly interface and capacity to carry out a variety of statistical analyses, will be used to conduct the data analysis (Arkkelin, 2014). The survey is multilingual (in English and Bahasa Malaysia) and is intended for Malaysian citizens above 18.

Data Collection Method

There are several approaches that can be used, but survey research is one that is frequently used because it is simple and affordable, especially when analysing large numbers of participants. One noteworthy example is a study conducted by the Pew Research Centre in 2021. The study employed survey research to look into how the Covid-19 epidemic affected people's mental health and found that tension and worry were higher, especially in younger folks. In a similar vein, this study uses a survey-based methodology to get data from participants about their experiences and perspectives of the Sepilok Orang Utan Rehabilitation Centre. The online survey's objective is to offer quantifiable information that can be used to compare and effectively observe how different individuals or social classes react to outside factors that affect their intention to return. The study follows Taherdoost's (2016) six-step sampling procedure.

Figure 2. Sampling process steps

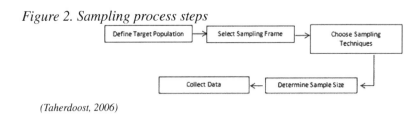

(Taherdoost, 2006)

Data Collection Procedure

Data collection, according to Bhandari (2020), is an essential procedure that entails obtaining observations or measurements in order to get firsthand knowledge and insights into a research subject. In order to determine the percentage of tourists who are satisfied and to obtain input on the destination's performance, the operationalized approach entails giving visitors' experiences at the Sepilok Orang Utan Rehabilitation Centre a 4-point.

Figure 3. Data collection procedures

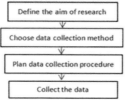

(Bhandari, 2020)

Study Population

This research are including visitors who visit the destination during the researcher site visit. It is provided to respondents with ages 18 years old and above and manage to understand the questions asked in the survey. Using the Rule of Thumb established by Jacob Cohen, the smallest number of respondents targeted would be 150, while this research successfully gain 231 respondents.

Study Sample

In research, a study sample defined as group of individuals selected in the study. The representative selected in the sample is crucial to guarantee the validity and generalization of research findings. The study sample for this research is the respondents include foreign and domestic tourists.

Sampling Method

There are two types of sampling method which are probability sampling and non-probability sampling (Kothari, 2014). The research used convenience sampling as main sampling method as it easily select participants who are willing to participate in the survey. This sampling provide easy access on survey of passers-by or visitors at the destination.

Study Instruments

The questionnaires in self-completed design are being used as the study instruments adapt from previous studies. The questionnaire adapt with quantitative methods, involving introduction section, social and demographic background section, and identified variables measurement section. The research will explain the purpose of the survey in the introduction. Section A refer to social and demographic data for the respondent. Section B refer to variables in the purpose of research. The section include 42 questions in a 4-point Likert scale anchored at 1 = strongly disagree and 4 = strongly agree with each four items in every variables of marketing activities, influences of media, views of family and friends, tourist satisfaction and intention to re-visit.

Table 1. Adaption of questionnaire with sources

Variable	Source	Total Items
Gender, age, marital status, ethnicity, religion, education background, level of income	Hendry, A. H. & Mogindol H. S. (2017), Mohaidin et al., (2017)	6
Marketing Activities **Influences of media** **Views of relatives and friends** **Tourist Satisfaction**	Sheila. (2019) Buphachat, P. (2013) Sheila. (2019) Amaresan, S. (2023) Hendry, A.H. & Mogindol H.S. (2017)	38
Total		44

Survey Forms

Section A: General Information

Table 2. Please CHOOSE the most appropriate response/answer.

Gender	A. Male
	B. Female
Age	A. 18 - 26
	B. 27 - 42
	C. 43 - 58
	D. Above 58
	E. Above 58
Marital Status	A. Single
	B. Married
	C. Divorced
	D. Widowed
Education Background	A. High school
	B. Certificate/diploma
	C. Bachelor Degree
	D. Master
	E. PHD/ others _____
Income Level	A. < RM 2500
	B. RM 2501 - RM 4350
	C. RM 4851 - RM 10970
	D. > RM 10970
Did you know any ecotourism destinations in Malaysia ?	A. Yes
	B. No

Section B: Factors That Effected Intention to Re-Visit at the Sepilok Orang Utans Rehabilitation Centre (SORC)

Table 3. This section is seeking your opinion regarding the factors that influence your intention to travel to the Sepilok Orang Utans Rehabilitation Centre, Sandakan as an ecotourism destination. Please indicate your (dis)agreement with each statement below based on 4-likert scale [(1) = strongly disagree; (2) = Disagree, (3) = Agree; (4) = Strongly Agree]

Factors		1	2	3	4
Marketing Activities (MA)					
MA1	Are you actively using social media/ digital platform right now ?				
MA2	Has you seen any marketing activities from the SORC ?				
MA3	Do you agree with the effectiveness of media platform towards SORC marketing activities ?				
MA4	Do you agree if the SORC have cooperation with influence in media social for the marketing activities ?				
Influences of Media (IM)					
IM1	Does interesting content persuade you to go SORC ?				
IM2	Does SORC easy to access on the portal ?				
IM3	Does SORC has clear content and easy to understand ?				
IM4	Does SORC have a popularity in destination?				
Views of relatives and friends (VRF)					
VRF1	Do you got recommendation from relatives and friends ?				
VRF2	Does SORC get a positive feedback from your close one ?				
VRF3	Do you go to SORC with your family and friends ?				
VRF4	Do your relatives and friends agree SORC is a good place ?				
Intention to Re-Visit					
1.	Have you go visit SORC before ?				
2.	Would you visit SORC again ?				
Tourist Satisfaction		1	2	3	4
1.	How likely you are to recommend us to family, friends, and colleagues ?				
2.	How satisfied were you with your experience ?				
3.	Would you go to SORC with family, friends, and colleague ? ?				
Education					
1.	Do you learn more about Eco-tourism ?				
2.	Do you understand the goals of SORC ?				
3.	Do you want to help SORC conserve the environment ?				
4.	Does SORC manage to teach more about sustainability habitat ?				
Facility					
1.	The centre offer good physical facilities (parking and platform)				
2.	The information counter have relevant information about the centre				
3.	The viewing platform are in good situation				

continued on following page

Table 3. Continued

Factors		1	2	3	4
Marketing Activities (MA)					
4.	The centre offer interesting visual associated with the service				
Responsiveness					
1.	Queries dealt with efficiently and promptly				
2.	Staff are responding to visitor request				
3.	Staff are willing to assist visitors				
4.	Staff provide services at a time it promises to do so				
Tangibility					
1.	The centre provide exactly what the media are promoting to				
2.	The centre has many attractions in Eco-tourism				
3.	The centre has worth it to go for				
4.	The centre provide useful information in ecotourism				
Activity					
1.	The centre have good security measures				
2.	Staff are friendly and courteous				
3.	Visiting hours are flexible to all visitors				
4.	The centre able to assist in the care and protection of the wild animals				
5.	The centre has environmentally safe facilities for wild animals and visitors.				

RESULT AND DISCUSSION

Demographic Profile

From the data collected at SORC, a total of 209 respondents of foreign and local tourists completed the survey, giving a response rate of 90.5%. The demographic information included the following characteristics of participants: gender, age, marital status, educational background, and income level. The survey characteristic information included how much do they know on any ecotourism destination in Malaysia.

Table 4. Demographic profile for SORC (N=270)

Demographic Background		Frequency	Percentage
Gender	Male	104	45.2
	Female	126	54.8
Age	18-26	80	34.6
	27-42	84	36.4
	43-58	60	26.0
	> 58	7	3.0
Marital Status	Single	112	48.7
	Married	107	46.5
	Divorced	8	3.5
	Widowed	3	1.3
Educational Background	Highschool	60	26.0
	Certificate/ Diploma	55	23.8
	Bachelor Degree	80	34.6
	Master	32	13.9
	PHD/ others	4	1.7
Income Level	< RM 2500	109	48.2
	RM 2501 – RM 4350	46	20.4
	RM 4851 – RM 10970	33	14.6
	> RM 10970	38	16.8
Did you know any ecotourism destinations in Malaysia ?	Yes	194	84.7
	No	35	15.3

Reliability Statistics

Cronbach's Alpha, a popular internal consistency metric, was utilized in this study to evaluate the survey instrument's reliability. With an aggregate Cronbach's Alpha of 0.961, the survey items were determined to have a good degree of reliability. This figure indicates a high degree of coherence in the responses provided by respondents, indicating that the survey's items were consistently assessing the relevant construct. Furthermore, the Cronbach's Alpha based on standardized items, which accounts for changes in item scales, 0.965, confirming the survey instrument's consistency. The strong Cronbach's Alpha ratings in both participants. This degree of internal consistency is essential to guaranteeing that the survey instrument captures the desired variables accurately and adds to the study's overall validity. Notably, the reliability of the survey instrument is further supported by the reliability coefficients achieved in this work, which are significantly higher than the generally acknowledged criterion 0.70 (Nunnally, 1978). The study's credibility is strengthened by these findings, which also increase confidence in the validity of the inferences made from survey replies.

Table 5. Reliability statistics based on Cronbach's Alpha test

Cronbach's Alpha	Cronbach's Alpha Based on Standardized Items	N of Items
0.961	0.965	38

Evaluate the Effectiveness of Media Influences

Descriptive statistics are used in the study discussion to summaries respondents' views and opinions about different areas of the Sepilok Orangutan Rehabilitation Centre (SORC). The central tendency of the participants' answers is shown by the mean scores, which provide information about the typical degree of agreement or disagreement. Interestingly, respondents use digital platforms and social media on average actively (Mean = 3.47), yet there is (Mean = 2.70) point to areas for increased efficacy or visibility. The average ratings for engaging with social media influences (3.30), convincing compelling material (3.27), and SORC accessibility on portals (3.07) are all somewhat positive. These findings provide a quantitative perspective, allowing researchers to assess general opinion and pinpoint specific areas where SORC could improve its marketing strategy or capitalist on its existing strengths.

Table 6. The effectiveness of media influences

	Mean	SD	N
Are you actively using social media/ digital platform right now ?	3.47	.714	209
Has you seen any marketing activities from the SORC ?	2.70	.985	209
Do you agree with the effectiveness of media platform towards SORC marketing activities ?	3.25	.800	209
Do you agree if the SORC have cooperation with influencer in media social for the marketing activites ?	3.30	.807	209
Does interesting content persuade you to go SORC ?	3.27	.763	209
Does SORC easy to access on the portal ?	3.07	.763	209
Does SORC has clear content and easy to understand ?	3.19	.692	209
Does SORC have a popularity in destination?	3.46	.643	209
Average Mean	**3.21**	**0.77**	**209**

Evaluate the Impacts of Social Influences

The Cronbach's Alpha test was used to analyse survey responses in order to determine the internal consistency and reliability of items pertaining to suggestions and opinions of the Sepilok Orangutan Rehabilitation Centre (SORC). Based on a sample size of 209 respondents, the average mean across these questions was determined to be 3.32, with a standard deviation of 0.74. The average mean scores show that, on average, participants frequently get recommendations to visit SORC from friends and family (Mean = 3.20), indicating that word-of-mouth influences their decision-making process in a good way. Furthermore, as indicated by the mean score of 3.42, respondents generally agree that SORC is a nice place and believe it receives positive feedback from their close connections (Mean = 3.30). This may resulting on mean score 3.37 participants gone to SORC with family and friends. These results strengthen the survey instrument's consistency, boosting the validity of inferences made from the data and offering a solid foundation for comprehending people's opinions and suggestions regarding the SORC.

Table 7. Impacts of social influences

	Mean	SD	N
Do you got recommendation from relatives and friends ?	3.20	.865	209
Does SORC get a positive feedback from your close one ?	3.30	.706	209
Do you go to SORC with your family and friends ?	3.37	.756	209
Do your relatives and friends agree SORC is a good place ?	3.42	.646	209
Average Mean	**3.32**	**0.74**	**209**

MEASURING THE INTENTION TO REVISIT AMONG PARTICIPANTS BASED ON SATISFACTION

The Cronbach Alpha Test results provide vital information into visitors' opinions regarding their experiences at the Sepilok Orangutan Rehabilitation Centre (SORC). A series of questions about past visits, intentions to revisit, recommendations to others, overall satisfaction, and the possibility of future visits with friends, family, and colleagues were posed to the participants. Based on a sample size of 209 respondents, the average mean score for all of these questions was determined to be 3.32 with a standard deviation of 0.75. After looking over each question individually, visitors reported a mean score of 2.83 for their previous visits to SORC, indicating a moderate amount of past experiences. Particularly, the mean scores for intentions to return (Mean = 3.40), suggesting SORC (Mean = 3.46), satisfaction with the experience (Mean = 3.46), and motivation to visit with others (Mean = 3.47), demonstrating generally moderate satisfaction and a moderate willingness for future engagement. A consistent pattern among participants is indicated by the low standard deviation, which suggests a relatively low degree of response variability.

According to the results, visitors appear to have a positive attitude about SORC, both in terms of their own experiences and their propensity to tell others about these good encounters. These findings add to a thorough knowledge of tourist attitudes and provide SORC management with insightful information to improve visitor satisfaction and promote favourable word-of-mouth referrals.

Table 8. Intention to revisit

	Mean	SD	N
Have you visit SORC before ?	2.83	1.112	209
Would you visit SORC again ?	3.40	.700	209
How likely you are to recommend us to family, friends, and colleagues ?	3.46	.635	209
How satisfied were you with your experience ?	3.46	.672	209
Would you go to SORC with family, friends, and colleague ? ?	3.47	.628	209
Average Mean	**3.32**	**0.75**	**209**

Determine the Cumulative Impact of Media and Social Influences on Tourist Satisfaction

The participants' responses are usually positive, as seen by the mean scores, which point to a positive overall perception of SORC. Statements about environmental conservation and Eco-tourism were met with moderate to high levels of agreement from the participants. The high mean score of 3.42 for "Do you want to help SORC conserve the environment?" indicates that respondents were willing to support SORC's conservation efforts. Furthermore, it appears that people view the centre as a teaching hub for sustainable practices, as indicated by the mean score of 3.36 for the question "Does SORC manage to teach more about sustainability habitat?". Positive assessments of SORC's physical facilities and services are also revealed by the findings. A satisfactory level of participant satisfaction is indicated by the mean scores for statements about well-maintained viewing platforms, interesting visuals related to the services, relevant information at the information counter, and good physical facilities (Mean = 3.35, 3.23, 3.36, and 3.30, respectively). The favourable interactions between visitors and staff members are indicated statements pertaining to staff assistance, responsiveness, and courtesy. Furthermore, participants believe the centre can help with the care and conservation of wild animals (Mean = 3.51) and find the visiting hours to be flexible (Mean = 3.20). In general, the favourable ratings and good impressions of SORC visitors lead to a more thorough awareness of the program's positive effects, which is consistent with Eco-tourism and environmental conservation objectives. The center's attempts to offer a constructive and instructive experience appear to be well-received by the participants, improving its standing and ability to draw in more business.

Table 9. Cumulative impact of media and social influences on tourist satisfaction

	Mean	SD	N
Do you learn more about ecotourism ?	3.22	.681	209
Do you understand the goals of SORC ?	3.23	.719	209
Do you want to help SORC conserve the environment ?	3.42	.623	209
Does SORC manage to teach more about sustainability habitat ?	3.36	.688	209
The centre offer good physical facilities (parking and platform)	3.35	.672	209
The information counter have relevant information about the centre	3.23	.758	209
The viewing platform are in good situation	3.36	.651	209
The centre offer interesting visual associated with the service	3.30	.656	209
Queries dealt with efficiently and promptly	3.34	.646	209
Staff are responding to visitor request	3.36	.680	209
Staff are willing to assist visitors	3.40	.644	209
Staff provide services at a time it promises to do so	3.39	.649	209
The centre provide exactly what the media are promoting to	3.26	.680	209
The centre has many attractions in ecotourism	3.28	.714	209
The centre has worth it to go for	3.44	.641	209
The centre provide useful information in ecotourism	3.33	.673	209
The centre have good security measures	3.36	.651	209
Staff are friendly and courteous	3.43	.677	209
Visiting hours are flexible to all visitors	3.20	.811	209
The centre able to assist in the care and protection of the wild animals	3.51	.613	209
The centre has environmentally safe facilities for wild animals and visitors.	3.46	.643	209
Average Mean	**3.34**	**0.67**	**209**

Identifying the Strategies Enhance Intention to Revisit Through Media Influences

Targeted initiatives must be put into place in order to increase the attraction and level of visitor involvement at Sepilok Orangutan Rehabilitation Centre (SORC). First and foremost, a deliberate attempt should be made to improve campaigns, especially on social networking sites. Potential visitors' awareness and interest in SORC can be increased by enhancing the center's exposure through engaging and dynamic campaigns (Kotler et al., 2017). This entails making the most of social media to produce captivating material that highlights SORC's dedication to Eco-tourism ideals in addition to showcasing the natural beauty of the area. Secondly, focusing on content that is simply comprehensible, instructive, and in line with the objectives and draws of Eco-tourism is crucial. This gives potential visitors a thorough grasp of all SORC has to offer, which can have a substantial impact on their decision-making process (Jamal & Robinson, 2009). A focus on high-quality information helps to create a favourable impression of the centre and encourages potential guests to feel confident and trustworthy. Finally, it is critical to maximize accessibility on digital platforms. Any problems locating and gaining access to SORC information on the internet should be resolved right away. According to Kotler et al. (2017), a smooth digital experience makes it easy for prospective guests to find and learn about the centre via a variety of digital platforms, enhancing the overall impression and promoting visits.

CONCLUSION

In summary, this study highlights the vital roles that the Sepilok Orangutan Rehabilitation Centre (SORC) performs in the preservation of species, demonstrating its adherence to national conservation guidelines while simultaneously preserving its standing as a well-known ecotourism location in Malaysia. The research highlights how media and social influence interact in complex ways, underscoring the importance of carefully taking these elements into account in order to improve visitor happiness. Interestingly, the study shows a positive relationship between the percentage of satisfied tourists and their desire to return, highlighting the importance of providing a great visitor experience. Using, Cronbach Alpha test, the intriguing result of it is that SORC is naturally promoted by word-of-mouth, even though the centre lacks any advertising. This emphasizes how beneficial visitor experiences can raise awareness and expectations among prospective traveller. Even though there were time limits throughout the data collection process, SORC's cooperative participation during the site visit made it possible to acquire reliable and insightful data. In the future habitat and ecosystem conservation. Given that more and more traveller are choosing entertainment over education, future studies should look into creative ways to include learning into travel experiences. By doing this, tourism industry professionals may simultaneously support environmental education and conservation initiatives and adapt their strategy to the changing demands of tourists. Future research projects aiming at tackling new trends in the tourism sector can build on these findings.

ACKNOWLEDGEMENT

First and foremost, sincere thankfulness is expressed to Allah for His plentiful blessings. The author would like to express sincere appreciation to the research supervisor, Dr. Zaliha Zainuddin, for her constant support, invaluable contributions, and abundance of knowledge offered during the study process, which has been wonderful privilege and honour.

REFERENCES

Arkkelin, D. (2014). Using SPSS to Understand Research and Data Analysis. Psychology Curricular Materials. 1.

Banerjee, A., & Chaudhury, S. (2010). Statistics without tears: Populations and samples. From Industrial Psychiatry Journal. *National Library of Medicine*, *19*(1), 60–65.

Berkman, L. F., Glass, T., Brissete, I., & Seeman, T. E. (2000). From social integration to health: Durkheim in the new millenium. *Social Science & Medicine*, *51*(6), 843–857. DOI: 10.1016/S0277-9536(00)00065-4 PMID: 10972429

Bhandari, P. (2020). Data Collection | Definition, Methods & Examples. Retrieved from https://scribbr.com/methodology/data-collection/

Bianchi, C. (2021). Antecedents of tourists' solo travel inentions. *Tourism Review*, *77*(3), 780–795. DOI: 10.1108/TR-12-2020-0611

Bigne, J. E., Sanchez, M. I., & Sanchez, J. (2001). Tourism image, evaluation variables, and after purchase behaviour: Inter-relationship. *Tourism Management*, *22*(6), 607–616. DOI: 10.1016/S0261-5177(01)00035-8

Buhalis, D., & Foerste, M. (2015). The Impact of Social Media on Tourism. *Journal of Travel Research*, *54*(5), 511–527. DOI: 10.1177/0047287514565159

Buhalis, D., & Law, R. (2008). Progress in information technology and tourism management: 20 years on and 10 years after the Internet—The state of eTourism research. *Tourism Management*, *29*(4), 609–623. DOI: 10.1016/j.tourman.2008.01.005

Chan, N. W. (2019). The Nature and Management of Ecotourism Attractions in Sabah, Malaysian Borneo. *Journal of Southeast Asian Studies*, *2019*, 1–17.

Chen, C. F., Chen, F. S., & Chen, P. J. (2016). An investigation of the factors affecting tourist satisfaction. *Journal of Travel Research*, *55*(4), 481–493.

Chen, C. F., & Tsai, D. C. (2007). How destination image and evaluative factors affect behavioral intentions? *Tourism Management*, *28*(4), 1115–1122. DOI: 10.1016/j.tourman.2006.07.007

Diamantis, M. E. (2022). Employed algorithms: A labor model of corporate liability for AI. *Duke Law Journal*, *72*, 797.

Dill, K. E. (2009). The impact of thin models in music videos on adolescent girls' body dissatisfaction. *Journal of Research on Adolescence*, *19*(3), 423–438.

Dixon, S. (2023). Number of global social network users 2017-2027. Statista. Retrieved from https://statista.com/statistics/278414/number-of-worldwide-social-network-users/

Druckman, J. N., & Parkin, M. (2005). The impact of media bias: How editorial slant affects voters. *The Journal of Politics*, *67*(4), 1030–1049. DOI: 10.1111/j.1468-2508.2005.00349.x

Fennel, D. A. (2015). *Ecotourism* (4th ed.). Routledge.

Fernandes, B., Biswas, U. N., Mansukhani, R. T., Casarín, A. V., & Essau, C. A. (2020). The impact of COVID-19 lockdown on internet use and escapism in adolescents. Revista de psicología clínica con niños y adolescentes, 7(3), 59-65.

Ferrarese, M. (2023). Malaysia's tourism recovery flops as Thailand, Indonesia cash in. Aljazeera. Retrieved from https://www.aljazeera.com/economy/2023/1/16/malaysia-tourism-recovery-lags-thailand-indonesia-vietnam

Friends of Orangutan. (2019). Sepilok orangutan tourism – here's what's wrong. Retrieved from https://www.fotomalaysia.org/sepilok-orangutan-tourism-heres-whats-wrong/

Gebara, C. H., & Laurent, A. (2023). National SDG-7 performance assessment to support achieving sustainable energy for all within planetary limits. *Renewable & Sustainable Energy Reviews*, *173*, 112934. DOI: 10.1016/j.rser.2022.112934

Gossling, S., Scott, D., & Hall, C. M. (2020). *Tourism and Water*. Channel View Publications.

Hendry, A. H., & Mogindol, H. S. (2017). Applying WILSERV in Measuring Visitor Satisfaction at Sepilok Orangutan Rehabilitation Centre (SORC). *International Journal of Social and Tourism Sciences*, *11*(8).

Hu, L., & Ritchie, J. B. (1993). Measuring destination attractiveness: A contextual approach. *Journal of Travel Research*, *32*(2), 25–34. DOI: 10.1177/004728759303200204

Jamal, T. B., & Robinson, M. (2009). *The SAGE Handbook of Tourism Studies*. Sage Publications. DOI: 10.4135/9780857021076

Javed, M., Tučková, Z., & Jibril, A. B. (2020). The role of social media on tourists' behavior: An empirical analysis of millennials from the Czech Republic. *Sustainability (Basel)*, *12*(18), 7735. DOI: 10.3390/su12187735

Josiassen, A., & Assaf, A. G. (2013). Look at me—I am flying: The influence of social visibility of consumption on tourism decisions. *Annals of Tourism Research*, *40*, 155–175. DOI: 10.1016/j.annals.2012.08.007

Khamis, S., Ang, L., & Weiling, R. (2017). Self-branding, 'micro-celebrity' and the rise of social media influencers. *Celebrity Studies*, *8*(2), 191–208. DOI: 10.1080/19392397.2016.1218292

Kim, D. Y., Vogt, C. A., & Knutson, B. J. (2015). Relationships among customer satisfaction, delight, and loyalty in the hospitality industry. *Journal of Hospitality & Tourism Research (Washington, D.C.)*, *39*(2), 170–197. DOI: 10.1177/1096348012471376

Kim, M. G., Lee, A. R., Kwon, H. J., Kim, J. W., & Kim, I. K. (2018, December). Sharing medical questionnaries based on blockchain. In *2018 IEEE International Conference on Bioinformatics and Biomedicine (BIBM)* (pp. 2767-2769). IEEE. DOI: 10.1109/BIBM.2018.8621154

Kothari, C. R. (2014). *Research Methodology: Methods and techniques*. New Age International.

Kotler, P., Bowen, J. T., & Makens, J. C. (2017). *Marketing for Hospitality and Tourism* (7th ed.). Pearson.

Kozak, M., & Rimmington, M. (2000). Tourist satisfaction with Mallorca, Spain, as an off-season holiday destination. *Journal of Travel Research*, *38*(3), 260–269. DOI: 10.1177/004728750003800308

Lin, N. (1999). Building a network theory of social capital. *Connections*, *22*(1), 28–51.

Mariani, M. M., Baggio, R., Fuchs, M., & Hoepflinger, F. (2019). The role of attitude and motivation in tourists' pro-environmental behaviour: A comparative analysis of Alpine and coastal destinations. *Journal of Sustainable Tourism*, *27*(9), 951–972.

Meng, F., Tepanon, Y., & Uysal, M. (2008). Measuring tourist satisfaction by attribute and motivation: The case of nature-based resort. *Journal of Travel Research*, *47*(1), 73–85.

Mohaidin, Z., Wei, K. T., & Ali Murshid, M. (2017). Factors influencing the tourists' intention to select sustainable tourism destination: A case study of Penang, Malaysia. *International Journal of Tourism Cities*, *3*(4), 442–465. DOI: 10.1108/IJTC-11-2016-0049

Muller, D., Buttler, F., & Boeck, H. (2020). COVID-19 and tourism: Impacts and implications for advancing and resetting industry and research. *Journal of Business Research*, *117*, 312–321. DOI: 10.1016/j.jbusres.2020.06.015 PMID: 32546875

Rajesh, R. (2013). Impact of Tourist Perceptions, Destination Image and Tourist Satisfaction on Destination Loyalty: A Conceptual Model. *Pasos (El Sauzal)*, *11*(3), 67–78. DOI: 10.25145/j.pasos.2013.11.039

Sigala, M. (2020). Tourism and COVID-19: Impacts and implications for advancing and resetting industry and research. *Journal of Business Research*, *117*, 312–321. DOI: 10.1016/j.jbusres.2020.06.015 PMID: 32546875

Taherdoost, H. (2016). Sampling Methods in Research Methodology; How to Choose a Sampling Technique for Research. SSRN Electronic Journal, 5(2), 18-27. DOI: 10.2139/ssrn.3205035

Wang, D., & Pizam, A. (2011). Tourism, Security and Safety:From Theory to Practice. Butterworth_Heinemann.

Weaver, D. (2018). Ecotourism. In Holden, A., & Fennel, D. (Eds.), *The Routledge Handbook of Transport and Tourism* (pp. 417–429). Routledge.

Yap, C. K., Tan, S. G., Suhaili, Z., Wong, C. H., & Leong, S. C. (2019). Rehabilitation of orphaned and displaced orangutans at the Sepilok Orangutan Rehabilitation Centre, Sabah, Malaysia. *Malaysian Applied Biology*, *48*(1), 1–9.

Yoon, Y., & Uysal, M. (2005). An examination of the effects of motivation and satisfaction on destination loyalty:A structural model. *Tourism Management*, *26*(1), 45–56. DOI: 10.1016/j.tourman.2003.08.016

Zeng, B., & Gerritsen, R. (2014). What do we know about social media in tourism? A review. *Tourism Management Perspectives*, *10*, 27–36. DOI: 10.1016/j.tmp.2014.01.001

Chapter 12
Impact of Customers' Interpersonal Interactions in Social Commerce on Purchase Intention of Tourism Products and Services

Md Shamim Hossain
https://orcid.org/0000-0003-1645-7470
Hajee Mohammad Danesh Science and Technology University, Bangladesh

Rafi Ahmed Reza
Hajee Mohammad Danesh Science and Technology University, Bangladesh

Md. Abdullah Al Noman
https://orcid.org/0000-0002-1377-7113
Hajee Mohammad Danesh Science and Technology University, Bangladesh

ABSTRACT

This study aims to determine the impact of customers' interpersonal interactions in social commerce on the purchase intention of tourism products and services. Additionally, our research explores the influence of interpersonal interaction variables (perceived expertise, familiarity, and similarity) on the development of flow experience and its corresponding effects on customers' purchasing intentions of tourism products and services in the areas of social commerce, using the stimulus-organism-response paradigm. To test the structural model, the authors used a

DOI: 10.4018/979-8-3693-3196-5.ch012

structural equation modeling technique. The study's primary data came from 391 Bangladeshi respondents who filled out questionnaires with seven points labelled "Likert type scale." The findings show that customers' interpersonal interactions have a positive impact on their perceived flow, which in turn has a positive impact on their intent to purchase tourism products and services. Theoretical consequences, practical suppositions, and possible research directions are all discussed based on the study results.

1. INTRODUCTION

Social commerce (SC) has risen considerably in recent decades, owing largely to the advent of a diverse set of SC outlets, including social network (SN) websites, internet communities, blogs, image and live streaming gateways, and reviews and rating groups. SC has also greatly changed the way travelers obtain information, organize their journeys, and, more crucially, share their travel experiences with others in the tourism sector (Mirzaalian & Halpenny, 2021). Currently, many modern travelers base their decision to take a holiday or trip on suggestions from friends and family, internet endorsements, opinions, and, to a lesser extent, information provided by a third party (Berhanu & Raj, 2020). Users can engage in a variety of product purchases, comparisons, and conversion activities that can take place either offline or online with the help of SC (Zhou et al., 2013). To cover the gap between travel agencies and travelers, travel companies developed sophisticated SC platforms as well as a distribution channel (Ponte et al., 2015). As a result, in today's world, SC assumes a significant job in the comprehensive marketing and expansion of the tourist business. At the moment, the contribution of SC is also seen in the extensive promotion and expansion of Bangladesh's tourist sector. People actively share their travel memories, photos of exotic journeys, hotel stay experiences, hotel facilities, etc. via some popular and dynamic social media platforms (Facebook, Twitter, LinkedIn, Instagram, and YouTube) that have a significant influence on others. The tourism industry in Bangladesh has received a positive response through SC because SC platforms are the most popular and dynamic means of communication. Through social media, it is possible to reach the masses with ideas about tourism products and services, which is of great benefit to tourists, tour agencies, and tour operators.

Purchasing tourism products and services has now become exceedingly easier for SC because attractive tourism products and services can be promoted to tourists on one platform through SC. The exponential evolution of new technologies has a significant impact on the behavioral interactions of consumers. Customers may use SC to buy any type of product or service, including tourist goods and services. Previous analysis has shown that SC has an effect on the selling of products and services because it provides an interpersonal interaction between a broad population and the flow experience to increase the purchase intention. The whole process is shown in this study using the S-O-R model for tourism products and services. The S-O-R model has been used in many past studies in different contexts, including the following: Behavioral Intention to use ChatGPT (Peng et al., 2025) potential customers' empathy behavior detection (Hossain and Rahman, 2022); organic food purchase intention analysis (Sultan et al., 2021); evaluating the purchase intention through QR code (Hossain, Zhou, and Rahman, 2018); factors influencing consumers' continuous purchase intention on fresh food e-commerce platforms (Lin et al., 2021); factors influencing consumers' continuous purchase intention on fresh food e-commerce platforms (Hewei and Youngsook, 2022). The stimulus-organization-response (S-O-R) paradigm is employed to investigate the purchase intention of tourism products and services in this study since it has been extensively used in similar investigations before, along with interpersonal interaction variables that relate to flow experience and thereby affect customer satisfaction and purchase intention.

In the current study, we are primarily characterized by three fundamental questions, (i) What is the role of social commerce (SC) in the tourism industry? (ii) How do interpersonal interactions of customers in social commerce (SC) influence flow experiences? (iii) How do the flow experiences of customers influence the buyer's purchase intention of tourism products and services? Therefore, the study has the following objectives: (i) To know the roles of social commerce (SC) in the tourism industry. (ii) To examine the impact of customers' interpersonal interactions in social commerce (SC) on consumer flow experiences. (iii) To investigate the impact of customer flow experiences on purchase intentions of tourism products and services.

2. REVIEW OF LITERATURE

2.1 Social Commerce:

SC is a subcategory of e-commerce that arose as a result of the growth of SN, so SC may be defined as activities undertaken on SN platforms (Chen et al., 2018). Lu et al. (2016) explain that SC restores the social aspect of purchase to e-commerce, increasing the quantity of social participation in the virtual environment. Prior studies showed that SC positively affects the users' purchase intention (Gan & Wang, 2017). SC is significant in the case of tourism products and services because most travelers now search SC sites before purchasing any type of tourism product or service and follow others' ratings, perspectives, and reviews. When a tourist shares all of his travel experiences on SC sites, it has a huge impact on the minds of others.

This flow has an impact on others in both positive and negative ways, resulting in customer satisfaction and purchasing intent.

In recent years, social commerce (SC) has seen a dramatic rise, particularly due to the widespread use of social media platforms. These platforms have become pivotal in shaping consumer purchasing behavior, particularly in tourism. Hu et al. (2023) highlight that social media usage plays a crucial role in cross-border social commerce, as it facilitates international consumers' engagement with brands and products across cultures. Their study suggests that cultural identity change and social support are key moderators in how consumers interact with social commerce platforms, influencing their purchase intention. This global perspective of SC aligns with Zhao et al. (2023), who emphasize the significance of the Stimulus-Organism-Response (S-O-R) framework in understanding how consumers' perceptions of social commerce factors drive their actions. These findings are particularly relevant for the tourism industry, as platforms where users share travel experiences and reviews can profoundly shape the purchase behaviors of potential customers. Similarly, Dincer and Dincer (2023) note that the rapid growth of smartphones and social media has led to the emergence of social commerce as a powerful tool to exchange information and facilitate social connections, which directly impact consumers' purchase intentions. The integration of peer reviews, ratings, and shared experiences in tourism SC platforms helps create a social influence that not only informs but often sways potential buyers. This reinforces the role of social interactions in shaping consumer behavior, a notion further corroborated by Rahman et al. (2023), who observe how trust and engagement in social commerce platforms influence consumers' decisions, even when purchasing perishable products. Collectively, these studies affirm that social commerce is a powerful driver of purchase intention, particularly in industries like tourism, where consumer decisions are significantly influenced by the experiences and opinions of others.

2.2 S-O-R Theoretical Framework:

This framework illustrates stimulation and human psychology (response and action) as being related by an organism aspect. The S-O-R paradigm offers a rigorous and systematic way of examining the impact of interpersonal communication variables as ecological indicators on consumer online actions and their eventual desire to buy from SC sites (Hossain & Rahman, 2022). As they reveal consumers' behavioral outputs, the responses are categorized as consumers' purchase intention and satisfaction (Gao & Bai, 2014). Stimuli are defined in the S–O–R paradigm as a set of qualities that impact customer experience (Mazursky & Jacoby, 1986). Such features serve as the beginning point for the process of consumer behavior, which implies they are stimuli that influence consumer perception and awaken them, expressly or implicitly, to a certain action (Oh et al., 2008). Therefore, interpersonal interaction considerations (perceived expertise, similarity, and familiarity) have been included as stimuli that influence consumers' purchasing intentions in the SC environment. The organism passes through a time of internal interference between the stimulus and the individual's reaction (Hossain, Rahman, & Zhou, 2021). However, a person turns stimuli into concrete information through this phase, which means that perceptions such as feelings and thoughts on various events will trigger a difference in the individual's emotional and cognitive state (Mehrabian & Russell, 1974; Hossain and Rahman, 2022). The organism consists of online user views shared by flow interactions (Gao & Bai, 2014; Hossain, Rahman, & Zhou, 2021). According to the previous analysis (Hoffman & Novak, 1996), flow is a mental state that changes based on the situation and may be affected by one person to another (Hossain & Rahman, 2022). SC sites are designed to attract customers with a lot of captivating pictures, videos, designs, and products. As a result, customers are easily satisfied and show the intention to purchase the product, which is called "flow" (Hossain, Rahman, & Zhou, 2021). Then consumer purchasing intention is tracked and regarded as a consumer behavioral response in our research.

2.3 Flow Experience:

A Hungarian-American psychologist, Milhaly Csikzentmihalyi, represented flow experience in 1975 and demonstrated that flow is a holistic feeling that people experience as they act fully involved (Csikzentmihalyi, 1975). The flow experience's importance in assisting individuals to feel more delight and participation is frequently utilized in online-consumer behavior platforms (Hossain, Rahman, & Zhou, 2021). Customers' flow state is completely involved, distinctly, action and loss of self-awareness. As a result, the flow has gained expanded recognition and has been used as a basis for creating persuasive interactions (Ding et al., 2009). Following these findings, we propose that this flow has an impact on users' intentions to engage in SC. From the definition of flow experience, it is pleasant and ideal. Nevertheless, the result of its appeal in absolute reality does not always produce beneficial results, and practical research has proved that flow experience is typically favorably connected with consumer approach and performance expectancy. In the context of Bangladesh, flow experience is immensely important in buying and selling products, which helps in increasing purchase intention.

2.4. Conceptual Model And Hypotheses

Figure 1: Conceptual framework

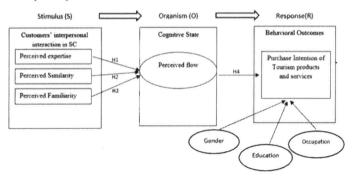

By using the S-O-R framework (Mehrabian & Russell, 1974), this study uses SC concept cues, flow experience, and purchase intention of tourism products and services customers. **Figure 1** depicts the conceptual framework created for the current investigation. The suggested framework investigates whether consumers' flow states (organisms) naturally derived from assessments of three SC cues (stimuli) impact purchase intention and satisfaction (responses). According to the early part of this passage, the author starts by explaining the three SC cues and then goes on to describe the influence of each of the three stimuli on flow and the impact of flow on a variety of behavioral consequences.

2.5 Stimulus: SC Cues As Environmental Stimuli (S)

One of the special features of SC is that it allows consumers to perform more checks and balances when purchasing products (Ng, 2013). That's why SN sites should increase their social engagement with more and more customers. Keeping member connections on a regular basis would surely improve the interpersonal attraction of organizations (Shen et al., 2010). Our study refers to interpersonal interaction characteristics that are linked to SC. We also focus on flow experience and response. In this section, we look at three types of interpersonal interactions: perceived expertise, similarity, and familiarity (Shen et al., 2010). Interpersonal contacts have a significant influence on tourist products and services. Perceived expertise is the degree to which a source is thought to be capable of forming a legitimate view (Hovland, 1951). Perceived similarity refers to the combining of one customer's preferences with those of another (Liu et al., 2016). Customers with similar tastes are more likely to interact with one another (Shen et al., 2010). As a result, consumers may appreciate one another more, ensuring a pleasant encounter.

Interacting with these similar peers may bring them additional happiness (Zhou, 2019). Perceived familiarity represents a regular connection with consumers in SC and fosters strong customer relationships (Gibreel et al., 2018).

2.6 Organism: Flow Experience As Customer Cognitive States (O)

Flow has been adequately proven as a crucial effect of an online buying experience (Hossain, Zhou, & Rahman, 2018). Thus, online shoppers who have a flow experience are surely less price-sensitive, have favorable views, and have a high consumption intention (Wang & Hsiao, 2012). From the definition of flow experience, it is pleasant and ideal. Nevertheless, the result of its appeal in the absolute world does not always produce beneficial results, and practical research has proved that flow experience is typically favorably connected with consumer approach and behavior intention. Customers are completely immersed in their flow state, taking distinct acts and losing sight of their own consciousness (Gao & Bai, 2014). The stimulus of formativeness is believed to influence buyers' cognitive states at the travel website, that is, user's flow experiences as demonstrated by the S-O-R framework, and consumers who are completely immersed in a travel website that is insightful or deemed to be beneficial may experience a coherent state of flow (Gao & Bai, 2014).

According to the hypothesis of similarity-attraction, people are drawn to others who are similar to them (Natour et al.,2005). Therefore, similarity of interests and preferences makes interactions with each other easy and helps build a stronger relationship (Shen et al., 2010). Strong relationships and beliefs are created by perceived similarity. Then again, if there are different preferences and interests among people in a society, it becomes difficult to develop a good relationship between them. People share their similarities when they meet someone who is similar to them because humans are social animals (Fu et al., 2018). In real life, people like sharing their diverse experiences with someone similar to them, just as people share diverse experiences with people of similarity through social media, which plays a significant role in establishing a strong relationship. On the contrary, people do not present themselves effectively in society and refrain from sharing their various experiences.

H1: Perceived similarity is significantly related to flow experience.

When perceived expertise relates to a source's ability to make true statements, perceived trustworthiness refers to the extent of conviction that a source is inspired to transmit a proper decision. Perceived expertise indicates someone's assessment of the skill and knowledge of other members (Hu et al., 2016). Additionally, someone gets confidence from a skilled community or member that they know a lot, and it ensures a positive experience. In the same way, when an experienced person comes in contact with another experienced person in society, trust is formed in them, which helps them to have a positive experience. People in society believe that if they are in touch with experienced people, they can get lots of valuable information and advice from them. Then again, no one expects more from less experienced people, and society has less trust in them.

H2: Perceived expertise is significantly related to flow experience.

In the context of SC, customers tend to maintain more contact with familiar members (Shen et al., 2010). Maintaining frequent contact with acquaintances in which trust is fully established helps them have an interesting experience (Kim & Kim, 2018). When a customer in SC interacts with an unfamiliar person, they may feel unsafe (Zhou, 2019). Therefore, customers often do not rely on the seller, so acquaintances are consulted when purchasing products (Fu et al., 2018). Perceived familiarity can reduce uncertainty and improve the belief in SC. Thus, we developed the following hypothesis:

H3: Perceived familiarity is significantly related to flow experience.

2.7 Response: Customers' Purchase Intention (R)

In the S-O-R model, the term "response" refers to an individual's final behavioral outcome, which might be positive or negative (Donovan & Rositter, 1982). From the S-O-R framework, it can be said that responses represent the behavioral outcomes based on the cognitive state of a customer. Meanwhile, purchasing decisions are critical behavioral outcomes (Yadav et al., 2013). Flow is so significant that it is widely used in information systems research (Zhou, 2019). This affects the behavior of the customers. When a customer is affected by the flow of SC, his purchase intention increases (Zhou, 2019). In other words, customers have to address a wide range of interpersonal attractive aspects and effects such as similarity, familiarity, expertise, informative affect, and moral significance, and these factors will affect subsequent consumer behavior (Liao et al., 2010). Prior research has shown that consumer purchase intention might be a measure of consumer behavioral outcomes. The resulting model equation, then, gives us purchase intention as a reaction in SC (Liu et al., 2016). Our findings are comparable with those of previous studies that used the S-O-R model and considered purchase intention to be the response (Hossain et al., 2018; Sultan et al., 2021; Han et al., 2022).

2.8 Flow Experience (O) Is Significantly Related To Purchase Intention (R)

The flow experience is a strong indicator of purchase intent (Martins et al., 2019). Webster et al. (1993) show that computer-mediated changes in behavior and learning can improve flow. Several studies have found that pleasant flow experiences may attract customers, reduce product price sensibility, and have a positive impact on attitudes and behavior (Novak et al., 2000). Previous research found that flow experience has a positive impact on customers' perceptions of the major site and the large firm (Mathwick & Rigdon, 2004). As a result, flow experience is undoubtedly connected with lengthy visits and greater time spent on the website (Kabadayi & Gupta, 2005). Experience and consumer online behavior are closely related to each other (Chen et al., 1999). O'Cass and Carlson (2010) ensured that the flow of experience leads directly to satisfaction from the website by increasing the positive perception of consumers. Ilsever et al. (2007) suggest that customers who encounter flow return to the website or re-purchase from it in the latter. As a result, the customer who experiences the flow visits the website again, and he/she makes purchases from the online or SC site again. Based on the preceding discussion, the following hypothesis is proposed:

H4: Flow experience is significantly related to purchase intention.

2.9 Flow Experience As Mediating Role

The current research explores the significance of flow experience as a mediator. Flow experiences entail the gradual transformation of potentially unpleasant situations into joyful ones. The S-O-R paradigm (Csikzentmihalyi, 1975) has a mediating influence on flow experience, and it has been demonstrated that interpersonal connection on SC can increase purchase intentions for tourist items and services. The S-O-R framework influences people's behavior by creating cognitive states and leading to a response (Loureiro et al., 2020). The online environment gesture influences consumer purchase intent through an online seller, and this influence is mediated by the customer's cognitive state (Chang & Chen, 2008). Flow experience, as a mediator, plays a crucial role in the relationship between stimuli and responses (Goi et al., 2018). (2003) investigated emotional and cognitive cognitive states and discovered a link between perceived virtual community and purchasing results, which mediates the cognitive states of online shoppers. Jang & Namkung (2009) investigated the impact of positive emotions as a moderator between perceived quality and behavioral intentions, and they discovered a link between stimuli and future behavioral outcomes with trust and fairness. Ha & Lennon (2010) proved that the relationship between website design and customer response behavior is mediated by affective states. Therefore, the S-O-R framework demonstrates that interpersonal interaction factors (stimuli) and customer response are mediated by customer internal states (organisms) (Ha & Lennon, 2010; Yoon, 2012). The current study implies that flow functions as a mediator between the interpersonal interaction portions of SC and response, based on the S–O–R paradigm and previous research on mediating implications for internal cognitive processes.

H5: Flow influences the connection between interpersonal interaction and purchase desire.

3. METHODOLOGY OF THIS STUDY

3.1. Measuring System

This study involved applying components that had previously been used in a survey. Existing research should be tailored to fit the SC context. To meet the commonly accepted guidelines on wording for questionnaire questions, we created and finalized the questionnaire accordingly (Fang et al., 2014). Liao et al. (2010) provided the items for evaluating perceived similarity, competence, and familiarity. Zhang et al. (2014) proposed the flow elements in this case and the customers' purchasing intent items were generated by Pavlou and Fygenson (2006). Annex A contains a list of all the measurements utilized in the study, as well as their sources. A Likert scale of seven points, including options such as "strongly disagree" and "strongly agree," was utilized to collect all the items in the survey. Multiple control factors were added to our framework to demonstrate that the statistical findings were not influenced by covariance with other factors. To measure purchasing intention, we chose gender, education, and occupation because these factors might have an impact on purchasing intention from SC. Because of the practical challenges connected with the execution of experimental and experimental designs, control variables have been included in the majority of earlier investigations (Bernerth and Aguinis, 2015). To get better results, we incorporated non-hypothesized control variables into our model to prevent our findings from correlating with other factors.

3.2. Survey Structure

To assess our hypotheses and model, we carried out a survey. because it claims to anticipate human behavior and discover relationships between variables and constructs. Aside from that, the survey approach has proven quite effective in analyzing consumer behavior in SC (Zhang et al., 2014). We conducted an online survey to acquire survey data for the present study, and our target population was those who use SC and purchase at least one product from SC. Therefore, we feel that conducting a survey is an acceptable strategy for the current investigation.

3.3. Data Collection

To collect data, we used a variety of social media platforms (Facebook, YouTube, Twitter, and We Chat). Before the main survey, we conducted pilot and pre-tests with 20 and 50 respondents, respectively. We amended certain questions depending on the results of the pilot and pre-tests. We have designed a questionnaire and sent it to the target population. We sent at least two hundred emails and share questionnaire links for collecting data. Finally, 391 valid responses were collected for our study. **In Table 1**, we can find the demographic characteristics of the respondents.

3.4. Data Analysis

To analyze our measurement and structural model, we employed the structural equation modeling approach, which employs partial least squares (PLS) estimation. For the current investigation, we employed the software Smart-PLS 2.0 to perform partial least squares (PLS) estimation. It can better cope with formative assessment and regulating connections using the Smart-PLS 2.0. A smart partial least squares (PLS) can develop a formative model for latent constructs, and further, it only requires a much lower level of verification to support it (Tamjidyamcholo et al., 2013). Therefore, we used Smart Partial Least Squares (PLS) 2.0 software in our study.

4. FINDINGS AND ANALYSIS

4.1. Common Method Variance (CMV)

CMV, or common method bias, is a kind of variance that is a widespread concern in quantitative approaches and other self-reported surveys (Ali, 2016). The greatest threat to validity may come when all data is perceptually acquired from a single source simultaneously (Podsakoff et al., 2003). To address the issue of CMV, the study employed Harman's One-Factor Test. Our statistical findings revealed that this study is free of CMV.

4.2. Measurement Model

Demographics of respondents: In the original dataset, there were 444 respondents. We filtered the data set based on the customers' past purchasing experiences online and their internet surfing experiences and finally got 391 final responses.

Table: 1. Demographics profile of respondents

Demographics	Frequency	(%)
Gender:		
Male	246	63.0%
Female	145	37.0%
Age:		
21-30 years	273	69.8%
31-40 years	81	20.7%
Less than 20 years	21	5.4%
41-50 years	14	3.6%
Above 50 years	2	0.5%
Education Qualification:		
Tertiary/University	225	57.5%
Postgraduate or above	134	34.3%
Post-secondary/Diploma Secondary	29	7.4%
	3	0.8%
Current Occupation:		
Student	220	56.3%
Private job	80	20.5%
Government job	50	12.8%
Currently not employed	32	8.2%
Businessman	5	1.3%
Retired person	3	0.7%
Housewife	1	0.2%
Years of social media networking:		
More than 6 years	300	76.7%
For last 5 years	71	18.2%
For last 3 years	17	4.3%
For last 2 years	3	0.8%
Have you surfed the internet before:	391	100%
Yes		
Like travel:	391	100%
Yes		
Purchased Product:	391	100%
Yes		

Confirmatory factor analysis (CFA) was used to evaluate the measurement model. We used three methods to evaluate the measurement model's content, convergent, and discriminant validity. All these components of convergent validity were calculated by assessing the correlation of the component loadings, composite reliability (CR), Cronbach's alpha, and the average variance extracted (AVE) (Liu et al., 2016). The

CFA findings indicated that all indicator loadings are greater than 0.7. Cronbach's alpha, CR, and AVE requirements are as follows: Cronbach's alpha = 0.7, CR = 0.7, and AVE = 0.5. (Fornell & Larcker, 1981). Cronbach's alpha and CR values larger than 0.8, and also an AVE score better than 0.7, are shown in **Table 2**. Based on the research findings, the findings might be interpreted as having convergent validity.

The fact that the measurements of a construct are unique from other constructs is an example of discriminant validity. Two different approaches are being employed here to analyze the validity of discrimination (Gefen & Straub, 2005). First, we determined the measurement model by evaluating correlation coefficients between constructs and the square root of the AVE (Fornell & Larcker, 1981). **Table 3** demonstrates that the square roots of the AVE are considerably more significant than the component correlations, demonstrating high discriminating validity. Second, we looked at the components in the item loadings and cross-loadings to see if there were any relationships. According to the results in **Table 4**, all of the construct item loadings with that resembling concealed factor have a higher value than the cross-loadings of the other concealed factors, suggesting adequate discriminant validity.

4.3. Structural Model

We employed smart partial least squares (PLS) to examine the expected relationships. The outcomes of the smart partial least squares (PLS) assessment on the entire data set are shown in **Figure 2**. As per result, perceived similarity ($\beta = 0.324$, $p < 0.001$), expertise ($\beta = 0.211$, $p < 0.001$) and familiarity ($\beta = 2.71$, $p<0.001$) all had beneficial effects on flow. As a consequence, each of the research hypotheses (H1, H2, and H3) is justified. According to the findings, perceived flow has a positive impact on purchase intention ($\beta = 0.546$, $p < 0.001$), suggesting that H4 is justified.

Additionally, we conducted separate structural tests for older and younger consumers. Age is a critical variable in how people respond (Heinonen and Strandvik,, 2007). The result of the study focused on younger folks (below 30 years) with more positive attitudes about purchase intention from SC than older users (above 30 years). In this study, 69.8% of respondents were below 30 years old, and 30.2% were above 30 years old **(Table 1)**.

Figure 3 illustrates that perceived similarity for younger SC users ($\beta = 0.391$, $p < 0.001$) and older users ($\beta = 0.302$, $p < 0.001$), perceived expertise for younger folks ($\beta = 0.148$, $p < 0.001$) and older users ($\beta = 0.251$, $p < 0.001$), perceived familiarity for younger folks ($\beta = 0.071$, $p < 0.001$) and older users ($\beta = 0.325$, $p < 0.001$). As shown in the findings, perceived familiarity has a significant influence on perceived flow for older users but has no effect on flow for younger folks. As a whole, perceived flow has a stronger influence on purchase intention among older users ($\beta = 0.573$, $p < 0.001$) than that for younger folks ($\beta = 0.421$, $p < 0.001$).

Table 2. Results of the CFA.

Constructs	Items	Loading	Cronbach's alpha	Composite reliability (CR)	AVE
PES	PES1	0.843	0.872	0.943	0.731
	PES2	0.821			
	PES3	0.913			
	PES4	0.854			
PEE	PEE1	0.832	0.923	0.956	0.825
	PEE2	0.911			
	PEE3	0.802			
	PEE4	0.812			
PEF	PEF1	0.841	0.883	0.964	0.891
	PEF2	0.862			
	PEF3	0.813			
	PEF4	0.825			
FWL	FWL1	0.901	0.942	0.957	0.692
	FWL2	0.821			
	FWL3	0.843			
	FWL4	0.814			
PSI	PSI1	0.943	0.921	0.977	0.835
	PSI2	0.902			
	PSI3	0.911			
	PSI4	0.921			

Perceived Similarity=PES, Perceived Expertise=PEE, Perceived Familiarity=PEF, Flow Experience=FWL, Purchase Intention=PSI

Table 3. Correlations among constructs.

Constructs	AVE	Cronbatch alpha	1	2	3	4	5
PES	0.731	0.872	0.832				
PEE	0.825	0.923	0.643	0.924			
PEF	0.891	0.883	0.532	0.635	0.887		
FWL	0.692	0.942	0.634	0.657	0.671	0.982	
PSI	0.835	0.921	0.523	0.572	0.602	0.621	0.902

Perceived Similarity=PES, Perceived Expertise=PEE, Perceived Familiarity=PEF, Flow Experience=FWL, Purchase Intention=PSI

Table 4. Item loadings and cross loadings.

Constructs	Items	PES	PEE	PEF	PWL	PSI
PES	PES1	0.843	0.531	0.502	0.464	0.472
	PES2	0.821	0.520	0.535	0.502	0.467
	PES3	0.913	.514	0.524	0.531	0.463
	PES4	0.854	0.501	0.521	0.403	0.434
PEE	PEE1	0.461	0.832	0.442	0.473	0.443
	PEE2	0.507	0.911	0.456	0.434	0.468
	PEE3	0.523	0.802	0.476	0.492	0.403
	PEE4	0.484	0.812	0.493	0.478	0.503
PEF	PEF1	0.464	0.468	0.841	0.407	0.433
	PEF2	0.504	0.485	0.862	0.524	0.441
	PEF3	0.524	0.521	0.813	0.503	0.467
	PEF4	0.437	0.513	0.825	0.472	0.445
FWL	FWL1	0.454	0.442	0.404	0.901	0.488
	FWL2	0.523	0.514	0.507	0.821	0.525
	FWL3	0.502	0.512	0.503	0.843	0.515
	FWL4	0.509	0.487	0.404	0.814	0.421
PSI	PSI1	0.487	0.486	0.465	0.464	0.943
	PSI2	0.479	0.485	0.523	0.476	0.902
	PSI3	0.503	0.515	0.523	0.503	0.911
	PSI4	0.504	0.511	0.522	0.513	0.921

Perceived Similarity=PES, Perceived Expertise=PEE, Perceived Familiarity=PEF, Flow Experience=FWL, Purchase Intention=PSI

4.4 Mediation Analyses

According to H5, the effect of interpersonal interactions on customer reaction behavior is influenced by the consumer flow experience. We utilized the bootstrapping method to analyze the effect that mediates between variables (Preacher & Hayes, 2008; Shrout & Bolger, 2002). **Table 5** demonstrates a significant association between flow experience and perceived similarity. The indirect influence of flow experience on the relationship between perceived similarity and purchase intention has a 95 percent bootstrap CI excluding zero (CI.95 = 0.053, 0.171); this observation shows that perceived similarity activates the flow experience, which influences purchase intention. Perceived expertise also indirectly affects purchase intention; it increases purchase intention (CI.95 = 0.044, 0.130). As well, perceived familiarity has a mediating influence (CI.95 = 0.032, 0.062).

Table 5. Results of bootstrapping

95% Bootstrap confidence intervals(CI) for indirect effect			
Flow experience			
	Effects	SE	CIs
PES	0.112	0.273	(0.053, 0.171)
PEE	0.082	0.031	(0.044, 0.130)
PEF	0.034	0.024	(0.032, 0.062)

Perceived Similarity=PES, Perceived Expertise=PEE, Perceived Familiarity=PEF

5. DISCUSSION

Using the S-O-R paradigm, this study analyzes the influence of flow on customer purchase intentions, with a focus on interpersonal interaction on SC sites. According to Liao et al. (2010), interpersonal interaction aspects are classified into three types: perceived similarity, perceived expertise, and perceived familiarity. We then explore how the interpersonal interaction components affect the flow and the link between flow and purchase intention across different age groups. Our findings supported all the hypotheses and thus support the claim that flow experiences are a helpful tool for predicting purchase intentions in SC. The results found in this study suggest that all three interpersonal interaction elements have a substantial effect on flow experiences in SC. This study demonstrates that perceived similarity is far more influential in purchasing SC than perceived expertise and perceived familiarity. According to Gao and Bai (2014), the perceived flow positively impacts purchase intention. Therefore, flow experience is significant in buying and selling products, which helps in increasing purchase intention.

Additionally, **Figure 3** demonstrates the disparities between the younger and older demographics. For young social purchasing consumers, it is vital to have recognized competence in the production of flow states, but perceived similarity has a greater influence. It was also discovered that the influence of perceived familiarity on flow was negligible for younger customers. Familiarity and similarity are more essential for older social buying consumers than perceived expertise in triggering flow. When members of a group are expected to be familiar with each other, older users experience a more substantial flow state than younger users. This may be because elderly customers place a higher priority on forming social ties. When there is a flow, older customers seem to be more inclined to buy from SC sites, whereas younger folks are less inclined. One related example is that when it comes to purchasing decisions, senior clients place a higher value on the flow experience than younger folks.

Figure 2. The outcomes of the study model test.

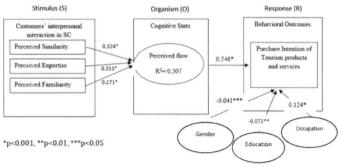

Figure 3. The outcomes of the study model test of young users (old users).

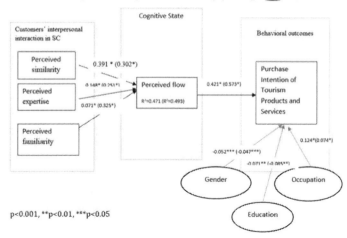

5.2 Implications of the Research

5.2.1 Theoretical Implications

This study makes several theoretical contributions to the intersection of technological innovation, social commerce (SC), and global cultural tourism. It expands on existing research by integrating interpersonal interaction variables—such as perceived expertise, familiarity, and similarity—into the flow experience model, particularly in the context of social commerce for tourism. The findings confirm that these interpersonal cues not only contribute to the development of flow but also have a direct impact on purchase intentions. This highlights the critical role of social and psychological engagement mechanisms within digital environments, especially in tourism, where experiences are central to consumer decision-making. Our research goes further by exploring these elements in the context of global cultural tourism, an area that has been underexplored in existing literature on flow in e-commerce and social media.

Moreover, our study extends the work of Liao et al. (2010) by showing that interpersonal interaction characteristics influence purchase intentions, not just loyalty or community engagement, within SC platforms focused on tourism products. This provides valuable theoretical insights into how peer influence and social connections function as stimuli that enhance flow and drive consumer behavior in a digital tourism setting. Additionally, we introduce new findings on age-related differences in consumer behavior. Younger consumers tend to place higher importance on perceived similarity, while older consumers are more attuned to familiarity, which in turn leads to a stronger flow experience and purchase intention. These results offer novel perspectives on age-based preferences in digital tourism commerce, an area that has not been sufficiently explored in previous studies.

Furthermore, this study contributes to the theoretical understanding of the Stimulus-Organism-Response (S-O-R) model, particularly in how social and psychological factors act as stimuli that influence consumer behavior in social commerce platforms within the tourism industry. By incorporating interpersonal interactions such as perceived expertise, familiarity, and similarity into the flow experience model, we underscore the importance of social presence in driving consumer engagement and decision-making. While previous research has primarily focused on product characteristics and website usability, our findings emphasize that social cues—such as advice from peers or the feeling of connection to others—serve as key stimuli that enhance the flow state and lead to higher purchase intentions. This insight enriches the S-O-R framework by highlighting the interactive and relational dimensions of consumer behavior in digital tourism environments. Moreover, our study lays the groundwork for further research into the role of social interactions in fostering digital trust and community-driven purchasing decisions, an area that remains underexplored, especially in the context of cultural tourism. These contributions not only deepen our understanding of the psychological mechanisms in digital consumer behavior but also open new avenues for investigating how social media and e-commerce can be used more effectively to enhance consumer engagement and conversion rates in the tourism sector.

5.2.2 Managerial Implications

From a managerial standpoint, the insights from this research provide valuable guidance for tourism service providers and social commerce platform developers seeking to enhance customer engagement and increase purchase intention. Tourism platforms should consider designing features that foster meaningful interpersonal interactions, such as interactive user profiles, peer recommendations, and group-based content sharing. These features can leverage perceived expertise and shared interests to create an environment where flow experiences are more easily triggered. Additionally, given the observed differences in behavior between younger and older consumers, tourism marketers should tailor their strategies to appeal to these distinct groups. Younger consumers are more likely to respond to similarity in peer interactions, while older consumers may value familiarity and social connection more in their decision-making process. Thus, social commerce platforms should integrate features that cater to both younger and older audiences by providing options that align with their specific social preferences and purchasing behaviors.

Furthermore, the study highlights the importance of technological inclusion in global tourism markets. While our research focused on Bangladesh, the findings have broader implications for social commerce in other regions, particularly in developing countries where technology is increasingly shaping consumer behaviors. Tourism service providers should consider leveraging social commerce platforms to connect local tourism offerings with a broader, international audience. This approach can help overcome geographic and cultural barriers, making tourism more accessible and engaging on a global scale. Finally, this research underscores the need for personalized customer experiences within the digital tourism space. By understanding how social interactions and flow influence purchase intentions, tourism marketers can create more immersive, tailored experiences that resonate with diverse consumer segments.

In addition, tourism service providers should focus on enhancing the interactive aspects of their platforms to better engage consumers in the digital tourism space. Features like peer reviews, ratings, and user-generated content should be emphasized, as they contribute to the flow experience by increasing social presence and trust. To further foster interpersonal interactions, platforms can incorporate community-building tools, such as discussion forums or travel groups, where users can share experiences and recommendations. These features not only boost engagement but also encourage a sense of belonging and shared interest, which is crucial in influencing purchase intentions. Moreover, tourism marketers should take into account the diverse social preferences of their users. Customizing interactions based on age and preferences—for example, highlighting familiarity for older consumers or similarity for younger consumers—will enable platforms to cater to both groups effectively. This targeted approach can help increase consumer satisfaction, loyalty, and ultimately, conversion rates in the competitive global tourism market.

6. CONCLUSION

This study has explored the impact of customers' interpersonal interactions in social commerce on their purchase intentions for tourism products and services, using the Stimulus-Organism-Response (S-O-R) model. The findings highlight that interpersonal interaction variables—perceived expertise, familiarity, and similarity—are critical in shaping consumers' flow experiences, which, in turn, significantly influence their purchase decisions. This research provides novel insights into the psychological mechanisms underlying consumer behavior in the context of digital tourism, particularly in emerging markets like Bangladesh. The study contributes to existing literature by expanding the understanding of flow experience within social commerce, particularly in relation to tourism. While previous studies have explored flow in e-commerce or social media, few have focused on how these dynamics play out in tourism-related SC platforms. By integrating interpersonal interaction factors, our research enriches the theoretical foundation and offers a fresh perspective on how social and psychological elements drive consumer behavior in the context of global cultural tourism. Moreover, the research highlights the importance of age-related differences in consumer responses to social commerce. While younger consumers tend to prioritize similarity, older consumers place greater emphasis on familiarity, which influences their flow experience and purchase intention. These insights provide a nuanced understanding of how social commerce platforms can cater to different demographic groups, creating personalized, engaging experiences that drive conversion. From a managerial perspective, the study underscores the importance of incorporating social interaction features into tourism platforms. By fostering a sense of community through shared interests, expertise, and familiarity, tourism providers can enhance user engagement and satisfaction, ultimately leading to higher purchase intentions. Furthermore, our findings suggest that tourism marketers should tailor their strategies to accommodate the different preferences of younger and older consumers, ensuring that both groups find value in the platform's social interactions.

While this research has provided valuable theoretical and practical contributions, it also opens up avenues for future investigation. Studies could explore the cross-cultural applicability of the findings, the influence of emerging technologies like augmented reality (AR) and virtual reality (VR), and the role of social influence and community trust in shaping consumer decisions. As social commerce continues to evolve, further research will be essential to understanding how technology and social dynamics intersect to transform the global tourism industry. Moreover, this study lays a strong foundation for future research in social commerce and tourism, offering both practical insights for industry professionals and theoretical advancements that enhance our understanding of consumer behavior in digital tourism platforms. As the field continues to grow, the integration of technological innovation with interpersonal interactions will play a key role in shaping the future of global cultural tourism.

REFERENCES

Ali, F. (2016). Hotel website quality, perceived flow, customer satisfaction and purchase intention. *Journal of Hospitality and Tourism Technology*, *7*(2), 213–228. DOI: 10.1108/JHTT-02-2016-0010

Berhanu, K., & Raj, S. (2020). The trustworthiness of travel and tourism information sources of social media: Perspectives of international tourists visiting Ethiopia. *Heliyon*, *6*(3), e03439. DOI: 10.1016/j.heliyon.2020.e03439 PMID: 32181382

Bernerth, J. B., & Aguinis, H. (2015). A Critical Review and Best-Practice Recommendations for Control Variable Usage. *Personnel Psychology*, *69*(1), 229–283. DOI: 10.1111/peps.12103

Buhalis, D., & Law, R. (2008, August). Progress in information technology and tourism management: 20 years on and 10 years after the Internet—The state of eTourism research. *Tourism Management*, *29*(4), 609–623. DOI: 10.1016/j.tourman.2008.01.005

Chang, H., & Chen, S. (2008). The impact of online store environment cues on purchase intention: Trust and perceived risk as a mediator. *Online Information Review*, *32*(6), 818–841. DOI: 10.1108/14684520810923953

Chang, S.-H., Chih, W.-H., Liou, D.-K., & Hwang, L.-R. (2014). The influence of web aesthetics on customers' PAD. *Computers in Human Behavior*, *36*, 168–178. DOI: 10.1016/j.chb.2014.03.050

Chen, C.-C., Hsiao, K.-L., & Wu, S.-J. (2018). Purchase intention in social commerce: An empirical examination of perceived value and social awareness. *Library Hi Tech*, *36*(4), 583–604. DOI: 10.1108/LHT-01-2018-0007

Chen, H., Wigand, R. T., & Nilan, M. S. (1999, September). Optimal experience of Web activities. *Computers in Human Behavior*, *15*(5), 585–608. DOI: 10.1016/S0747-5632(99)00038-2

Csikzentmihalyi, M. (1975). *Beyond boredom and anxiety*. Jossey-Bass.

Dincer, C., & Dincer, B. (2023). Social Commerce and Purchase Intention: A Brief Look at the Last Decade by Bibliometrics. *Sustainability (Basel)*, *15*(1), 846. Advance online publication. DOI: 10.3390/su15010846

Ding, D., Hu, P.-H., Verma, R., & Wardell, D. (2009). The Impact of Service System Design and Flow Experience on Customer Satisfaction in Online Financial Services. *Journal of Service Research*, *13*(1), 96–110. DOI: 10.1177/1094670509350674

Donovan, R., & Rositter, J. (1982). Store atmosphere: An environmental psychology approach. *Journal of Retailing*, *58*(1), 34–57.

Eroglu, S., Machleit, K., & Davis, L. (2003). Empirical Testing of a Model of Online Store Atmospherics and Shopper Responses. *Psychology and Marketing*, *20*(2), 139–150. DOI: 10.1002/mar.10064

Fang, Y., Qureshi, I., Sun, H., McCole, P., Ramsey, E., & Lim, K. (2014). Trust, Satisfaction, and Online Repurchase Intention: The Moderating Role of Perceived Effectiveness of E-Commerce Institutional Mechanisms. *Management Information Systems Quarterly*, *38*(2), 407–428. https://www.jstor.org/stable/26634932. DOI: 10.25300/MISQ/2014/38.2.04

Fornell, C., & Larcker, D. (1981). Evaluating Structural Equation Models with Unobservable Variables and Measurement Error. *JMR, Journal of Marketing Research*, *18*(1), 39–50. DOI: 10.1177/002224378101800104

Fu, S., Yan, Q., & Feng, G. C. (2018, June). Who will attract you? Similarity effect among users on online purchase intention of movie tickets in the social shopping context. *International Journal of Information Management*, *40*, 88–102. DOI: 10.1016/j.ijinfomgt.2018.01.013

Gan, C., & Wang, W. (2017). The influence of perceived value on purchase intention in social commerce context. *Internet Research*, *27*(4), 772–785. DOI: 10.1108/IntR-06-2016-0164

Gao, L., & Bai, X. (2014). Online consumer behaviour and its relationship to website atmospheric induced flow: Insights into online travel agencies in China. *Journal of Retailing and Consumer Services*, *21*(4), 653–665. DOI: 10.1016/j.jretconser.2014.01.001

Gefen, D., & Straub, D. (2005). A Practical Guide To Factorial Validity Using PLS-Graph: Tutorial And Annotated Example. *Communications of the Association for Information Systems*, *16*(1), 91–109. DOI: 10.17705/1CAIS.01605

Gibreel, O., Alotaibi, D. A., & Altmann, J. (2018, January–February). Social commerce development in emerging markets. *Electronic Commerce Research and Applications*, *27*, 152–162. DOI: 10.1016/j.elerap.2017.12.008

Goi, M., Kalidas, V., & Yunus, N. (2018). Mediating roles of emotion and experience in the stimulus-organism-response framework in higher education institutions. *Journal of Marketing for Higher Education*, *28*(5), 1–23. DOI: 10.1080/08841241.2018.1425231

Ha, Y., & Lennon, S. (2010). Online visual merchandising (VMD) cues and consumer pleasure and arousal: Purchasing versus browsing situation. *Psychology and Marketing*, *27*(2), 141–165. DOI: 10.1002/mar.20324

Han, M. S., Hampson, D. P., Wang, Y., & Wang, H. (2022). Consumer confidence and green purchase intention: An application of the stimulus-organism-response model. *Journal of Retailing and Consumer Services*, *68*, 103061. DOI: 10.1016/j.jretconser.2022.103061

Heinonen, K., & Strandvik, T. (2007). Consumer responsiveness to mobile marketing. *International Journal of Mobile Communications*, *5*(6), 603–617. DOI: 10.1504/IJMC.2007.014177

Hewei, T., & Youngsook, L. (2022). Factors affecting continuous purchase intention of fashion products on social E-commerce: SOR model and the mediating effect. *Entertainment Computing*, *41*, 100474. DOI: 10.1016/j.entcom.2021.100474

Hoffman, D., & Novak, T. (1996). Marketing in Hypermedia Computer-Mediated Environments: Conceptual Foundations. *Journal of Marketing*, *60*(3), 50–68. DOI: 10.1177/002224299606000304

Hossain, M., & Rahman, M. (2022). Detection of potential customers' empathy behavior towards customers' reviews. *Journal of Retailing and Consumer Services*, *65*, 102881. DOI: 10.1016/j.jretconser.2021.102881

Hossain, M., Zhou, X., & Rahman, M. (2018). Examining the impact of QR codes on purchase intention and customer satisfaction on the basis of perceived flow. *International Journal of Engineering Business Management*, *10*, 1–11. DOI: 10.1177/1847979018812323

Hossain, M. S., Rahman, M. F., & Zhou, X. (2021). Impact of customers' interpersonal interactions in social commerce on customer relationship management performance. *Journal of Contemporary Marketing Science*, *4*(1), 161–181. DOI: 10.1108/JCMARS-12-2020-0050

Hovland, C. I., & Weiss, W. (1951). The influence of source credibility on communication effectiveness. *Public Opinion Quarterly*, *15*(4), 635–650. DOI: 10.1086/266350

Hsieh, J.-K., Hsieh, Y.-C., Chiu, H.-C., & Yang, Y.-R. (2014). Customer Response to Web Site Atmospherics: Task-relevant Cues, Situational Involvement and PAD. *Journal of Interactive Marketing*, *28*(3), 225–236. DOI: 10.1016/j.intmar.2014.03.001

Hsu, C. L., Chang, K. C., & Chen, M. C. (2011). The impact of website quality on customer satisfaction and purchase intention: Perceived playfulness and perceived flow as mediators. *Information Systems and e-Business Management*, *10*(4), 549–570. DOI: 10.1007/s10257-011-0181-5

Hu, S., Akram, U., Ji, F., Zhao, Y., & Song, J. (2023). Does social media usage contribute to cross-border social commerce? An empirical evidence from SEM and fsQCA analysis. *Acta Psychologica*, *241*, 104083. DOI: 10.1016/j.actpsy.2023.104083 PMID: 37972439

Hu, X., Huang, Q., Zhong, X., Davison, R. M., & Zhao, D. (2016, December). The influence of peer characteristics and technical features of a social shopping website on a consumer's purchase intention. *International Journal of Information Management*, *36*(6), 1218–1230. DOI: 10.1016/j.ijinfomgt.2016.08.005

Huang, T.-L., & Liao, S.-L. (2017). Creating e-shopping multisensory flow experience through augmented-reality interactive technology. *Internet Research*, *27*(2), 449–475. DOI: 10.1108/IntR-11-2015-0321

Ilsever, J., Cyr, D., & Parent, M. (2007). EXTENDING MODELS OF FLOW AND E-LOYALTY. *Journal of Information Science and Technology*, *4*(2), 3–22.

Jang, S., & Namkung, Y. (2009). Perceived quality, emotions, and behavioral intentions: Application of an extended Mehrabian–Russell model to restaurants. *Journal of Business Research*, *62*(4), 451–460. DOI: 10.1016/j.jbusres.2008.01.038

Kabadayi, S., & Gupta, R. (2005). Website loyalty: An empirical investigation of its antecedents. *International Journal of Internet Marketing and Advertising*, *2*(4), 321–345. DOI: 10.1504/IJIMA.2005.008105

Kaur, P., Dhir, A., & Rajala, R. (2016). Assessing flow experience in social networking site based. *Computers in Human Behavior*, *64*, 217–225. DOI: 10.1016/j.chb.2016.06.045

Kim, N., & Kim, W. (2018, April). Do your social media lead you to make social deal purchases?Consumer-generated social referrals for sales via social commerce. *International Journal of Information Management*, *39*, 38–48. DOI: 10.1016/j.ijinfomgt.2017.10.006

Kim, S.-H., Whaley, J., & Choi, Y. (2022). Managing the restaurant experience: Re-specifying the role of food, interaction, and atmosphere as contributors to the optimal flow experience. *Journal of Foodservice Business Research*, •••, 1–22. DOI: 10.1080/15378020.2022.2047573

Koufaris, M. (2002). Applying the Technology Acceptance Model and Flow Theory to Online Consumer Behavior. *Information Systems Research*, *13*(2), 115–225. DOI: 10.1287/isre.13.2.205.83

Liao, H.-C., Shen, Y.-C., & Chu, C.-Y. H.-H. (2010). Virtual Community Loyalty: An Interpersonal-Interaction Perspective. *International Journal of Electronic Commerce*, *15*(1), 49–74. DOI: 10.2753/JEC1086-4415150102

Lin, J., Li, T., & Guo, J. (2021). Factors influencing consumers' continuous purchase intention on fresh food e-commerce platforms: An organic foods-centric empirical investigation. *Electronic Commerce Research and Applications*, *50*, 101103. DOI: 10.1016/j.elerap.2021.101103

Liu, C., Bao, Z., & Zheng, C. (2019). Exploring consumers' purchase intention in social commerce: An empirical study based on trust, argument quality, and social presence. *Asia Pacific Journal of Marketing and Logistics*, *31*(2), 378–397. DOI: 10.1108/APJML-05-2018-0170

Liu, H., Chu, H., Huang, Q., & Chen, X. (2016, May). Enhancing the flow experience of consumers in China through interpersonal interaction in social commerce. *Computers in Human Behavior*, *58*, 306–314. DOI: 10.1016/j.chb.2016.01.012

Loureiro, S. M., Sarmento, E. M., & Rosário, J. F. (2020). Incorporating VR, AR, and Related Technologies in the Tourism Industry: State of the Art. *Managerial Challenges and Social Impacts of Virtual and Augmented Reality*, 211-233. DOI: 10.4018/978-1-7998-2874-7.ch013

Lu, B., Fan, W., & Zhou, M. (2016). Social presence, trust, and social commerce purchase intention: An empirical research. *Computers in Human Behavior*, *56*, 225–237. DOI: 10.1016/j.chb.2015.11.057

Maia, C., Lunardi, G., Longaray, A., & Munhoz, P. (2018). Factors and characteristics that influence consumers' participation in social commerce. *Revista de Gestão*, *25*(2), 194–211. DOI: 10.1108/REGE-03-2018-031

Martins, J., Costa, C., Oliveira, T., Gonçalves, R., & Branco, F. (2019). How smartphone advertising influences consumers' purchase intention. *Journal of Business Research*, *94*, 378–387. DOI: 10.1016/j.jbusres.2017.12.047

Mathwick, C., & Rigdon, E. (2004, September). Play, Flow, and the Online Search Experience. *The Journal of Consumer Research*, *31*(2), 324–332. DOI: 10.1086/422111

Mazursky, D., & Jacoby, J. (1986). Exploring the development of store images. *Journal of Retailing*.

Mehrabian, A., & Russell, J. (1974). *An approach to environmental psychology.* The MIT Press.

Mirzaalian, F., & Halpenny, E. (2021, June). Exploring destination loyalty: Application of social media analytics in a nature-based tourism setting. *Journal of Destination Marketing & Management*, *20*, 100598. Advance online publication. DOI: 10.1016/j.jdmm.2021.100598

Natour, S. A., Benbasat, I., & Cenfetelli, R. T. (2005). The Role of Similarity in e-Commerce Interactions:The Case of Online Shopping Assistants. *SIGHCI 2005 proceedings.4.* Retrieved from https://aisel.aisnet.org/sighci2005/4

Ng, C. S.-P. (2013). Intention to purchase on socia lcommerce websites across cultures: Across-regional study. *Information & Management*, *50*(8), 609–620. DOI: 10.1016/j.im.2013.08.002

Novak, T., Hoffman, D., & Duhachek, A. (2003). The Influence of Goal-Directed and Experiential Activities on Online Flow Experiences. *Journal of Consumer Psychology*, *13*(1), 3–16. DOI: 10.1207/153276603768344744

Novak, T. P., Hoffman, D. L., & Yung, Y.-F. (2000). Measuring the Customer Experience in Online Environments: A Structural Modeling Approach. *Marketing Science*, *19*(1), 22–42. DOI: 10.1287/mksc.19.1.22.15184

O'Cass, A., & Carlson, J. (2010, April). Examining the effects of website-induced flow in professional sporting team websites. *Internet Research*, *20*(2), 115–134. DOI: 10.1108/10662241011032209

Oh, J., Fiorito, S., Cho, H., & Hofackerd, C. (2008). Effects of design factors on store image and expectation of merchandise quality in web-based stores. *Journal of Retailing and Consumer Services*, *15*(4), 237–249. DOI: 10.1016/j.jretconser.2007.03.004

Oppland, M. (2021, February 15). *8 Ways To Create Flow According to Mihaly Csikszentmihalyi.* Retrieved March 5, 2021, from positivepsychology.com: https://positivepsychology.com/mihaly-csikszentmihalyi-father-of-flow/

Pavlou, P., & Fygenson, M. (2006). Understanding and Predicting Electronic Commerce Adoption: An Extension of the Theory of Planned Behavior. *MIS Quarterly*, *30*(1). *Management Information Systems Quarterly*, *30*(1), 115. Advance online publication. DOI: 10.2307/25148720

Peng, S., Le, L., Hossain, M. S., & Zabin, S. (2025). Investigating Students' Behavioral Intention to use ChatGPT for Educational purposes. *Sustainable Futures : An Applied Journal of Technology, Environment and Society, 9*, 1–14. DOI: 10.1016/j.sftr.2025.100531

Ponte, E. B., Trujillo, E. C., & Rodríguez, T. E. (2015). Influence of trust and perceived value on the intention to purchase travel online: Integrating the effects of assurance on trust antecedents. *Tourism Management, 47*, 286–302. DOI: 10.1016/j.tourman.2014.10.009

Preacher, K., & Hayes, A. (2008). Asymptotic and resampling strategies for assessing and comparing indirect effects in multiple mediator models. *Behavior Research Methods, 40*(3), 879–891. DOI: 10.3758/BRM.40.3.879 PMID: 18697684

Rahman, F. B. A., Hanafiah, M. H., Zahari, M. S. M., & Jipiu, L. B. (2023). Social commerce adoption: A study on consumer's online purchase behaviour of perishable pastry products. *British Food Journal, 125*(1), 318–344. DOI: 10.1108/BFJ-07-2021-0796

Shen, Y.-C., Huang, C.-Y., Chu, C.-H., & Liao, H.-C. (2010). Virtual community loyalty: An interpersonal-interaction perspective. *International Journal of Electronic Commerce, 15*(1), 49–74. DOI: 10.2753/JEC1086-4415150102

Shrout, P., & Bolger, N. (2002). Mediation in experimental and nonexperimental studies: New procedures and recommendations. *Psychological Methods, 7*(4), 422–445. DOI: 10.1037/1082-989X.7.4.422 PMID: 12530702

Su, Y.-S., Chiang, W.-L., Lee, C.-T., & Chang, H.-C. (2016). The effect of flow experience on player loyalty in mobile game application. *Computers in Human Behavior, 63*, 240–248. DOI: 10.1016/j.chb.2016.05.049

Sultan, P., Wong, H. Y., & Azam, M. S. (2021). How perceived communication source and food value stimulate purchase intention of organic food: An examination of the stimulus-organism-response (SOR) model. *Journal of Cleaner Production, 312*, 127807. DOI: 10.1016/j.jclepro.2021.127807

Tamjidyamcholo, A., Gholipour, R., Baba, M., & Yamchello, H. (2013). Information security professional perceptions of knowledge-sharing intention in virtual communities under social cognitive theory. *International Conference on Research and Innovation in Information Systems (ICRIIS),* (pp. 416-421). Kuala Lumpur, Malaysia: IEEE. DOI: 10.1109/ICRIIS.2013.6716746

Wang, L., & Hsiao, D. F. (2012). Antecedents of flow in retail store shopping. *Journal of Retailing and Consumer Services*, *19*(4), 381–389. DOI: 10.1016/j.jretconser.2012.03.002

Webster, J., Trevino, L. K., & Ryan, L. (1993, Winter). The dimensionality and correlates of flow in human-computer interactions. *Computers in Human Behavior*, *9*(4), 411–426. DOI: 10.1016/0747-5632(93)90032-N

Yadav, M. S., Valck, K., Thurau, T. H., Hoffman, D. L., & Spann, M. (2013, November). Social Commerce: A Contingency Framework for Assessing Marketing Potential. *Journal of Interactive Marketing*, *27*(4), 311–323. DOI: 10.1016/j.intmar.2013.09.001

Yoon, E. (2012). Effects of Website Environmental Cues on Consumers' Response and Outcome Behaviors. *Public Access Theses, Dissertations, and Student Research from the College of Education and Human Sciences*. Retrieved from https://digitalcommons.unl.edu/cehsdiss/163/

Zhang, H., Lu, Y., Gupta, S., & Zhao, L. (2014). What motivates customers to participate in social commerce? The impact of technological environments and virtual customer experiences. *Information & Management*, *51*(8), 1017–1030. DOI: 10.1016/j.im.2014.07.005

Zhao, W., Hu, F., Wang, J., Shu, T., & Xu, Y. (2023). A systematic literature review on social commerce: Assessing the past and guiding the future. *Electronic Commerce Research and Applications*, *57*, 101219. Advance online publication. DOI: 10.1016/j.elerap.2022.101219

Zhou, L., Zhang, P., & Zimmermann, H.-D. (2013). Social commerce research: An integrated view. *Electronic Commerce Research and Applications*, *12*(2), 61–68. DOI: 10.1016/j.elerap.2013.02.003

Zhou, T. (2019). The effect of flow experience on users' social commerce intention. [[doi:]. *Kybernetes*, *49*(10), 2349–2363. DOI: 10.1108/K-03-2019-0198

KEY TERMS AND DEFINITIONS

Social Commerce (SC): Social commerce refers to the use of social media platforms and online communities to facilitate the buying and selling of goods and services, with a focus on peer-to-peer interactions, user-generated content, and social influence. In the context of tourism, SC leverages these elements to enhance consumer decision-making, creating a digital environment where interactions between users can influence the purchase of tourism products and services.

Flow Experience: Flow experience is a psychological state in which a person is fully immersed in an activity, resulting in heightened focus, enjoyment, and involvement. In the context of social commerce for tourism, flow refers to the deep engagement consumers feel when interacting with a platform, driven by interpersonal interactions, personalized content, and emotional connection to the travel experience being offered.

Perceived Expertise: Perceived expertise refers to the extent to which consumers view an individual or platform as knowledgeable, skilled, or experienced in a specific area, such as tourism products and services. In social commerce, perceived expertise enhances trust and influences consumer behavior, as users are more likely to make purchasing decisions based on the advice and recommendations of experts or perceived authority figures within a community.

Familiarity: Familiarity refers to the degree to which consumers feel comfortable with and recognize the identities or brands they encounter during their social commerce interactions. In tourism-related SC, familiarity influences consumer trust and engagement, as consumers tend to be more likely to purchase products or services from sources they perceive as familiar or trustworthy, such as friends, family, or familiar brands.

Similarity: Similarity refers to the extent to which individuals perceive others as sharing common interests, backgrounds, or preferences. In social commerce, perceived similarity fosters connection, enhances communication, and increases the likelihood of forming relationships that can lead to increased purchase intentions. In the context of tourism, similarity can influence consumers' willingness to engage with and purchase from platforms that reflect their personal preferences and values.

Purchase Intention: Purchase intention refers to the likelihood or willingness of a consumer to buy a product or service based on various influencing factors, including emotional and social influences, perceived value, and external recommendations. In the context of social commerce, purchase intention is shaped by the interaction between flow experience, interpersonal factors, and consumer attitudes towards the tourism products and services being offered.

Interpersonal Interaction in Social Commerce: Interpersonal interaction in social commerce refers to the communication and social engagement between users or consumers within an online platform, which can include sharing experiences, offering recommendations, or engaging in discussions about products and services. In the context of tourism, interpersonal interactions are vital in shaping consumer perceptions, enhancing trust, and influencing purchase decisions, as consumers often rely on peer recommendations and social cues when making decisions related to travel.

APPENDIX: QUESTIONNAIRE ITEMS

Table 6.

Constructs	Items Measures	Sources
Perceived similarity (PES)	PES1: As regards the styles in tourism products and services, you are similar to some members on these SN sites.	
	PES2: As regards the tastes in tourism products and services, you are similar to some members on these SN sites.	(Liao, Shen, & Chu, 2010)
	PES3: As regards your likes and dislikes about tourism products and services, you are similar to some members on these SN sites.	
	PES4: As regards preferences in tourism products and services, you are similar to some members on these SN sites.	
Perceived expertise (PEE)	PEE1: Some members on these SN sites are very knowledgeable about tourism products and services.	
	PEE2: Some members on these SN sites are experts regarding the tourism products and services	(Liao, Shen, & Chu, 2010)
	PEE3: Some member on these SN sites are highly experienced in tourism products and services?	
	PEE4: Compared with other sites, these SN sites contains much information and knowledge about tourism products and services.	
Perceived familiarity (PEF)	PEF1: Members of these SN sites as familiar to you as good friends.	
	PEF2: you have frequent interactions with other members of these SN sites by writing or replying to articles.	(Liao, Shen, & Chu, 2010)
	PEF3: The members on these SN sites are familiar to you.	
	PEF4: You keep close contact with these SN sites members.	
Flow experience (FWL)	FWL1: It is fun to interact on these SN sites.	
	FWL2: The interaction on these SN sites is interesting	(Zhang, Lu, Gupta, & Zhao, 2014)
	FWL3: You may enjoy the pleasure of exploration when shopping on these SN sites.	
	FWL4: When you purchase on these SN sites, you become completely engrossed.	
Purchase intention (PSI)	PSI1: You aim to acquire products from these SN sites whenever you need to shop.	
	PSI2: Whenever you need to shop, you make a plan to purchase products on these SN sites.	(Pavlou & Fygenson, 2006)

continued on following page

Table 6. Continued

Constructs	Items Measures	Sources
	PSI3: You can expect that you'll buy anything from one of these SN sites.	
	PSI4: It's very possible that you'll buy anything from one of these SN websites.	

Chapter 13
Decision to Visit Ecotourism Among Generation Z:
The Role of Environment Sustainability and Social Sustainability

Genoveva Genoveva
President University, Indonesia

Tandi Gunadi
President University, Indonesia

ABSTRACT

Sustainability issues, related to the triple bottom line that occurred nowadays can affect the tourist's intention on visiting the ecotourism destination in Indonesia before it turns to visit decision-making. The researchers will choose generation Z who intend to visit ecotourism sites, such as Komodo National Park, Raja Ampat, Way Kambas, Kawah Ijen, Tanjung Puting and Gunung Leuser. However, in this study it was limited to visitors to Komodo National Park which is the most popular ecotourism in Indonesia and is protected by UNESCO. Enviromental sustanaibility and social sutanaibility are incorporated in this study in order to understand how they influence visit intention and visit decision. This research used a quantitative method using Smart PLS 3.0 (PLS-SEM) to analyze total 278 respondents from Generation Z in greater Jakarta. The results show that environmental sustainability and social sustainability developed by ecotourism positively affect tourist visit intention and also positive indirect effect on visit decision.

DOI: 10.4018/979-8-3693-3196-5.ch013

INTRODUCTION

Indonesia is well known as one of the largest maritime country in the world. The geographic condition of the country supports the country to be rich in culture diversity until the nature and biodiversity. The variety of the social and natural resources in Indonesia then create the opportunity for the country to develop tourism business, especially in ecotourism business. Ecotourism is a tourism activity that takes responsibility to the relative environment and the local people on the site. Ecotourism itself is claimed to be most expanding sector in tourism industry (Honey, 2008). Ecotourism provide insight into the influence of people on the environment, and promote a larger appreciation of the nature habitats, inclusive of ecotourism is responsible for minimizing the terrible aspects of traditional tourism on the environment programs, in addition to strengthening the cultural harmony of the neighborhood population and comparison of environmental factors (Bazazo, Nasseef, Al-Zawaideh, Al-Zawaideh, & Al-Dhomaidat, 2017). The right implementation of ecotourism industry is proofed to help the conservation funding for the nature, create social and cultural awareness, promote local communities, help to fund developing country, and educate tourists (Honey, 2008). The concept of environmental and sustainable tourism has driven to pull in visitors in huge numbers within the different countries of the world. It then characterized by the government and the local community awareness towards the great care, development, promoting and advancement for ecotourism destination, which would make all dependable parties are mindful of what will happen as a result (Su, Wall, & Ma, 2014).

A study by Mihanyar, Rahman, & Aminudin (2015) show that environmentally sustainable development in tourism sector can create tourism awareness and behavioral visit intention. For environmental sustainability, the most environmental sustainability threats that facing the global are pollution, climate changes, natural resources exploitation, and emitted carbon and methane (Durant, Fiorino, & O'Leary, 2017). Previous research found out that climate change and land use can affecting the biodiversity situation in complex mechanism (Oliver & Morecroft, 2014). Unfortunately, Indonesia is currently facing quite serious environmental issues. A report found that Indonesia is the top 11 air polluted country in the world and the most air populated country in South East Asia (IQ Air AirVisual, 2019). A report by international institution, Yale, Indonesia's environmental quality still need improvement as it have 46.92 score of 100 for the *environmental performance index (EPI)*. The scored is calculated based on comparing and analyzing environmental condition of countries around the world. In ASEAN, Indonesia EPI got 7th position below than other neighbor countries such as Singapore, Brunei Darussalam, Malaysia, Philippine, Thailand, Timor Leste, and Vietnam, while it get 29th position in Asia and rank 133 (out of 180) in the world (Yale, 2018). Beside of air pollution, another threat by water pollution also following Indonesia. Report by NatureResearch, found out that Indonesia is the second water polluted country after China, while 4 of Indonesia's river included in the 20 most polluted river in the world because of the plastic waste pollution (Lebreton, et al., 2017). Water pollution that exist will cause the low level of water quality and disease (Sharma & Sanghi, 2012). In tourism industry, beside of advertisement and site development, attractiveness become key indicator to create intention and action for satisfaction. Attractiveness from tourism comes from the recreation resource and uniqueness that come from the society, service, or facility that may create intention to visit in order to achieve satisfaction (Hultman, Kazeminia, & Ghasemi, 2015).

Second is the challenge in social sustainability to attract tourist in ecotourism. Unfortunately, social sustainability is less concerned than economic and environmental sustainability while actually people participation is the key to achieve sustainable development (Dilard, Dujon, & King, 2009). Social sustainability challenge in tourism sector including reducing poverty, deleting social barriers and tourism development through people participation (Saarinen, 2014). A study by Reddy & Thomson (2015) show that social sustainability aspects such as living standards, health, cohesion, norms, and society values affecting social capital in achieving sustainable development. Previous research show that people participation and community involvement on ecotourism development increase destination image and improving service quality of ecotourism in Kintamani, Bali (Kencana & Mertha, 2014). Other research show that activity that involved nature, culture and local community in ecotourism affected tourist travel behavior (Lee & Jan, 2018). Another previous research uncover that consumers' ecotourism attitude would emphatically impact ecotourism intention, ecotourism interest, and readiness to pay a premium for ecotourism (Lu, Gursoy, & Chiappa, 2016). Ecotourism attitude of tourist can be described as pro environmental attitudes such respecting the environment as a system that have correlation between wildlife and natural habitats, have greater awareness and interest toward environment, and more likely to spend time in nature (Packer, Ballantyne, & Hughes, 2014).

Therefore, this research will take social sustainability and environment sustainability that become core of attractiveness of ecotourism towards generation Z visit intention before it turns to visit decision making. The researcher chooses Komodo National Park as one of the emerging ecotourism destinations because Komodo National Park is one of the world heritage sites by UNESCO and the only national park in the world that nurturing Komodo Dragon *(Varanus komodoensis),* the historic animal that almost faces the extinction. Besides, Komodo National Park is now facing high level sustainability threat. A report by IUCN's World Heritage Outlook (2017) found out that Komodo National Park (KNIP) is facing over-fishing of reef resources, destructive fishing practices, poaching, cutting forests for firewood, and fresh water supply shortages that endangered the ecosystem stability. A report by The JakartaPost (2017) also indicates waste management problem by developer because of the massive non-organic waste in Komodo National Park area.

The researchers select generation Z as the research sample because generation Z is forecasted to be the largest group of consumers at 2020 (Miller & Lu, 2018). Generation Z is the generation born between the year of 1995 and 2009 (Bassiouni & Hackley, 2014). Generation Z is known with their tendency to try something new, because of their tech savvy behavior (Fromm & Read, 2018). The report by Miller & Lu also stated that the 32% of world's population is composed by Generation Z with total 7.7 billion population. In Indonesia, the travelers population started to increase as described in domestic travelers distribution based on the age classification, as served by Indonesia Central Bureau of Statistics/ BPS (Badan Pusat Statistik) data below (Fitriani, Indriati, & Barudin, 2017).

Another report also explain that the millennial generation population are slightly surpassed by Generation Z (Elkind, 2019). A research by Fromm (2018), reported that 93% of family purchase decisions are affected by Generation Z with estimated direct spending from $29 billion until $143. For the demographic sample, researcher will choose generation Z people that live in Jabodetabek area because this area is known as largest business center area in Indonesia and also Jakarta, as the capital city of Indonesia is including to this area, which makes Jabodetabek area as the one of the most populated area in Indonesia (Handayani, Suleeman, Priadi, & Darmajanti, 2017). Jabodetabek is Jakarta metropolitan area that consist of Jakarta, Bogor, Tangerang, and Bekasi. Jakarta as the capital city, together with Depok, Bekasi city from West Java province (Jawa Barat), and also Tangerang from Banten province, are included in the top 5 of travelers' population based on the province origin (Fitriani, Indriati, & Barudin, 2017).

The first section of this study is the introduction that highlights the rationale for selecting the topic and the challenges facing generation Z to visit ecotourism. The second section is a literature review, in which we discuss the theories that underpin this study. The third section is theresearch methodology, in which we elaborate the steps we took to collect and analyse the data. The fourth section is the result and discussion, where we present and discuss the statistical results. Finally, we summarize our study's findings in the conclusion section.

LITERATURE REVIEW AND HYPOTHESIS DEVELOPMENT

Sustainability is a concern to balance the needs/condition between the present situations while at the same time keeping the next generation the same opportunity to fulfill their needs (Kenton, 2019). The science of sustainability is an emerging study that has been discussed more than decades ago yet still being developed until now. This field yet become even larger topic as the concern need major participation by shareholders, and citizens to achieve the field study, which is being sustainable (Clark & Wokaun, 2003). There are three main pillars on achieving sustainability, which are social, economic, and environmental sustainability. Further concern related to social sustainability and environmental sustainability will be discussed one after one on the next literature.

Social Sustainability itself is a concern of development and growth that correlated with society especially civil society to reduce inequalities, increase social awareness and social integration. There are three concepts in ideas of social sustainability which are social capital, social cohesive and social exclusion (Bagaeen & Uduku, 2010).

Social Sustainability

Social sustainability as an approach that focus on human or social relationship. The social sustainability approach concerns to analyze human needs, quality life problems, and also environmental awareness. Social sustainability concerns between individuals with environment, and individuals with institutional or organization (Manzi, Lucas, Lloyd, & Allen, 2010). Human activities, working system and society need to be considered in social sustainability as it also have long term impact to the long term social and environmental development (J.Zink, 2008). Besides, social sustainability can be described as dynamical process to maximize social resources, such as social values, culture and community. The social resources should contribute to 'viability, health, and functioning' (Baldwin & King, 2018). There are few drivers of social sustainability, which are community funding and support, community involvement, education and personal development, diversity and equal opportunities (Popovic, Povoa, Krawslawski, & Carvalho, 2018).

Environmental Sustainability

Environmental Sustainability is a concern to create systemic condition to maintain human activity without damaging the natural cycle in a regional level or even planetary level so that it can be exist for future generation (Vezzoli & Manzini, 2008). Environment sustainability also can be interpret as system designed by human to ensure the nature resource and its cycle without giving negative impact on society, environment, and human health. Environmental issues, such as water pollution, global warming, and limited energy supply are some obstacles of environment sustainability to achieve sustainable development (Klemes, 2015). Environment sustainability is an ability to maintain sustainable resource in order to fulfill nature resource supply and demand. Environment sustainability ecosystem are strongly affected by climate change, pollutions, carrying capacity and biodiversity (Dong & Hauschild, 2017).

Visit Intention

Intention is a robust goals/aim that supported by determination to achieved targeted result. People with intention can be interpret as having strong will to not let any intervention inhibit their inner desire (Dyer, 2010). In planning theory of intention, intention is defined as part of partial plan of action concerning the current and upcoming establishment. The theory characterized intention roles to shaping ongoing reasoning and decision making (Bratman, 1999).

In travel/tourism sector, visit Intention is described as consumer plan for future travel behavior. Future visit intention is strongly related with consumer attitudes. The attitudes from consumer towards destination will create consumer behavior to visit a destination (Kim & Kwon, 2018). Individual's visit intention based on theory of planned behavior, is affected by 3 factors, which are the attitudes towards behavior, norm subjectivity and behavioral control (Pramanik, Hossain, & Azam, 2016). Other theory classify the visit intention on ecotourism as a progressive function of pro-environment and ecotourism attitudes. Previous research proofed that tourist behaviors, intentions, and attitudes toward ecotourism affect their visit intention on ecotourism (Hultman, Kazeminia, & Ghasemi, 2015).

Visit Decision

Decision making is situational consideration that consist of various complexity level involving different objectives. Decision making is part of our life because it happens in daily activities of individuals and multiple ranges of groups in society (Chankong & Haimas, 2008). Decision making is choosing the set of potential result and also other alternative from a process. Decision making process was identified to have similar decision process, including visit decision (Rubright, Kline, Viren, Naar, & Oliver, 2016). Decision making for eco-tourist can be affected by perspectives, preferences and values. Decision making for eco-tourist also can be influence by environment (Solomon, Bamossy, Askegaard, & Hogg, 2016). Previous research by (Satyarini, Rahmanita, & Setarnawat, 2017) show that visit intention will affect visit decision towards tourism destination. Several indicators are also can drive the decision making process. Uncertainty avoidance, sensation seeking, novelty seeking, and risk-taking propensity is figured to give effect toward decision making (Karl, 2018).

Based on the above literature, the hypotheses are as follows:

H$_1$: There is direct influence between Social Sustainability and Visit Intention
H$_2$: There is direct influence between Environment Sustainability and Visit Intention
H$_3$: There is direct influence between Visit Intention and Visit Decision
H$_4$: There is direct influence between Social Sustainability and Visit Decision
H$_5$: There is direct influence between Enviromental Sustainability and Visit Decision
H$_6$: There is indirect influence of Social Sustainability toward Visit Decision mediated by Visit Intention
H$_7$: There is indirect influence of Environment Sustainability toward Visit Intention mediated by Visit intention

Figure 1. Theoretical framework

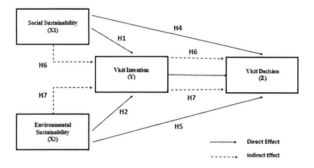

METHODOLOGY

This research uses quantitative method by spreading questionnaire to obtain the data. The questionnaire composed of 28 questions with a 5-point Likert Scale, that consist of strongly disagree, disagree, neutral, agree, and strongly agree. This questionnaire corresponds through sample visit intention to Komodo National Park. The questionnaire was preceded by three screening questions, so that the respondent who filled it out was in accordance with the criteria, namely having visited the Komodo National Park, aged 10-25 years and residing in Jabodetabek (greater Jakarta).

To gain more information for this research, the researchers decides to focus on the population of the sample from generation Z people that have or haven't visit Komodo National Park, especially in Jabodetabek area. Researchers use non-probability sampling to distribute the research questions. The sampling distribution using networks to get certain data collection (Etikan & Bala, 2017). Since the population of this research isn't identified, Hair sampling method (Hair, Black, Babin, & Anderson, 2010) used by researchers to decide the sample size, by calculating 5 times (Total questions) of all variables. The formula is N = Number of question x 5-10. The total questions in this research is 28. Therefore, the minimum question in this research is 140.

This research uses the Smart PLS 3.0 data analysis Partial Least Square-Structural Equation Model (PLS-SEM) to evaluate the results of data collection. The evaluation of PLS-SEM method will use outer and inner model measurement. Outer model measurements are divided into three, namely convergent validity, discriminant validity, and reliability. Convergent validity test can be done looking at outer loading factor and AVE score, Discriminant validity test can be done through Fornell-Lecker criterion and cross loading factor score, while reliability test can be done by looking through construct reliability (CR) and *cronbach alpha* score. Inner models/ structural models are used to predict relationships between variables. The inner model evaluation can be tested by evaluating the determination coefficient, path coefficient, and goodness of fit. Determination Coefficient is measured through R^2 for endogenous constructs. Path Coefficient can be evaluated if the p-value <0.05. The goodness of fit can be seen through the SRMR /Standardized Root Mean Square Residual score that below 0.08.

RESULT AND DISCUSSION

Respondent Profile

Table 1 below shows the profile of the respondents. The first profile background question shows the respondent's gender majority male consist of 145 (52.16%), the rest is female consist of 133 (47.84%). The second question show that, the majority of the respondents' age 21-25 consist of 197 (70.86%), then age 16-20 years old consist of 78 (28.06%), and age 10-15 years old only 3 (1.08%). The last question in respondent profile is occupation. They are employee numbering 187 (67.27%), then student totaling 64 (19.79%), and from student totaling 64 (19.795).

Table 1. Respondent profile

Profile	Category	Frequency	Percentage (%)
Gender	Male	145	52.16%
	Female	133	47.84%
Age	10-15	3	1.08%
	16-20	78	28.06%
	21-25	197	70.86%
Occupation	Student	64	19.79%
	Employee	187	67.27%
	Entrepreneur	27	12.94%

Descriptive Statistics

Table 2 shows the general mean and standard deviation score for each variable tested in the research. There are total of 278 respondents analyzed by this research. Environmental Sustainability is the variable with highest mean score (4.2503) while visit intention get the lowest mean score (4.0701).

Table 2. Descriptive statistics

Variable	Mean	Standard Deviation
Social Sustainability	4.193	0.671
Enironmental. Sustanaibiity	4.250	0.667
Visit Intention	4.070	0.786
Visit decision	4.114	0.761

Outer Model Evaluation

Figure 2. Outer model

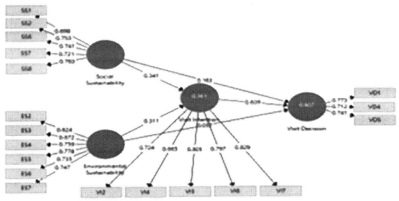

Convergent Validity Test

Convergent validity test results are measured based on the value of the loading factor (outer loading) of the construct indicator. According to Hair, Ringle, & Sarstedt (2013), the parameter for convergent validity is an outer loading value > 0.6. Table 3 show that all of question > 0.6, meaning the data can be use for the next process.

Tabel 3. Convergent validity result

Variable	Indicator	Outer Loading	Description
Environmental Sustainability	ES2	0.624	Valid
	ES3	0.672	Valid
	ES4	0.759	Valid
	ES5	0.778	Valid
	ES6	0.735	Valid
	ES7	0.747	Valid
Social Sustainability	SS1	0.698	Valid
	SS2	0.753	Valid
	SS6	0.741	Valid
	SS7	0.721	Valid
	SS8	0.763	Valid

continued on following page

Tabel 3. Continued

Variable	Indicator	Outer Loading	Description
Visit Decision	VD1	0.773	Valid
	VD4	0.712	Valid
	VD5	0.741	Valid
Visit Intention	VI2	0.724	Valid
	VI4	0.665	Valid
	VI5	0.805	Valid
	VI6	0.797	Valid
	VI7	0.829	Valid

Further tests on convergent validity are shown at the AVE value in the below table (table 4). Table shows the results of AVE for each variable and stated all variables are valid. The parameter for valid is a value of AVE> 0.5. The results above show an overall AVE value > 0.5.

Table 4. AVE score

Variable	AVE Score	Description
Social Sustainability	0.541	Valid
Environmental Sustainability	0.520	Valid
Visit Intention	0.587	Valid
Visit Decision	0.551	Valid

Discriminant Validity Test

The second test of the measurement model quality is the Discriminant Validity test which is assessed based on the value of cross loading or by looking at the results of cross loading factor and *Fornell-Lacker* test on table 5 below. The value of each indicator and variables should be higher than the other score on each construct. Based on Table 5 below shows the correlation value of indicators with latent variables in the block is greater than the correlation value of indicators with latent variables in other blocks. For the example, loading factor ES2 (environmental sustainability) is 0.624 greater than the latent variable in the other blocks, namely social sustainability (0.455), visit decision (0.265), and visit intention (0.379).

Table 5. Cross loading table

	Environmental Sustainability	Social Sustainability	Visit Decision	Visit Intention
ES2	0.624	0.455	0.265	0.379
ES3	0.672	0.507	0.287	0.311
ES4	0.759	0.546	0.374	0.375
ES5	0.778	0.52	0.456	0.459
ES6	0.735	0.476	0.412	0.398
ES7	0.747	0.524	0.417	0.431
SS1	0.444	0.698	0.367	0.387
SS2	0.557	0.753	0.436	0.344
SS6	0.453	0.741	0.459	0.463
SS7	0.565	0.721	0.377	0.414
SS8	0.554	0.763	0.409	0.434
VD1	0.477	0.478	0.773	0.605
VD4	0.417	0.409	0.712	0.512
VD5	0.26	0.352	0.741	0.574
VI2	0.353	0.375	0.577	0.724
VI4	0.546	0.518	0.494	0.665
VI5	0.318	0.304	0.609	0.805
VI6	0.379	0.427	0.588	0.797
VI7	0.484	0.491	0.639	0.829

Reliability Test

A reliability analysis using Cronbach's Alpha test and Composite Reliability was performed in this report. Cronbach's Alpha results are reported to have passed a minimum limit of 0.5, the results in the table 6 show that all variables have results above 0.5, this study meets the requirements for reliability.

Table 6. Cronbach's alpha

	Cronbach's Alpha	rho_A	Composite Reliability
Environmental Sustainability	0.815	0.825	0.866
Social Sustainability	0.788	0.791	0.855
Visit Decision	0.594	0.598	0.786
Visit Intention	0.822	0.825	0.876

Inner Model Evaluation (Structural Model)

Figure 3. Inner model

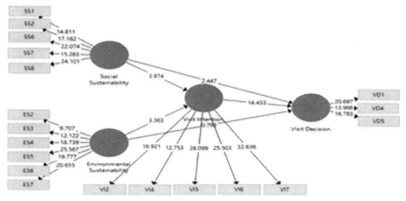

Determination Coefficient

Determination Coefficient is measured through R^2 for endogenous constructs. The R-Square test results can be seen in table 7 below. R-square value of visit intention variable is 0.361 including moderate (>0.33). This means that tourist visit intention can be explained by social sustainability and environmental sustainability by 36.1%. The R-square variable value for visit decision is 0.607, including moderate (>0.33). That is, visit intention can be explained by social sustainability and environmental sustainability by 60.7%.

Table 7. R- square

Variable	R-square
Visit Intention	0.361
Visit Decision	0.607

Path Coefficient

In Table 8 below, there are five hypotheses tested. The path coefficient results show that there is one hypothesis that is not proven, namely Environment Sustainability has no influence on the Visit Decision (H_5) as shown by the P value 0.428 >

0.05 and the T-Statistics result is 0.793 <1.96. The P-Value must be <0.05, while the T-Value must be > 1.96.

The other hypothesis shows that the P-Value and T-Statistic meet the requirements, where Environmental Sustainability affects Visit Intentionis (H_2) means that an environment that is cared for and maintained in a sustainable manner is attractive to Gen Z who live in a metropolitan city (greater Jakarta), because it gives a clean, green and refreshing impression, so there is a tendency to want to visit. This result is in line with the previous study from (Lee & Jan, 2018).

Likewise, Social Sustainability has an influence on the Visit Decision. This is indicated by the T-test of 3.974> 1.96 with a p value or significance level of 0,000, then the hypothesis (H_4) is accepted. This result has similar result with previous research by (Rubright, Kline, Viren, Naar, & Oliver, 2016) that analyze the impact of sustainable attraction toward visit decision. The other factor is needed to effect visit decision. Researcher interpret that other variables is needed to build indirect effect toward visit decision, such as visit intention as the mediating variables, or even other variables that may be moderating variables. Environmental sustainability concern by Komodo National Park may directly affecting generation Z visit intention, however the result may be different if it related with visit decision. ES2 which stated about Komodo National Park condition that rich terrestrial and marine biodiversity, will not affecting generation Z's visit decision if they don't have visit intention at the beginning.

Next is Social Sustainability which also has an influence on Visit Intention (H_1). The first hypothesis test results from data analysis show that social sustainability developed by Komodo National Park have a significant influence on tourist visit intention in Indonesia. This is indicated by the T-test of 3.974> 1.96 with a p value or significance level of 0,000, then the hypothesis (H1) is accepted. This hypothesis result proof that the ecotourism with well concerned social sustainability factor can attract more visit intention of tourism. This hypothesis is supported by the previous research (Doran & Larsen, 2015) that proof social value created by ecotourism will affecting tourist visit intention.

The third hipotesis show that Visit Intention influence Visit Decision (H_3). Result of data analyze show 14.433 T value score and P value which indicate the hypothesis is accepted. This hypothesis is supported by previous research (Satyarini, Rahmanita, & Setarnawat, 2017) that proofed positive impact of visit intention toward visit decision on tourist destination.

To get better interpretation of the hypothesis result, researcher evaluate the relation of indicator VI2, VI4, VI5, VI6, and VI7 from visit intention variable toward visit decision. The highest mean score is VI4 with score of 4.39, which stated motivation to visit Komodo National Park to get rid of daily activities or realities. It can be interpreted that the most affecting factor of generation Z visit intention in Jabodetabek area towards Komodo National Park is because of their motivation to get rid of their reality. The interpretation can be supported by the fact of Jabodetabek as the most populated area and also the central of business area in Indonesia. In addition, VI2 is the indicator with least mean score of 4.15. VI2 stated about visit intention to Komodo National Park based on the feelings of want and needs. This one of the self-motivation is not the most affecting factor of Generation Z in Jabodetabek area to visit Komodo National Park.

Table 8. Total path coefficient (direct effect)

	Original Sample (O)	Sample Mean (M)	Standard Deviation (STDEV)	T Statistics (|O/STDEV|)	P Values	Description
Environmental Sustainability -> Visit Decision	0.057	0.051	0.071	0.793	0.428	Not Significant
Environmental Sustainability -> Visit Intention	0.311	0.316	0.093	3.363	0.001	Significant
Social Sustainability -> Visit Decision	0.163	0.166	0.066	2.447	0.015	Significant
Social Sustainability -> Visit Intention	0.341	0.342	0.086	3.974	0.000	Significant
Visit Intention -> Visit Decision	0.639	0.643	0.044	14.433	0.000	Significant

There are 2 indirect effect exist in this model which are indirect effect between Environmental Sustainability to visit decision and indirect of Social Sustainability to Visit Decision. The result shows that the 2 indirect effect are significant, with the T value score above 1.96, and P value score below 0.5. The next hypothesis result shows that there is an indirect influence of social sustainability toward visit decision by the visit intention (H_6). This hypothesis is accepted since T value is 3.608 (> 1.96) and 0 P value/ significance level. This hypothesis has similar result with research by (Zgolli & Zaiem, 2018) that examine the effect of social engagement and public power toward destination choice by behavioral intention.

Based on the result of hypothesis 1, hypothesis 4 and hypothesis 6, researcher interpret that social sustainability concern by Komodo National Park have a significant impact toward visit intention and visit decision of generation Z in Jabodetabek. This is because the variable of social sustainability is not only has direct effect to each variables of visit intention and visit decision, but also the social sustainability have indirect effect to visit decision. By promoting local product and service, education to tourist, respecting diversity and giving equal opportunities in Komodo National Park, it will attract generation Z, which has high social awareness to visit Komodo National Park. Indicator SS7 that related to participation of cultural festival in Komodo National Park, indeed also bring the indirect effect toward visit decision by visit intention with the highest mean score by 4.25, while SS8 which stated about participation to support creation of local job is the least indicator that affecting the generation Z visit intention to Komodo National Park with 4.18 mean score.

The last hypothesis shows that the there is significant indirect influence of environmental sustainability toward visit decision by the visit intention (H_7). This is proofed by the T value score which is 3.608 and 0.001 P value that indicates the hypothesis accepted. The result of this hypothesis testing has similar result with previous research done by Hultman, Kazeminia, & Ghasemi (2015) that analyze the indirect impact of pro environmental behavior toward willingness to pay premium by having the visit intention.

As discussed on the interpretation result of hypothesis 2 and 5, the environmental sustainability concern in ecotourism can bring direct impact of generation visit intention. However, the environmental sustainability is not bringing direct influence toward generation Z visit decision. Other factor such as mediating and moderating variable is needed so that environmental sustainability concern in Komodo National Park can obtain Generation Z visit intention. The result of hypothesis 7 proof that environmental sustainability concern can affecting generation Z visit decision if it is mediated by visit intention. Therefore, researcher also interpret the relation of environmental sustainability indicator analyzed in this research, which are ES2, ES3, ES4, ES5, ES6, and ES7. The indicator with highest mean score, which is ES6, indicates the most affecting indicator toward visit intention and also visit decision, however, ES6 is also effecting the indirect of visit decision by the visit intention.

Table 9. Total indirect effect

	Original Sample (O)	Sample Mean (M)	Standard Deviation (STDEV)	T Statistics (IO/ STDEVI)	P Values	Description
Environmental Sustainability -> Visit Intention -> Visit Decision	0.199	0.204	0.061	3.28	0.001	Significant
Social Sustainability -> Visit Intention -> Visit Decision	0.218	0.216	0.06	3.608	0.000	Significant

Goodness of Fit

The goodness of fit can be seen through the SRMR /Standardized Root Mean Square Residual score that below 0.080. The calculation results show the score SRMR of 0.077 that below 0.080. If the score of SRMR is below 0.80 the model can be considered to have a good fit.

Tabel 10. Goodness of fit

	Saturated Model	Estimated Model
SRMR	0.077	0.077
d_ULS	1.127	1.127
d_G	0.303	0.303
Chi-Square	372.572	372.572
NFI	0.767	0.767

CONCLUSION & RECOMMENDATION

After several result concluded by this research, we can see that sustainability concern for ecotourism development is essential. Social and environmental sustainability is proofed to have significant influence toward visit intention. The social and environmental sustainability also have indirect effect toward visit decision by the visit intention. Therefore, researchers suggest that developer of ecotourism in Indonesia also focusing on the ecotourism development rather than just doing the marketing strategy to attract tourist. The development of ecotourism can bring impact to attract tourists and also can increase brand image that may help to boost the marketing strategy for developer.

Besides of Environmental and Social Sustainability, researchers suggest future research to add economic development variable to fulfill the triple bottom line concept analysis. Researcher would also suggest for further research to take sampling of generation Z that have experienced in ecotourism, since the research done by researcher only take the sampling of generation Z generally without filtering the ecotourism experienced of the tourist. Researcher also suggest ecotourism developer to increase more environmental and social awareness by promoting their ecotourism to obtain visit intention of potential tourist and also for government, enhancing education can also be the key factor to improve environmental and social awareness in society, while at the same time may also attract more visit intention toward ecotourism in Indonesia.

REFERENCES

Baldwin, C., & King, R. (2018). *Social Sustainability, Climate Resilience and Community-Based Urban Development*. Routledge. DOI: 10.4324/9781351103329

Bassiouni, D. H., & Hackley, C. (2014). Generation Z children's adaptation to digital consumer culture. *Journal of Customer Behaviour*, *13*(2), 113–133. DOI: 10.1362/147539214X14024779483591

Bazazo, I., Nasseef, M. A., Al-Zawaideh, A., Al-Zawaideh, A., & Al-Dhomaidat, M. (2017). The Impact of the Attitudes towards Ecotourism Benefits on Destination. *Journal of Management and Strategy*, *8*(3), 67–79. DOI: 10.5430/jms.v8n3p67

Bratman, M. E. (1999). *Faces of Intention: Selected Essays on Intention and Agency*. Cambridge University Press. DOI: 10.1017/CBO9780511625190

Chankong, V., & Haimas, Y. Y. (2008). *Multiobjective Decision Making: Theory and Methodology* (Vol. 8). Dover Publication.

Dilard, J., Dujon, V., & King, M. C. (2009). *Understanding the Social Dimension of Sustainability*. Routledge.

Dong, Y., & Hauschild, M. Z. "Indicators for Environmental Sustainability," *The 24th CIRP Conference on Life Cycle Engineering,* vol. 61, pp. 697-702, 2017. DOI: 10.1016/j.procir.2016.11.173

Doran, R., & Larsen, S. (2015). The Relative Importance of Social and Personal Norms in Explaining Intentions to Choose Eco-Friendly Travel Options. *International Journal of Tourism Research*, *18*(2), 159–166. DOI: 10.1002/jtr.2042

Durant, R. F., Fiorino, D. J., & O'Leary, R. (2017). *Environmental Governance Reconsidered: Challenges, Choices, and Opportunities*. The MIT Press.

Dyer, D. W. W. (2010). The Power of Intention, Gift Edition ed., J. Pyle, Ed., New York: Hay House.

Elkind, D. (2019). "Travel Trends: On The Go With Generation Z,". Online. Available: https://www.cmo.com/features/articles/2019/5/15/generation-z-travel.html#gs.28tjb9

Fitriani, I. A., & Indriati, D. (2017). "Kajian Data Pasar Wisatawan Nusantara 2017," Kementrian Pariwisata, Jakarta.

Fromm, J. (2018, January). How much financial influence does Gen Z have? *Forbes*.

Fromm, J., & Read, A. (2018). *Marketing to Gen Z: The Rules for Reaching This Vast and Very Different Genereations of Influencers.* AMACOM.

Hair, J. F.Jr, Ringle, C. M., & Sarstedt, M. (2013). Partial Least Squares Structural Equation Modeling: Rigorous Applications, Better Results and Higher Acceptance. *Long Range Planning*, *46*(1-2), 1–12. DOI: 10.1016/j.lrp.2013.01.001

Handayani, R., Suleeman, E., Priadi, C., & Darmajanti, L. (2017). *Water Recycling Opportunity in the Business Sectors of Greater Jakarta.* International Journal of Technology. DOI: 10.14716/ijtech.v8i6.743

Honey, M. Ecotourism and Sustainable Development, Second Edition: Who Owns Paradise? 2nd edition, 2nd ed., Washington: Island Press, 2008.

Hultman, M., Kazeminia, A., & Ghasemi, V. (2015). Intention to visit and willingness to pay premium for ecotourism. *Journal of Business Research*, *68*(9), 1854–1861. DOI: 10.1016/j.jbusres.2015.01.013

IQ Air AirVisual. (2019). *2018 World Air Quality Report.* IQ Air.

Karl, M. (2018). Risk and Uncertainty in Travel Decision-Making: Tourist and Destination Perspective. *Journal of Travel Research*, *57*(1), 129–146. DOI: 10.1177/0047287516678337

Kencana, I. P. E. N., & Mertha, I. W. (2014). People Participation as Social Capital Form for Realizing Sustainable Ecotourism. *International Journal of Social, Management, Economics and Business Engineering*, *8*(10), 3014–3020.

Kim, S.-B., & Kwon, K.-J. (2018). Examining the Relationships of Image and Attitude on Visit Intention to Korea among Tanzanian College Students. *Sustainability (Basel)*, *10*(360), 360. DOI: 10.3390/su10020360

Klemes, J. J. (2015). *Assessing and Measuring Environmental Impact and Sustainability.* Elsevier.

Lebreton, L. C., Zwet, J. d., Damsteeg, J.-W., Slat, B., Andrady, A., & Reisser, J. "River plastic emissions to the world's oceans," 7th June 2017. Online. Available: https://www.nature.com/articles/ncomms15611

Lee, T. H., & Jan, F.-H. (2018). Ecotourism Behavior of Nature-Based Tourists: An Integrative Framework. *Journal of Travel Research*, *57*(6), 792–810. DOI: 10.1177/0047287517717350

Lu, A. C. C., Gursoy, D., & Chiappa, G. D. (2016). The Influence of Materialism on Ecotourism Attitudes and Behaviors. *Journal of Travel Research*, *55*(2), 176–189. DOI: 10.1177/0047287514541005

Makur, M. "New Study Aims to Solve Waste Problems in Komodo National Park," 07 November 2017. Online. Available: https://www.thejakartapost.com/news/2017/11/07/new-study-aims-to-solve-waste-problems-in-komodo-national-park.html

Mihanyar, P., Rahman, S. A., & Aminudin, N. (2015). "The Influence of Sustainable Tourism Awareness and Environmental Sustainability Dimensions on Behavioural Intentions Among Domestic Tourists in Developing Countries," *ourism. Leisure and Global Change*, 2, TOC-119.

Miller, L. J., & Lu, W. "Gen Z Is Set to Outnumber Millennials Within a Year," Bloomberg, 20 August 2018. Online. Available: https://www.bloomberg.com/news/articles/2018-08-20/gen-z-to-outnumber-millennials-within-a-year-demographic-trends

Oliver, T. H., & Morecroft, M. D. (2014). Interactions Between Climate Change and Land Use Change. *Wiley Interdisciplinary Reviews: Climate Change*, 5(3), 318–329. DOI: 10.1002/wcc.271

Packer, J., Ballantyne, R., & Hughes, K. (2014). Chinese and Australian tourists' attitudes to nature, animals and environmental issues: Implications for the design of nature-based tourism experiences. *Tourism Management*, 44, 101–107. DOI: 10.1016/j.tourman.2014.02.013

Popovic, T., Povoa, A. P., Krawslawski, A., & Carvalho, A. (2018, April). Quantitative Indicators for Social Sustainability Assessment of Supply. *Journal of Cleaner Production*, 180, 748–768. DOI: 10.1016/j.jclepro.2018.01.142

Pramanik, S. A. K., Hossain, E., & Azam, S. (2016). The Impacts of Visitors' Attitude on Visit Intention in the Context of Museum Applying SEM: Offering an Alternative Visit Intention Model. *Bangladesh Journal of Tourism*, 1(1).

Reddy, T. L., & Thomson, R. J. "Environmental, Social and Economic Sustainability: Implications for Actuarial Science," in *ASTIN, AFIR/ERM and IACA Colloquia*, Sydney, 2015.

Rubright, H. L., Kline, C., Viren, P. P., Naar, A., & Oliver, J. (2016). Attraction Sustainability In North Carolina And Its Impact On Decision-Making. *Tourism Management Perspectives*, 19, 1–10. DOI: 10.1016/j.tmp.2016.04.002

Saarinen, J. (2014). Critical Sustainability: Setting the Limits to Growth and Responsibility in Tourism. *Sustainability (Basel)*, 6(1), 1–17. DOI: 10.3390/su6010001

Satyarini, N. W. M., Rahmanita, M., & Setarnawat, S. (2017). The Influence of Destination Image on Tourist Intention and Decision to Visit Tourist Destination (A Case Study of Pemuteran Village in Buleleng, Bali, Indonesia). *TRJ Tourism Research Journal*, *1*(1), 81–97. DOI: 10.30647/trj.v1i1.10

Sharma, S. K., & Sanghi, R. (2012). *Advance in Water Treatment and Pollution Prevention*. Springer. DOI: 10.1007/978-94-007-4204-8

Solomon, M. R., Bamossy, G. J., Askegaard, S. T., & Hogg, M. K. Consumer Behaviour-A European Perspective, Sixth Edition ed., Harlow: Pearson, 2016.

Su, M. M., Wall, G., & Ma, Z. (2014). Assessing Ecotourism from a Multi Stakeholder Perspective: Xingkai Lake National Nature Reserve. *Environmental Management*, *54*(5), 1190–1207. DOI: 10.1007/s00267-014-0360-5 PMID: 25248933

Vezzoli, C. A., & Manzini, E. (2008). *Design for Environmental Sustainability*. Springer.

World Heritage Outlook, I. U. C. N. "Komodo National Park," 09 November 2017. Online. Available: https://worldheritageoutlook.iucn.org/explore-sites/wdpaid/67725

Yale, "Environmental Performance Index Results," 2018. Online. Available: https://epi.envirocenter.yale.edu/epi-indicator-report/EPI?country=

Zgolli, S., & Zaiem, I. (2018). The Responsible Behavior of Tourist: The Role of Personnel Factors and Public Power and Effect on The Choice of Destination. *The Arab Economics and Business Journal*, *13*(2), 168–178. DOI: 10.1016/j.aebj.2018.09.004

Zink, P. D. K. J. (2008). *Corporate Sustainability as a Challenge for Comprehensive Management*. Springer. DOI: 10.1007/978-3-7908-2046-1

Chapter 14
Emerging Technologies in Metaverse Tourism:
Opportunities and Challenges

Nilanjan Ray
https://orcid.org/0000-0002-6109-6080
JIS University, India

Tanmoy Majumder
https://orcid.org/0009-0008-6524-255X
JIS University, India

Moumita Roy
https://orcid.org/0009-0005-0066-9200
JIS University, India

ABSTRACT

Artificial Intelligence (AI) in particular has revolutionised a number of industries, bringing concepts like the "sharing economy," "Internet of Things," and "Internet of People" to life. With chatbots and smart systems being used widely in travel agencies and airlines to improve consumer experiences, artificial intelligence (AI) has had a huge impact on the travel and tourism industry. According to projections, AI will keep advancing individualised solutions and completely changing the travel and tourism sector. This is part of a larger, continuous technological revolution that promises constant innovation and transformation. Information technology (IT) has also significantly changed how businesses operate internationally. The tourist sector is a prime example of how IT may improve communication with potential clients by using destination imagery.In the present market scenario, the tourism industry has also merged many parameters with the usage of information technology aiming to reduce the middlemen in marketing travel schemes to consumers.

DOI: 10.4018/979-8-3693-3196-5.ch014

INTRODUCTION

The Advent of Informational Technology and Artificial intelligence in the tourism industry has taken this industry to a new zenith positioning it as one of the rapidly growing industries in the current industrial 4.0 era. Digitalization and the expanding travel industry are driving the use of AI in the tourism industry. AI is being used by Indian travel agencies to increase client interaction, optimize workflows, and maintain their competitiveness. Global service distribution began with the introduction of computerised reservation systems (CRSs) by airlines in the 1970s, among other technological advances. (Masood.A.Naqvi and Hongyan. Jia,2014). Indian tourist enterprises are benefiting from AI-driven data analytics solutions that help them comprehend consumer behaviour, market trends, and rivals. To maintain their competitiveness in the market, businesses can use this data to inform strategic decisions about product development, marketing, and pricing. The tourism sector has experienced notable changes on a worldwide and Indian level due to the amalgamation of Artificial Intelligence (AI) and Information Technology (IT).(Technology in Tourism Management, 2023) It has transformed operations by improving customer experiences, optimising resource management, and enabling improved revenue strategies. With increased traveller demand and the digitalisation of platforms, AI is becoming more widely used in India's tourism industry. (Lakshay Agarwal et al., 2024) With the increasing usage of these technologies, countries shall experience competition in tourism destinations, increased operational effectiveness and efficiency and customer co-creation in gaining a positive travel experience. AI has a wide-ranging impact on the Indian tourist industry, from safety improvements to customized marketing, making it a more efficient and safe business. It is also contributing to increased earnings, attracting increased tourist footfall. (Villamarin Rodriguez & Nagaraj, 2020)

LITERATURE REVIEW

The advent of information technology has had a significant impact on destination marketing, allowing tourism organisations to communicate with a worldwide audience in ways never seen before. Platforms like social media, websites, and mobile apps have transformed how places promote their attractions, events, and experiences in real time. Notably, professionals such as Buhalis and Law (2008) emphasise the critical significance of Web 2.0 technology in enabling user-generated content, which complements destination marketing initiatives. Platforms like TripAdvisor and Yelp have evolved as critical areas for travellers to share their opinions and recommendations, impacting the travel decisions of others. To identify the emerging themes in research for tourism and hospitality, AI is used as stated in the study by Knani et al. (2022) studded the artificial neural network and data mining sentiment analysis and upcoming subjects like the robotic services. Law et al. (2014) states that tourism industry marketers try to bring in competitive advantages by the usage of IT tools facilitating innovation in sectors like the online booking, revenue management platforms, customer management, and improving the decision-making process. With integration of AI, these sectors have been enhanced as studied by (Wang, Y., Li, J., & Li, C, 2019) it states the function of AI in the travel sector is covered in this article. It investigates how AI may help both travellers and businesses. AI helps travellers access relevant information, make informed decisions, and personalise their experiences. Businesses can use AI for tasks such as growth optimisation, price predictions, and better customer service. ((Bulchand-Gidumal, 2020) states an overview of how AI assists in travel related recommendations by chatbots and intelligent travel assistants. its emphasis on the potential of customised travel experience, improved accessibility and resource management. (Singh and Bashar, 2021) This disparity draws attention to the necessity of a thorough synthesis of the literature in order to present a cohesive "big picture" of the interaction between tourism and information technology. The last few years have seen a rise in publications that highlight the major trends in the tourism industry, including smart tourism, robotic implementation, robust recommender systems, the use of virtual and augmented reality in tourism, social network sites, 3D visualisation and web personalisation, digital architecture, human less interaction in tourism, tourism 4.0, and so forth. (Abreu, A., Costa, E., & Borges, I,2020) The author in his study emphasized the effects of AI for planning, booking and assessing a tourists journey, accessing the overall satisfaction .Additionally, one of the most well-liked subjects in tourism study these days is "sustainability through technology" (Corte et al., 2019; SeguAmortegui et al., 2019; Serrano et al., 2019). Palomoa et al. (2017) discussed how, for the previous 20 years, data mining, big data, and structural equation modelling have all been used in tourist research.

METHODOLOGY

The study aims to provide a comprehensive picture of the impact of artificial intelligence and information technology on the tourism business. It assesses the significance of using these techniques in a broader theoretical context. It also explores how different tools can be integrated into different parameters of the tourism sector, such as service provider performance, destination decision-making, tourism experience via augmented reality, and various IT and AI tools for structural improvements. Various secondary data sources have been used to draw inferences for the study.

IT & AI IN TOURISM MANAGEMENT: THEORETICAL BACKGROUND

AI is significantly changing the travel and tourism field in terms of enhanced services optimization, improved personnel and customer services, and systematic data-based decision-making. The major AI application cases in this business segment include personalized trips, convenient travel disruptions handling, and revenue generation, as well as scheduled data processing, voice digital support, face recognition for employee verification and VIP identification, instant check-in and fast online purchasing, and managing customer review content. Information technology significantly impacts the tourism industry, influencing services, management, marketing, and public relations. It plays a crucial role for managers and entrepreneurs across service and production sectors. These factors also establish scheduled data processing, real-time customer opinions and preferences, and routine tasks automation, allowing travel and tourism companies to stay competitive. Let us discuss the above in the light of various contexts of the tourism industry.

In the Context of Destination

Information Technology (IT) and Artificial Intelligence (AI) has transformed tourism, enhancing marketing, management, and traveler experiences. AI technologies like machine learning and predictive analytics forecast trends, personalize services, and optimize operations. IT enables destinations to gather insights from tourist data, customize marketing, and predict behavior. In India, AI-driven platforms like PaxPulse offer augmented reality experiences, while AI tools tailor travel plans based on preferences and mood. Sustainable tourism is promoted through AI-controlled robots and chatbots, analyzing social media trends to influence destination choices ((Villamarin Rodriguez & Nagaraj, 2020) Destination often forms the first step, that creates the urge in tourists to move from their place of domicile to a different destination in search of their desired experience. The experience can be categorized under many strata, like spiritual, educational, etc. Integration of IT and AI promotes better customer relationship management through virtual communities, hence increasing links between customers and destination management organisations (DMOs). Web 2.0 plays an important role in marketing and promoting tourist destinations by increasing not just travel-related content, but also applications and technology for effective destination marketing. Mobile technology has also enhanced the tourism experience of a destination by providing application based customized language translators, real-time services and instant recommendations (Xiang, Du, and Ma,2017). IT and AI have also enhanced several operational processes in destination management through integration. Some reservation systems use advanced algorithms, and many payment platforms are digitized, while AI operates customer service chatbots to reduce resource waste. AI algorithms underpin the functionality of machine learning tools, which help people to predict demand. This enables managers to plan and optimize resource allocation during seasons and hence prevent overcrowding of destinations at peak.

In the Context of Tourist Information

The advancement of AI, mobile tech, NLP, and speech recognition has made smart travel assistants feasible. These apps understand user preferences and offer tailored suggestions, even coordinating various services at destinations within budget constraints. However, a key challenge is determining whether these assistants serve the user or the developer, leading to the emergence of a new marketing approach focused on targeting travel assistants rather than tourists. Another evidence from the Orissa Tourism Website which was revamped to highlight the state's tourism offerings and collaborate with the National Informatics Centre (NIC). Electronic tourism distribution channels prioritise ease of transaction over product differentiation. (Bhuali 1998) we can draw instances that operating systems like DOS and Windows, form the backbone of tourism operations. Systems like CRS (Computerized Reservation System) play a pivotal role, enabling storage, retrieval, and transaction processing related to air travel, including schedules, fares, and passenger data.

GIS plays a crucial role in tourism planning and management by providing visual representations and advanced analyses of digital geospatial data related to tourist destinations.(Satpalda, 2024) It enables comprehensive insights into tourist sites by processing data on electronic maps.(Jovanović, 2016) GIS, as part of GIT, serves as an information system that enhances flexibility in providing information on travel, accommodation, dining, and trip management(Jovanović, 2016)

Information technology extends beyond operational realms, influencing tactical and strategic management within the tourism industry. By fostering direct and efficient communication among stakeholders, including travellers and suppliers, IT offers competitive advantages and software components, such as CRS (Computerized Reservation System), play a pivotal role in enabling storage, retrieval, and transaction processing related to air travel. (Jakkilinki et.al 2007, Cho & Fesenmaier 2001).

Table 1. Software used in CRS

Major systems	Created by	Users
Amadeus	Air France, Iberia, Lufthansa, SAS	Online travel agencies including ebookers, Expedia, Opodo Flights
Sabre	American Airlines, All Nippon Airways, Cathay Pacific Airways, China Airlines, Singapore Airlines	Expedia, Travelocity ,Kayak
Galileo	Aer Lingus, Air Canada, Alitalia, Swissair, TAP, United Airlines	Cheap Tickets , ebookers, Ixeo
World span	Delta, Northwest	Orbitz , Hotwire, Priceline

Source: Ray et.al (2011) International Conference on Management and Service Science, Wuhan, China

Travel agencies optimize operations using back-office software for accounting, commission tracking, and customer management, enhancing service quality. Group Decision Support Systems (GDSS) aid in efficient decision-making through real-time discussions and idea generation, improving collaboration. Geographical Information Systems (GIS) within Information and Communication Technology (ICT) revolutionize tourism by enabling data management, analysis, and problem-solving. The Internet's influence on ICT transforms communication and relationships in the tourism sector, fostering enhanced interactions among stakeholders, regulators, and customers for mutual benefits. (Copperchips & root, 2023)

In the Context of Hotels and Hospitality Industry

Robots have begun to give people a broader look at the future of many businesses and industries, including but not limited to, the hotel industry.

The use of AI in the hospitality industry has the most dramatic use of which has been in the hotel aspect.

The hotel industry had been incorporating AI to the industry in pandemic at many national and international associations, However the idea of AI in the hotel industry has been met with much skepticism. Industry leaders, owners, managers and academics agreed the industry needed a solution and AI was the resolution. Also, mobile and Wi-Fi technologies provide unparalleled convenience for travellers, facilitating access to tour-related information via GSM, WAP, and GPRS networks, empower travellers to seamlessly book accommodations, transportation, and other travel necessities

Table 2. Software used in hotel industries

ASI FrontDesk Freeware 6.0	With features including reservation administration, check-ins, billing, and reporting, ASI FrontDesk Freeware 6.0 is a free hotel management programme designed for small hotels and guesthouses. Its goal is to increase efficiency through front-office automation without requiring a large capital outlay.
eZee FrontDesk Hotel Software 5.2	eZee FrontDesk Hotel Software 5.2 is a comprehensive hotel property management system that includes front-office operations, reservations, guest management, invoicing, and housekeeping. It may also include reporting, analytics, and integration with POS and online booking channels, all with the goal of increasing productivity and guest satisfaction for hotels of all sizes and types.
SIMSOFT Hotel pro 2006	all-in-one software for hotels that simplifies tasks like booking reservations, managing the front desk, coordinating housekeeping, handling bills and invoices, and generating reports
Room Master 2000 Hotel Reservation Software 12	Manage advance reservations and deposits. Email And printing confirmation for Group blocks, Revenue management,
EXSS Facility Manager 5.2	EXSS Facility Manager is intended primarily for small hotels, universities, fitness centres, SPAs, sports stadiums, gymnasiums, rent-a-cars, service areas, sanatoriums, pensions, rental facilities, and so on.

Source: Ray et.al (2011) International Conference on Management and Service Science, Wuhan, China

IMPACT OF IT AND ARTIFICIAL INTELLIGENCE ON TOURISM INDUSTRY

The study highlights the transformative impact of the Internet on the tourism industry. It emphasizes how the Internet has revolutionized marketing by enabling two-way communication between businesses and consumers, empowering consumers with more choices and information. The Internet has opened up the entry barriers, increased competition, and enhanced distribution channels, leading to a more efficient and competitive marketplace. Businesses can now offer personalized products by blending various travel components, and customer experience. However, challenges such as government regulations on privacy and security, legal risks, and economic fluctuations impact the industry. To fully leverage e-commerce in tourism, addressing security, copyright, and legal issues is crucial. The role of Central Reservation Systems (CRS) and Global Distribution Systems (GDS) in managing inventory and enhancing information accessibility within the tourism sector has paved the way for electronic travel agencies, reshaping how tourism products are produced and distributed. Overall, the Internet's evolution the below mentioned points summarises the positive impacts ((De Carvalho et al., 2021)

- Personalised Travel Planning: AI-powered chatbots and virtual assistants make personalised recommendations based on the traveler's preferences, budget, and previous experiences.
- Efficient Booking and Reservation Systems: Online booking platforms and mobile applications simplify the booking process by allowing for real-time comparisons of rates, availability, and reviews.
- Improved Customer Service: AI-powered chatbots and virtual assistants respond instantly to basic inquiries, freeing up human workers to handle more difficult issues. (Bulchand-Gidumal et al., 2023)
- Improved Travel Experience: GIS technology generates interactive maps and navigation systems, AR and VR applications allow for previews of attractions and lodgings, and IoT gadgets provide seamless interactions.
- Data-Driven Decision Making: Tourism organisations may make more informed decisions by analysing data on travel trends, client preferences, and market situations using IT systems and AI algorithms. (García-Madurga & Grilló-Méndez, 2023)

As we know that, every positive aspect has some negative in it, the Integration of AI and IT also has few negative implications in the tourism sector they can be summarised as.

Privacy and Security Concerns: AI and IT systems raise concerns about privacy and security, especially regarding customer data.

Technology Acceptance: Just like any new innovation, tourists can fall into different categories based on their willingness to adopt new technology. Some are quick to embrace it, while others are more cautious. Studies have identified three main types of users: those who are hesitant about AI, those who are enthusiastic about its benefits, and those who are realistic about both the advantages and risks

CONCLUSION

The tourism industry has been completely transformed by information technology: accessibility and ease of booking have improved, the use of data analysis allows creation of a unique experience for each client, and business processes have become more functional and efficient. For instance, "morning traffic jams at tourist spots, congested CBDs, long queues to check in for flights. All of these are now a thing of the dawn and the 4th industrial revolution". Improvements have been made to the planning side for travelers with the emergence of mobile applications, easy online booking systems, and necessary guidance provided by smart devices. Additionally, "a new reality for hoteliers and airlines is hyper-personalization: combating the decline of customer loyalty by using artificial intelligence. However, some of the changes "can lead to overall lower spending in local economies or a decline in cultural immersion". Therefore, the tourism industry should carefully balance enhancing and negative impacts of existing technologies to provide the best possible experience for the tourist.

The integration of AI and IT in the tourism industry has revolutionized services, customer interactions, and decision-making processes. It has transformed destination marketing, operational processes, and customer experiences, offering personalized travel plans, augmented reality experiences, and seamless booking processes.

Future Scope of Research

Sustainability through Technology: Future research could delve deeper into how AI and IT can promote sustainable tourism practices, focusing on environmental conservation and responsible travel.

Ethical Considerations: Exploring the ethical implications of AI and IT in the tourism industry, such as privacy concerns, data security, and the impact on local communities.

Innovative Technologies: Investigating the potential of emerging technologies like virtual reality, blockchain, and Internet of Things (IoT) in further enhancing the tourism experience.

Smart Tourism: Research could focus on the development of smart tourism initiatives, leveraging AI and IT to create seamless, interconnected travel experiences for tourists.

Policy Implications: Studying the regulatory frameworks needed to govern the use of AI and IT in the tourism sector, ensuring responsible and sustainable growth.

The significant role of Information Technology (IT) in the travel industry underscores the necessity for travel businesses to adopt suitable technologies that streamline processes, reduce costs, and enhance service flexibility, ultimately improving the overall travel experience for customers. The influence of Information and Communication Technology (ICT) in tourism cannot be overstated. For example, tour guides require historical and cultural information about destinations, tour agencies need data for reservations and accommodation, and tourists seek information through various channels such as cell phone applications, the internet, and GPS. IT plays a crucial role in facilitating the dissemination of tourism information to potential travelers through platforms like FAX, GPS, and websites. One such informative IT tool is Geospatial Information Technology (GIT), particularly Geographic Information Systems (GIS), which provides visual representations and advanced analyses of digital geospatial information through integrated electronic maps of tourist sites. The benefits of Web GIS, including Geospatial Mashups, outweigh its challenges, as it enables maximum information dissemination to potential tourists while empowering travel agents to promote lesser-known locations as popular tourist spots. Potential tourists can analyze demographic, economic, and market characteristics of locations with just a click, supporting strategic planning, collaborative information sharing, online marketing techniques, and enhancing efficiency in tourism management.

The future research scope outlined in this paper emphasizes the application of Web GIS and Geospatial Mashups as analytical and strategic tools in tourism management and promotion.

REFERENCES

Abreu, A., Costa, E., & Borges, I. (2020). The Impact of Artificial Intelligence on the Tourism Industry: A Systematic Review. *Advances in Tourism, Technology and Systems: Selected Papers from ICOTTS20, 1*(208), 458.

(•••). Analysis in data mining, big data and structural equations models. *Ereview of Tourism Research*, 8, 1–5.

Balogun, V. F., Thompson, A. F., & Sarumi, O. A. (2010). A 3D Geo-Spatial Virtual Reality System for Virtual Tourism. *Pacific Journal of Science and Technology*, *11*(2), 601–609.

Buhalis, D., & Law, R. (2008). Progress in information technology and tourism management: 20 years on and 10 years after the internet—The state of eTourism research. *Tourism Management*, *29*(4), 609–623. DOI: 10.1016/j.tourman.2008.01.005

Bulchand-Gidumal, J., William Secin, E., O'Connor, P., & Buhalis, D. (2023). Artificial intelligence's impact on hospitality and tourism marketing: Exploring key themes and addressing challenges. *Current Issues in Tourism*, *0*(0), 1–18. DOI: 10.1080/13683500.2023.2229480

Chaudhuri, S., & Ray, N. (2015). Application of web-based Geographical Information System (GIS) in tourism development. In *Encyclopedia of Information Science and Technology, Third Edition* (pp. 7026-7036). IGI Global.

Chaudhuri, S., & Ray, N. (Eds.). (2018). *GIS applications in the tourism and hospitality industry*. IGI Global. DOI: 10.4018/978-1-5225-5088-4

Chen, Y., Cottam, E., & Lin, Z. (2020). The effect of resident-tourist value cocreation on residents' well-being. *Journal of Hospitality and Tourism Management*, *44*, 30–37. DOI: 10.1016/j.jhtm.2020.05.009

Cho, Y., & Fesenmaier, D. R. (2001). A new paradigm for tourism and electronic commerce: Experience marketing using the virtual tour. In Laws, E., & Buhalis, D. (Eds.), *tourism distribution channels: practices, issues and transformation* (pp. 351–370). Thomson.

Copperchips, & root. (2023, March 14). Role of Geographic Information Systems (GIS) in Tourism Planning. *Copperchips*. https://copperchips.com/role-geographic-information-systems-tourism-planning/

Corte, V. D., Gaudio, G. D., Sepe, F., & Sciarelli, F. (2019). Sustainable Tourism in the Open Innovation Realm: A Bibliometric analysis. *Sustainability (Basel)*, *11*(21), 6114. DOI: 10.3390/su11216114

Davin, K. (1997).. . *Effects of Computer Support on Group Decisions Journal of Hospitality and Tourism Research.*, *21*(2), 44–57.

De Carvalho, J. V., Rocha, Á., Liberato, P., & Peña, A. (Eds.). (2021). *Advances in Tourism, Technology and Systems: Selected Papers from ICOTTS20* (Vol. 1). Springer Singapore., DOI: 10.1007/978-981-33-4256-9

Durán-Sánchez, A., Álvarez-García, J., del Río-Rama, M. D. L. C., & Rosado-Cebrián, B. (2019). Science mapping of the Knowledge Base on Tourism Innovation. *Sustainability (Basel)*, *11*(12), 3352. DOI: 10.3390/su11123352

Fajuyigbe, O., Balogun, V. F., & Obembe, O. M. (2007). Web-based geographical information system (GIS) for tourism in Oyo State, Nigeria. *Information Technology Journal*, *6*(5), 613–622. DOI: 10.3923/itj.2007.613.622

Fodor, O., & Werthner, H. (2005). Harmonise: A step toward an interoperable tourism Marketplace. *International Journal of Electronic Commerce*, *9*(2), 11–39. DOI: 10.1080/10864415.2005.11044324

García-Madurga, M.-Á., & Grilló-Méndez, A.-J. (2023). Artificial Intelligence in the Tourism Industry: An Overview of Reviews. *Administrative Sciences*, *13*(8).

Jakkilinki, R., Georgievski, M., & Sharda, N. (2007). Connecting Destinations with an Ontology-Based e-Tourism Planner. In M. Sigala, L. Mich, & J. Murphy (Eds). Information and Communication Technologies in Tourism 2007, (pp. 21-32), Springer-Verlag Wien.

Jovanović, V. (2016). The application of GIS and its components in tourism. *Yugoslav Journal of Operations Research, 18*(2).

Kim, E., Nam, D., & Stimpert, J. L. (2004). The Applicability of Porter's Generic Strategies in the Digital Age: Assumptions, Conjectures and Suggestions. *Journal of Management*, *30*(5), 569–589. DOI: 10.1016/j.jm.2003.12.001

Law, R., Buhalis, D., & Cobanoglu, C. (2014). Progress on information and communication technologies in hospitality and tourism. *International Journal of Contemporary Hospitality Management*, *26*(5), 727–750. DOI: 10.1108/IJCHM-08-2013-0367

Longmatey, D., Samuel, A., & Prah, B. K. (2002), Management and Promotion of Tourism in Ghana: A GIS Approach from African Tourism Websites. Retrieved on May 20, 2015. http://www.africantourism.com/ghana.htm

Mehraliyev, F., Chan, I. C. C., Choi, Y., Koseoglu, M. A., & Law, R. (2020). A state-of-the-art review of smart tourism research. *Journal of Travel & Tourism Marketing*, *37*(1), 78–91. DOI: 10.1080/10548408.2020.1712309

Nusair, K., Butt, I., & Nikhashemi, S. R. (2019). A bibliometric analysis of social media in hospitality and tourism research. *International Journal of Contemporary Hospitality Management*, *31*(7), 2691–2719. DOI: 10.1108/IJCHM-06-2018-0489

Ortega-Fraile, F. J., Ríos-Martín, M. Á., & Ceballos-Hernandez, C. (2018). Tourism and mobile devices: Provenance of academic research through a bibliometric study. *Journal of Tourism Analysis*, *25*(1), 91–112. DOI: 10.1108/JTA-02-2018-0008

Palomoa, J., Figueroa-Domecqa, C., FlechaBarrioa, M. D., & Segovia-Pérez, M. (2017). The use of new data analysis techniques in tourism: A Bibliometric

Pandey, O. K., & Chakraborty, R. (2007), GIS: Information technology for planning management and development of GOA tourism master plan in next millennium. Retrieved on May 20, 2015. http://www.gisdevelopment.net/application

Pierce, T., Dobson, G., & Phillips, M. (2009), GIS Mashups on the Web: Using Google, ESRI, and Open Source to Develop Weather and Climate Applications for the Web, *Geospatial Infrastructure Solutions Conference*, April 2009, Tampa FL

Ray, N., Das, D. K., Ghosh, S., & Banerjee, A. (2011). A Study on Application of Information Technology on Tourism Development, IEEE Proceeding Catalog No: CFP1141H-ART ISBN978-1-4244-6579- China

Satpalda. (2024, March 4). *GIS in Tourism—SATPALDA*. https://satpalda.com/blogs/gis-in-tourism/

Seguí-Amortegui, L., Clemente-Almendros, J. A., Medina, R., & Gala, M. G. (2019). Sustainability and competitiveness in the tourism industry and tourist destinations: A Bibliometric Study. *Sustainability (Basel)*, *11*(22), 1–30. DOI: 10.3390/su11226351

Serrano, L., Sianes, A., & Ariza-Montes, A. (2019). Using bibliometric methods to shed light on the concept of sustainable tourism. *Sustainability (Basel)*, *11*(24), 6964. DOI: 10.3390/su11246964

Sigala, M. (2010). Web 2.0, social marketing strategies and distribution channels for city destinations: Enhancing the participatory role of travelers and exploiting their collective intelligence. In *Web technologies: Concepts, methodologies, tools, and applications* (pp. 1249–1273). IGI Global. DOI: 10.4018/978-1-60566-982-3.ch068

Singh, S., & Bashar, A. (2021). A bibliometric review on the development in e-tourism research. *International Hospitality Review*, *37*(1), 71–93. DOI: 10.1108/IHR-03-2021-0015

Stabb, S., & Werthner, H. (2002). Intelligent Systems for Tourism. IEEE Intelligent Systems, November/December, 53-55. *Statistics*. Retrieved April 16, 2005, from

Strandberg, C., Nath, A., Hemmatdar, H., & Jahwash, M. (2018). Tourism research in the new millennium: A bibliometric review of literature in Tourism and Hospitality Research. *Tourism and Hospitality Research*, *18*(3), 269–285. DOI: 10.1177/1467358416642010

Villamarin Rodriguez, R., & Nagaraj, S. (2020). *Impact of AI and Robotics in the Tourism sector: A Critical Insight*.

Xiang, Z., Du, Q., & Ma, Y. (2017). ICT-enabled seamless travel: A conceptual framework and its applications. *Journal of Hospitality and Tourism Technology*, *8*(1), 63–75.

ADDITIONAL READING

ALsarayreh, M. N., Jawabreh, O. A., ALkharabsheh, K. S., & Aldahamsheh, M. M. (2011). Tourism promotion through the internet (websites)(Jordan as a case study). *Asian Social Science*, *7*(6), 125.

Chaudhuri, S., & Ray, N. (2017). Geospatial mashups in Web GIS for tourism infrastructure: Internet-based channel perspective promotional measures. In *Business infrastructure for sustainability in developing economies* (pp. 272–295). IGI Global. DOI: 10.4018/978-1-5225-2041-2.ch015

Dixit, M., Belwal, R., & Singh, G. (2006). Online tourism and travel (analyzing trends from marketing perspective). *Skyline Business School Journal*, *3*(1), 89–99.

Ray, N., Banerjee, A., Ghosh, S., & Das, D. K. (2011, August). A study on application of information technology on tourism development. In *2011 International Conference on Management and Service Science* (pp. 1-7). IEEE. DOI: 10.1109/ICMSS.2011.5998707

Ray, N., Das, D. K., & Chaudhuri, S. (2015). Tourism promotion through web. In *Hospitality, travel, and tourism: concepts, methodologies, tools, and applications* (pp. 366–375). IGI Global. DOI: 10.4018/978-1-4666-6543-9.ch022

KEY TERMS AND DEFINITIONS

Artificial Intelligence (AI): Artificial Intelligence is the simulation of human intelligence in machines that are programmed to think, learn, and make decisions. AI encompasses areas such as machine learning, natural language processing, robotics, and computer vision.

Geospatial Information Technology: Geospatial Information Technology involves the collection, analysis, and visualization of data that is associated with a specific location on the Earth's surface. It includes tools such as Geographic Information Systems (GIS), Global Positioning Systems (GPS), remote sensing, and spatial analysis to support planning, decision-making, and resource management.

Information Technology (IT): Information Technology refers to the use of computers, software, networks, and other electronic systems to store, retrieve, transmit, and manipulate data. It plays a critical role in modern businesses, education, healthcare, and communication systems.

Tourism: Tourism is the activity of traveling to and staying in places outside one's usual environment for leisure, business, or other purposes. It involves the services and infrastructure that cater to travelers, including transportation, accommodation, and entertainment.

Compilation of References

Aas, C., Ladkin, A., & Fletcher, J. (2005). Stakeholder collaboration and heritage management. *Annals of Tourism Research*, *32*(1), 28–48. DOI: 10.1016/j.annals.2004.04.005

Abad, P. E. S., & Borbon, N. M. D. (2021, October 1). Influence of travel vlog: Inputs for destination marketing model. *International Journal of Research Studies in Management*, *9*(3). Advance online publication. DOI: 10.5861/ijrsm.2021.m7729

Abdurakhmanova, G. K., Astanakulov, O. T., Goyipnazarov, S. B., & Irmatova, A. B. (2022, December 15). Tourism 4.0: Opportunities For Applying Industry 4.0 Technologies In Tourism. *Proceedings of the 6th International Conference on Future Networks & Distributed Systems*. DOI: 10.1145/3584202.3584208

Abisuga-Oyekunle, O. A., & Fillis, I. R. (2017). The role of handicraft micro-enterprises as a catalyst for youth employment. *Creative Industries Journal*, *10*(1), 59–74. DOI: 10.1080/17510694.2016.1247628

Abou-Shouk, M., & Soliman, M. (2021). The impact of gamification adoption intention on brand awareness and loyalty in tourism: The mediating effect of customer engagement. *Journal of Destination Marketing & Management*, *20*, 100559. Advance online publication. DOI: 10.1016/j.jdmm.2021.100559

Abraham, V., Pizam, A., & Medeiros, M. (2021). The impact of attitudes, motivational factors, and emotions on the image of a dark tourism site and the desire of the victims' descendants to visit it. *Journal of Heritage Tourism*, *17*(2), 264–282.

Abreu, A., Costa, E., & Borges, I. (2020). The Impact of Artificial Intelligence on the Tourism Industry: A Systematic Review. *Advances in Tourism, Technology and Systems: Selected Papers from ICOTTS20*, *1*(208), 458.

Adler, P. (1998). Beyond cultural identity: Reflections on multiculturalism. *Basic concepts of intercultural communication: Selected readings*, 225-245.

Agag, G., & El-Masry, A. A. (2016). Understanding consumer intention to participate in the online travel community and effects on consumer intention to purchase travel online and WOM: An integration of innovation diffusion theory and TAM with trust. *Computers in Human Behavior*, *60*, 97–111. DOI: 10.1016/j.chb.2016.02.038

Akhtar, N., Khan, N., Mahroof Khan, M., Ashraf, S., Hashmi, M. S., Khan, M. M., & Hishan, S. S. (2021, May 11). Post-COVID 19 Tourism: Will Digital Tourism Replace Mass Tourism? *Sustainability (Basel)*, *13*(10), 5352. DOI: 10.3390/su13105352

Akorio, F. A., Turyamureeba, S., Tugume, A., & Eze, V. H. U. (2024). Rural Tourism and Socio-Economic Development in Kalapatta Sub County Kabong District of Uganda. [JHASS]. *Journal of the Humanities and Social Sciences*, *6*(1), 31–38. DOI: 10.36079/lamintang.jhass-0601.606

Alcala, K., D'Achille, A., & Bruckman, A. (2023). The Stage and the Theatre: AltspaceVR and its Relationship to Discord. *Proceedings of the ACM on Human-Computer Interaction, 7*(CSCW1), 1-21. DOI: 10.1145/3579529

Ali, F. (2016). Hotel website quality, perceived flow, customer satisfaction and purchase intention. *Journal of Hospitality and Tourism Technology*, *7*(2), 213–228. DOI: 10.1108/JHTT-02-2016-0010

Alla, L., Bentalha, B., & Bouhtati, N. (2022). Assessing supply chain performance in the covid 19 context: a prospective model. In 2022 14th International Colloquium of Logistics and Supply Chain Management (LOGISTIQUA) (pp. 1-6). IEEE. DOI: 10.1109/LOGISTIQUA55056.2022.9938083

Alrihani, N. (2022). *Interactive mixed reality experiences: integrated digital representations of tangible/intangible Cultural Heritage assets and immersive technology applications to improve heritage visitor experiences*. The University of Liverpool.

Al-Romeedy, B. S., & Hashem, T. (2024). From Insight to Advantage: Harnessing the Potential of Marketing Intelligence Systems in Tourism. In *Marketing and Big Data Analytics in Tourism and Events* (pp. 80-98). IGI Global.

Amalia, D., Nesya, N., & Tyrta, M. (2023). Implementasi Kota Pintar (Smart City) Di Kota Surabaya. *Jurnal Birokrasi & Pemerintahan Daerah*, *5*(1), 57–63.

Amaro, S., Barroco, C., & Fonseca, P. (2021). The use of information and communication technologies in religious tourism. In *The Routledge Handbook of Religious and Spiritual Tourism* (pp. 372–384). Routledge. DOI: 10.4324/9780429201011-31

Amendola, C., La Bella, S., Joime, G. P., Frattale Mascioli, F. M., & Vito, P. (2022). An Integrated Methodology Model for Smart Mobility System Applied to Sustainable Tourism. *Administrative Sciences*, *12*(1), 40. Advance online publication. DOI: 10.3390/admsci12010040

Amirou, R. (2000). *Imaginaire du tourisme culturel*. Puf.

Android | Ministry of Tourism | Government of India. (n.d.). https://tourism.gov.in/important-links-latest-program-application-download/android

Appel, G., Grewal, L., Hadi, R., & Stephen, A. T. (2019, October 12). The future of social media in marketing. *Journal of the Academy of Marketing Science*, *48*(1), 79–95. DOI: 10.1007/s11747-019-00695-1 PMID: 32431463

Applboim, T., & Poria, Y. (2020). Witnesses in uniform: Are Israeli defense forces officers in favor of their soldiers visiting Holocaust heritage sites in Poland? *Journal of Heritage Tourism*, *15*(4), 438–449. DOI: 10.1080/1743873X.2019.1666134

Archer, B., Cooper, C., & Ruhanen, L. (1998). The positive and negative impacts of tourism. *Global tourism*, *2*, 63-81.

Arkkelin, D. (2014). Using SPSS to Understand Research and Data Analysis. Psychology Curricular Materials. 1.

Asplet, M., & Cooper, M. (2000). Cultural designs in New Zealand souvenir clothing: The question of authenticity. *Tourism Management*, *21*(3), 307–312. DOI: 10.1016/S0261-5177(99)00061-8

Asriyani, H., & Verheijen, B. (2020). Protecting the Mbau Komodo in Riung, Flores: Local Adat, National Conservation and Ecotourism Developments. *Forest and Society*, *4*(1), 20–34. DOI: 10.24259/fs.v4i1.7465

Auschwitz-Birkenau Memorial and Museum. (2021). Visitor numbers. https://auschwitz.org/en/museum/history-of-the-memorial/the-first-years-of-the-memorial/visitor-numbers (Accessed January 13, 2023).

Ayuningtyas, D. I., & Dharmawan, A. H. (2011). Dampak Ekowisata Terhadap Kondisi Sosio-Ekonomi Dan Sosio-Ekologi Masyarakat Di Taman Nasional Gunung Halimun Salak. *Sodality: Jurnal Transdisiplin Sosiologi, Komunikasi, Dan Ekologi Manusia*, *05*(03).

Bachleitner, R., & Zins, A. (1999). Cultural tourism in rural communities: The residents' perspective. *Journal of Business Research*, *44*(3), 199–209. DOI: 10.1016/S0148-2963(97)00201-4

Baldwin, C., & King, R. (2018). *Social Sustainability, Climate Resilience and Community-Based Urban Development*. Routledge. DOI: 10.4324/9781351103329

Balletto, G., Milesi, A., Ladu, M., & Borruso, G. (2020). A dashboard for supporting slow tourism in green infrastructures. A methodological proposal in Sardinia (Italy). *Sustainability (Basel)*, *12*(9), 3579. Advance online publication. DOI: 10.3390/su12093579

Baloglu, S. (2000). A path analytic model of visitation intention involving information sources, socio-psychological motivations, and destination image. *Journal of Travel & Tourism Marketing*, *8*(3), 81–90. DOI: 10.1300/J073v08n03_05

Balogun, V. F., Thompson, A. F., & Sarumi, O. A. (2010). A 3D Geo-Spatial Virtual Reality System for Virtual Tourism. *Pacific Journal of Science and Technology*, *11*(2), 601–609.

Banerjee, A., & Chaudhury, S. (2010). Statistics without tears: Populations and samples. From Industrial Psychiatry Journal. *National Library of Medicine*, *19*(1), 60–65.

Bappenas. (2015). *Rencana Pembangunan Jangka Menengah Nasional (RPJMN) 2015-2019*. Perpres No 2 Tahun 2015. Jakarta: Bappenas.

Barney, J. (1991). Firm resources and sustained competitive advantage. *Journal of Management*, *17*(1), 99–120. DOI: 10.1177/014920639101700108

Bascom, W. (1965). The forms of folklore: Prose narratives. *Journal of American Folklore*, *78*(307), 3–20. DOI: 10.2307/538099

Bassiouni, D. H., & Hackley, C. (2014). Generation Z children's adaptation to digital consumer culture. *Journal of Customer Behaviour*, *13*(2), 113–133. DOI: 10.1362/147539214X14024779483591

Bauer, I. L. (2021). Death as attraction: The role of travel medicine and psychological travel health care in dark tourism. *Tropical Diseases, Travel Medicine and Vaccines*, *7*(1), 1–14. DOI: 10.1186/s40794-021-00149-z PMID: 34380578

Bazazo, I., Nasseef, M. A., Al-Zawaideh, A., Al-Zawaideh, A., & Al-Dhomaidat, M. (2017). The Impact of the Attitudes towards Ecotourism Benefits on Destination. *Journal of Management and Strategy*, *8*(3), 67–79. DOI: 10.5430/jms.v8n3p67

Beddaa, M., & Bentalha, B. (2025). Optimizing Local Attractiveness Through Territorial Digital Communication. In Sustainable and Intelligent Territorial Marketing and Entrepreneurship (pp. 159-192). IGI Global.

Beeman, W. O. (1993). The anthropology of theater and spectacle. *Annual Review of Anthropology*, 22(1), 369–393. DOI: 10.1146/annurev.an.22.100193.002101

Beeton, S. (2005). *Film-Induced Tourism*. Channel View. DOI: 10.21832/9781845410162

Benjelloun, A. (2019). Le patrimoine culturel, levier d'attractivité pour la destination touristique «Fès». Revue du contrôle, de la comptabilité et de l'audit, 3(2).

Benjelloun, A., Kaddari, F., & El Gharbaoui, B. (2021). La pédagogie numérique comme solution à la continuité pédagogique en temps du COVID-19 (Cas des étudiants de la ville de Fès). *Alternatives Managériales Economiques*, 3(1), 650–666.

Bentalha, B. (2023). Motivating Factors for Hotel Employees: A Fuzzy Logic Approach. In Strategic Human Resource Management in the Hospitality Industry: A Digitalized Economic Paradigm (pp. 159-178). IGI Global. DOI: 10.4018/978-1-6684-7494-5.ch008

Bentalha, B. (2024). Contribution des randonnées au développement d'un tourisme durable dans la région Fès Meknès. Numérisation et durabilité, Vers une économie responsable et innovante, 226-245.

Bentalha, B. (2025). Artificial Intelligence in B2B Sales: A Survey of Current Applications and Future Trends. AI, Economic Perspectives, and Firm Business Management, 143-164.

Bentalha, B., & Boukare, M. (2024). AI-Driven Territorial Intelligence: An Integrated Approach to Enhancing Digital Sovereignty. In Generative AI and Implications for Ethics, Security, and Data Management (pp. 231-261). IGI Global.

Bentalha, B., & Alla, L. (2024). Revealing the subtleties: The art of qualitative studies in science and management. In *Applying qualitative research methods to management science* (pp. 1–21). IGI Global. DOI: 10.4018/979-8-3693-5543-5.ch001

Bentalha, B., Hmioui, A., & Alla, L. (2020). La performance des entreprises de services: Un cadrage théorique d'un concept évolutif. *Alternatives Managériales Economiques*, 2(1), 58–78.

Berhanu, K., & Raj, S. (2020). The trustworthiness of travel and tourism information sources of social media: Perspectives of international tourists visiting Ethiopia. *Heliyon*, 6(3), e03439. DOI: 10.1016/j.heliyon.2020.e03439 PMID: 32181382

Berkman, L. F., Glass, T., Brissete, I., & Seeman, T. E. (2000). From social integration to health: Durkheim in the new millenium. *Social Science & Medicine*, 51(6), 843–857. DOI: 10.1016/S0277-9536(00)00065-4 PMID: 10972429

Bernerth, J. B., & Aguinis, H. (2015). A Critical Review and Best-Practice Recommendations for Control Variable Usage. *Personnel Psychology*, *69*(1), 229–283. DOI: 10.1111/peps.12103

Berondo, R. G. (2023). *The Impact of Socio–economic and Traditional Practices of the Local Folks in the Tourism Industry*. Cultural Landscapes Insights. DOI: 10.59762/cli901324531220231205131244

Bhandari, P. (2020). Data Collection | Definition, Methods & Examples. Retrieved from https://scribbr.com/methodology/data-collection/

Bhardwaj, S., Sharma, I., Kaur, G., & Sharma, S. (2025). Personalization in Tourism Marketing Based on Leveraging User-Generated Content With AI Recommender Systems. In *Redefining Tourism With AI and the Metaverse* (pp. 317–346). IGI Global Scientific Publishing. DOI: 10.4018/979-8-3693-8482-4.ch010

Bhatia, A. K. (2002). *Tourism development: Principles and practices*. Sterling Publishers Pvt. Ltd.

Bhimrajka, A. (2024). *Battle of the Super Apps: Gojek vs. Grab – Who Comes Out on Top?* Miracuves: https://miracuves.com/battle-of-the-super-apps-gojek-vs-grab/ . Accessed on 10 May 2025.

Bianchi, C. (2021). Antecedents of tourists' solo travel inentions. *Tourism Review*, *77*(3), 780–795. DOI: 10.1108/TR-12-2020-0611

Bigne, J. E., Sanchez, M. I., & Sanchez, J. (2001). Tourism image, evaluation variables, and after purchase behaviour: Inter-relationship. *Tourism Management*, *22*(6), 607–616. DOI: 10.1016/S0261-5177(01)00035-8

Bilotta, E., Bertacchini, F., Gabriele, L., Giglio, S., Pantano, P. S., & Romita, T. (2021, November). Industry 4.0 technologies in tourism education: Nurturing students to think with technology. *Journal of Hospitality, Leisure, Sport and Tourism Education*, *29*, 100275. DOI: 10.1016/j.jhlste.2020.100275

Blomstrom (1983). Strategic market planning in the hospitality industry. Educational Institute for the American Hotel and Motel Association, Michigan.

Bonink, C. (1992). Cultural tourism development and government policy. *Unpublished ma dissertation). Rijksuniversiteit, Utrecht, The Netherlands.*

Bonsón Ponte, E., Carvajal-Trujillo, E., & Escobar-Rodríguez, T.Bonsón. (2015). Influence of trust and perceived value on the intention to purchase travel online: Integrating the effects of assurance on trust antecedents. *Tourism Management*, *47*, 286–302. DOI: 10.1016/j.tourman.2014.10.009

Boudri, R., Bentalha, B., Andaloussi, O. B., & Abbass, Z. (2025). Leveraging the "Made in Morocco" Label for Smart Marketing and Sustainable Territorial Attractiveness. In Sustainable and Intelligent Territorial Marketing and Entrepreneurship (pp. 69-94). IGI Global.

Boudri, R., Bentalha, B., & Benjelloun, O. (2024). Phygital marketing and the pain of paying: An Amazon Go netnographic case study. In *AI and data engineering solutions for effective marketing* (pp. 348–363). IGI Global. DOI: 10.4018/979-8-3693-3172-9.ch017

Bouhtati, N., Alla, L., & Bentalha, B. (2023). Marketing Big Data Analytics and Customer Relationship Management: A Fuzzy Approach. In Integrating Intelligence and Sustainability in Supply Chains (pp. 75-86). IGI Global. DOI: 10.4018/979-8-3693-0225-5.ch004

Bounia, A., Nikonanou, N., & Oikonomou, M. (2008). *Technology in the service of cultural heritage*. Kaleidoscope.

Boxo. (2024). *15 Most Popular Super Apps in the World in 2024.* https://www.boxo.io/blog/most-popular-superapps-in-the-world. Accessed on 10 May 2025.

Bradford, G., Gary, M., & Wallach, G. (2000). *The politics of culture: Policy perspectives for individuals, institutions and communities*. New Press.

Bramwell, B., & Lane, B. (1993). Rural tourism and sustainable rural development. *Journal of Sustainable Tourism*, *1*(1), 1–4. DOI: 10.1080/09669589309450696

Bratman, M. E. (1999). *Faces of Intention: Selected Essays on Intention and Agency*. Cambridge University Press. DOI: 10.1017/CBO9780511625190

Brown, F., & Hall, D. (2008). Tourism and development in the global South: The issues. In Brown, F., & Hall, D. (Eds.), *Tourism and development in the Global South* (pp. 1–24). Routledge. DOI: 10.1080/01436590802105967

Buhalis, D. (2000). Marketing the competitive destination of the future. *Tourism Management*, *21*(1), 97–116. DOI: 10.1016/S0261-5177(99)00095-3

Buhalis, D. (2020). Technology in tourism-from information communication technologies to eTourism and smart tourism towards ambient intelligence tourism: A perspective article. *Tourism Review*, *75*(1), 267–272. DOI: 10.1108/TR-06-2019-0258

Buhalis, D., & Amaranggana, A. (2014). Smart tourism destinations. *Information and Communication Technologies in Tourism*, *2014*, 553–564.

Buhalis, D., & Amaranggana, A. (2014, December 27). Smart Tourism Destinations Enhancing Tourism Experience Through Personalisation of Services. *Information and Communication Technologies in Tourism*, 2015, 377–389. DOI: 10.1007/978-3-319-14343-9_28

Buhalis, D., & Foerste, M. (2015). The Impact of Social Media on Tourism. *Journal of Travel Research*, 54(5), 511–527. DOI: 10.1177/0047287514565159

Buhalis, D., & Law, R. (2008). Progress in information technology and tourism management: 20 years on and 10 years after the Internet—The state of eTourism research. *Tourism Management*, 29(4), 609–623. DOI: 10.1016/j.tourman.2008.01.005

Buhalis, D., & Yen, C. (2020). Smart tourism: AI, Big Data, and innovation. *Journal of Travel & Tourism Marketing*, 37(1), 1–6.

Bulchand-Gidumal, J. (2020). Impact of Artificial Intelligence in Travel, Tourism, and Hospitality. *Handbook of e-Tourism*, 1–20. https://doi.org/DOI: 10.1007/978-3-030-05324-6_110-1

Bulchand-Gidumal, J., William Secin, E., O'Connor, P., & Buhalis, D. (2023). Artificial intelligence's impact on hospitality and tourism marketing: Exploring key themes and addressing challenges. *Current Issues in Tourism*, 0(0), 1–18. DOI: 10.1080/13683500.2023.2229480

Butcher, J. (2001). 'Cultural baggage and cultural tourism', in Innovations in Cultural Tourism, Proceedings of the 5th ATLAS International Conference, Rethymnon, Crete, 1998, Tilburg: ATLAS, pp. 11–18.

Butler, R., & Hinch, T. (Eds.). (1996). *Tourism and Indigenous Peoples*. International Thomson Business Press.

Butler, R., & Hinch, T. (Eds.). (2007). *Tourism and Indigenous Peoples: Issues and Implications*. Butterworth-Heinemann. DOI: 10.4324/9780080553962

Cáceres, J. A., & Duran, J. (2021). The role of rural tourism in promoting sustainable development in Peru. *Tourism Management Perspectives*, 39, 100854.

Calza, F., Trunfio, M., Pasquinelli, C., Sorrentino, A., Campana, S., & Rossi, S. (2022). *Technology-driven innovation. Exploiting ICTs tools for digital engagement, smart experiences, and sustainability in tourism destinations. SLIOB*. Enzo Albano Edizioni Naples.

Canturk, D., Karagoz, P., Kim, S. W., & Toroslu, I. H. (2023). Trust-aware location recommendation in location-based social networks: A graph-based approach. *Expert Systems with Applications*, 213, 119048. DOI: 10.1016/j.eswa.2022.119048

Casillo, M., Colace, F., Lorusso, A., Santaniello, D., & Valentino, C. (2025). Integrating Physical and Virtual Experiences in Cultural Tourism: An Adaptive Multimodal Recommender System. *IEEE Access : Practical Innovations, Open Solutions, 13*, 28353–28368. DOI: 10.1109/ACCESS.2025.3539205

Chalana, M., & Sprague, T. S. (2013). Beyond Le Corbusier and the modernist city: Reframing Chandigarh's 'World Heritage' legacy. *Planning Perspectives, 28*(2), 199–222. DOI: 10.1080/02665433.2013.737709

Chang, H., & Chen, S. (2008). The impact of online store environment cues on purchase intention: Trust and perceived risk as a mediator. *Online Information Review, 32*(6), 818–841. DOI: 10.1108/14684520810923953

Chang, S.-H., Chih, W.-H., Liou, D.-K., & Hwang, L.-R. (2014). The influence of web aesthetics on customers' PAD. *Computers in Human Behavior, 36*, 168–178. DOI: 10.1016/j.chb.2014.03.050

Chankong, V., & Haimas, Y. Y. (2008). *Multiobjective Decision Making: Theory and Methodology* (Vol. 8). Dover Publication.

Chan, N. W. (2019). The Nature and Management of Ecotourism Attractions in Sabah, Malaysian Borneo. *Journal of Southeast Asian Studies, 2019*, 1–17.

Chaudhuri, S., & Ray, N. (2015). Application of web-based Geographical Information System (GIS) in tourism development. In *Encyclopedia of Information Science and Technology, Third Edition* (pp. 7026-7036). IGI Global.

Chaudhuri, S., & Ray, N. (Eds.). (2018). *GIS applications in the tourism and hospitality industry*. IGI Global. DOI: 10.4018/978-1-5225-5088-4

Chen, C. C., & Tsai, J. L. (2019). Determinants of behavioral intention to use the Personalized Location-based Mobile Tourism Application: An empirical study by integrating TAM with ISSM. *Future Generation Computer Systems, 96*, 628–638. DOI: 10.1016/j.future.2017.02.028

Chen, C. F., Chen, F. S., & Chen, P. J. (2016). An investigation of the factors affecting tourist satisfaction. *Journal of Travel Research, 55*(4), 481–493.

Chen, C. F., & Tsai, D. C. (2007). How destination image and evaluative factors affect behavioral intentions? *Tourism Management, 28*(4), 1115–1122. DOI: 10.1016/j.tourman.2006.07.007

Chen, C.-C., Hsiao, K.-L., & Wu, S.-J. (2018). Purchase intention in social commerce: An empirical examination of perceived value and social awareness. *Library Hi Tech, 36*(4), 583–604. DOI: 10.1108/LHT-01-2018-0007

Chen, H., & Rahman, I. (2018). Cultural tourism: An analysis of engagement, cultural contact, memorable tourism experience and destination loyalty. *Tourism Management Perspectives*, *26*, 153–163. DOI: 10.1016/j.tmp.2017.10.006

Chen, H., Wigand, R. T., & Nilan, M. S. (1999, September). Optimal experience of Web activities. *Computers in Human Behavior*, *15*(5), 585–608. DOI: 10.1016/S0747-5632(99)00038-2

Chen, N. (2020). Application of big data technology in smart Tourism. *Journal of Physics: Conference Series*, *1648*(4), 042101. Advance online publication. DOI: 10.1088/1742-6596/1648/4/042101

Chen, S., & Xu, H. (2020). The moral gaze in commercialized dark tourism. *Current Issues in Tourism*, *24*(2), 1–20.

Chen, Y., Cottam, E., & Lin, Z. (2020). The effect of resident-tourist value co-creation on residents' well-being. *Journal of Hospitality and Tourism Management*, *44*, 30–37. DOI: 10.1016/j.jhtm.2020.05.009

Chen, Y., Ding, D., Meng, L., Li, X., & Zhang, S. (2021). Understanding consumers' purchase intention towards online paid courses. *Information Development*. Advance online publication. DOI: 10.1177/02666669211027206

Ching-Fu, C., & Wu, C. C. (2009). How motivations, constraints, and demographic factors predict seniors' overseas travel propensity. *Asia Pacific Management Review*, *14*(3).

Chi, O. H., Gursoy, D., & Chi, C. G. (2022). Tourists' Attitudes toward the Use of Artificially Intelligent (AI) Devices in Tourism Service Delivery: Moderating Role of Service Value Seeking. *Journal of Travel Research*, *61*(1), 170–185. DOI: 10.1177/0047287520971054

Chopra, A., Avhad, V., & Jaju, A. S. (2020, June 15). Influencer Marketing: An Exploratory Study to Identify Antecedents of Consumer Behavior of Millennial. *Business Perspectives and Research*, *9*(1), 77–91. DOI: 10.1177/2278533720923486

Chowdhary, K. (2020, April 4). Fundamentals of Artificial Intelligence. *Springer Nature*. http://books.google.ie/books?id=8SfbDwAAQBAJ&printsec=frontcover&dq=Fundamentals+of+Artificial+Intelligence&hl=&cd=1&source=gbs_api

Cho, Y., & Fesenmaier, D. R. (2001). A new paradigm for tourism and electronic commerce: Experience marketing using the virtual tour. In Laws, E., & Buhalis, D. (Eds.), *tourism distribution channels: practices, issues and transformation* (pp. 351–370). Thomson.

Choy, D. J. (1995). The quality of tourism employment. *Tourism Management, 16*(2), 129–137. DOI: 10.1016/0261-5177(94)00023-4

Christou, L. (2012). Is it possible to combine mass tourism with alternative forms of tourism: The case of Spain, Greece, Slovenia and Croatia. *Journal of Business Administration Online, 11*, 1.

Christou, P. A. (2020). *Philosophies of hospitality and tourism: Giving and receiving*. Channel View Publications.

Chung, N., Tyan, I., & Lee, S. J. (2019). Eco-innovative museums and visitors' perceptions of corporate social responsibility. *Sustainability (Basel), 11*(20), 1–16. DOI: 10.3390/su11205744

Chu, S. C., Deng, T., & Cheng, H. (2020, September 24). The role of social media advertising in hospitality, tourism and travel: A literature review and research agenda. *International Journal of Contemporary Hospitality Management, 32*(11), 3419–3438. DOI: 10.1108/IJCHM-05-2020-0480

Cohen, E. (1988). Authenticity and commoditization in tourism. *Annals of Tourism Research, 15*(3), 371–386. DOI: 10.1016/0160-7383(88)90028-X

Cole, S. (2006). Cultural tourism, community participation and empowerment. *Cultural tourism in a changing world: Politics, participation and (re) presentation*, 89-103.

Collins-Kreiner, N. (2020). Pilgrimage tourism-past, present and future rejuvenation: A perspective article. *Tourism Review, 75*(1), 145–148. DOI: 10.1108/TR-04-2019-0130

Cooper, C. (1994). Tourism product life cycle. In Seaton, A. (Eds.), *Tourism: The state of the art* (pp. 340–346). J., Wiley.

Cooper, C., Fletcher, J., Gilbert, D., & Wanhill, S. (1993). *Turism Principles and Practice*. Pitman.

Cooper, C., & Jackson, S. (1989). Destination life cycle: The Isle of Man case study. *Annals of Tourism Research, 16*(3), 377–398. DOI: 10.1016/0160-7383(89)90051-0

Copperchips, & root. (2023, March 14). Role of Geographic Information Systems (GIS) in Tourism Planning. *Copperchips*. https://copperchips.com/role-geographic-information-systems-tourism-planning/

Corte, V. D., Gaudio, G. D., Sepe, F., & Sciarelli, F. (2019). Sustainable Tourism in the Open Innovation Realm: A Bibliometric analysis. *Sustainability (Basel), 11*(21), 6114. DOI: 10.3390/su11216114

Craik, J. (2002). The culture of tourism. In *Touring cultures* (pp. 123–146). Routledge.

Crompton, J. L. (1995). Economic impact analysis of sports facilities and events: Eleven sources of misapplication. *Journal of Sport Management, 9*(1), 14–35. DOI: 10.1123/jsm.9.1.14

Csikzentmihalyi, M. (1975). *Beyond boredom and anxiety*. Jossey-Bass.

Cuomo, M. T., Tortora, D., Foroudi, P., Giordano, A., Festa, G., & Metallo, G. (2021). Digital transformation and tourist experience co-design: Big social data for planning cultural tourism. *Technological Forecasting and Social Change, 162*, 120345. DOI: 10.1016/j.techfore.2020.120345

Cynthia, M., Ingrid, P., & Alicia, Y. (2021). *Digitization trends in hospitality and tourism*. Smart Tourism., DOI: 10.54517/st.v2i2.1709

D'Amore, L. J. (1988). Tourism—A vital force for peace. *Tourism Management, 9*(2), 151–154. DOI: 10.1016/0261-5177(88)90025-8

D'Antonio, A., Monz, C. A., Crabb, B., Baggio, J. A., & Howe, P. D. (2022). Proof of concept study using GPS-based tracking data to build agent-based models of visitors' off-trail behavior in nature-based tourism settings. *Applied Geography (Sevenoaks, England), 147*, 102771. DOI: 10.1016/j.apgeog.2022.102771

Dahiru, T. (2011, March 3). P-Value, a true test of statistical significance? a cautionary note. *Annals of Ibadan Postgraduate Medicine, 6*(1). Advance online publication. DOI: 10.4314/aipm.v6i1.64038 PMID: 25161440

Dahles, H. (2002). Tourism, small enterprises and community development. In *Tourism and sustainable community development* (pp. 172–187). Routledge.

Damanik, J., & Helmut, F. W. (2006). *Perencanaan Ekowisata Dari Teori ke Aplikasi*. Andi Offset.

Damanik, J., & Yusuf, M. (2022). Effects of perceived value, expectation, visitor management, and visitor satisfaction on revisit intention to Borobudur Temple, Indonesia. *Journal of Heritage Tourism, 17*(2), 174–189. DOI: 10.1080/1743873X.2021.1950164

Dant, T. (1999). *Material culture in the social world*. McGraw-Hill Education.

Danyun, L., & Jiun, C. Y. (2016, October). Historical cultural art heritage come alive: Interactive design in Taiwan palace museum as a case study. In *2016 22nd International Conference on Virtual System & Multimedia (VSMM)* (pp. 1-8). IEEE.

Das, J., & Chakraborty, S. (2021). Scope of dark tourism as a revival strategy for the industry: A study with special reference to Rajasthan. *Business Studies, XLII*(1 & 2).

Dash, G., Kiefer, K., & Paul, J. (2021, January). Kiefer, Kip., & Paul, J. (2021). Marketing-to-Millennials: Marketing 4.0, customer satisfaction and purchase intention. *Journal of Business Research*, *122*, 608–620. Advance online publication. DOI: 10.1016/j.jbusres.2020.10.016

Dashper, K. (2014). Rural tourism: Opportunities and challenges. *Journal of Rural Studies*, *36*(1), 32–40.

Davin, K. (1997).. . *Effects of Computer Support on Group Decisions Journal of Hospitality and Tourism Research.*, *21*(2), 44–57.

Davis, F. D. (1989). Perceived usefulness, perceived ease of use, and user acceptance of information technology. *Management Information Systems Quarterly*, *13*(3), 319–340. DOI: 10.2307/249008

Davlembayeva, D., Chari, S., & Papagiannidis, S. (2025). Virtual influencers in consumer behaviour: A social influence theory perspective. *British Journal of Management*, *36*(1), 202–222. DOI: 10.1111/1467-8551.12839

De Ascaniis, S., Mutangala, M.-M., & Cantoni, L. (2018). ICTs in the tourism experience at religious heritage sites: A review of the literature and an investigation of pilgrims' experiences at the sanctuary of Loreto (Italy). Church. *Communication and Culture*, *3*(3), 310–334. DOI: 10.1080/23753234.2018.1544835

De Carvalho, J. V., Rocha, Á., Liberato, P., & Peña, A. (Eds.). (2021). *Advances in Tourism, Technology and Systems: Selected Papers from ICOTTS20* (Vol. 1). Springer Singapore., DOI: 10.1007/978-981-33-4256-9

de Jesus Duenas-Garcia, M. (2022). *Living in Borderlands. Archaeology and Meaningful Divulgation of the Northern Frontier of Mesoamerica*. University of California, Merced.

De las Heras-Pedrosa, C., Millán-Celis, E., Iglesias-Sánchez, P. P., & Jambrino-Maldonado, C. (2020). Importance of Social Media in the Image Formation of Tourist Destinations from the Stakeholders' Perspective. *Sustainability (Basel)*, *12*(10), 4092. DOI: 10.3390/su12104092

Derrett, R. (2003). Festivals & regional destinations: How festivals demonstrate a sense of community & place. *Rural Society*, *13*(1), 35–53. DOI: 10.5172/rsj.351.13.1.35

Dessylla, H. (2004). *Griekenland: Nieuwe Vormen Van Toerisme. Elke*. The Hellenic Center for Investment.

Dhatrak, S. P. (2020). Dark tourism sites in India: A review. *Shanlax International Journal of Arts, Science and Humanities*, *8*(2).

Dhonju, H. K., Xiao, W., Sarhosis, V., Mills, J. P., Wilkinson, S., Wang, Z., Thapa, L., & Panday, U. S. (2017). Feasibility study of low-cost image-based heritage documentation in Nepal. *The International Archives of the Photogrammetry, Remote Sensing and Spatial Information Sciences*, *42*(W3), 237–242. DOI: 10.5194/isprs-archives-XLII-2-W3-237-2017

Diamantis, M. E. (2022). Employed algorithms: A labor model of corporate liability for AI. *Duke Law Journal*, *72*, 797.

Dilard, J., Dujon, V., & King, M. C. (2009). *Understanding the Social Dimension of Sustainability*. Routledge.

Dill, K. E. (2009). The impact of thin models in music videos on adolescent girls' body dissatisfaction. *Journal of Research on Adolescence*, *19*(3), 423–438.

Dincer, C., & Dincer, B. (2023). Social Commerce and Purchase Intention: A Brief Look at the Last Decade by Bibliometrics. *Sustainability (Basel)*, *15*(1), 846. Advance online publication. DOI: 10.3390/su15010846

Ding, D., Hu, P.-H., Verma, R., & Wardell, D. (2009). The Impact of Service System Design and Flow Experience on Customer Satisfaction in Online Financial Services. *Journal of Service Research*, *13*(1), 96–110. DOI: 10.1177/1094670509350674

Dixon, S. (2023). Number of global social network users 2017-2027. Statista. Retrieved from https://statista.com/statistics/278414/number-of-worldwide-social-network-users/

Dobrica, J. (2014). Cultural tourism in the context of relations between mass and alternative tourism. *Current Issues in Tourism*, *12*(1), 1–8.

Dong, Y., & Hauschild, M. Z. "Indicators for Environmental Sustainability," *The 24th CIRP Conference on Life Cycle Engineering*, vol. 61, pp. 697-702, 2017. DOI: 10.1016/j.procir.2016.11.173

Donnelly, J. H. J. (1976). Marketing intermediaries in channels of distribution for services. *Journal of Marketing*, *40*, 55–70.

Donovan, R., & Rositter, J. (1982). Store atmosphere: An environmental psychology approach. *Journal of Retailing*, *58*(1), 34–57.

Doran, R., & Larsen, S. (2015). The Relative Importance of Social and Personal Norms in Explaining Intentions to Choose Eco-Friendly Travel Options. *International Journal of Tourism Research*, *18*(2), 159–166. DOI: 10.1002/jtr.2042

Dorcic, J., Komsic, J., & Markovic, S. (2019). Mobile technologies and applications towards smart tourism – state of the art. *Tourism Review*, *74*(1), 82–103. DOI: 10.1108/TR-07-2017-0121

Dorokhov, O., Malyarets, L., Ukrainski, K., Petrova, M., Yevstrat, D., & Aliyeva, A. (2023). Consumer expectations and real experiences: Case of Ukrainian tourists in Turkey. *Access Journal*, *4*(1), 102–114. DOI: 10.46656/access.2023.4.1(8)

Douglas, K. (2020). Youth, trauma and memorialisation: The selfie as witnessing. *Memory Studies*, *13*(3), 384–399. DOI: 10.1177/1750698017714838

Doush, I. A., Alshattnawi, S., & Barhoush, M. (2015). Non-visual navigation interface for completing tasks with a predefined order using mobile phone: A case study of pilgrimage. *International Journal of Mobile Network Design and Innovation*, *6*(1), 1. DOI: 10.1504/IJMNDI.2015.069207

Dresler, E. (2023). Multiplicity of moral emotions in educational dark tourism. *Tourism Management Perspectives*, *46*, 46. DOI: 10.1016/j.tmp.2023.101094

Druckman, J. N., & Parkin, M. (2005). The impact of media bias: How editorial slant affects voters. *The Journal of Politics*, *67*(4), 1030–1049. DOI: 10.1111/j.1468-2508.2005.00349.x

Durán-Sánchez, A., Álvarez-García, J., del Río-Rama, M. D. L. C., & Rosado-Cebrián, B. (2019). Science mapping of the Knowledge Base on Tourism Innovation. *Sustainability (Basel)*, *11*(12), 3352. DOI: 10.3390/su11123352

Durant, R. F., Fiorino, D. J., & O'Leary, R. (2017). *Environmental Governance Reconsidered: Challenges, Choices, and Opportunities*. The MIT Press.

Dyer, D. W. W. (2010). The Power of Intention, Gift Edition ed., J. Pyle, Ed., New York: Hay House.

Eagleton, T. (2000). *The Idea of Culture*. Blackwell.

Edensor, T. (2001). Performing tourism, staging tourism: (re)producing tourist space and practice. *Tourist Studies*, *1*(1), 59–81. DOI: 10.1177/146879760100100104

Edgell, D. L.Sr. (2019). *Managing sustainable tourism: A legacy for the future*. Routledge.

El Archi, Y., Benbba, B., Nizamatdinova, Z., Issakov, Y., Vargáné, G. I., & Dávid, L. D. (2023). Systematic Literature Review Analysing Smart Tourism Destinations in Context of Sustainable Development: Current Applications and Future Directions. *Sustainability (Basel)*, *15*(6), 5086. DOI: 10.3390/su15065086

Eliot, T. S. (2010). *Notes towards the Definition of Culture*. Faber & Faber.

Elkind, D. (2019). "Travel Trends: On The Go With Generation Z,". Online. Available: https://www.cmo.com/features/articles/2019/5/15/generation-z-travel.html#gs.28tjb9

Eroglu, S., Machleit, K., & Davis, L. (2003). Empirical Testing of a Model of Online Store Atmospherics and Shopper Responses. *Psychology and Marketing*, *20*(2), 139–150. DOI: 10.1002/mar.10064

Fabros, M. G. M., Lopez, E. L. F., & Roma, M. N. (2023). Dark tourism in the Philippine context: Indicators, motivations, and spectrum. *Social Sciences & Humanities Open*, *7*(1), 100452. DOI: 10.1016/j.ssaho.2023.100452

Fabry, N., & Zeghni, S. (2017). "Le tourisme du futur: entre mobilité et proximité". inGerardin H. et Montalieu T. (éditeurs), Mobilités et soutenabilité du développement, Paris, Karthala, 2017

Faidat, N., & Khozin, M. (2018). Analisa Strategi Pengembangan Kota Pintar (Smart City): Studi Kasus Kota Yogyakarta. *JIP (Jurnal Ilmu Pemerintahan). Kajian Ilmu Pemerintahan Dan Politik Daerah*, *3*(2), 171–180. DOI: 10.24905/jip.3.2.2018.171-180

Fajuyigbe, O., Balogun, V. F., & Obembe, O. M. (2007). Web-based geographical information system (GIS) for tourism in Oyo State, Nigeria. *Information Technology Journal*, *6*(5), 613–622. DOI: 10.3923/itj.2007.613.622

Fang, J., Zhao, Z., Wen, C., & Wang, R. (2017). Design and performance attributes driving mobile travel application engagement. *International Journal of Information Management*, *37*(4), 269–283. DOI: 10.1016/j.ijinfomgt.2017.03.003

Fang, Y., Qureshi, I., Sun, H., McCole, P., Ramsey, E., & Lim, K. (2014). Trust, Satisfaction, and Online Repurchase Intention: The Moderating Role of Perceived Effectiveness of E-Commerce Institutional Mechanisms. *Management Information Systems Quarterly*, *38*(2), 407–428. https://www.jstor.org/stable/26634932. DOI: 10.25300/MISQ/2014/38.2.04

Farmaki, A. (2012). An exploration of tourist motivation in rural settings: The case of Troodos, Cyprus. *Tourism Management Perspectives*, *2*, 72–78. DOI: 10.1016/j.tmp.2012.03.007

Farooq, M., & Altintas, V. (2022). Role of Technology on Religious Tourism in Turkey. In Ramos, C., Quinteiro, S., & Gonçalves, A. (Eds.), *ICT as Innovator Between Tourism and Culture* (pp. 67–80). IGI Global., DOI: 10.4018/978-1-7998-8165-0.ch005

Fennell, D. A. (2020). *Ecotourism*. Routledge. DOI: 10.4324/9780429346293

Fernandes, B., Biswas, U. N., Mansukhani, R. T., Casarín, A. V., & Essau, C. A. (2020). The impact of COVID-19 lockdown on internet use and escapism in adolescents. Revista de psicología clínica con niños y adolescentes, 7(3), 59-65.

Fernández-Díaz, E., Jambrino-Maldonado, C., Iglesias-Sánchez, P. P., & de las Heras-Pedrosa, C. (2023). Digital accessibility of smart cities - tourism for all and reducing inequalities: Tourism Agenda 2030. *Tourism Review*, 78(2), 361–380. DOI: 10.1108/TR-02-2022-0091

Ferrarese, M. (2023). Malaysia's tourism recovery flops as Thailand, Indonesia cash in. Aljazeera. Retreived from https://www.aljazeera.com/economy/2023/1/16/malaysia-tourism-recovery-lags-thailand-indonesia-vietnam

Ferreira, L., Oliveira, T., & Neves, C. (2023). Consumer's intention to use and recommend smart home technologies: The role of environmental awareness. *Energy*, 263, 125814. DOI: 10.1016/j.energy.2022.125814

Fitriani, I.A., & Indriati, D. (2017). "Kajian Data Pasar Wisatawan Nusantara 2017," Kementrian Pariwisata, Jakarta.

Flying, S. (2020). "United couldfollow American withearly 757 & 767 retirement". https://simpleflying.com/united-757-767-early-retirement/

Fodor, O., & Werthner, H. (2005). Harmonise: A step toward an interoperable tourism Marketplace. *International Journal of Electronic Commerce*, 9(2), 11–39. DOI: 10.1080/10864415.2005.11044324

Fornell, C., & Larcker, D. (1981). Evaluating Structural Equation Models with Unobservable Variables and Measurement Error. *JMR, Journal of Marketing Research*, 18(1), 39–50. DOI: 10.1177/002224378101800104

Friends of Orangutan. (2019). Sepilok orangutan tourism – here's what's wrong. Retreived from https://www.fotomalaysia.org/sepilok-orangutan-tourism-heres-whats-wrong/

Fromm, J. (2018, January). How much financial influence does Gen Z have? *Forbes*.

Fromm, J., & Read, A. (2018). *Marketing to Gen Z: The Rules for Reaching This Vast and Very Different Genereations of Influencers*. AMACOM.

Fuchs, M., Höpken, W., & Lexhagen, M. (2014). Big Data analytics for knowledge generation in tourism destinations. *Journal of Destination Marketing & Management*, 3(4), 198–209. DOI: 10.1016/j.jdmm.2014.08.002

Fujimatsu, I., Levy, J., Park, J., & Waddelow, T. (2024). *An ecosystem approach to accelerating sustainable tourism.* Visa Economic Empowerment Institute.

Fu, S., Yan, Q., & Feng, G. C. (2018, June). Who will attract you? Similarity effect among users on online purchase intention of movie tickets in the social shopping context. *International Journal of Information Management*, *40*, 88–102. DOI: 10.1016/j.ijinfomgt.2018.01.013

Galí-Espelt, N. (2012). Identifying cultural tourism: A theoretical methodological proposal. *Journal of Heritage Tourism*, *7*(1), 45–58. DOI: 10.1080/1743873X.2011.632480

Gan, C., & Wang, W. (2017). The influence of perceived value on purchase intention in social commerce context. *Internet Research*, *27*(4), 772–785. DOI: 10.1108/IntR-06-2016-0164

Gant, A. C. (2016). Holiday rentals: The new gentrification battlefront. *Sociological Research Online*, *21*(3), 112–120. DOI: 10.5153/sro.4071

Gao, L., & Bai, X. (2014). Online consumer behaviour and its relationship to website atmospheric induced flow: Insights into online travel agencies in China. *Journal of Retailing and Consumer Services*, *21*(4), 653–665. DOI: 10.1016/j.jretconser.2014.01.001

García-Madurga, M.-Á., & Grilló-Méndez, A.-J. (2023). Artificial Intelligence in the Tourism Industry: An Overview of Reviews. *Administrative Sciences*, *13*(8).

Garlick, K. (2022). *Morbid curiosity: Exploring the ethics of dark tourism. West Chester University Digital Commons.* Doctoral Projects.

Gazzaz, O. B., & Mohamed, H. S. (2022). Patterns of Touch Screen Technology Use in Religious Tourism and Pilgrimage. *International Journal of Customer Relationship Marketing and Management*, *13*(1), 1–21. DOI: 10.4018/IJCRMM.300830

Gebara, C. H., & Laurent, A. (2023). National SDG-7 performance assessment to support achieving sustainable energy for all within planetary limits. *Renewable & Sustainable Energy Reviews*, *173*, 112934. DOI: 10.1016/j.rser.2022.112934

Geertz, C. (1973). From the native's point of view: On the nature of anthropological understanding. In Rabinow, P., & Sullivan, W. M. (Eds.), *Interpretive social science: A reader* (pp. 225–241). University of California Press.

Gefen, D., & Straub, D. (2005). A Practical Guide To Factorial Validity Using PLS-Graph: Tutorial And Annotated Example. *Communications of the Association for Information Systems*, *16*(1), 91–109. DOI: 10.17705/1CAIS.01605

Gholipour, H. F., & Tajaddini, R. (2014). Cultural dimensions and outbound tourism. *Annals of Tourism Research*, *49*(November), 203–205. DOI: 10.1016/j.annals.2014.08.006

Giaccardi, E. (2012). *Heritage and social media: Understanding heritage in a participatory culture*. Routledge. DOI: 10.4324/9780203112984

Giampiccoli, A., & Kalis, J. H. (2012). Tourism, food, and culture: Community-based tourism, local food, and community development in m pondoland. *Culture, Agriculture, Food and Environment*, *34*(2), 101–123. DOI: 10.1111/j.2153-9561.2012.01071.x

Gibreel, O., Alotaibi, D. A., & Altmann, J. (2018, January–February). Social commerce development in emerging markets. *Electronic Commerce Research and Applications*, *27*, 152–162. DOI: 10.1016/j.elerap.2017.12.008

Global Sustainable Tourism Council (GSTC). (2013). *GSTC Destination Criteria*. https://www.gstcouncil.org/gstc-criteria/gstc-destination-criteria/. Accessed on 27 December 2023.

Global sustainable Tourism Council. (2013). *GSTC Hotel & Tour Operator Criteria*. https://www.gstcouncil.org/gstc-criteria/gstc-industry-criteria/. Accessed on 27 December 2023.

GlobeNewswire. (2024). *Indonesia Ecommerce Market Databook 2024, Featuring Bukalapak, JD.id, Lazada, Shopee, Tokopedia, GoFood, GrabFood, Kulina, Wahyoo, Agoda, Bobobox, PegiPegi, Tiket and Traveloka*. https://www.globenewswire.com/de/news-release/2024/06/12/2897607/28124/en/Indonesia-Ecommerce-Market-Databook-2024-Featuring-Bukalapak-JD-id-Lazada-Shopee-Tokopedia-GoFood-GrabFood-Kulina-Wahyoo-Agoda-Bobobox-PegiPegi-Tiket-and-Traveloka.html. Accessed on 10 May 2025.

Glossary of tourism terms | UNWTO. (n.d.). https://www.unwto.org/glossary-tourism-terms (Accessed: March 13, 2024)

Godovykh, M., Baker, C., & Fyall, A. (2022). VR in tourism: A new call for virtual tourism experience amid and after the COVID-19 pandemic. *Tourism and Hospitality*, *3*(1), 265–275. DOI: 10.3390/tourhosp3010018

Goi, M., Kalidas, V., & Yunus, N. (2018). Mediating roles of emotion and experience in the stimulus-organism-response framework in higher education institutions. *Journal of Marketing for Higher Education*, *28*(5), 1–23. DOI: 10.1080/08841241.2018.1425231

Goodwin, H. (1998, October). Sustainable tourism and poverty elimination. In *DFID/DETR Workshop on Sustainable Tourism and Poverty* (Vol. 13). London: Department for International Development.

Góraj, K. (2024). The Impact of Computer-Generated Influencers on Social Media Advertising. *Social Communication*, 25(1), 137–144. DOI: 10.57656/sc-2024-0014

Gössling, S. (2021, January 20). Tourism, technology and ICT: A critical review of affordances and concessions. *Journal of Sustainable Tourism*, 29(5), 733–750. DOI: 10.1080/09669582.2021.1873353

Gossling, S., Scott, D., & Hall, C. M. (2020). *Tourism and Water*. Channel View Publications.

Green, T. A. (Ed.). (1997). *Folklore: an encyclopedia of beliefs, customs, tales, music, and art* (Vol. 1). Abc-clio. DOI: 10.5040/9798216190714

Greenwood, D. J. (1977). Culture by the pound: An anthropological perspective on tourism as cultural commodification. In Smith, V. L. (Ed.), *Hosts and Guests: The Anthropology of Tourism* (pp. 129–138). University of Pennsylvania Press.

Gretzel, U. (2011). Intelligent systems in tourism: A social science perspective. *Annals of Tourism Research*, 38(3), 757–779. DOI: 10.1016/j.annals.2011.04.014

Gretzel, U., Sigala, M., Xiang, Z., & Koo, C. (2015, August 1). Smart tourism: Foundations and developments. *Electronic Markets*, 25(3), 179–188. DOI: 10.1007/s12525-015-0196-8

Grundner, L., & Neuhofer, B. (2021). The bright and dark sides of artificial intelligence: A futures perspective on tourist destination experiences. *Journal of Destination Marketing & Management*, 19, 100511. DOI: 10.1016/j.jdmm.2020.100511

Guccio, C., Lisi, D., Mignosa, A., & Rizzo, I. (2018). Does cultural heritage monetary value have an impact on visits? An assessment using official Italian data. *Tourism Economics*, 24(3), 297–318. DOI: 10.1177/1354816618758729

Gujarati, D. N., & Porter, D. C. (2009). *Basic Econometrics* (5th ed.). McGraw Hill Inc.

Gunlu, E., & Okumus, F. (2010). The Hajj experience of Turkish female pilgrim. *Tourism in the Muslim World Bridging Tourism Theory and Practice*, 2, 223–236.

Hadi, C. E., Reinarto, R., & Rahadi, R. A. (2021). Conceptual Analysis of Sustainable Tourism Management in Indonesia. *JHTHEM*, 6(23), 35–41. DOI: 10.35631/JTHEM.623004

Hair, J. F.Jr, Ringle, C. M., & Sarstedt, M. (2013). Partial Least Squares Structural Equation Modeling: Rigorous Applications, Better Results and Higher Acceptance. *Long Range Planning*, *46*(1-2), 1–12. DOI: 10.1016/j.lrp.2013.01.001

Hall, C. M. (2019). Constructingsustainabletourismdevelopment: The 2030 agenda and the managerialecology of sustainabletourism. *Journal of Sustainable Tourism*, *27*(7), 1044–1060. DOI: 10.1080/09669582.2018.1560456

Hamid, R. A., Albahri, A., Alwan, J. K., Al-qaysi, Z., Albahri, O., Zaidan, A., Al-noor, A., Alamoodi, A., & Zaidan, B. (2021, February). How smart is e-tourism? A systematic review of smart tourism recommendation system applying data management. *Computer Science Review*, *39*, 100337. DOI: 10.1016/j.cosrev.2020.100337

Hammoud, G., Refai, H., & Hammad, M. (2021). Using rumours and dark stories to promote tourism: Applied to Egyptian dark tourism sites. *Journal of Association of Arab Universities for Tourism and Hospitality*, *20*(1), 27–36. DOI: 10.21608/jaauth.2021.56728.1114

Hamouda, M. (2022). Mobile Applications in Tourism. *International Journal of Technology and Human Interaction*, *18*(1), 1–13. DOI: 10.4018/IJTHI.293198

Handayani, R., Suleeman, E., Priadi, C., & Darmajanti, L. (2017). *Water Recycling Opportunity in the Business Sectors of Greater Jakarta*. International Journal of Technology. DOI: 10.14716/ijtech.v8i6.743

Handriana, T., Yulianti, P., & Kurniawati, M. (2020). Exploration of pilgrimage tourism in Indonesia. *Journal of Islamic Marketing*, *11*(3), 783–795. DOI: 10.1108/JIMA-10-2018-0188

Han, M. S., Hampson, D. P., Wang, Y., & Wang, H. (2022). Consumer confidence and green purchase intention: An application of the stimulus-organism-response model. *Journal of Retailing and Consumer Services*, *68*, 103061. DOI: 10.1016/j.jretconser.2022.103061

Harahab, N., & Setiawan, S. (2017). Suitability Index Of Mangrove Ecotourism In Malang Regency. *Ecsofim: Journal of Economic and Social of Fisheries and Marine*, *04*(02), 153–165. DOI: 10.21776/ub.ecsofim.2017.004.02.05

Harrison, D. (2008). Pro-poor tourism: A critique. *Third World Quarterly*, *29*(5), 851–868. DOI: 10.1080/01436590802105983

Hashem, T. N., Albattat, A., Valeri, M., & Sharma, A. (Eds.). (2024). *Marketing and Big Data Analytics in Tourism and Events*. IGI Global. DOI: 10.4018/979-8-3693-3310-5

Hashem, T., & Suleiman, H. (2025). *Promotion of Jordan's Golden Triangle via Recreational and Religious Tourism Marketing Strategies*. Tourism Ethics and Responsible Community Development, GoodFellow Publishers.

Hassannia, R., Barenji, A. V., Li, Z., & Alipour, H. (2019). Web-based recommendation system for smart tourism: Multiagent technology. *Sustainability (Basel)*, *11*(2), 323. Advance online publication. DOI: 10.3390/su11020323

Hausmann, A. (2007). Cultural tourism: Marketing challenges and opportunities for German cultural heritage. *International Journal of Heritage Studies*, *13*(2), 170–184. DOI: 10.1080/13527250601121351

Ha, Y., & Lennon, S. (2010). Online visual merchandising (VMD) cues and consumer pleasure and arousal: Purchasing versus browsing situation. *Psychology and Marketing*, *27*(2), 141–165. DOI: 10.1002/mar.20324

Hays, S., Page, S. J., & Buhalis, D. (2013). Social Media as a Destination Marketing Tool: Its Use by National Tourism Organisations. *Current Issues in Tourism*, *16*(3), 211–239. DOI: 10.1080/13683500.2012.662215

Heinonen, K., & Strandvik, T. (2007). Consumer responsiveness to mobile marketing. *International Journal of Mobile Communications*, *5*(6), 603–617. DOI: 10.1504/IJMC.2007.014177

Hendry, A. H., & Mogindol, H. S. (2017). Applying WILSERV in Measuring Visitor Satisfaction at Sepilok Orangutan Rehabilitation Centre (SORC). *International Journal of Social and Tourism Sciences*, *11*(8).

Hewapathirana, I. U., & Perera, N. (2024). Navigating the age of AI influence: A systematic literature review of trust, engagement, efficacy and ethical concerns of virtual influencers in social media.

Hewei, T., & Youngsook, L. (2022). Factors affecting continuous purchase intention of fashion products on social E-commerce: SOR model and the mediating effect. *Entertainment Computing*, *41*, 100474. DOI: 10.1016/j.entcom.2021.100474

Hewison, R. (1987). *The Heritage Industry: Britain in a Climate of Decline* (1st ed.). Routledge.

Hicks, R. (2025). *Post-COVID boom in visitors sparks over-tourism fears in Asia*. Reuters: https://www.reuters.com/sustainability/land-use-biodiversity/post-covid-boom-visitors-sparks-over-tourism-fears-asia-2025-05-06. Accessed on 10 May 2025.

Hijriati, E., & Mardiana, R. (2014). Community Based Ecotourism influence the condition of Ecology, Social, and Economic Batusuhunan village, Sukabumi. Sodality: *Jurnal Sosiologi Pedesaan, 2*(3).

Hindersah, H., Agustina, I. H., & Chofyan, I. (2021). The spiritual path of pilgrimage tourism for sustainable development: Case-desa Astana-Cirebon, Indonesia. *International Journal of Sustainable Development and Planning, 16*(4), 751–758. DOI: 10.18280/ijsdp.160415

Hjalager, A. M. (2010). A review of innovation research in tourism. *Tourism Management, 31*(1), 1–12. DOI: 10.1016/j.tourman.2009.08.012

Hmioui, A., Alla, L., & Bentalha, B. (2017). Pilotage de la touristicité territoriale au Maroc Proposition d'un indice de touriscticité pour la destination Fès. Entrepreneuriat, Innovation, Gouvernance et Développement territorial, 120-143.

Hmioui, A., Alla, L., & Bentalha, B. (2022). Perception of sustainable tourism by international clients: Case of the visit to a hotel establishment. Reconfigurations du tourisme en contexte de la crise du Covid-19: Quelles démarches pour quelles résiliences au Maroc et ailleurs ?, 1 (1), pp.5-38

Hmioui, A., Alla, L., & Bentalha, B. (2019). La performance touristique territoriale: Cas de la destination Fès. *Alternatives Managériales Economiques, 1*(1), 3–21.

Hodder, I. (1994). The interpretation of documents and material culture. *Sage biographical research, 1*, 393-402.

Hoffman, D., & Novak, T. (1996). Marketing in Hypermedia Computer-Mediated Environments: Conceptual Foundations. *Journal of Marketing, 60*(3), 50–68. DOI: 10.1177/002224299606000304

Hojeghan, S. B., & Esfangareh, A. N. (2011). Digital economy and tourism impacts, influences and challenges. *Procedia: Social and Behavioral Sciences, 19*, 308–316. DOI: 10.1016/j.sbspro.2011.05.136

Homsi, D., Freihat, S. M. S. S., Hashem, T. N., & Alshayyab, A. A. (2022). Touristic marketing through blogging and vlogging; does it attract customers' trust? *Calitatea, 23*(190), 170–178.

Honey, M. Ecotourism and Sustainable Development, Second Edition: Who Owns Paradise? 2nd edition, 2nd ed., Washington: Island Press, 2008.

Ho, R. C., Amin, M., Ryu, K., & Ali, F. (2021). Integrative model for the adoption of tour itineraries from smart travel apps. *Journal of Hospitality and Tourism Technology, 12*(2).

Hospitality Sector, Tourism In India | IBEF. India Brand Equity Foundation. https://www.ibef.org/industry/tourism-hospitality-india

Hossain, M. S., & Rahman, M. F. (2022). Detection of potential customers' empathy behavior towards customers' reviews. *Journal of Retailing and Consumer Services, 65*, 102881. Advance online publication. DOI: 10.1016/j.jretconser.2021.102881

Hossain, M. S., Rahman, M. F., & Zhou, X. (2021). Impact of customers' interpersonal interactions in social commerce on customer relationship management performance. *Journal of Contemporary Marketing Science, 4*(1), 161–181. DOI: 10.1108/JCMARS-12-2020-0050

Hossain, M., Zhou, X., & Rahman, M. (2018). Examining the impact of QR codes on purchase intention and customer satisfaction on the basis of perceived flow. *International Journal of Engineering Business Management, 10*, 1–11. DOI: 10.1177/1847979018812323

Hovland, C. I., & Weiss, W. (1951). The influence of source credibility on communication effectiveness. *Public Opinion Quarterly, 15*(4), 635–650. DOI: 10.1086/266350

Hsieh, J.-K., Hsieh, Y.-C., Chiu, H.-C., & Yang, Y.-R. (2014). Customer Response to Web Site Atmospherics: Task-relevant Cues, Situational Involvement and PAD. *Journal of Interactive Marketing, 28*(3), 225–236. DOI: 10.1016/j.intmar.2014.03.001

Hsu, C. L., Chang, K. C., & Chen, M. C. (2011). The impact of website quality on customer satisfaction and purchase intention: Perceived playfulness and perceived flow as mediators. *Information Systems and e-Business Management, 10*(4), 549–570. DOI: 10.1007/s10257-011-0181-5

Huang, T.-L., & Liao, S.-L. (2017). Creating e-shopping multisensory flow experience through augmented-reality interactive technology. *Internet Research, 27*(2), 449–475. DOI: 10.1108/IntR-11-2015-0321

Hughes, H. L. (2000). *Arts, Entertainment and Tourism.* Butterworth Heinemann.

Hughes, M., & Carlsen, J. (2010). The business of cultural heritage tourism: Critical success factors. *Journal of Heritage Tourism, 5*(1), 17–32. DOI: 10.1080/17438730903469805

Hu, L., & Ritchie, J. B. (1993). Measuring destination attractiveness: A contextual approach. *Journal of Travel Research, 32*(2), 25–34. DOI: 10.1177/004728759303200204

Hultman, M., Kazeminia, A., & Ghasemi, V. (2015). Intention to visit and willingness to pay premium for ecotourism. *Journal of Business Research, 68*(9), 1854–1861. DOI: 10.1016/j.jbusres.2015.01.013

Hunt, E. D. (1984). Travel, tourism and piety in the Roman Empire: A context for the beginnings of Christian pilgrimage. *Echos du monde classique. Échos du Monde Classique*, *28*(3), 391–417.

Hu, S., Akram, U., Ji, F., Zhao, Y., & Song, J. (2023). Does social media usage contribute to cross-border social commerce? An empirical evidence from SEM and fsQCA analysis. *Acta Psychologica*, *241*, 104083. DOI: 10.1016/j.actpsy.2023.104083 PMID: 37972439

Hussein, S., & Ahmed, E. (2022). Mobile Application for Tourism. *International Journal of Customer Relationship Marketing and Management*, *13*(1), 1–29. DOI: 10.4018/IJCRMM.290415

Hussin, N., Padlee, S. F., & Zulkiffli, S. N. A. (2021). Benefit Segmentation in Seaside Destination: A Domestic Tourism Perspective. *Estudios de Economía Aplicada*, *39*(10). Advance online publication. DOI: 10.25115/eea.v39i10.5341

Hu, X., Huang, Q., Zhong, X., Davison, R. M., & Zhao, D. (2016, December). The influence of peer characteristics and technical features of a social shopping website on a consumer's purchase intention. *International Journal of Information Management*, *36*(6), 1218–1230. DOI: 10.1016/j.ijinfomgt.2016.08.005

Hyde, K. F., & Harman, S. (2011). Motives for a secular pilgrimage to the gallipoli battlefields. *Tourism Management*, *32*(6), 1343–1351. DOI: 10.1016/j.tourman.2011.01.008

Ibrahim, I., Zukhri, N., & Rendy, R. (2019). From Nature Tourism to Ecotourism: Assessing The Ecotourism Principles Fulfillment of Tourism Natural Areas In Bangka Belitung. *Society*, *7*(2), 281–302. DOI: 10.33019/society.v7i2.111

Iliev, D. (2021). Consumption, motivation and experience in dark tourism: A conceptual and critical analysis. *Tourism Geographies*, *23*(5), 963–984. DOI: 10.1080/14616688.2020.1722215

Ilsever, J., Cyr, D., & Parent, M. (2007). EXTENDING MODELS OF FLOW AND E-LOYALTY. *Journal of Information Science and Technology*, *4*(2), 3–22.

Inskeep, E. (1991). *Tourism Planning: An Integrated and Sustainable Development Approach. VNR Tourism and Commercial Recreation Series*. Van Nostrad Reinhold.

Intelligence, A. (2024). *Who is the biggest OTA in Asia?* https://aggregateintelligence.com/who-is-the-biggest-ota-in-asia/. Accessed on 10 May 2025.

International Tourism to Reach Pre-Pandemic Levels in 2024 https://www.unwto.org/news/international-tourism-to-reach-pre-pandemic-levels-in-2024#:~:text=International%20tourism%20hit%20US%241.4,earned%20by%20destinations%20in%202019. (Accessed: March 13, 2024)

IPCC. (2007). IPCC Fourth Assessment Report: Climate change. In: Solomon, S., D, Q. (Eds.), *The Physical Science Basis.* Intergovernmental Panel on Climate Change. Cambridge.

IQ Air AirVisual. (2019). *2018 World Air Quality Report.* IQ Air.

Ivars-Baidal, J. A., Celdrán-Bernabeu, M. A., Femenia-Serra, F., Perles-Ribes, J. F., & Vera-Rebollo, J. F. (2023). Smart city and smart destination planning: Examining instruments and perceived impacts in Spain. *Cities (London, England), 137*(1), 104266. DOI: 10.1016/j.cities.2023.104266

Jakkilinki, R., Georgievski, M., & Sharda, N. (2007). Connecting Destinations with an Ontology-Based e-Tourism Planner. In M. Sigala, L. Mich, & J. Murphy (Eds). Information and Communication Technologies in Tourism 2007, (pp. 21-32), Springer-Verlag Wien.

Jamal, T. B., & Robinson, M. (2009). *The SAGE Handbook of Tourism Studies.* Sage Publications. DOI: 10.4135/9780857021076

Jang, S., & Namkung, Y. (2009). Perceived quality, emotions, and behavioral intentions: Application of an extended Mehrabian–Russell model to restaurants. *Journal of Business Research, 62*(4), 451–460. DOI: 10.1016/j.jbusres.2008.01.038

Javed, M., Tučková, Z., & Jibril, A. B. (2020). The role of social media on tourists' behavior: An empirical analysis of millennials from the Czech Republic. *Sustainability (Basel), 12*(18), 7735. DOI: 10.3390/su12187735

Jeong, M., & Shin, H. H. (2019, November 8). Tourists' Experiences with Smart Tourism Technology at Smart Destinations and Their Behavior Intentions. *Journal of Travel Research, 59*(8), 1464–1477. DOI: 10.1177/0047287519883034

Jiang, Q., & McCabe, S. (2023). Exploring fundamental motives of tourists visiting dark tourism sites. *Asia Pacific Journal of Tourism Research, 28*(6), 610–624. DOI: 10.1080/10941665.2023.2255313

Jia, S., Chi, O. H., Martinez, S. D., & Lu, L. (2025). When "old" meets "new": Unlocking the future of innovative technology implementation in heritage tourism. *Journal of Hospitality & Tourism Research (Washington, D.C.), 49*(3), 640–661. DOI: 10.1177/10963480231205767

Jiménez-Barreto, J., Rubio, N., Campo, S., & Molinillo, S. (2020, August). Linking the online destination brand experience and brand credibility with tourists' behavioral intentions toward a destination. *Tourism Management, 79*, 104101. DOI: 10.1016/j.tourman.2020.104101

Jordan, E. J., & Prayag, G. (2022). Residents' cognitive appraisals, emotions, and coping strategies at local dark tourism sites. *Journal of Travel Research, 61*(4), 887–902. DOI: 10.1177/00472875211004761

Josiassen, A., & Assaf, A. G. (2013). Look at me—I am flying: The influence of social visibility of consumption on tourism decisions. *Annals of Tourism Research, 40*, 155–175. DOI: 10.1016/j.annals.2012.08.007

Jovanović, V. (2016). The application of GIS and its components in tourism. *Yugoslav Journal of Operations Research, 18*(2).

Jureniene, V., & Radzevicius, M. (2022). Peculiarities of sustainable cultural development: A case of dark tourism in Lithuania. *Journal of Risk and Financial Management, 15*(6), 264. DOI: 10.3390/jrfm15060264

Kabadayi, S., & Gupta, R. (2005). Website loyalty: An empirical investigation of its antecedents. *International Journal of Internet Marketing and Advertising, 2*(4), 321–345. DOI: 10.1504/IJIMA.2005.008105

Kaplan, A. M., & Haenlein, M. (2010). Users of the world, unite! The challenges and opportunities of Social Media. *Business Horizons, 53*(1), 59–68. DOI: 10.1016/j.bushor.2009.09.003

Karali, E., Das, S., & Roy, A. (2021). The impact of climate change on rural tourism: Adaptation strategies and sustainability. *Tourism Management Perspectives, 40*(2), 100824.

Karl, M. (2018). Risk and Uncertainty in Travel Decision-Making: Tourist and Destination Perspective. *Journal of Travel Research, 57*(1), 129–146. DOI: 10.1177/0047287516678337

Kaur, P., Dhir, A., & Rajala, R. (2016). Assessing flow experience in social networking site based. *Computers in Human Behavior, 64*, 217–225. DOI: 10.1016/j.chb.2016.06.045

Kazak, A., Chetyrbok, P. V., & Oleinikov, N. N. (2020). Artificial intelligence in the tourism sphere. *IOP Conference Series. Earth and Environmental Science, 421*(4), 042020. Advance online publication. DOI: 10.1088/1755-1315/421/4/042020

Kemp, A., Gravios, R., Syrdal, H., & McDougal, E. (2023). Storytelling is not just for marketing: Cultivating a storytelling culture throughout the organization. *Business Horizons*, *66*(3), 313–324. Advance online publication. DOI: 10.1016/j.bushor.2023.01.008

Kencana, I. P. E. N., & Mertha, I. W. (2014). People Participation as Social Capital Form for Realizing Sustainable Ecotourism. *International Journal of Social, Management, Economics and Business Engineering*, *8*(10), 3014–3020.

Khamis, S., Ang, L., & Weiling, R. (2017). Self-branding, 'micro-celebrity' and the rise of social media influencers. *Celebrity Studies*, *8*(2), 191–208. DOI: 10.1080/19392397.2016.1218292

Khan, E. A., & Shambour, M. K. Y. (2018, January 1). An analytical study of mobile applications for Hajj and Umrah services. *Applied Computing and Informatics*. Elsevier B.V. DOI: 10.1016/j.aci.2017.05.004

Kim, D. Y., Vogt, C. A., & Knutson, B. J. (2015). Relationships among customer satisfaction, delight, and loyalty in the hospitality industry. *Journal of Hospitality & Tourism Research (Washington, D.C.)*, *39*(2), 170–197. DOI: 10.1177/1096348012471376

Kim, D., & Wang, Z. (2023). The ethics of virtuality: Navigating the complexities of human-like virtual influencers in the social media marketing realm. *Frontiers in Communication*, *8*, 1205610. DOI: 10.3389/fcomm.2023.1205610

Kim, E., Nam, D., & Stimpert, J. L. (2004). The Applicability of Porter's Generic Strategies in the Digital Age: Assumptions, Conjectures and Suggestions. *Journal of Management*, *30*(5), 569–589. DOI: 10.1016/j.jm.2003.12.001

Kim, M. G., Lee, A. R., Kwon, H. J., Kim, J. W., & Kim, I. K. (2018, December). Sharing medical questionnaries based on blockchain. In *2018 IEEE International Conference on Bioinformatics and Biomedicine (BIBM)* (pp. 2767-2769). IEEE. DOI: 10.1109/BIBM.2018.8621154

Kim, M. J., Lee, C. K., & Jung, T. (2020). Exploring consumer behavior in virtual reality tourism using an extended stimulus-organism-response model. *Journal of Travel Research*, *59*(1), 69–89. DOI: 10.1177/0047287518818915

Kim, N., & Kim, W. (2018, April). Do your social media lead you to make social deal purchases?Consumer-generated social referrals for sales via social commerce. *International Journal of Information Management*, *39*, 38–48. DOI: 10.1016/j.ijinfomgt.2017.10.006

Kim, S.-B., & Kwon, K.-J. (2018). Examining the Relationships of Image and Attitude on Visit Intention to Korea among Tanzanian College Students. *Sustainability (Basel)*, *10*(360), 360. DOI: 10.3390/su10020360

Kim, S.-H., Whaley, J., & Choi, Y. (2022). Managing the restaurant experience: Re-specifying the role of food, interaction, and atmosphere as contributors to the optimal flow experience. *Journal of Foodservice Business Research*, •••, 1–22. DOI: 10.1080/15378020.2022.2047573

Klemes, J. J. (2015). *Assessing and Measuring Environmental Impact and Sustainability*. Elsevier.

Kontogianni, A., & Alepis, E. (2020). Smart tourism: State of the art and literature review for the last six years. *Array (New York, N.Y.)*, *6*(February), 100020. DOI: 10.1016/j.array.2020.100020

Korstanje, M. E., & Seraphin, H. (2020). The dark tourist: Consuming dark spaces in the periphery. In Korstanje, M. E., & Seraphin, H. (Eds.), *Tourism, terrorism and security* (pp. 135–150). Emerald Publishing Limited. DOI: 10.1108/978-1-83867-905-720201009

Kothari, C. R. (2014). *Research Methodology: Methods and techniques*. New Age International.

Kotler, P., Bowen, J. T., & Makens, J. C. (2017). *Marketing for Hospitality and Tourism* (7th ed.). Pearson.

Koufaris, M. (2002). Applying the Technology Acceptance Model and Flow Theory to Online Consumer Behavior. *Information Systems Research*, *13*(2), 115–225. DOI: 10.1287/isre.13.2.205.83

Koushik, A. N., Manoj, M., & Nezamuddin, N. (2020, January 7). Machine learning applications in activity-travel behaviour research: A review. *Transport Reviews*, *40*(3), 288–311. DOI: 10.1080/01441647.2019.1704307

Koutsou, S. (2019). The socio-economic impact of rural tourism in Greece: Opportunities and challenges. *International Journal of Tourism Research*, *21*(1), 30–40.

Kozak, M., & Rimmington, M. (2000). Tourist satisfaction with Mallorca, Spain, as an off-season holiday destination. *Journal of Travel Research*, *38*(3), 260–269. DOI: 10.1177/004728750003800308

Kumaj Jena, P. (2010). Indian handicrafts in globalization times: An analysis of global-local dynamics. *Interdisciplinary Description of Complex Systems: INDECS*, *8*(2), 119–137.

Kumar, A., Prakash, G., & Kumar, G. (2021). Does environmentally responsible purchase intention matter for consumers? A predictive sustainable model developed through an empirical study. *Journal of Retailing and Consumer Services*, *58*, 102270. DOI: 10.1016/j.jretconser.2020.102270

Kumar, D., Zulkifli, N., & Ray, N. (2023). Identifying Critical Factors for Sustainable Tourism and Local Community Development: Evidence from Select Destinations in Bangladesh. *ASEAN Journal on Hospitality and Tourism*, *21*(1), 124–135. DOI: 10.5614/ajht.2023.21.1.09

Kuo, C. M., Chen, L. C., & Tseng, C. Y. (2017). Investigating an innovative service with hospitality robots. *International Journal of Contemporary Hospitality Management*, *29*(5), 1305–1321. DOI: 10.1108/IJCHM-08-2015-0414

Kurtz, L. R. (2015). *Gods in the global village: the world's religions in sociological perspective*. Sage Publications.

Lacanienta, A., Ellis, G., Hill, B., Freeman, P., & Jiang, J. (2020). Provocation and related subjective experiences along the dark tourism spectrum. *Journal of Heritage Tourism*, *15*(6), 626–647. DOI: 10.1080/1743873X.2020.1739055

Lages, C. R., Perez-Vega, R., Kadić-Maglajlić, S., & Borghei-Razavi, N. (2023). A systematic review and bibliometric analysis of the dark side of customer behavior: An integrative customer incivility framework. *Journal of Business Research*, *161*, 113779. DOI: 10.1016/j.jbusres.2023.113779

Lam, J. M. S., Ismail, H., & Lee, S. (2020). From desktop to destination: User-generated content platforms, co-created online experiences, destination image and satisfaction. *Journal of Destination Marketing & Management*, *18*, 100490. DOI: 10.1016/j.jdmm.2020.100490

Lamsiah, A., & Bentalha, B. (2022). Dakhla: A Growing Touristic Destination with a Diplomatic Sway. *Alternatives Managériales Economiques*, *1*, 94–115.

Lane, B. (1994). What is rural tourism? *Journal of Sustainable Tourism*, *2*(1-2), 7–21. DOI: 10.1080/09669589409510680

Lane, B., & Kastenholz, E. (2015). Rural tourism: The evolution of practice and research approaches – towards a new generation concept? *Journal of Sustainable Tourism*, *23*(8-9), 1133–1156. DOI: 10.1080/09669582.2015.1083997

Lavvas, G. P. (2001). *Cultural heritage*. Department of Communication and Mass Media, University of Athens. (in Greek)

Law, R., Buhalis, D., & Cobanoglu, C. (2014). Progress on information and communication technologies in hospitality and tourism. *International Journal of Contemporary Hospitality Management, 26*(5), 727–750. DOI: 10.1108/IJCHM-08-2013-0367

Leask, A., & Fyall, A. (Eds.). (2006). *Managing World Heritage Sites*. Butterworth-Heinemann. DOI: 10.4324/9780080461755

Lebreton, L. C., Zwet, J. d., Damsteeg, J.-W., Slat, B., Andrady, A., & Reisser, J. "River plastic emissions to the world's oceans," 7th June 2017. Online. Available: https://www.nature.com/articles/ncomms15611

Lee, P., Hunter, W. C., & Chung, N. (2020, May 12). Smart Tourism City: Developments and Transformations. *Sustainability (Basel), 12*(10), 3958. DOI: 10.3390/su12103958

Lee, S., Han, H., Radic, A., & Tariq, B. (2020). Corporate social responsibility (CSR) as a customer satisfaction and retention strategy in the chain restaurant sector. *Journal of Hospitality and Tourism Management, 45*, 348–358. DOI: 10.1016/j.jhtm.2020.09.002

Lee, T. H., & Jan, F.-H. (2018). Ecotourism Behavior of Nature-Based Tourists: An Integrative Framework. *Journal of Travel Research, 57*(6), 792–810. DOI: 10.1177/0047287517717350

Lee, W. J., & Kim, Y. H. (2021, January 15). Does VR Tourism Enhance Users' Experience? *Sustainability (Basel), 13*(2), 806. DOI: 10.3390/su13020806

Lee, W., & Jeong, C. (2019). Beyond the correlation between tourist eudaimonic and hedonic experiences: Necessary condition analysis. *Tourism Management, 73*, 2182–2194.

Lee, W., & Jeong, C. (2020). Beyond the correlation between tourist eudaimonic and hedonic experiences: Necessary condition analysis. *Current Issues in Tourism, 23*(18), 2182–2194. DOI: 10.1080/13683500.2019.1611747

Lemy, D. M., Teguh, F., & Pramezwary, A. (2020). Tourism Development in Indonesia. *Establishment of Sustainable Strategies. Emerald Publishing Ltd, 11*, 91–108.

Lennon, J. J., & Powell, R. (2018). Dark tourism and cities. *International Journal of Tourism Cities, 4*(1), 1–3. DOI: 10.1108/IJTC-03-2018-086

Lewis, RC (1980). Benefit segmentation for restaurant Advertisement. *Cornell HRA Quarterly,* 6-12

Lewis, H., Schrier, T., & Xu, S. (2022). *Dark tourism: Motivations and visit intentions of tourists*. International Hospitality Review.

Liao, H.-C., Shen, Y.-C., & Chu, C.-Y. H.-H. (2010). Virtual Community Loyalty: An Interpersonal-Interaction Perspective. *International Journal of Electronic Commerce*, *15*(1), 49–74. DOI: 10.2753/JEC1086-4415150102

Light, D. (2017). Progress in dark tourism and thanatourism research: An uneasy relationship with heritage tourism. *Tourism Management*, *61*, 275–301. DOI: 10.1016/j.tourman.2017.01.011

Li, M., Yin, D., Qiu, H., & Bai, B. (2021). A systematic review of AI technology-based service encounters: Implications for hospitality and tourism operations. *International Journal of Hospitality Management*, *95*, 102930. Advance online publication. DOI: 10.1016/j.ijhm.2021.102930

Lin, J., Li, T., & Guo, J. (2021). Factors influencing consumers' continuous purchase intention on fresh food e-commerce platforms: An organic foods-centric empirical investigation. *Electronic Commerce Research and Applications*, *50*, 101103. DOI: 10.1016/j.elerap.2021.101103

Lin, N. (1999). Building a network theory of social capital. *Connections*, *22*(1), 28–51.

Lin, Y. K., & Nawijn, J. (2020). The impact of travel motivation on emotions: A longitudinal study. *Journal of Destination Marketing & Management*, *16*, 16. DOI: 10.1016/j.jdmm.2019.05.006

Liu, C., Bao, Z., & Zheng, C. (2019). Exploring consumers' purchase intention in social commerce: An empirical study based on trust, argument quality, and social presence. *Asia Pacific Journal of Marketing and Logistics*, *31*(2), 378–397. DOI: 10.1108/APJML-05-2018-0170

Liu, H., Chu, H., Huang, Q., & Chen, X. (2016, May). Enhancing the flow experience of consumers in China through interpersonal interaction in social commerce. *Computers in Human Behavior*, *58*, 306–314. DOI: 10.1016/j.chb.2016.01.012

Liu, Z., & Wang, C. (2019). Design of traffic emergency response system based on internet of things and data mining in emergencies. *IEEE Access : Practical Innovations, Open Solutions*, *7*, 113950–113962. DOI: 10.1109/ACCESS.2019.2934979

Li, Y., Lau, C., & Su, P. (2020). Heritage tourism stakeholder conflict: A case of a World Heritage Site in China. *Journal of Tourism and Cultural Change*, *18*(3), 267–287. DOI: 10.1080/14766825.2020.1722141

Li, Z., Wang, D., Abbas, J., Hassan, S., & Mubeen, R. (2022). Tourists' health risk threats amid COVID-19 era: Role of technology innovation, Transformation, and recovery implications for sustainable tourism. *Frontiers in Psychology*, *12*, 769175. DOI: 10.3389/fpsyg.2021.769175 PMID: 35465147

Longmatey, D., Samuel, A., & Prah, B. K. (2002), Management and Promotion of Tourism in Ghana: A GIS Approach from African Tourism Websites. Retrieved on May 20, 2015. http://www.africantourism.com/ghana.htm

Looi, J., & Kahlor, L. A. (2024). Artificial intelligence in influencer marketing: A mixed-method comparison of human and virtual influencers on Instagram. *Journal of Interactive Advertising*, *24*(2), 107–126. DOI: 10.1080/15252019.2024.2313721

Lordkipanidze, M., Brezet, H., & Backman, M. (2005). The entrepreneurship factor in sustainable tourism development. *Journal of Cleaner Production*, *13*(8), 787–798. DOI: 10.1016/j.jclepro.2004.02.043

Loulanski, T. (2006). Revising the concept for cultural heritage: The argument for a functional approach. *International Journal of Cultural Property*, *13*(2), 207–233. DOI: 10.1017/S0940739106060085

Loureiro, S. M. C., Guerreiro, J., & Ali, F. (2020). 20 years of research on virtual reality and augmented reality in tourism context: A text-mining approach. *Tourism Management*, *77*(October 2019). DOI: 10.1016/j.tourman.2019.104028

Loureiro, S. M., Sarmento, E. M., & Rosário, J. F. (2020). Incorporating VR, AR, and Related Technologies in the Tourism Industry: State of the Art. *Managerial Challenges and Social Impacts of Virtual and Augmented Reality*, 211-233. DOI: 10.4018/978-1-7998-2874-7.ch013

Lovelock & Wright. (1999). *Principals of Service Marketing and Management translated by AbolfazalTajzadeh*. Samt Publication.

Lu, A. C. C., Gursoy, D., & Chiappa, G. D. (2016). The Influence of Materialism on Ecotourism Attitudes and Behaviors. *Journal of Travel Research*, *55*(2), 176–189. DOI: 10.1177/0047287514541005

Lu, B., & Chen, Z. (2021). Live streaming commerce and consumers' purchase intention: An uncertainty reduction perspective. *Information & Management*, *58*(7), 103509. DOI: 10.1016/j.im.2021.103509

Lu, B., Fan, W., & Zhou, M. (2016). Social presence, trust, and social commerce purchase intention: An empirical research. *Computers in Human Behavior*, *56*, 225–237. DOI: 10.1016/j.chb.2015.11.057

Lukman, H. (2017). Partisipasi Masyarakat Dalam Pembangunan Desa Sukamerta Kecamatan Rawamerta Kabupaten Karawang. *Jurnal Politikom Indonesiana*, *2*(2), 43–53.

Luz, N. (2020). Pilgrimage and religious tourism in Islam. *Annals of Tourism Research*, *82*, 102915. DOI: 10.1016/j.annals.2020.102915

Lv, X., Lu, R., Xu, S., Sun, J., & Yang, Y. (2022). Exploring visual embodiment effect in dark tourism: The influence of visual darkness on dark experience. *Tourism Management*, *89*, 89. DOI: 10.1016/j.tourman.2021.104438

MacDonald, R., & Joliffe, L. (2003). Cultural rural tourism: Evidence from Canada. *Annals of Tourism Research*, *30*(2), 307–322. DOI: 10.1016/S0160-7383(02)00061-0

Maczynska, P. (2024). Holistic Travel Wellness: Designing Wearable Technologies to Improve Long-Distance Flight Comfort.

Magano, J., Fraiz-Brea, J. A., & Ângela Leite, . (2023). Dark tourism, the Holocaust, and well-being: A systematic review. *Heliyon*, *9*(1), e13064. DOI: 10.1016/j.heliyon.2023.e13064 PMID: 36711286

Magano, J., Fraiz-Brea, J. A., & Leite, Â. (2022). Dark tourists: Profile, practices, motivations, and wellbeing to visit it. *International Journal of Environmental Research and Public Health*, *19*(19), 12100. DOI: 10.3390/ijerph191912100 PMID: 36231400

Magasic, M., & Gretzel, U. (2020). Travel connectivity. *Tourist Studies*, *146879761989934*(1), 3–26. Advance online publication. DOI: 10.1177/1468797619899343

Maheshwari, N., Singh, V., Singh, A., & Ansari, A. I. (2024). Understanding Artificial Intelligence Adoption in Tourism Services and Marketing: Boon or Bane? In Nadda, V., Tyagi, P., Singh, A., & Singh, V. (Eds.), *AI Innovations in Service and Tourism Marketing* (pp. 359–374). IGI Global., DOI: 10.4018/979-8-3693-7909-7.ch018

Maia, C., Lunardi, G., Longaray, A., & Munhoz, P. (2018). Factors and characteristics that influence consumers' participation in social commerce. *Revista de Gestão*, *25*(2), 194–211. DOI: 10.1108/REGE-03-2018-031

Mak, J. (2008). *Developing a dream destination: Tourism and tourism policy planning in Hawaii*. University of Hawaii Press. DOI: 10.21313/hawaii/9780824832438.001.0001

Makur, M. "New Study Aims to Solve Waste Problems in Komodo National Park," 07 November 2017. Online. Available: https://www.thejakartapost.com/news/2017/11/07/new-study-aims-to-solve-waste-problems-in-komodo-national-park.html

Manaf, N. A., Situmorang, D. S., & Rosalina, M. (2018). Rural tourism entrepreneurship: Exploring the role of local communities. *International Journal of Tourism Research*, *20*(6), 732–745.

Mardhiyah, D., Hartini, S., & Kristanto, D. (2020). An integrated model of the adoption of information technology in travel service. *International Journal of Innovation. Creativity and Change*, *11*(11), 283–299.

Mariani, M. M., Baggio, R., Fuchs, M., & Hoepflinger, F. (2019). The role of attitude and motivation in tourists' pro-environmental behaviour: A comparative analysis of Alpine and coastal destinations. *Journal of Sustainable Tourism*, *27*(9), 951–972.

Market Research Future. (2025). *Indonesia Travel and Tourism Market Overview Source*. https://www.marketresearchfuture.com/reports/indonesia-travel-and-tourism-market-44301. Accessed on 10 May 2025.

Martins, J., Costa, C., Oliveira, T., Gonçalves, R., & Branco, F. (2019). How smartphone advertising influences consumers' purchase intention. *Journal of Business Research*, *94*, 378–387. DOI: 10.1016/j.jbusres.2017.12.047

Mathwick, C., & Rigdon, E. (2004, September). Play, Flow, and the Online Search Experience. *The Journal of Consumer Research*, *31*(2), 324–332. DOI: 10.1086/422111

Mazursky, D., & Jacoby, J. (1986). Exploring the development of store images. *Journal of Retailing*.

Mazzetto, S. (2024). Integrating Emerging Technologies with Digital Twins for Heritage Building Conservation: An Interdisciplinary Approach with Expert Insights and Bibliometric Analysis. *Heritage*, *7*(11), 6432–6479. DOI: 10.3390/heritage7110300

McIntosh, R., & Goeldner, C. (1990). *Tourism: Principles, Practices, Philosophies* (6th ed.). John Wiley & Sons, Inc.

McKercher, B. (2002). Towards a classification of cultural tourists. *International Journal of Tourism Research*, *4*(1), 29–38. DOI: 10.1002/jtr.346

McKercher, B., & Du Cros, H. (2002). *Cultural tourism: The partnership between tourism and cultural heritage management*. Routledge.

McKercher, B., & Du Cros, H. (2003). Testing a cultural tourism typology. *International Journal of Tourism Research*, *5*(1), 45–58. DOI: 10.1002/jtr.417

Mehrabian, A., & Russell, J. (1974). *An approach to environmental psychology*. The MIT Press.

Mehraliyev, F., Chan, I. C. C., Choi, Y., Koseoglu, M. A., & Law, R. (2020). A state-of-the-art review of smart tourism research. *Journal of Travel & Tourism Marketing*, *37*(1), 78–91. DOI: 10.1080/10548408.2020.1712309

Mele, C. (2000). *Selling the lower east side: Culture, real estate, and resistance in New York City* (Vol. 5). U of Minnesota Press.

Meng, F., Tepanon, Y., & Uysal, M. (2008). Measuring tourist satisfaction by attribute and motivation: The case of nature-based resort. *Journal of Travel Research*, *47*(1), 73–85.

Meskell, L. (2002). Negative heritage and past mastering in archaeology. *Anthropological Quarterly*, *75*(3), 557–574. DOI: 10.1353/anq.2002.0050

Meziane, B., Alla, L., & Bentalha, B. (2025). Transformational Trends of Territorial Economic Intelligence Strategies in the Digital Era: A Systematic Theoretical Exploration. In Utilizing Technology to Manage Territories (pp. 455-490). IGI Global.

Middleton, V. T. C. (1994). *Marketing in Travel and Tourism*. Butterworth-Heinemann.

Mihajlovic, I. (2012). The impact of information and communication technology (ICT) as a key factor of tourism development on the role of Croatian travel agencies. *International Journal of Business and Social Science*, *3*(24).

Mihanyar, P., Rahman, S. A., & Aminudin, N. (2015). "The Influence of Sustainable Tourism Awareness and Environmental Sustainability Dimensions on Behavioural Intentions Among Domestic Tourists in Developing Countries," *ourism. Leisure and Global Change*, *2*, TOC-119.

Milano, C., Novelli, M., & Cheer, J. M. (2019). Overtourism and tourismphobia: A journey through four decades of tourism development, planning and local concerns. *Tourism Planning & Development*, *16*(4), 353–357. DOI: 10.1080/21568316.2019.1599604

Miller, L. J., & Lu, W. "Gen Z Is Set to Outnumber Millennials Within a Year," Bloomberg, 20 August 2018. Online. Available: https://www.bloomberg.com/news/articles/2018-08-20/gen-z-to-outnumber-millennials-within-a-year-demographic-trends

Mill, R. C. (1990). *Tourism: The international business*. Prentice Hall.

Mill, R. C., & Morrison, A. M. (1992). *The Tourism System*.

Mill, R. C., & Mossison, A. M. (1992). *The Tourism System: An Introductory text* (2nd ed.). Prentice Hall.

Min, J., Yang, K., & Thapa Magar, A. (2021). Dark tourism segmentation by tourists' motivations for visiting earthquake sites in Nepal: Implications for dark tourism. *Asia Pacific Journal of Tourism Research*, *26*(8), 866–878. DOI: 10.1080/10941665.2021.1925315

Mirzaalian, F., & Halpenny, E. (2021, June). Exploring destination loyalty: Application of social media analytics in a nature-based tourism setting. *Journal of Destination Marketing & Management*, *20*, 100598. Advance online publication. DOI: 10.1016/j.jdmm.2021.100598

Mitchell, T. M. (1997, January 1). *Machine Learning*. http://books.google.ie/books?id=EoYBngEACAAJ&dq=machine+learning+by+Tom+Mitchell&hl=&cd=1&source=gbs_api

Mohaidin, Z., Wei, K. T., & Ali Murshid, M. (2017). Factors influencing the tourists' intention to select sustainable tourism destination: A case study of Penang, Malaysia. *International Journal of Tourism Cities*, *3*(4), 442–465. DOI: 10.1108/IJTC-11-2016-0049

Mohseni, S., Jayashree, S., Rezaei, S., Kasim, A., & Okumus, F. (2018). Attracting tourists to travel companies' websites: The structural relationship between website brand, personal value, shopping experience, perceived risk and purchase intention. *Current Issues in Tourism*, *21*(6), 616–645. DOI: 10.1080/13683500.2016.1200539

Mora, J. A., Nieto, A., & León-Gómez, A. (2023). A bibliometric analysis and systematic review of dark tourism: Trends, impact, and prospects. *Administrative Sciences*, *13*(11).

Morgan, C., & Morgan, D. C. (1990). *Athletes and oracles: The transformation of Olympia and Delphi in the eighth century BC*. Cambridge University Press.

Morrison, A. M., Taylor, S., Morrison, A. J., & Morrison, A. D. (1999). Marketing small hotels on the World Wide Web. *Information Technology & Tourism*, *2*(2), 97–113.

Mousavi, S. S., Doratli, N., Mousavi, S. N., & Moradiahari, F. (2016, December). Defining cultural tourism. In *International Conference on Civil, Architecture and Sustainable Development* (Vol. 1, No. 2, pp. 70-75).

Muaz, H., Rinekso, S. A., & Susilo, H. (2017). Potensi Daya Tarik Ekowisata Suaka Margasatwa Bukit Batu Kabupaten Bengkalis Provinsi Riau. *Jurnal Penelitian Sosial Dan Ekonomi Kehutanan*, *14*(1), 39–56. DOI: 10.20886/jpsek.2017.14.1.39-56

Mullis, B. (2017). *The growth paradox: can tourism ever be sustainable?* World Economic Forum: https://www.weforum.org/stories/2017/08/the-growth-paradox-can-tourism-ever-be-sustainable/. Accessed on 10 May 2025.

Munjal, P. G. (2021). Charting the role of digital platforms for cultural heritage tourism in India. *Worldwide Hospitality and Tourism Themes*, *13*(2), 186–198. DOI: 10.1108/WHATT-10-2020-0126

Muthoo, A., & Onul, B. (1996). Rural tourism and its role in economic development. *Tourism Economics*, *2*(4), 309–321.

Myers, F. R. (2002). *Painting culture: the making of an aboriginal high art*. Duke University Press.

Nadkarni, S., & Teare, R. (2019). Reflections on the theme issue outcomes: Expo 2020: what will be the impact on Dubai? *Worldwide Hospitality and Tourism Themes*, *11*(3), 346–350. DOI: 10.1108/WHATT-03-2019-0013

Nag, A., & Mishra, S. (2024). Sustainable competitive advantage in heritage tourism: Leveraging cultural legacy in a data-driven world. [). Emerald Publishing Limited.]. *Review of Technologies and Disruptive Business Strategies*, *3*, 137–162. DOI: 10.1108/S2754-586520240000003008

Nandasena, R., Morrison, A. M., & Coca-Stefaniak, J. A. (2022). Transformational tourism – a systematic literature review and research agenda. *Journal of Tourism Futures*, *8*(3), 282–297. DOI: 10.1108/JTF-02-2022-0038

Natour, S. A., Benbasat, I., & Cenfetelli, R. T. (2005). The Role of Similarity in e-Commerce Interactions:The Case of Online Shopping Assistants. *SIGHCI 2005 proceedings.4*. Retrieved from https://aisel.aisnet.org/sighci2005/4

Nautiyal, R., & Polus, R. (2022). Virtual tours as a solidarity tourism product? *Annals of Tourism Research Empirical Insights*, *3*(2), 100066. DOI: 10.1016/j.annale.2022.100066

Navarrete, T. (2019). Digital heritage tourism: Innovations in museums. *World Leisure Journal*, *61*(3), 200–214. DOI: 10.1080/16078055.2019.1639920

Nayyar, A., Mahapatra, B., Le, D., & Suseendran, G. (2018). Virtual Reality (VR) & Augmented Reality (AR) technologies for tourism and hospitality industry. *International journal of engineering & technology, 7*(2.21), 156-160.

Negi, J. (1990). Rural tourism in the Third World: Promises and problems. *Annals of Tourism Research*, *17*(4), 476–484.

Neto, F. (2003, August). A new approach to sustainable tourism development: Moving beyond environmental protection. [). Oxford, UK: Blackwell Publishing Ltd.]. *Natural Resources Forum*, 27(3), 212–222. DOI: 10.1111/1477-8947.00056

Ng, C. S.-P. (2013). Intention to purchase on socia lcommerce websites across cultures: Across-regional study. *Information & Management*, 50(8), 609–620. DOI: 10.1016/j.im.2013.08.002

Nguyen, M. H., Armoogum, J., Madre, J. L., & Garcia, C. (2020, August). Reviewing trip purpose imputation in GPS-based travel surveys. [English Edition]. *Journal of Traffic and Transportation Engineering*, 7(4), 395–412. DOI: 10.1016/j.jtte.2020.05.004

Nguyen, T. H. H., & Cheung, C. (2014). The classification of heritage tourists: A case of Hue city, Vietnam. *Journal of Heritage Tourism*, 9(1), 35–50. DOI: 10.1080/1743873X.2013.818677

Nhlabathi, S. S., & Maharaj, B. (2020). The dark tourism discipline: A creative brand in a competitive academic environment? *Current Issues in Tourism*, 23(19), 2428–2439. DOI: 10.1080/13683500.2019.1636770

Niemczyk, A. (2013). Cultural tourists: "An attempt to classify them". *Tourism Management Perspectives*, 5, 24–30. DOI: 10.1016/j.tmp.2012.09.006

Noor, N. M. M., lina Ahm, I. A., Ali, N. H., & Ismail, F. (2010). Intelligent decision support system for tourism destination choice: A preliminary study. In *2010 International Symposium on Information Technology* (Vol. 3, pp. 1357-1361). IEEE. DOI: 10.1109/ITSIM.2010.5561594

Nørfelt, A., Kock, F., Karpen, I. O., & Josiassen, A. (2022). Pleasure through pain: An empirical examination of benign masochism in tourism. *Journal of Travel Research*.

Novak, T. P., Hoffman, D. L., & Yung, Y.-F. (2000). Measuring the Customer Experience in Online Environments: A Structural Modeling Approach. *Marketing Science*, 19(1), 22–42. DOI: 10.1287/mksc.19.1.22.15184

Novak, T., Hoffman, D., & Duhachek, A. (2003). The Influence of Goal-Directed and Experiential Activities on Online Flow Experiences. *Journal of Consumer Psychology*, 13(1), 3–16. DOI: 10.1207/153276603768344744

Nugroho, I., & Dahuri, I. (2012). *Pembangunan Wilayah: Perspektif ekonomi, sosial, dan lingkungan (second ed)*. Jakarta: LP3ES, Jakarta.

Nugroho, I., & Negara, P. D. (2015). *Pengembangan Desa Melalui: Dilengkapi dengan peraturan perundangan tentang pedoman pengembangan desa wisata*. Solo: Era Adicitra Intermedia.

Nugroho, I. (2011). *Ekowisata dan pembangunan berkelanjutan* (1st ed.). Pustaka Pelajar, Yogyakarta.

Nugroho, I., Negara, P. D., & Yuniar, H. R. (2018). The Planning and The Development of The Ecotourism and Tourism Village in Indonesia: A Policy Review. *Journal of Socioeconomics and Development*, *1*(1), 43–51. DOI: 10.31328/jsed.v1i1.532

Nugroho, I., Pramukanto, F. H., Negara, P. D., Purnomowati, W., & Wulandari, W. (2016). Promoting the Rural Development through the Ecotourism Activities in Indonesia. *American Journal of Tourism Management*, *5*(1), 9–18.

Nuraini, Satria, A., & Sri, W. E. (2019). Mekanisme Akses Dan Kekuasaan Dalam Memperkuat Kinerja Institusi Pengelolaan Ekowisata Bahari. *Sodality: Jurnal Sosiologi Pedesaan*, 65–77.

Nusair, K., Butt, I., & Nikhashemi, S. R. (2019). A bibliometric analysis of social media in hospitality and tourism research. *International Journal of Contemporary Hospitality Management*, *31*(7), 2691–2719. DOI: 10.1108/IJCHM-06-2018-0489

O'Cass, A., & Carlson, J. (2010, April). Examining the effects of website-induced flow in professional sporting team websites. *Internet Research*, *20*(2), 115–134. DOI: 10.1108/10662241011032209

OECD. (2009). *The Impact of Tourism on Culture*. OECD.

Oh, J., Fiorito, S., Cho, H., & Hofackerd, C. (2008). Effects of design factors on store image and expectation of merchandise quality in web-based stores. *Journal of Retailing and Consumer Services*, *15*(4), 237–249. DOI: 10.1016/j.jretconser.2007.03.004

Oklevik, O., Gössling, S., Hall, C. M., Steen Jacobsen, J. K., Grøtte, I. P., & McCabe, S. (2019).

Oklevik, O., Gössling, S., Hall, C. M., Steen Jacobsen, J. K., Grøtte, I. P., & McCabe, S. (2019, December 02). Overtourism, optimisation, and destination performance indicators: A case study of activities in Fjord Norway. *Journal of Sustainable Tourism*, *27*(12), 1804–1824. DOI: 10.1080/09669582.2018.1533020

Oliveira, T., Araujo, B., & Tam, C. (2020, June). Why do people share their travel experiences on social media? *Tourism Management*, *78*, 104041. DOI: 10.1016/j.tourman.2019.104041 PMID: 32322615

Oliver, T. H., & Morecroft, M. D. (2014). Interactions Between Climate Change and Land Use Change. *Wiley Interdisciplinary Reviews: Climate Change*, 5(3), 318–329. DOI: 10.1002/wcc.271

Omran, W., Casais, B., & Ramos, R. F. (2025). Attributes of Virtual and Augmented Reality Tourism Mobile Applications Predicting Tourist Behavioral Engagement. *International Journal of Human-Computer Interaction*, •••, 1–14. DOI: 10.1080/10447318.2025.2470293

Oppland, M. (2021, February 15). *8 Ways To Create Flow According to Mihaly Csikszentmihalyi*. Retrieved March 5, 2021, from positivepsychology.com: https://positivepsychology.com/mihaly-csikszentmihalyi-father-of-flow/

Oren, G., Shani, A., & Poria, Y. (2021). Dialectical emotions in a dark heritage site: A study at the Auschwitz death camp. *Tourism Management*, 82, 104194. DOI: 10.1016/j.tourman.2020.104194

Origet de Cluzeau, C. (1998). *Le Tourisme Culturel*. Puf.

Ortega-Fraile, F. J., Ríos-Martín, M. Á., & Ceballos-Hernandez, C. (2018). Tourism and mobile devices: Provenance of academic research through a bibliometric study. *Journal of Tourism Analysis*, 25(1), 91–112. DOI: 10.1108/JTA-02-2018-0008

Otoo, F. E., Kim, S. S., & King, B. E. M. (2021). African diaspora tourism: How motivations shape experiences. *Journal of Destination Marketing & Management*, 20, 100565. DOI: 10.1016/j.jdmm.2021.100565

Ozturk, I., Aslan, A., & Altinoz, B. (2022). Investigating the nexus between CO_2 emissions, economic growth, energy consumption and pilgrimage tourism in Saudi Arabia. *Ekonomska Istrazivanja*, 35(1), 3083–3098. DOI: 10.1080/1331677X.2021.1985577

Packer, J., Ballantyne, R., & Hughes, K. (2014). Chinese and Australian tourists' attitudes to nature, animals and environmental issues: Implications for the design of nature-based tourism experiences. *Tourism Management*, 44, 101–107. DOI: 10.1016/j.tourman.2014.02.013

Pack, S. D. (2010). Revival of the Pilgrimage to Santiago de Compostela: The Politics of Religious, National, and European Patrimony, 1879–1988. *The Journal of Modern History*, 82(2), 335–367. DOI: 10.1086/651613

Padlee, S. F., Thaw, C. Y., & Zulkiffli, S. N. A. (2019). The relationship between service quality, customer satisfaction and behavioural intentions. *Tourism and Hospitality Management*, 25(1), 121–139. DOI: 10.20867/thm.25.1.9

Padmaja, N., Sudha, T., & Saurab, S. S. (2020). Application of Big Data in Forecasting the Travel Behaviour of International Tourists. *Learning and Analytics in Intelligent Systems, 263–271.*https://doi.org/DOI: 10.1007/978-3-030-46943-6_30

Page, M. J., Moher, D., Bossuyt, P. M., Boutron, I., Hoffmann, T. C., Mulrow, C. D., Shamseer, L., Tetzlaff, J. M., Akl, E. A., Brennan, S. E., Chou, R., Glanville, J., Grimshaw, J. M., Hróbjartsson, A., Lalu, M. M., Li, T., Loder, E. W., Mayo-Wilson, E., McDonald, S., & McKenzie, J. E. (2021). PRISMA 2020 explanation and elaboration: Updated guidance and exemplars for reporting systematic reviews. *British Medical Journal, 372,* 160. DOI: 10.1136/bmj.n160 PMID: 33781993

Page, S., & Getz, D. (1997). The business of rural tourism: International perspectives. *Journal of Sustainable Tourism, 5*(1), 35–48.

Pai, H. I. (2014). *Heritage management in Korea and Japan: The politics of antiquity and identity.* University of Washington Press. DOI: 10.1515/9780295804835

Pallud, J. (2017). Impact of interactive technologies on stimulating learning experiences in a museum. *Information & Management, 54*(4), 465–478. DOI: 10.1016/j.im.2016.10.004

Palomoa, J., Figueroa-Domecqa, C., FlechaBarrioa, M. D., & Segovia-Pérez, M. (2017). The use of new data analysis techniques in tourism: A Bibliometric

Pandey, O. K., & Chakraborty, R. (2007), GIS: Information technology for planning management and development of GOA tourism master plan in next millennium. Retrieved on May 20, 2015. http://www.gisdevelopment.net/application

Panigrahy, A., & Verma, A. (2025). Tourist experiences: a systematic literature review of computer vision technologies in smart destination visits. *Journal of Tourism Futures.*

Pan, S.-Y., Gao, M., Kim, H., Shah, K. J., Pei, S.-L., & Chiang, P.-C. (2018). Advances and Challenges in Sustainable Tourism toward a Green Economy. *The Science of the Total Environment, 635,* 452–469. DOI: 10.1016/j.scitotenv.2018.04.134 PMID: 29677671

Parady, G., Suzuki, K., Oyama, Y., & Chikaraishi, M. (2023). Activity detection with google maps location history data: Factors affecting joint activity detection probability and its potential application on real social networks. *Travel Behaviour & Society, 30,* 344–357. DOI: 10.1016/j.tbs.2022.10.010

Paresishvili, O., Kvaratskhelia, L., & Mirzaeva, V. (2017). Rural tourism as a promising trend of small business in Georgia: Topicality, capabilities, peculiarities. *Annals of Agrarian Science, 15*(3), 344–348. DOI: 10.1016/j.aasci.2017.07.008

Park, H. Y. (2013). *Heritage Tourism*. Routledge. DOI: 10.4324/9781315882093

Pavlou, P., & Fygenson, M. (2006). Understanding and Predicting Electronic Commerce Adoption: An Extension of the Theory of Planned Behavior. *MIS Quarterly, 30*(1). *Management Information Systems Quarterly, 30*(1), 115. Advance online publication. DOI: 10.2307/25148720

Payton, B. (2025). *To the ends of the Earth: The Arctic's battle for sustainable tourism*. Reuters: https://www.reuters.com/sustainability/society-equity/ends-earth-arctics-battle-sustainable-tourism-2025-04-29/. Accessed on 10 May 2025.

Peeters, P., & Dubois, G. (2010). Tourism travel under climate change mitigation constraints. *Journal of Transport Geography, 18*(3), 447–457. DOI: 10.1016/j.jtrangeo.2009.09.003

Pei, Y., & Zhang, Y. (2021, April 1). A Study on the Integrated Development of Artificial Intelligence and Tourism from the Perspective of Smart Tourism. *Journal of Physics: Conference Series, 1852*(3), 032016. DOI: 10.1088/1742-6596/1852/3/032016

Pencarelli, T. (2019, November 27). The digital revolution in the travel and tourism industry. *Information Technology & Tourism, 22*(3), 455–476. DOI: 10.1007/s40558-019-00160-3

Peng, S., Le, L., Hossain, M. S., & Zabin, S. (2025). Investigating Students' Behavioral Intention to use ChatGPT for Educational purposes. *Sustainable Futures : An Applied Journal of Technology, Environment and Society, 9*, 1–14. DOI: 10.1016/j.sftr.2025.100531

Perreault, W.Jr, & McCarthy, J. E. (1999). *Basic Marketing—A Global Managerial Approach*. Irwin/McGraw Hill.

Petrillo, P. L. (Ed.). (2019). *The Legal Protection of the Intangible Cultural Heritage: A Comparative Perspective*. Springer. DOI: 10.1007/978-3-319-72983-1

Pierce, T., Dobson, G., & Phillips, M. (2009), GIS Mashups on the Web: Using Google, ESRI, and Open Source to Develop Weather and Climate Applications for the Web, *Geospatial Infrastructure Solutions Conference*, April 2009, Tampa FL

Pillai, R., & Sivathanu, B. (2020). Adoption of AI-based chatbots for hospitality and tourism. *International Journal of Contemporary Hospitality Management, ahead-of-print*(ahead-of-print). https://doi.org/DOI: 10.1108/IJCHM-04-2020-0259

Podoshen, J. S., Yan, G., Andrzejewski, S. A., Wallin, J., & Venkatesh, V. (2018). Dark tourism, abjection and blood: A festival context. *Tourism Management, 64*, 346–356. DOI: 10.1016/j.tourman.2017.09.003

Popovic, T., Povoa, A. P., Krawslawski, A., & Carvalho, A. (2018, April). Quantitative Indicators for Social Sustainability Assessment of Supply. *Journal of Cleaner Production, 180*, 748–768. DOI: 10.1016/j.jclepro.2018.01.142

Porter, M. E., & Heppelmann, J. E. (2014). How smart, connected products are transforming competition. *Harvard Business Review, 92*(11), 64–88.

Pramanik, S. A. K., Hossain, E., & Azam, S. (2016). The Impacts of Visitors' Attitude on Visit Intention in the Context of Museum Applying SEM: Offering an Alternative Visit Intention Model. *Bangladesh Journal of Tourism, 1*(1).

Prayag, G., Buda, D.-M., & Jordan, E. J. (2021). Mortality salience and meaning in life for residents visiting dark tourism sites. *Journal of Sustainable Tourism, 29*(9), 1508–1528. DOI: 10.1080/09669582.2020.1823398

Preacher, K., & Hayes, A. (2008). Asymptotic and resampling strategies for assessing and comparing indirect effects in multiple mediator models. *Behavior Research Methods, 40*(3), 879–891. DOI: 10.3758/BRM.40.3.879 PMID: 18697684

Prebensen, N., Woo, E., & Uysal, M. S. (2014). Experience value: Antecedents and consequences. *Current Issues in Tourism, 17*(10), 910–928. DOI: 10.1080/13683500.2013.770451

Priatmoko, S., Rosalina, M., & Situmorang, D. (2023). Post-Covid sustainability and rural tourism: A focus on new trends. *Journal of Sustainable Tourism, 31*(2), 239–256.

Qalati, S. A., Vela, E. G., Li, W., Dakhan, S. A., Hong Thuy, T. T., & Merani, S. H. (2021). Effects of perceived service quality, website quality, and reputation on purchase intention: The mediating and moderating roles of trust and perceived risk in online shopping. *Cogent Business & Management, 8*(1), 1869363. Advance online publication. DOI: 10.1080/23311975.2020.1869363

Qian, L., Guo, J., Qiu, H., Zheng, C., & Ren, L. (2023). Exploring destination image of dark tourism via analyzing user generated photos: A deep learning approach. *Tourism Management Perspectives, 48*, 101147. DOI: 10.1016/j.tmp.2023.101147

Qian, L., Zheng, C., Wang, J., Pérez Sánchez, M. D. L. Á., Parra López, E., & Li, H. (2021). Dark tourism destinations: The relationships between tourists' on-site experience, destination image and behavioural intention. *Tourism Review*.

Qi, S., Law, R., & Buhalis, D. (2008). Usability of Chinese destination management organization websites. *Journal of Travel & Tourism Marketing*, 25(2), 182–198. DOI: 10.1080/10548400802402933

Rahman, M. K., Akter, S., Hossain, M. M., & Hassan, A. (2022). Pilgrimage and Halal Tourism Event: Application of Technology. In *Technology Application in Tourism Fairs, Festivals and Events in Asia* (pp. 63–75). Springer Nature. https://doi.org/DOI: 10.1007/978-981-16-8070-0_4

Rahman, F. B. A., Hanafiah, M. H., Zahari, M. S. M., & Jipiu, L. B. (2023). Social commerce adoption: A study on consumer's online purchase behaviour of perishable pastry products. *British Food Journal*, 125(1), 318–344. DOI: 10.1108/BFJ-07-2021-0796

Raine, R. (2013). A dark tourist spectrum. *International Journal of Culture, Tourism and Hospitality Research*, 7(3), 242–256. DOI: 10.1108/IJCTHR-05-2012-0037

Rajesh, R. (2013). Impact of Tourist Perceptions, Destination Image and Tourist Satisfaction on Destination Loyalty: A Conceptual Model. *Pasos (El Sauzal)*, 11(3), 67–78. DOI: 10.25145/j.pasos.2013.11.039

Rathore, S. (2020). Analyzing the influence of user-generated-content (UGC) on social media platforms in travel planning. https://doi.org/DOI: 10.5937/turizam24-24429

Rausch, T. M., & Kopplin, C. S. (2021, January). Rausch, Theresa Maria., & Kopplin, C. (2021). Bridge the gap: Consumers' purchase intention and behavior regarding sustainable clothing. *Journal of Cleaner Production*, 278, 123882. Advance online publication. DOI: 10.1016/j.jclepro.2020.123882

Ray N & Das D K (2011). 3Hs Tourism, An Alternative Approach of Developing Rural Tourism at Kamarpukur: An Empirical Study, South *Asian Journal of Tourism and Heritage Referred International Journal*, 4(2), India.

Ray N & Das D K, Ghosh S, Sengupta P P. (2012): Rural tourism and its Impact on Socio- Economic Condition: Evidence from West Bengal, India *Global Journal of Business Research* the IBFR, 6(2), Hilo, USA

Ray, N., Das, D. K., Ghosh, S., & Banerjee, A. (2011). A Study on Application of Information Technology on Tourism Development, IEEE Proceeding Catalog No: CFP1141H-ART ISBN978-1-4244-6579- China

Ray, N., Das, D. K., Sengupta, P. P., & Ghosh, S. (2011). Information Technology and Its Impact on Tourism: An Overview. In Khurana, R., Agrawal, R., & Debnath, C. (Eds.), *Computing Business Application and Legal Issues*. Excel Book Publication.

Reader, I. (2007). Pilgrimage growth in the modern world: Meanings and implications. *Religion*, *37*(3), 210–229. DOI: 10.1016/j.religion.2007.06.009

Reddy, T. L., & Thomson, R. J. "Environmental, Social and Economic Sustainability: Implications for Actuarial Science," in *ASTIN, AFIR/ERM and IACA Colloquia*, Sydney, 2015.

Rehman Khan, H. U., Lim, C. K., Ahmed, M. F., Tan, K. L., & Bin Mokhtar, M. (2021, July 21). Systematic Review of Contextual Suggestion and Recommendation Systems for Sustainable e-tourism. *Sustainability (Basel)*, *13*(15), 8141. DOI: 10.3390/su13158141

Reisinger, Y. (1994). Tourist—Host contact as a part of cultural tourism. *World Leisure & Recreation*, *36*(2), 24–28. DOI: 10.1080/10261133.1994.9673910

Remoaldo, P., Freitas, I., Matos, O., Lopes, H., Silva, S., Fernández, M. D. S., & Ribeiro, V. (2017). The planning of tourism on rural areas: The stakeholders' perceptions of the Boticas municipality (northeastern Portugal). *European Countryside*, *9*(3), 504–525. DOI: 10.1515/euco-2017-0030

Remoaldo, P., Serra, J., Marujo, N., Alves, J., Gonçalves, A., Cabeça, S., & Duxbury, N. (2020). Profiling the participants in creative tourism activities: Case studies from small and medium sized cities and rural areas from Continental Portugal. *Tourism Management Perspectives*, *36*, 100746. DOI: 10.1016/j.tmp.2020.100746 PMID: 32953432

Renaghan, L. M., & Kay, M. Z. (1987). What meeting planners want: The conjoint-analysis approach. *The Cornell Hotel and Restaurant Administration Quarterly*, *28*(1), 66–76.

Report on National Digital Tourism Mission (NDTM) | Ministry of Tourism | Government of India. (n.d.). https://tourism.gov.in/whats-new/report-national-digital-tourism-mission-ndtm

Reuters. (2024). *Driving sustainability in the critical world of digital infrastructure*. https://www.reuters.com/plus/acumen-stories/cop-28/eunetworks. Accessed on 10 May 2025.

Rhee, S., Kitchener, D., Brown, T., Merrill, R., Dilts, R., & Tighe, S., & USAID-Indonesia. (2004). (Submitted in). Report on Biodiversity and Tropical Forests in Indonesia. *Accordance with Foreign Assistance Act Sections*, *118/119*, 1–316.

Ribeiro, M. A., Woosnam, K. M., Pinto, P., & Silva, J. A. (2018). Tourists' destination loyalty through emotional solidarity with residents: An integrative moderated mediation model. *Journal of Travel Research*, *57*(3), 279–295. DOI: 10.1177/0047287517699089

Richards, G. (2001c) Creative Tourism as a Factor in Destination Development, ATLAS 10th Anniversary International Conference papers, 4–6 October, Dublin.

Richards, G. (1996). *Cultural Tourism in Europe*. CAB International.

Richards, G. (2001). *Cultural attractions and European tourism*. CABI. DOI: 10.1079/9780851994406.0000

Richards, G. (2007). *Globalisation, localisation and cultural tourism. Destinations revisited. Perspectives on developing and managing tourist areas*. ATLAS Reflections.

Richards, G. (2011). Creativity and tourism: The state of the art. *Annals of Tourism Research*, *38*(4), 1225–1253. DOI: 10.1016/j.annals.2011.07.008

Richards, G. (2013). Tourism development trajectories: From culture to creativity? In Smith, M. K., & Richards, G. (Eds.), *Routledge Handbook of Cultural Tourism* (pp. 297–303). Routledge.

Richards, G. (2014). *Tourism trends: The convergence of culture and tourism*. Academy for Leisure NHTV University of Applied Sciences.

Richards, G. (2015). Evolving gastronomic experiences: From food to foodies to foodscapes. *Journal of Gastronomy and Tourism*, *1*(1), 5–17. DOI: 10.3727/216929715X14298190828796

Richards, G. (2018). Cultural tourism: A review of recent research and trends. *Journal of Hospitality and Tourism Management*, *36*, 12–21. DOI: 10.1016/j.jhtm.2018.03.005

Richards, G. (2021). Business Models for Creative Tourism. *Journal of Hospitality and Tourism*, *19*(1), 1–13.

Richards, G. (Ed.). (2007). *Cultural tourism: Global and local perspectives*. Psychology Press.

Richards, G., & Hall, D. (2000). *Tourism and Sustainable Community Development*. Routledge.

Richards, G., & van der Ark, L. A. (2013). Dimensions of cultural consumption among tourists: Multiple correspondence analysis. *Tourism Management*, *37*, 71–76. DOI: 10.1016/j.tourman.2013.01.007

Rinschede, G. (1992). Forms of religious tourism. *Annals of Tourism Research*, *19*(1), 51–67. DOI: 10.1016/0160-7383(92)90106-Y

Roberts, L., & Hall, D. (2001). Rural tourism and recreation: Principles to practice. *Tourism and Hospitality Management*, *7*(3), 212–218.

Robinson, M., & Andersen, H. (Eds.). (2004). *Literature and Tourism: Essays in the Reading and Writing of Tourism*. Thomson International.

Rosli, A. B. A., & Zaki, N. A. M. (2022). Understanding The Impacts Of Covid-19 Pandemic On Consumer Behaviour In Malaysia. TIJARI International Journal of Islamic Economics, Bussiness and Entrepreneurship, 2(4).

Rosli, N. A., Zainuddin, Z., Yusliza, M. Y., Muhammad, Z., & Saputra, J. (2023). Investigating the effect of destination image on revisit intention through tourist satisfaction in Laguna Redang Island Resort, Terengganu. *International Journal of Advanced and Applied Sciences*, *10*(6), 17–27. DOI: 10.21833/ijaas.2023.06.003

Ross, S., & Wall, G. (1999). Ecotourism: Towards congruence between theory and practice. *Tourism Management*, *20*(1), 123–132. DOI: 10.1016/S0261-5177(98)00098-3

Rothberg, D. (1999). *Enhanced and Alternative Financing Mechanisms Strengthening National Park Management in Indonesia*.

Rowley, G., & El-Hamdan, S. A. S. (1978). The Pilgrimage to Mecca: An Explanatory and Predictive Model. Environment and Planning A. *Environment & Planning A*, *10*(9), 1053–1071. DOI: 10.1068/a101053 PMID: 12262752

Roy, G., Datta, B., Mukherjee, S., Basu, R., & Shrivastava, A. K. (2021). Effect of eWOM valence on purchase intention: The moderating role of product. *International Journal of Technology Marketing*, *15*(2-3), 158–180. DOI: 10.1504/IJTMKT.2021.118201

Rubright, H. L., Kline, C., Viren, P. P., Naar, A., & Oliver, J. (2016). Attraction Sustainability In North Carolina And Its Impact On Decision-Making. *Tourism Management Perspectives*, *19*, 1–10. DOI: 10.1016/j.tmp.2016.04.002

Ruiz-Real, J. L.. (2021). Climate change and rural tourism: Challenges and opportunities. *Journal of Tourism Futures*, *7*(1), 24–37.

Saarinen, J. (2014). Critical Sustainability: Setting the Limits to Growth and Responsibility in Tourism. *Sustainability (Basel)*, *6*(1), 1–17. DOI: 10.3390/su6010001

Saarinen, J.. (2017). Historical perspectives on rural tourism: Exploring the evolution of rural destinations. *Journal of Rural Tourism Studies*, *5*(3), 109–125.

Salameh, A. A., Al Mamun, A., Hayat, N., & Ali, M. H. (2022). Modelling the significance of website quality and online reviews to predict the intention and usage of online hotel booking platforms. *Heliyon, 8*(9), e10735. DOI: 10.1016/j.heliyon.2022.e10735 PMID: 36177224

Saluveer, E., Raun, J., Tiru, M., Altin, L., Kroon, J., Snitsarenko, T., Aasa, A., & Silm, S. (2020). Methodological framework for producing national tourism statistics from mobile positioning data. *Annals of Tourism Research, 81*, 102895. Advance online publication. DOI: 10.1016/j.annals.2020.102895

Samala, A. D., Ricci, M., Angel Rueda, C. J., Bojić, L., Ranuharja, F., & Agustiarmi, W. (2024). Exploring campus through web-based immersive adventures using virtual reality photography: A low-cost virtual tour experience. *International journal of online and biomedical engineering, 20*(1).

Sanyal, B. (2005). Hybrid planning cultures: The search for the global cultural commons. In *Comparative planning cultures* (pp. 27–50). Routledge.

Satpalda. (2024, March 4). *GIS in Tourism—SATPALDA*. https://satpalda.com/blogs/gis-in-tourism/

Satyarini, N. W. M., Rahmanita, M., & Setarnawat, S. (2017). The Influence of Destination Image on Tourist Intention and Decision to Visit Tourist Destination (A Case Study of Pemuteran Village in Buleleng, Bali, Indonesia). *TRJ Tourism Research Journal, 1*(1), 81–97. DOI: 10.30647/trj.v1i1.10

Saxena, S. K., Gupta, V., & Kumar, S. (2024). Enhancing Guest Loyalty in the Hotel Industry Through Artificial Intelligence-Drive Personalization. In *New Technologies in Virtual and Hybrid Events* (pp. 335–350). IGI Global. DOI: 10.4018/979-8-3693-2272-7.ch017

Seaton, A. V. (2002). Tourism as metempsychosis and metensomatosis: The personae of eternal recurrence. In Dann, G. M. S. (Ed.), *The tourist as a metaphor of the social world* (pp. 135–168). CABI. DOI: 10.1079/9780851996066.0135

Seaton, T. (2021). Remembrancing, remembrance gangs and co-opted encounters: Loading and reloading dark tourism experiences. In Sharpley, R. (Ed.), *Routledge handbook of the tourist experience* (pp. 328–350). Routledge. DOI: 10.4324/9781003219866-28

Seguí-Amortegui, L., Clemente-Almendros, J. A., Medina, R., & Gala, M. G. (2019). Sustainability and competitiveness in the tourism industry and tourist destinations: A Bibliometric Study. *Sustainability (Basel), 11*(22), 1–30. DOI: 10.3390/su11226351

Sehyeon, D. (2024). *Gojek, Indonesia's Super App Giant*. Medium: https://medium.com/%40davidsehyeonbaek/gojek-indonesias-super-app-giant-81283f63e3d5. Accessed on 10 May 2025.

Seraphin, H., & Korstanje, M. E. (2021). Dark tourism tribes: Social capital as a variable. In Pforr, P., Dowling, R. K., & Volgger, M. (Eds.), *Consumer tribes in tourism: Contemporary perspectives on special-interest tourism* (pp. 83–99). Springer. DOI: 10.1007/978-981-15-7150-3_7

Serrano, L., Sianes, A., & Ariza-Montes, A. (2019). Using bibliometric methods to shed light on the concept of sustainable tourism. *Sustainability (Basel)*, *11*(24), 6964. DOI: 10.3390/su11246964

Sesser, W. E., & Morgan, I. P. (1977). The Bermuda Triangle of food service chain. *The Cornell Hotel and Restaurant Administration Quarterly*, *17*(February), 56–61. DOI: 10.1177/001088047701700410

Shamim, R., & Bentalha, B. (2023). Blockchain-Enabled Machine Learning Framework for Demand Forecasting in Supply Chain Management. In Integrating Intelligence and Sustainability in Supply Chains (pp. 28-48). IGI Global. DOI: 10.4018/979-8-3693-0225-5.ch002

Shamim, N., Gupta, S., & Shin, M. M. (2024). Evaluating user engagement via metaverse environment through immersive experience for travel and tourism websites. *International Journal of Contemporary Hospitality Management*.

Sharma, M., & Singh, A. (2024). Embracing Technological Innovation: A Review of Hi-Tech Services in Hospitality Industry. *Evergreen*, *11*(4), 2818–2830. DOI: 10.5109/7326926

Sharma, R., & Singh, A. (2024a). Use of Digital Technology in Improving Quality Education: A Global Perspectives and Trends. In Nadda, V., Tyagi, P., Moniz Vieira, R., & Tyagi, P. (Eds.), *Implementing Sustainable Development Goals in the Service Sector* (pp. 14–26). IGI Global., DOI: 10.4018/979-8-3693-2065-5.ch002

Sharma, S. K., & Sanghi, R. (2012). *Advance in Water Treatment and Pollution Prevention*. Springer. DOI: 10.1007/978-94-007-4204-8

Sharpley, R., & Sharpley, J. (1997). Rural tourism: An introduction. *International Journal of Tourism Research*, *9*(4), 213–230.

Shetty, P. (2020). Dark tourism in India. *International Journal of Disaster Recovery and Business Continuity*, *11*(1), 622–627.

Shrout, P., & Bolger, N. (2002). Mediation in experimental and nonexperimental studies: New procedures and recommendations. *Psychological Methods*, *7*(4), 422–445. DOI: 10.1037/1082-989X.7.4.422 PMID: 12530702

Sia, P. Y. H., Saidin, S. S., & Iskandar, Y. H. P. (2023). Systematic review of mobile travel apps and their smart features and challenges. *Journal of Hospitality and Tourism Insights*, *6*(5), 2115–2138. DOI: 10.1108/JHTI-02-2022-0087

Sigala, M. (2010). Web 2.0, social marketing strategies and distribution channels for city destinations: Enhancing the participatory role of travelers and exploiting their collective intelligence. In *Web technologies: Concepts, methodologies, tools, and applications* (pp. 1249–1273). IGI Global. DOI: 10.4018/978-1-60566-982-3.ch068

Sigala, M. (2020). Tourism and COVID-19: Impacts and implications for advancing and resetting industry and research. *Journal of Business Research*, *117*, 312–321. DOI: 10.1016/j.jbusres.2020.06.015 PMID: 32546875

Silberberg, T. (1995). Cultural tourism and business opportunities for museums and heritage sites. *Tourism Management*, *16*(5), 361–365. DOI: 10.1016/0261-5177(95)00039-Q

SimilarWeb. (2025). *Traveloka*.https://www.similarweb.com/company/traveloka.com/. Accessed on 10 May 2025.

Singh, B., Kaunert, C., & Lal, S. (2025). AI-Driven Solutions for Virtual Tourism: Balancing Visitor Experience and Ecosystem Conservation. In *Integrating Architecture and Design Into Sustainable Tourism Development* (pp. 21-40). IGI Global Scientific Publishing.

Singh, A. (2024). Virtual Research Collaboration and Technology Application: Drivers, Motivations, and Constraints. In Chakraborty, S. (Ed.), *Challenges of Globalization and Inclusivity in Academic Research* (pp. 250–258). IGI Global., DOI: 10.4018/979-8-3693-1371-8.ch016

Singh, A., & Das, R. (2025). Women's Participation in Cultural Preservation and Commercialization of Rural Tourism: A Study on West Bengal. In Hassan, V. (Ed.), *Navigating Mass Tourism to Island Destinations: Preservation and Cultural Heritage Challenges* (pp. 313–340). IGI Global Scientific Publishing., DOI: 10.4018/979-8-3693-9107-5.ch012

Singh, A., & Hassan, S. C. (2024). Service Innovation Through Blockchain Technology in the Tourism and Hospitality Industry: Applications, Trends, and Benefits. In Singh, S. (Ed.), *Service Innovations in Tourism: Metaverse, Immersive Technologies, and Digital Twin* (pp. 205–214). IGI Global., DOI: 10.4018/979-8-3693-1103-5.ch010

Singh, R. (2018). Community-based tourism and its impact on rural development in India. *Journal of Tourism and Cultural Change, 16*(1), 43–59.

Singh, S., & Bashar, A. (2021). A bibliometric review on the development in e-tourism research. *International Hospitality Review, 37*(1), 71–93. DOI: 10.1108/IHR-03-2021-0015

Situmorang, D. S.. (2019). Rural tourism and local development: A community approach. *Tourism Review, 74*(1), 90–104.

Slimani, H. (2020). L'impact du facteur humain sur le développement de l'entreprise Touristique Cas: Les NTIC dans le secteur Touristique. *Revue Internationale des Sciences de Gestion, 3*(2).

Smith, C., & Watmough, S. (2019). Indigenous cultural tourism in rural Canada: A case study of community empowerment. *Journal of Rural Studies, 68,* 125–133.

Smith, M. K. (2003). *Issues in cultural tourism studies.* Routledge. DOI: 10.4324/9780203402825

Sofronov, B. (2018). The development of the travel and tourism industry in the world. *Annals of Spiru Haret University.Economic Series, 18*(4), 123–137.

Solomon, M. R., Bamossy, G. J., Askegaard, S. T., & Hogg, M. K. Consumer Behaviour-A European Perspective, Sixth Edition ed., Harlow: Pearson, 2016.

Soraya, I. (2015). Faktor-Faktor yang Mempengaruhi Minat Masyarakat Jakarta dalam Mengakses Fortal Media Jakarta Smart City. *Jurnal Komunikasi, 6*(1), 10–23.

Soulard, J., Stewart, W., Larson, M., & Samson, E. (2022). Dark tourism and social mobilization: Transforming travelers after visiting a Holocaust museum. *Journal of Travel Research, 62*(4), 632–646.

Spilanis, G. (2000). Tourism and regional development. The case of the Aegean islands. In Tsartas, P. (Ed.), *Tourism development, multidisciplinary approaches.* Exantas.

Srivastava, R. (2023). *FEATURE-Bhutan seeks to balance economy and environment with tourist tax.* Reuters: https://www.reuters.com/article/markets/oil/feature-bhutan-seeks-to-balance-economy-and-environment-with-tourist-tax-idUSL8N3A93GD/. Accessed on 10 May 2025.

Stabb, S., & Werthner, H. (2002). Intelligent Systems for Tourism. IEEE Intelligent Systems, November/December, 53-55. *Statistics.* Retrieved April 16, 2005, from

Stankov, U., & Gretzel, U. (2020, July 25). Tourism 4.0 technologies and tourist experiences: A human-centered design perspective. *Information Technology & Tourism*, *22*(3), 477–488. DOI: 10.1007/s40558-020-00186-y

State of travel influencer marketing: Top 5 trends for travel influencers to keep in mind. (2022, November 16). ETHospitalityWorld.com. https://hospitality.economictimes.indiatimes.com/news/speaking-heads/state-of-travel-influencer-marketing-top-5-trends-for-travel-influencers-to-keep-in-mind/95547388#:~:text=Travel%20influencers%20are%20again%20being,INR%2022%20billion%20by%202025

Statista. (2024a). *Most Popular Online Travel Agencies among Consumers in Indonesia as of June 2023.* https://www.statista.com/statistics/1200620/indonesia-most-used-online-travel-agencies/. Accessed on 10 May 2025.

Statista. (2024b). *Most preferred accommodation booking methods for year-end holiday travel in Indonesia as of November 2022.* https://www.statista.com/statistics/1379871/indonesia-preferred-accommodation-booking-methods/. Accessed on 10 May 2025.

Štefko, R., Kiráľová, A., & Mudrík, M. (2015). Strategic Marketing Communication in Pilgrimage Tourism. *Procedia: Social and Behavioral Sciences*, *175*, 423–430. DOI: 10.1016/j.sbspro.2015.01.1219

Stone, P. R., & Morton, C. (2022). Portrayal of the female dead in dark tourism. *Annals of Tourism Research*, *97*, 103506. DOI: 10.1016/j.annals.2022.103506

Stone, P., & Sharpley, R. (2008). Consuming dark tourism: A thanatological perspective. *Annals of Tourism Research*, *35*(2), 574–595. DOI: 10.1016/j.annals.2008.02.003

Strandberg, C., Nath, A., Hemmatdar, H., & Jahwash, M. (2018). Tourism research in the new millennium: A bibliometric review of literature in Tourism and Hospitality Research. *Tourism and Hospitality Research*, *18*(3), 269–285. DOI: 10.1177/1467358416642010

Stylianou-Lambert, T. (2011). Gazing from home: Cultural tourism and art museums. *Annals of Tourism Research*, *38*(2), 403–421. DOI: 10.1016/j.annals.2010.09.001

Su, L., Cheng, J., & Swanson, S. R. (2020). The impact of tourism activity type on emotion and storytelling: The moderating roles of travel companion presence and relative ability. *Tourism Management*, *81*, 104138. DOI: 10.1016/j.tourman.2020.104138

Sultan, P., Wong, H. Y., & Azam, M. S. (2021). How perceived communication source and food value stimulate purchase intention of organic food: An examination of the stimulus-organism-response (SOR) model. *Journal of Cleaner Production*, *312*, 127807. DOI: 10.1016/j.jclepro.2021.127807

Su, M. M., Wall, G., & Ma, Z. (2014). Assessing Ecotourism from a Multi Stakeholder Perspective: Xingkai Lake National Nature Reserve. *Environmental Management, 54*(5), 1190–1207. DOI: 10.1007/s00267-014-0360-5 PMID: 25248933

Sun, J., & Lv, X. (2021). Feeling dark, seeing dark: Mind–body in dark tourism. *Annals of Tourism Research, 86*, 103087. DOI: 10.1016/j.annals.2020.103087

Supera, M., Guerra, E., Villamar, E., & Saranza, C. (2024). Rural Tourism Development in the Philippines: Balancing Economic Growth with Ecological and Socio-Cultural Sustainability. *Journal of Economics. Finance and Management Studies., 7*(6), 3307–3322. DOI: 10.47191/jefms/v7-i6-25

Su, X. (2011). Commodification and the selling of ethnic music to tourists. *Geoforum, 42*(4), 496–505. DOI: 10.1016/j.geoforum.2011.03.006

Su, X., Li, X., & Kang, Y. (2019). A bibliometric analysis of research on intangible cultural heritage using CiteSpace. *SAGE Open, 9*(2), 2158244019840119. DOI: 10.1177/2158244019840119

Su, Y.-S., Chiang, W.-L., Lee, C.-T., & Chang, H.-C. (2016). The effect of flow experience on player loyalty in mobile game application. *Computers in Human Behavior, 63*, 240–248. DOI: 10.1016/j.chb.2016.05.049

Swarbrooke, J., & Horner, S. (2001). *Business travel and tourism*. Routledge. DOI: 10.1016/B978-0-7506-4392-4.50012-4

Taber, K. S. (2017, June 7). The Use of Cronbach's Alpha When Developing and Reporting Research Instruments in Science Education. *Research in Science Education, 48*(6), 1273–1296. DOI: 10.1007/s11165-016-9602-2

Taherdoost, H. (2016). Sampling Methods in Research Methodology; How to Choose a Sampling Technique for Research. SSRN Electronic Journal, 5(2), 18-27. DOI: 10.2139/ssrn.3205035

Tamjidyamcholo, A., Gholipour, R., Baba, M., & Yamchello, H. (2013). Information security professional perceptions of knowledge-sharing intention in virtual communities under social cognitive theory. *International Conference on Research and Innovation in Information Systems (ICRIIS)*, (pp. 416-421). Kuala Lumpur, Malaysia: IEEE. DOI: 10.1109/ICRIIS.2013.6716746

Tan, S. (2024). *Indonesia: Which online travel agencies are best at turning awareness to purchase intent in Q1 2024?* YouGov: https://business.yougov.com/content/49688-indonesia-online-travel-agencies-best-at-turning-awareness-to-purchase-intent-q1-2024. Accessed on 10 May 2025.

Team, C. (2018, September 28). *How airlines price their tickets; AI's role in optimising airline revenue management and ticketing - CRN - India*. CRN - India. https://www.crn.in/thought-leader/how-airlines-price-their-tickets-ais-role-in-optimising-airline-revenue-management-and-ticketing/

Tham, A., Croy, G., & Mair, J. (2013). Social media in destination choice: Distinctive electronic word-of-mouth dimensions. *Journal of Travel & Tourism Marketing*, *30*(1-2), 144–155. DOI: 10.1080/10548408.2013.751272

Tham, A., Mair, J., & Croy, G. (2019). Social media influence on tourists' destination choice: Importance of context. *Tourism Recreation Research*. Advance online publication. DOI: 10.1080/02508281.2019.1700655

Throsby, D. (2001). *Economics and culture*. Cambridge university press.

Timothy, D. J. (2011). *Cultural Heritage and Tourism: An Introduction*. Channel View. DOI: 10.21832/9781845411787

Timothy, D. J., & Olsen, D. H. (Eds.). (2006). *Tourism, Religion and Spiritual Journeys*. Routledge. DOI: 10.4324/9780203001073

Timothy, D. J., & Ron, A. S. (2013). Heritage cuisines, regional identity and sustainable tourism. In *Sustainable Culinary Systems* (pp. 275–290). Routledge.

Timothy, D., & Teye, V. (2009). *Tourism and the lodging sector*. Routledge.

Tonkin, E. (1995). *Narrating our pasts: The social construction of oral history* (No. 22). Cambridge university press.

Tripathi, R., Tripathi, M. A., & Rawat, A. (2022). Performance of women artisans as entrepreneurs in ODOP in Uttar Pradesh to boost economy: Strategies and away towards global handicraft index for small business. *Academy of Marketing Studies Journal*, *26*(1), 1–19.

Trunfio, M., Jung, T., & Campana, S. (2022). Mixed reality experiences in museums: Exploring the impact of functional elements of the devices on visitors' immersive experiences and post-experience behaviours. *Information & Management*, *59*(8), 103698. DOI: 10.1016/j.im.2022.103698

Tsai, F. M., & Bui, T. D. (2020, March 1). Impact of word of mouth via social media on consumer intention to purchase cruise travel products. *Maritime Policy & Management*, *48*(2), 167–183. DOI: 10.1080/03088839.2020.1735655

Tsartas, P. (2003). Cultural tourism and regional development: Problems, possibilities, prospects. In Deffner, A., Konstandakopoulos, D., & Psycharis, Y. (Eds.), *Culture and regional economic development in Europe*. University of Thessaly Press.

Turner, V. (1973). The center out there: Pilgrim's goal in rural tourism. *Journal of Anthropological Research*, *29*(1), 137–151.

Tussyadiah, I. P., & Fesenmaier, D. R. (2008). Marketing places through first-person stories—An analysis of Pennsylvania roadtripper blog. *Journal of Travel & Tourism Marketing*, *25*(3-4), 299–311. DOI: 10.1080/10548400802508358

UNESCO. (2017), "UNESCO and the International Year of Sustainable Tourism", *UNESCO*, 16 January, available at: https://en.unesco.org/iyst4d (accessed 5 February 2023).

UNWTO. (2005). *Making Tourism More Sustainable - A Guide for Policy Makers*. United Nations World Tourism Organization.

UNWTO. (2017a). *Discussion Paper on the Occasion of the International Year of Sustainable Tourism for Development 2017*. United Nations World Tourism Organization, Madrid, Spain, p. 84.

UNWTO. (2017b). *UNWTO Annual Report 2016*. World Tourism Organization.

UNWTO. (2018). *Report on tourism and culture synergies*. UNWTO.

UNWTO. (2019), Faits saillants du tourisme, édition 2019, [On line], https://www.unwto.org/fr/publication/faits-saillants-du-tourisme-2019 (Consulted 11/01/2024)

Van Nuenen, T., & Scarles, C. (2021). Advancements in technology and digital media in tourism. *Tourist Studies*, *21*(1), 119–132. DOI: 10.1177/1468797621990410

Varadarajan, R., Welden, R. B., Arunachalam, S., Haenlein, M., & Gupta, S. (2022). Digital product innovations for the greater good and digital marketing innovations in communications and channels: Evolution, emerging issues, and future research directions. *International Journal of Research in Marketing*, *39*(2), 482–501. DOI: 10.1016/j.ijresmar.2021.09.002

Vărzaru, A. A., Bocean, C. G., & Cazacu, M. (2021). Rethinking tourism industry in pandemic COVID-19 period. *Sustainability (Basel)*, *13*(12), 6956. DOI: 10.3390/su13126956

Verma, A., Shukla, V. K., & Sharma, R. (2021, January 1). Convergence of IOT in Tourism Industry: A Pragmatic *Analysis.Journal of Physics: Conference Series*, *1714*(1), 012037. DOI: 10.1088/1742-6596/1714/1/012037

Vezzoli, C. A., & Manzini, E. (2008). *Design for Environmental Sustainability*. Springer.

Villamarin Rodriguez, R., & Nagaraj, S. (2020). *Impact of AI and Robotics in the Tourism sector: A Critical Insight.*

Volpentesta, A. P., & Felicetti, A. M. (2012). Identifying opinion leaders in time-dependent commercial social networks. In *Collaborative Networks in the Internet of Services: 13th IFIP WG 5.5 Working Conference on Virtual Enterprises, PRO-VE 2012, Bournemouth, UK, October 1-3, 2012.* [Springer Berlin Heidelberg.]. *Proceedings, 13*, 571–581.

Volpentesta, A. P., Felicetti, A. M., & Ammirato, S. (2017). Intelligent food information provision to consumers in an internet of food era. In *Collaboration in a Data-Rich World: 18th IFIP WG 5.5 Working Conference on Virtual Enterprises, PRO-VE 2017, Vicenza, Italy, September 18-20, 2017* [Springer International Publishing.]. *Proceedings, 18*, 725–736.

Von Hohenberg, B. C., & Guess, A. M. (2023). When do sources persuade? The effect of source credibility on opinion change. *Journal of Experimental Political Science, 10*(3), 328–342. DOI: 10.1017/XPS.2022.2

Vyslobodska, H., Brychka, B., & Bulyk, O. (2022). Rural tourism as an alternative direction of activity diversification of agricultural products producers. *Scientific Messenger of LNU of Veterinary Medicine and Biotechnologies.Series Economical Sciences, 24*(99), 10–14.

Wamwara, H., & Ndung'u, N. (2020). The socio-economic impact of cultural tourism on local communities in Kenya. *African Journal of Hospitality, Tourism and Leisure, 9*(1), 1–15.

Wang, D., & Pizam, A. (2011). Tourism, Security and Safety:From Theory to Practice. Butterworth_Heinemann.

Wang, J., Huang, X., Gong, Z., & Cao, K. (2020). Dynamic assessment of tourism carrying capacity and its impacts on tourism economic growth in urban tourism destinations in China. *Journal of Destination Marketing & Management, 15*, 100383. DOI: 10.1016/j.jdmm.2019.100383

Wang, L., & Hsiao, D. F. (2012). Antecedents of flow in retail store shopping. *Journal of Retailing and Consumer Services, 19*(4), 381–389. DOI: 10.1016/j.jretconser.2012.03.002

Wang, T., Duong, T. D., & Chen, C. C. (2016). Intention to disclose personal information via mobile applications: A privacy calculus perspective. *International Journal of Information Management, 36*(4), 531–542. DOI: 10.1016/j.ijinfomgt.2016.03.003

Wardana, I.-M., Sukaatmadja, I.-P.-G., Ekawati, N.-W., Yasa, N.-N.-K., Astawa, I.-P., & Setini, M. (2021). Policy Models for Improving Ecotourism Performance to Build Quality Tourism Experience and Sustainable Tourism. *Management Science Letters*, *11*, 595–608. DOI: 10.5267/j.msl.2020.9.007

Weaver, D. (2006). *Sustainable Tourism: Theory and Practice*. Elsevier Ltd.

Weaver, D. (2018). Ecotourism. In Holden, A., & Fennel, D. (Eds.), *The Routledge Handbook of Transport and Tourism* (pp. 417–429). Routledge.

Weber-Sabil, J., & Han, D. I. D. (2021). Immersive Tourism-State of the Art of Immersive Tourism Realities through XR Technology.

Webster, J., Trevino, L. K., & Ryan, L. (1993, Winter). The dimensionality and correlates of flow in human-computer interactions. *Computers in Human Behavior*, *9*(4), 411–426. DOI: 10.1016/0747-5632(93)90032-N

Wei, Z., Zhang, J., Huang, X., & Qiu, H. (2023). Can gamification improve the virtual reality tourism experience? Analyzing the mediating role of tourism fatigue. *Tourism Management*, *96*, 104715. DOI: 10.1016/j.tourman.2022.104715

Weng, L., He, B. J., Liu, L., Li, C., & Zhang, X. (2019). Sustainability assessment of cultural heritage tourism: Case study of pingyao ancient city in China. *Sustainability (Basel)*, *11*(5), 1392. DOI: 10.3390/su11051392

Wight, A. C. (2020). Visitor perceptions of European Holocaust heritage: A social media analysis. *Tourism Management*, *81*, 104142. DOI: 10.1016/j.tourman.2020.104142

Williams, M. N., Grajales, C. A. G., & Kurkiewicz, D. (2013). Assumptions of Multiple Regression: Correcting Two Misconceptions. *Practical Assessment, Research & Evaluation*, *18*(11). http://pareonline.net/getvn.asp?v=18&n=11

Williams, S. (1998). *Tourism geography*. Psychology Press.

Wirentake, M. P., & Arfani, S. (2024). *Exploring English through tourist attractions: Motivating students to speak*. Jakad Media Publishing.

Withiam, G. (1985). *Hotel companies aim for multiple markets: The current proliferation of brand names to an effort by hotels to become*. Cornell HRA Quarterly.

Wong, J. W. C., Lai, I. K. W., & Tao, Z. (2019, August 1). Sharing memorable tourism experiences on mobile social media and how it influences further travel decisions. *Current Issues in Tourism*, *23*(14), 1773–1787. DOI: 10.1080/13683500.2019.1649372

World Economic Forum. (2023, October 9). World Economic Forum. https://www.weforum.org/publications/the-travel-tourism-competitiveness-report-2019/

World Heritage Outlook, I. U. C. N. "Komodo National Park," 09 November 2017. Online. Available: https://worldheritageoutlook.iucn.org/explore-sites/wdpaid/67725

World Travel & Tourism Council (WTTC) | Travel & Tourism Representative Council. (n.d.). World Travel & Tourism Council. https://wttc.org/news-article/india-travel-and-tourism-could-surpass-pre-pandemic-levels-by-the-end-of-2022

Xiang, Z., & Fesenmaier, D. R. (2022). Travel Information Search. *Handbook of E-Tourism*, 921–940. https://doi.org/DOI: 10.1007/978-3-030-48652-5_55

Xiang, Z., Du, Q., & Ma, Y. (2017). ICT-enabled seamless travel: A conceptual framework and its applications. *Journal of Hospitality and Tourism Technology*, *8*(1), 63–75.

Xin, B., Hao, Y., & Xie, L. (2024). Virtual influencers and corporate reputation: From marketing game to empirical analysis. *Journal of Research in Interactive Marketing*, *18*(5), 759–786. DOI: 10.1108/JRIM-10-2023-0330

Yadav, M. S., Valck, K., Thurau, T. H., Hoffman, D. L., & Spann, M. (2013, November). Social Commerce: A Contingency Framework for Assessing Marketing Potential. *Journal of Interactive Marketing*, *27*(4), 311–323. DOI: 10.1016/j.intmar.2013.09.001

Yale, "Environmental Performance Index Results," 2018. Online. Available: https://epi.envirocenter.yale.edu/epi-indicator-report/EPI?country=

Yan, Y., Shah, M. I., Sharma, G. D., Chopra, R., Fareed, Z., & Shahzad, U. (2022). Can tourism sustain itself through the pandemic: Nexus between tourism, COVID-19 cases and air quality spread in the 'Pineapple State' Hawaii. *Current Issues in Tourism*, *25*(3), 421–440. DOI: 10.1080/13683500.2021.1965553

Yap, C. K., Tan, S. G., Suhaili, Z., Wong, C. H., & Leong, S. C. (2019). Rehabilitation of orphaned and displaced orangutans at the Sepilok Orangutan Rehabilitation Centre, Sabah, Malaysia. *Malaysian Applied Biology*, *48*(1), 1–9.

Yesawich, P. C. (1987). Hospitality Marketing for the '90s: Effective Marketing Research. *The Cornell Hotel and Restaurant Administration Quarterly*, *28*(1), 48–57.

Ying, C. W. (2024, July). Preliminary Exploration of Intelligent Virtual Avatars in the Virtual Influencer Industry. In *2024 IEEE 24th International Conference on Software Quality, Reliability, and Security Companion (QRS-C)* (pp. 1284-1291). IEEE. DOI: 10.1109/QRS-C63300.2024.00167

Yoon, E. (2012). Effects of Website Environmental Cues on Consumers' Response and Outcome Behaviors. *Public Access Theses, Dissertations, and Student Research from the College of Education and Human Sciences*. Retrieved from https://digitalcommons.unl.edu/cehsdiss/163/

Yoon, Y., & Uysal, M. (2005). An examination of the effects of motivation and satisfaction on destination loyalty: A structural model. *Tourism Management*, 26(1), 45–56. DOI: 10.1016/j.tourman.2003.08.016

You, X. (2025). *How renewable energy is helping China's tourism industry go green*. Reuters: https://www.reuters.com/sustainability/climate-energy/how-renewable-energy-is-helping-chinas-tourism-industry-go-green-2025-05-08/. Accessed on 10 May 2025.

Yusuf, R. M. S., & Jumhur, H. M. (2018). Penerapan E-Government Dalam Membangun Smart City Pada Kota Bandung Tahun 2018 E- Government Implementation in Building Smart City in Bandung 2018. *E-Proceeding of Management*, 5(3), 3126–3130.

Zakia. (2021). Ecotourism in Indonesia: Local Community Involvement and the Affecting Factors. *Journal of Governance and Public Policy*, 8(2), 93-105.

Zeithaml, V. A. (1988). Consumer Perceptions of Price, Quality, and Value: A means-End Model and Synthesis of Evidence. *Journal of Marketing*, 52(3), 2–22. DOI: 10.1177/002224298805200302

Zeithaml, V., & Bitner, M. J. (1996). *Services Marketing*. McGraw-Hill.

Zeng, B., & Gerritsen, R. (2014). What do we know about social media in tourism? A review. *Tourism Management Perspectives*, 10, 27–36. DOI: 10.1016/j.tmp.2014.01.001

Zeppel, H. (2006). *Indigenous Ecotourism: Sustainable Development and Management*. CABI. DOI: 10.1079/9781845931247.0000

Zgolli, S., & Zaiem, I. (2018). The Responsible Behavior of Tourist: The Role of Personnel Factors and Public Power and Effect on The Choice of Destination. *The Arab Economics and Business Journal*, 13(2), 168–178. DOI: 10.1016/j.aebj.2018.09.004

Zhang, H., Lu, Y., Gupta, S., & Zhao, L. (2014). What motivates customers to participate in social commerce? The impact of technological environments and virtual customer experiences. *Information & Management*, 51(8), 1017–1030. DOI: 10.1016/j.im.2014.07.005

Zhang, S., Tan, Y., Zhong, Y., Yuan, J., & Ding, Y. (2023). Psychological recovery effects of 3D virtual tourism with real scenes—A comparative study. *Information Technology & Tourism*, *25*(1), 71–103. DOI: 10.1007/s40558-023-00246-z

Zhang, Y. (2021). Unpacking visitors' experiences at dark tourism sites of natural disasters. *Tourism Management Perspectives*, *40*, 100880. DOI: 10.1016/j.tmp.2021.100880

Zhang, Y. (2022). Experiencing human identity at dark tourism sites of natural disasters. *Tourism Management*, *89*, 104451. DOI: 10.1016/j.tourman.2021.104451

Zhan, L., & Ning, K. (2021). Minority Tourist Information Service and Sustainable Development of Tourism under the Background of Smart City. *Mobile Information Systems*, *2021*, 1–14. Advance online publication. DOI: 10.1155/2021/6547186

Zhao, X. (2022). Virtual fashion influencers: towards a more sustainable consumer behaviour of generation Z?

Zhao, W., Hu, F., Wang, J., Shu, T., & Xu, Y. (2023). A systematic literature review on social commerce: Assessing the past and guiding the future. *Electronic Commerce Research and Applications*, *57*, 101219. Advance online publication. DOI: 10.1016/j.elerap.2022.101219

Zhou, L., Zhang, P., & Zimmermann, H.-D. (2013). Social commerce research: An integrated view. *Electronic Commerce Research and Applications*, *12*(2), 61–68. DOI: 10.1016/j.elerap.2013.02.003

Zhou, T. (2019). The effect of flow experience on users' social commerce intention. [[doi:]. *Kybernetes*, *49*(10), 2349–2363. DOI: 10.1108/K-03-2019-0198

Zhuang, X., Yao, Y., & Li, J. (2019). Sociocultural impacts of tourism on residents of world cultural heritage sites in China. *Sustainability (Basel)*, *11*(3), 840. DOI: 10.3390/su11030840

Zink, P. D. K. J. (2008). *Corporate Sustainability as a Challenge for Comprehensive Management*. Springer. DOI: 10.1007/978-3-7908-2046-1

Zopiatis, A., Pericleous, K., & Theofanous, Y. (2021). COVID-19 and hospitality and tourism research: An integrative review. *Journal of Hospitality and Tourism Management*, *48*, 275–279. DOI: 10.1016/j.jhtm.2021.07.002

About the Contributors

Ahmad Albattat is an Associate Professor and Program Leader in School of Global Hospitality and Tourism, Asia Pacific University of Technology and Innovation, Kuala Lumpur, Malaysia. He is a Visiting Professor and External Examiner in Medan Academy of Tourism (Akpar Medan). He is a Doctoral Supervisor in European Global Institute of Innovation & Technology, Malta, and Rushford Business School, Switzerland. He received PhD in Hospitality Management "Disaster and Emergency Planning and Preparedness" from University Sains Malaysia (USM), Malaysia. He worked as an Associate Professor in Graduate School of Management, Post Graduate Centre, Management and Science University, Shah Alam, Selangor, Malaysia. Assistant Professor, Ammon Applied University College, Amman, Jordan. Senior Lecturer and Research Coordinator in School of Hospitality & Creative Arts, Management and Science University, Shah Alam, Selangor, Malaysia, and Researcher at Sustainable Tourism Research Cluster (STRC), Pulau Pinang, Malaysia. He was working for the Jordanian hospitality industry for 17 years. His teaching and consultancy fields include hospitality management, events management, research methodology, strategic management and final research projects. His research areas include hospitality management, hotel, tourism, events, emergency planning, disaster management, sustainable development goals and human resource. He is an active member of several Scientific and Editorial Board of International journals, reviewer, author and editor for book projects with Emeralds, Routledge, and IGI Global. His latest works have been published in the refereed international journals, conference proceedings, books and book chapters.

***

Syaza Marina Abdul Kadir holds a Bachelor of Accounting from the Universiti Putra Malaysia. Currently, she works as an account executive at a private company in Kuala Lumpur.

Shazrul Ekhmar Abdul Razak is currently a lecturer at Asia Pacific University of Technology & Innovation (APU), Kuala Lumpur. He holds a PhD in Accounting from Universiti Putra Malaysia, and a Master of Science in Accounting at Putra Business School, Universiti Putra Malaysia, Malaysia. His research interests encompass management accounting systems, sustainability, and risk management

Teuku Afrizal is a reseacher in public policy of Diponegoro University.

Khairil Wahidin Awang, PhD, is a Professor of Tourism at the Faculty of Hospitality, Tourism and Wellness, Universiti Malaysia Kelantan, Kota Bharu. He obtained his BSc in Geology and MA in Geography from the University of Nebraska, the U.S., and PhD in Tourism Geography from the University of Wales-Aberystwyth, the U.K. Professor Khairil specializes in the tourism-sustainability agenda. His research interest covers the arena of spatial tourism development, focusing on intertwined issues rooted in varies tourism subsectors, and of particular the small and medium-sized accommodation and attraction entities. These span across different forms of tourism; ecotourism, community-based tourism, green-tourism, rural tourism and Islamic tourism. Professor Khairil had been engaged on different capacities by the World-Wide Fund for Nature, the Cambodian Government, the Organization of Islamic Cooperation, the United Nations World Tourism Organization and local and private organizations. Professor Khairil had been in the past a Research Associate at the Islamic Tourism Centre, the Ministry of Tourism and Culture Malaysia, a Dean, a Deputy Dean, a Head of Department and a Visiting Professor. Currently he teaches tourism subjects and Business Research Methodology besides supervising postgraduate students at the Universiti Malaysia Kelantan.

Sofea Cheah Azlan is a graduate in Bachelor of Management (Tourism) and Master of Science Tourism Planning with experience in the field of management and tourism. She is a reliable, consistent, and hardworking person with good time management skills. Eager and enthusiastic to make use of the knowledge and skills to develop and maintain the reputation of the company as a dedicated employee.

Ahmed Benjelloun is a teacher-researcher at the National School of Business and Management of Fez, Sidi Mohamed de Ben Abdellah University. He has been involved in cultural events since 2009 and in professional training and higher education since 2013. His areas of expertise cover strategic, territorial, tourism, cultural and digital marketing. He is author of the book "Fez, cultural tourism destination" and several articles and scientific publications in national and international specialized journals. He is committed to promoting the interactions between the university and the professional world through concrete and impactful initiatives. Since 2023, he has also been dedicated to supporting startups and organizing events dedicated to entrepreneurship, hoping to contribute to the development of an innovative and successful entrepreneurial ecosystem in the Fez-Meknes region.

Badr Bentalha teaches Supply Chain and Operations Management at National School of Business and Management – Fez, Sidi Mohamed Ben Abdellah University – Morocco. Dr. Bentalha investigates the structural dynamics and control of complex networks, applying his findings to supply chain management, Industry 4.0, risk analysis, and digital supply chains. His work emphasizes the intersection of supply chain management, operations research, industrial engineering, and digital technology. As a professor, he teaches undergraduate, graduate, and doctoral courses in operations management, supply chain management, logistics, management information systems, and strategic management. Through guest lectures, webinars, and scholarly presentations, he engages students and fosters an active learning environment. Professor Bentalha specializes in supply chain and operations management, operations research, and service management. He is passionate about integrating knowledge across disciplines to solve real-world problems. He has delivered numerous invited plenary talks, keynotes, and panel discussions at conferences and global webinars.

Indranil Bose, a Fellow of the Higher Education Academy UK (FHEA) has over twenty years of experience in academia and research, contributing significantly to management education in India, the UK, and the UAE. Dr. Bose is also a 'Certified Management and Business Educator (CMBE)' by Chartered Association of Business Schools (CABS, UK). He has authored and published numerous peer-reviewed articles, and research papers in prestigious journals and books indexed with SCOPUS, ABDC and Web of Science. He has also presented his research at international conferences across Asia and Europe. Dr. Bose is a sought-after speaker for faculty development programs and has addressed nearly fifty institutions worldwide. He evaluates PhD theses in areas like Human Resources and Technology-Enabled HR Strategies for various universities. His accolades include the Dewang Mehta Best Professor Award, the MTC Global Distinguished Faculty Award, the Turnitin Global Innovation Award, ATHE Star Assessor Award UK. He also serves on the editorial boards of several prestigious publications, including Emerald UK and Springer USA. He is also an advisory council member of Harvard Business Review and a Fellow of the Association of Indian Management Professionals, New Delhi.

T. K. Chatterjee is an MBA in Marketing from Patna University and holds a PhD in Management from National Law University, Jodhpur. Currently he is an Associate Professor in Marketing Area with IMT Nagpur. He has twenty years of experience in corporate and has been in academics for last eighteen years. He has published several research articles in National and International journals, most of them in ABDC including one in A*. He has presented several papers in National and International Conferences. He is author of a book and is an avid networker. He has delivered several talks in various forums as Plenary speaker, Guest of Honour, Keynote speaker etc.

Bouteïna El Gharbaoui is a Teacher-Researcher at Université Moulay Ismail de Meknes.

Sahil Gautam is a research scholar in the School of Tourism, Travel and Hospitality Management, Department of Tourism and Travel Management, Central University of Himachal Pradesh. His research interests include Homestay tourism and Tourist motivation & satisfaction.

Genoveva has a Doctoral qualification in Marketing. She has about 28 years of experience in teaching, research, and training, including 4 years as Vice Rector, 4 years as Director of Quality Assurance, and 5 years as Marketing Director. She also has about 20 years of experience in entrepreneurship, including 12 years as an entrepreneur in her own family business and 16 years as a consultant in the Feasibility Study & Business Plan for a start-up company.

Tandi Gunadi is affiliated with President University in Indonesia.

Tareq Nael Hashem is a Full Professor of Marketing at Applied Science Private University, Amman, Jordan and holds PH.D. from Amman Arab University, Jordan. He is Permanent Member Senior Consultant For Development programs(EABAFF) in European Arab Business Fellowship Foundations.(2007-up to now), Member in EMBRI/EMAB &Emerald (EMAB Associate Fellow- AF-EMAB),Membership in American Association of International Researchers (AAIR),Member of European Marketing Academy (EMAC),Member in European Institute for Advanced Studies in Management (EIASM),Member in International Corporate and Marketing Communication Association (ICMCA),Member in European Retail Academy and Member of IGI Global Editorial Advisory Review Board

Augustin Rina Herawati is lecturer in digital public service management at the public administration department of FISIP Diponegoro University.

Md Shamim Hossain is a Professor in the Department of Marketing, Hajee Mohammad Danesh Science and Technology University (HSTU), Bangladesh. In 2019, he received his Ph.D. in Business Management from the University of

International Business and Economics (UIBE), Beijing, China. His research interests include operations management, online business, e-marketing, self-service technologies (SSTs), e-commerce, m-banking, online customer behavior, and machine learning in marketing. Dr. Hossain is a pioneer in the field of machine learning-based marketing and is actively engaged in research related to this area.

Priyanka Kanjilal is a faculty in Department of Management studies in Asansol Engineering College and also a research scholar in JIS University India.

Tanmoy Majumder is an Assistant Professor at JIS University, Kolkata, with over 13 years of comprehensive experience spanning both corporate and academic spheres. He holds a Bachelor's degree in Hospital Management from the West Bengal University of Technology, a Master's in Hospital Administration from the West Bengal University of Health Sciences, and a Master of Business Management from West Bengal State University. He is currently pursuing a Ph.D. in Healthcare Marketing Management at JIS University. Mr. Majumder's core research interests lie in the areas of Marketing Management and Hospital Management. His academic contributions include several research papers published in national and international journals. He has actively participated in numerous conferences, presenting his work across multidisciplinary domains including business, technology, and social sciences.

Shubhra Mishra serves as an Assistant Professor and Research Scholar at Babu Banarasi Das University, School of Management, focusing on Marketing. With experience in digital and content marketing, she is presently pursuing a PhD on the Applications of AI in Marketing. Her research interests delve into the intersection of AI, consumer behavior, and emerging trends in marketing.

Soumya Mukherjee is an Associate Professor of Swami Vivekananda University, Barrackpore, West Bengal, India. He is an accomplished educator with demonstrated ability and experience to teach, motivate, and direct students while maintaining high interest and achievement. He has more than 15 years of experience in academics. He has authored two books and has several research articles in journal and conference proceedings to his credit.

Mazlina Mustapha is an Associate Professor at the School of Business and Economics, Universiti Putra Malaysia. Prior to joining the academic line, she worked as an auditor at Big 5 firm and accountant at a listed company. She served as MIA Council member from 2019 until 2023. She was appointed as head of department for Department of Accounting and Finance, UPM, from 2017 to 2020. Her works and research interests include audit, corporate governance, corporate sustainability, risk management, performance management and accounting education.

Nurul Binti Napatah is an University Lecturer at Universiti Malaysia Terengganu based in Kuala Terengganu, Terengganu. Previously, Nurul was an Industrial Trainee at Tourism Malaysia and also held positions at Event Management Companies, Kuala Lumpur Convention Centre. Nurul received a Bachelor of Tourism Planning and Hospitality Management degree from International Islamic University Malaysia and a Master of Science - Master of Science from Universiti Teknologi Malaysia.

Md Abdullah Al Noman, currently studying for an MSc in International Business with Advanced Practice at Ulster University, U.K., holds a distinguished academic background with a B.B.A major in Finance from the Department of Finance and Banking, Hajee Mohammad Danesh Science and Technology University, Dinajpur, Bangladesh. His research interests are deeply rooted in customer satisfaction, customer sentiment analysis, business analytics, and marketing. Mr. Noman has contributed significantly to these areas, which is evident in his scholarly articles and active participation in prestigious research conferences such as the International Conference on Business and Economic Challenges. His dedication to research is unwavering, and he is keenly interested in collaborations and discussions related to his expertise.

Mario Ossorio is an Assistant Professor of Management at University of Campania "Luigi Vanvitelli", where he earned his Ph. D. in Innovation and Entrepreneurship. His last works are published in Journals such as Management Decision, Journal of Family Business Strategy, Global Business Review, European Journal of Innovation Management. He regularly serves as Chair and Discussant at international conferences of management.

Noor Fazliza Rasim is affiliated with the Department of Tourism Management, Faculty of Business, Economic, and Social Development at University Malaysia Terengganu.

Nilanjan Ray is from Kolkata, India and presently associated as an Associate Professor at Department of Management Studies, JIS University. Prior joining to JIS University Dr Ray was at Institute of Leadership Entrepreneurship and Development as Associate Professor and HoD and additional responsibility as Director IQAC before that he was also associated at Adamas University as Associate Professor of Marketing Management and Centre Coordinator for Research in Business Analytics at Adamas University in Department of Management, School of Business and Economics, West Bengal, India. Dr Ray has obtained certified Accredited Management Teacher Award from All India Management Association, New Delhi, India. He has obtained his PhD(Mktg); M.Com (Mktg); MBA (Mktg), STC FMRM (IIT-Kgp). He has more than 12 years teaching and 6 years Research experience, awarded 2 Doctoral Scholars and guided around 56 Post Graduate students' project also. Dr. Ray has contributed over 90 research papers in reputed National and International Referred, Peer Reviewed Journals, Proceedings and 13 Edited Research Hand Books from Springer, IGI-Global USA and Apple Academic Publisher CRC Press .

Rafi Ahmed Reza holds a BBA and an MBA in Marketing from Hajee Mohammad Danesh Science and Technology University, both completed in 2020. He currently works as a Business Development Executive at an IT firm, where he contributes to business growth and the development of strategic partnerships. His career reflects a strong commitment to excellence and a passion for harnessing business opportunities in the ever-evolving technology sector.

Moumita Roy is a distinguished academic and researcher with 18 years of expertise in Organizational Behavior and Human Resource Management. Currently an Assistant Professor at JIS University, she has played a pivotal role in shaping future business leaders through her innovative teaching and research. Her expertise spans workplace dynamics, leadership strategies, employee motivation, organizational culture, and change management. She has designed and delivered impactful courses that integrate theory with practical applications, ensuring students grasp modern business challenges effectively. Dr. Roy has an extensive portfolio of research publications in national and international journals, addressing critical issues such as employee engagement, work-life fusion, and strategic HR practices. A frequent speaker at conferences and seminars, she is dedicated to bridging the gap between research and practice. Her commitment to academic excellence, mentorship, and thought leadership continues to inspire students and professionals alike.

Nirmal Chandra Roy is currently serving in the Department of Business Administration (Human Resource) at The University of Burdwan, West Bengal, India. He graduated from the University of North Bengal, Darjeeling, and was awarded the UGC-JRF in 2015. He holds Diplomas in Labour Laws and Hospitality Management. Dr. Roy is a life member of the Indian Commerce Association (ICA) and the Indian Accounting Association (IAA). He has authored three books: Human Resource Management in the Indian Tea Industry, Organizational Behavior, and Production and Operations Management. Additionally, he has published over 35 research articles and management case studies in Scopus, Web of Science, and

ABDC-listed journals of national and international repute, through publishers such as Inderscience, Sage, and Publishing India. Dr. Roy has presented over 50 research articles at various national and international conferences. Dr. Roy has authored a design patent on 'Data Processing Device for Receiving and Analyzing Consumer Feedback' from the Patent Office, Government of India on 27/11/2024. He also serves as a reviewer for several esteemed journals, including Management and Labour Studies (Sage Publications), FIIB Business Review (Sage Publications), Global Business Review (Sage Publications), International Journal of Contemporary Hospitality Management (Emerald Publications), International Journal of Rural Management (Sage Publications), and Humanities and Social Science Studies (UGC Care Listed). Furthermore, Dr. Roy is a member of the editorial board of two international journals. His research interests include Human Resource Management, Labour Laws, Industrial Relations, Organizational Behavior, Entrepreneurship, and Tourism Management.

Suman Sharma is Dean & Professor in School of Tourism, Travel and Hospitality Management, Department of Tourism and Travel Management, Central University of Himachal Pradesh. His research interests include Destination Branding and Tourism Marketing.

Amrik Singh is working as Professor in the School of Hotel Management and Tourism at Lovely Professional University, Punjab, India. He obtained his Ph.D. degree in Hotel Management from Kurukshetra University, Kurukshetra. He started his academic career at Lovely Professional University, Punjab, India in the year 2007. He has published more than 70 research papers in UGC and peer-reviewed and Scopus/Web of Science) journals. He has published 12 patents and 01 patent has been granted in the inter-disciplinary domain. Dr. Amrik Singh participated and acted as a resource person in various national and international conferences, seminars, research workshops, and industry talks. His area of research interest is accommodation management, ergonomics, green practices, human resource management in hospitality, waste management, AR VR in hospitality, etc. He is currently guiding 8Ph.D. scholars and 7 Ph.D. scholars have been awarded Ph.D.

Hajar Slimani is a University Professor at the National School of Commerce and Management -UMI -Meknes. She has conducted several training programs for professionals and worked in several international companies. She has written several articles in my field of interest, in national and international journals.

Rohit Thakur is a research scholar in the School of Tourism, Travel and Hospitality Management, Department of Tourism and Travel Management, Central

University of Himachal Pradesh. His research interests include Cultural Heritage Tourism and Tourism planning.

Rinki Verma is a proficient academician in the field of management and has extensive research experience. She carries a wide experience of 15 years in academics and corporate. She shouldered responsibilities from IQAC and NAAC in her current and prior serving institutions. She served as the Project Director for an ICSSR-funded project. Currently, she is an Associate Professor at Babu Banarasi Das University, Lucknow. She holds a doctorate from an institute of national importance, MNNIT, Allahabad. She has qualified UGC NET in Management. She has many national and international research papers in her credit, which are published in ABDC, Scopus, UGC CARE, and reputed peer-reviewed journals. She made significant contributions to the academic field as the editor, publishing two books centered on the theme of digital transformation. She is passionate, purposeful, high-spirited and has a never-ending approach to learning. She has supervised many students for their PhD and Masters dissertations. Publications

Nina Widowati is lecturer in public administration from Diponegoro University

Zaliha Zainuddin is a PhD holder and works as a Senior Lecturer and as the Head of Tourism Department, Faculty of Business, Economics, and Social Development Universiti Malaysia.

Index

A

Augmented Reality 27, 28, 30, 36, 42, 43, 45, 63, 126, 130, 139, 146, 149, 183, 184, 189, 190, 191, 192, 193, 195, 203, 204, 205, 206, 207, 208, 209, 237, 238, 240, 296, 302, 335, 336, 341

B

Bangladesh 101, 199, 277, 278, 281, 295, 296, 330

Big Data 28, 35, 37, 42, 61, 62, 82, 124, 143, 144, 145, 146, 147, 149, 150, 154, 155, 156, 157, 160, 161, 164, 165, 166, 171, 172, 174, 175, 176, 177, 180, 184, 189, 193, 238, 242, 335, 343

C

Consumer Decision Making 155, 159, 164, 165, 166, 167, 169, 170, 171, 172

COVID-19 13, 14, 45, 62, 64, 65, 66, 67, 68, 69, 70, 71, 72, 74, 78, 79, 80, 81, 83, 84, 90, 156, 159, 184, 196, 197, 220, 245, 252, 255, 256, 258, 260, 273, 275

CRS 337, 338, 339

Cultural Heritage Tourism 187, 219, 220, 221, 222, 225, 226, 227, 237, 238, 239, 240, 242, 245, 246, 249

Cultural Narratives 1, 4, 13, 14, 22, 29, 237

Cultural Tourism 8, 23, 24, 25, 26, 27, 28, 30, 31, 32, 33, 34, 35, 37, 39, 61, 87, 88, 90, 91, 92, 93, 95, 100, 103, 104, 105, 183, 184, 185, 186, 187, 188, 189, 193, 194, 195, 196, 235, 236, 237, 238, 243, 244, 245, 246, 247, 288, 293, 294, 296

Culture 9, 19, 21, 25, 26, 29, 37, 39, 55, 79, 88, 89, 91, 92, 97, 101, 102, 103, 105, 107, 110, 111, 112, 114, 117, 119, 121, 152, 184, 185, 186, 187, 188, 196, 206, 207, 214, 216, 219, 220, 221, 222, 223, 224, 225, 226, 227, 228, 229, 233, 234, 235, 236, 242, 243, 244, 245, 246, 247, 248, 257, 312, 313, 315, 328

D

Dark Tourism 2, 3, 4, 5, 6, 7, 9, 10, 11, 12, 13, 14, 15, 16, 17, 18, 19, 20, 21, 22

Dark Tourism Impact 21, 22

Dark Tourism Motive 22

decision-making criteria 66

Digitalization 124, 126, 133, 144, 145, 151, 152, 154, 158, 159, 160, 161, 169, 171, 172, 174, 175, 183, 184, 189, 334

Digital technologies 21, 43, 45, 71, 124, 135, 159, 183, 184, 185, 189, 193, 239

E

Economic effects 4, 14, 22, 87

Ecotourism 89, 116, 117, 118, 119, 120, 121, 122, 123, 124, 133, 134, 135, 137, 138, 139, 140, 141, 142, 163, 253, 254, 259, 263, 265, 266, 270, 271, 272, 273, 275, 311, 312, 313, 314, 316, 319, 324, 326, 327, 328, 329, 331

Environment 15, 19, 46, 53, 63, 74, 75, 76, 77, 78, 79, 105, 107, 108, 109, 110, 111, 113, 116, 117, 121, 131, 140, 141, 144, 154, 174, 189, 217, 225, 227, 231, 235, 245, 253, 258, 264, 269, 270, 279, 281, 285, 295, 298, 304, 306, 311, 312, 313, 315, 316, 317, 323, 324, 347

G

Geospatial Information Technology 341, 347

GIS 239, 241, 337, 338, 340, 341, 342, 343, 344, 345, 346, 347

H

Heritage 2, 7, 9, 11, 12, 14, 16, 17, 18, 19, 20, 23, 24, 25, 26, 27, 28, 29, 30, 31, 32, 33, 34, 35, 36, 37, 38, 45, 46, 61, 62, 63, 69, 88, 89, 91, 92, 93, 97, 98, 102, 104, 105, 109, 113, 117, 118, 119, 120, 121, 124, 125, 126, 163, 184, 185, 186, 187, 190, 193, 194, 196, 203, 204, 205, 210, 212, 214, 219, 220, 221, 222, 223, 224, 225, 226, 227, 228, 229, 231, 233, 235, 237, 238, 239, 240, 241, 242, 243, 244, 245, 246, 247, 248, 249, 313, 331
Heritage Preservation 23, 27, 31, 45, 93
hospitality services 5, 199, 200, 205, 207, 208, 209

I

ICT 131, 143, 144, 145, 146, 148, 151, 152, 154, 158, 159, 160, 161, 169, 171, 172, 174, 175, 176, 178, 195, 205, 209, 214, 226, 227, 338, 341, 346
Influencer 45, 50, 55, 63, 64, 151, 158, 178, 181, 267
Information Technology 37, 45, 64, 84, 103, 155, 180, 181, 194, 195, 272, 298, 333, 334, 335, 336, 337, 340, 341, 343, 344, 345, 346, 347
Interactivity 41, 43, 46, 48, 49, 52, 54, 56, 57, 58, 59, 147, 149, 240

M

media influences 252, 253, 254, 255, 256, 257, 259, 260, 267, 270
Moderator 260, 285
Morocco 65, 66, 67, 69, 74, 79, 82
Multimedia Content 41, 43, 47, 48, 49, 52, 54, 56, 57, 58, 59, 203

P

perceived flow 278, 289, 292, 298, 300, 301
Personalization 30, 41, 42, 43, 47, 48, 49, 52, 54, 56, 57, 58, 59, 61, 63, 128, 129, 131, 135, 147, 160, 199, 200, 240, 340
Personalized Experiences 59, 130, 135, 147, 148
pilgrimage tourism experiences 199, 200, 205, 206, 207, 208, 209
purchase intention 65, 67, 71, 72, 73, 74, 76, 77, 78, 79, 80, 82, 83, 84, 277, 279, 280, 281, 282, 284, 285, 289, 290, 291, 292, 294, 295, 296, 298, 299, 300, 301, 302, 304, 306, 308

R

Realism 41, 43, 46, 48, 49, 56, 57, 58, 59
restaurants 5, 66, 67, 72, 199, 200, 207, 228, 230, 234, 301
Revisit intention 61, 84, 259
Rural Tourism 21, 38, 88, 89, 90, 91, 93, 94, 95, 99, 100, 101, 102, 103, 104, 105, 106, 132, 220, 226, 247

S

Smart Tourism 37, 42, 124, 125, 132, 135, 138, 139, 144, 145, 147, 148, 149, 157, 177, 178, 179, 180, 194, 214, 215, 335, 341, 345
Social 3, 5, 6, 7, 8, 13, 17, 20, 22, 24, 25, 27, 29, 31, 38, 41, 43, 44, 45, 47, 48, 49, 51, 52, 54, 55, 56, 57, 58, 59, 61, 62, 66, 67, 71, 72, 73, 80, 83, 89, 91, 92, 94, 95, 100, 101, 105, 106, 107, 108, 109, 112, 113, 118, 119, 120, 121, 137, 138, 139, 143, 144, 145, 147, 151, 152, 154, 155, 156, 157, 158, 159, 160, 161, 162, 163, 166, 167, 169, 171, 172, 174, 175, 176, 177, 178, 179, 180, 181, 184, 189, 191, 193, 194, 195, 197, 200, 204, 205, 206, 208, 209, 211, 214, 216, 217, 220, 223, 224, 225, 229, 233, 238, 239, 240, 241, 242, 244, 245, 248, 251, 252, 253, 254, 255, 256, 257, 258, 259, 260, 262, 264, 267, 268, 269, 270, 271, 272, 273, 274, 275, 277, 278, 279, 280, 282, 283, 287, 288, 292, 293, 294, 295, 296,

297, 298, 299, 300, 301, 302, 303, 304, 305, 306, 307, 311, 312, 313, 315, 317, 319, 320, 321, 322, 323, 324, 325, 326, 327, 328, 329, 330, 334, 335, 336, 345, 346

Social commerce 277, 278, 279, 280, 293, 294, 295, 296, 297, 298, 299, 300, 301, 302, 304, 305, 306, 307

social influences 252, 253, 255, 258, 259, 260, 267, 268, 269, 270, 306

Social Interaction 41, 43, 47, 48, 49, 52, 54, 56, 57, 58, 206, 208, 296

Social Media 13, 20, 27, 29, 43, 44, 55, 58, 62, 71, 72, 73, 80, 143, 144, 145, 151, 152, 154, 155, 157, 158, 159, 160, 161, 162, 163, 166, 167, 169, 171, 172, 174, 175, 176, 177, 178, 179, 180, 181, 194, 204, 205, 206, 209, 211, 229, 233, 238, 239, 240, 241, 242, 245, 248, 251, 252, 256, 257, 264, 267, 271, 272, 274, 275, 278, 280, 283, 287, 288, 294, 296, 298, 301, 303, 306, 334, 336, 345

Socio-cultural impact 106, 233

Sustainability 2, 14, 24, 27, 29, 31, 32, 33, 35, 42, 61, 64, 70, 72, 73, 82, 84, 90, 93, 101, 102, 104, 108, 109, 112, 113, 115, 116, 117, 125, 126, 134, 135, 136, 137, 139, 140, 141, 142, 175, 177, 178, 179, 180, 184, 194, 215, 239, 240, 249, 264, 269, 270, 274, 298, 311, 312, 313, 314, 315, 316, 317, 319, 320, 321, 322, 323, 324, 325, 326, 327, 328, 329, 330, 331, 335, 341, 344, 345, 346

Sustainable Development Goals 24, 32, 38, 70, 107, 112

Sustainable tourism 19, 27, 29, 42, 63, 70, 83, 87, 100, 101, 102, 107, 108, 109, 110, 111, 112, 113, 114, 115, 116, 122, 124, 126, 128, 131, 132, 133, 134, 135, 137, 138, 140, 142, 178, 189, 200, 201, 212, 217, 220, 226, 244, 245, 246, 247, 248, 274, 275, 312, 330, 336, 341, 344, 345

T

Technology 28, 29, 30, 33, 34, 36, 37, 38, 39, 41, 42, 43, 44, 45, 54, 55, 61, 62, 64, 71, 83, 84, 103, 115, 132, 133, 135, 139, 143, 144, 145, 146, 147, 148, 149, 153, 154, 155, 156, 158, 159, 160, 161, 164, 169, 171, 172, 174, 175, 176, 177, 178, 179, 180, 181, 189, 194, 195, 199, 200, 201, 203, 204, 205, 206, 207, 208, 209, 210, 211, 212, 213, 214, 215, 216, 217, 219, 220, 226, 233, 234, 237, 238, 239, 240, 242, 245, 272, 277, 295, 297, 298, 301, 302, 304, 329, 333, 334, 335, 336, 337, 338, 340, 341, 343, 344, 345, 346, 347

Tourism 1, 2, 3, 4, 5, 6, 7, 8, 9, 10, 11, 12, 13, 14, 15, 16, 17, 18, 19, 20, 21, 22, 23, 24, 25, 26, 27, 28, 29, 30, 31, 32, 33, 34, 35, 37, 38, 39, 41, 42, 43, 44, 45, 46, 47, 48, 49, 50, 51, 53, 54, 55, 56, 57, 58, 60, 61, 62, 63, 64, 65, 66, 67, 68, 69, 70, 71, 72, 73, 74, 75, 77, 78, 79, 80, 82, 83, 84, 87, 88, 89, 90, 91, 92, 93, 94, 95, 96, 98, 99, 100, 101, 102, 103, 104, 105, 106, 107, 108, 109, 110, 111, 112, 113, 114, 115, 116, 117, 118, 119, 120, 121, 122, 123, 124, 125, 126, 128, 131, 132, 133, 134, 135, 136, 137, 138, 139, 140, 141, 142, 143, 144, 145, 146, 147, 148, 149, 150, 151, 152, 153, 154, 155, 156, 157, 158, 159, 160, 163, 166, 169, 176, 177, 178, 179, 180, 181, 182, 183, 184, 185, 186, 187, 188, 189, 190, 193, 194, 195, 196, 197, 199, 200, 201, 202, 203, 204, 205, 206, 207, 208, 209, 210, 211, 212, 213, 214, 215, 216, 217, 218, 219, 220, 221, 222, 225, 226, 227, 228, 229, 230, 231, 232, 233, 234, 235, 236, 237, 238, 239, 240, 242, 243, 244, 245, 246, 247, 248, 249, 252, 253, 254, 255, 256, 257, 258, 259, 262, 264, 265, 269, 271, 272, 273, 274, 275, 277, 278,

279, 280, 282, 288, 293, 294, 295, 296, 297, 298, 302, 303, 304, 306, 307, 308, 312, 313, 316, 324, 328, 330, 331, 333, 334, 335, 336, 337, 338, 339, 340, 341, 342, 343, 344, 345, 346, 347

Tourism Industry 4, 12, 42, 44, 64, 65, 71, 72, 73, 88, 98, 99, 100, 107, 108, 110, 116, 121, 142, 146, 153, 154, 156, 157, 159, 160, 166, 169, 176, 180, 181, 183, 184, 185, 189, 195, 220, 226, 227, 229, 230, 231, 232, 234, 235, 248, 252, 257, 258, 271, 278, 279, 280, 294, 297, 302, 312, 313, 333, 334, 335, 336, 337, 339, 340, 341, 343, 344, 345

tourism products and services 99, 111, 277, 278, 279, 282, 296, 306, 308

tourism recovery 69, 70, 273

tourism strategy 65, 74, 75, 77, 78, 113

tourist satisfaction 84, 124, 251, 253, 255, 257, 258, 259, 260, 262, 264, 269, 270, 272, 274, 275

tourists behaviors 188

U

Use of technology 199, 205, 208, 209, 210, 211, 212, 238

User-Friendly Interface 41, 43, 48, 49, 52, 55, 56, 57, 58, 260

User-Generated Content 61, 143, 145, 151, 154, 155, 157, 158, 160, 166, 167, 169, 171, 172, 174, 175, 179, 238, 257, 295, 306, 334

V

Virtual Assistants 23, 24, 26, 31, 43, 149, 340

Virtual Tourism 41, 42, 43, 45, 46, 47, 48, 49, 50, 51, 53, 54, 55, 56, 57, 58, 60, 62, 63, 64, 343

Visit intention 311, 312, 313, 316, 317, 319, 321, 322, 323, 324, 325, 326, 327, 329, 330